# STORIES ABOUT BIRDS
# AND BIRD WATCHERS

# STORIES ABOUT BIRDS

FROM *Bird Watcher's Digest*

ILLUSTRATED BY BOB HINES

# AND BIRD WATCHERS

EDITED BY *Mary Beacom Bowers*

**FOREWORD BY ROGER TORY PETERSON**

NEW YORK   1981   *Atheneum*

*Library of Congress Cataloging in Publication Data*
*Main entry under title:*

*Stories about birds and bird watchers from Bird*
  *watcher's digest.*
  *1. Bird watching. I. Bowers, Mary Beacom.*
*II. Bird watcher's digest.*
*QL677.5.S76        598'.07'234        80-7925*
*ISBN 0-689-11093-6*

*Published simultaneously in Canada by McClelland and Stewart Ltd.*
*Composition by American–Stratford Graphic Services, Brattleboro, Vermont*
*Printed and bound by Fairfield Graphics, Fairfield, Pennsylvania*
*Designed by Kathleen Carey*
*First Edition*

*For William, Andrew, and Laura Thompson*
*and for Susanna Beacom*

# Acknowledgments

*Bird Watcher's Digest* would like to thank, for their special help and interest:

Neil and Doris Christy
Bruce DeMoll
Jim Dunn
Jenny Eaton
Cynthia Meredith
Randall and Jane Metcalf
Laura Miller
Larry Mills
Pat Murphy

Roger Tory and Virginia Peterson
Ed and Rosalie Pitner
Bob Richardson
Bill and Laura Riley
Larry Sheehan
Bill and Jenny Sheppard
Margaret Thompson
Tom and Joyce Vadakin

. . . and

# *Foreword*

## ROGER TORY PETERSON

FORTY years ago, my friend the late James Fisher, the distinguished British ornithologist, quipped that the observation of birds may be many things—a superstition, a tradition, an art, a science, a pleasure, a hobby, or even a bore—depending on the observer.

Professor Joseph Hickey of the University of Wisconsin, himself a lifelong ornithophile, commented in his *Guide to Bird Watching*, published in 1943, that watching birds is regarded by some "as a mild paralysis of the central nervous system which can be cured only by rising at dawn and sitting in a bog. Others regard it as a harmless occupation of children, into which maiden aunts may sometimes relapse." The truth is that it is anything you care to make it.

Many names have been used to designate those who watch birds—*ornithologist, bird lover, bird watcher, birder,* etc. *Ornithologist,* except in rare cases, presumes too much. It is as loosely used as the terms *artist* and *scientist.* One must be engaged in the scientific investigation of birds to merit the status of ornithologist.

*Bird lover* bothers me because loving implies reciprocation or at least the hope of reciprocation. Birds do not reciprocate. *Birder* is usually applied to those who make a sport of identifying birds, ticking them off on their checklists. The list is the thing.

The term *bird watcher*, to some, evokes an image of little old ladies in mackintoshes and running shoes. This stereotype is way off base. In this day of awakening environmental awareness, people of all ages and all walks of life watch birds, and the person who does not have at least a peripheral interest in them is the one who is out of step with the times.

It seems to me that the most appropriate and inclusive term is still *bird watcher*. It embraces observers of all stripes and hues, from academic ethologists like Lorenz and Tinbergen, recipients of the Nobel Prize, down to the white-breasted nuthatch type of bird watcher who puts sunflower seeds outside the kitchen window. We might argue that even the several million duck hunters may be included, although their bird watching is usually restricted to a few aquatic species.

There are journals and publications that cater to all these levels of interest. *The Auk, The Wilson Bulletin,* and the *Condor* are vehicles for the academically inclined, although it is doubtful whether some of the papers with their charts, graphs, and computerized data are conscientiously digested by more than a few dozen readers. *American Birds,* an excellent publication of the National Audubon Society, monitors in detail the changing fortunes of birds, their populations, range extensions and declines, with all their environmental implications. *Birding,* the organ of the American Birding Association, is primarily for the lister who makes a game of it or watches birds for the sheer fun.

Overlapping these, but attempting to carve out niches of their own, are *Western Birds, Birding News Survey,* and most re-

*Foreword*

cently, *Continental Birdlife*. I subscribe to all of these and many
more, including the more general conservation magazines such
as *Audubon, Defenders of Wildlife,* and *National Wildlife*. But
none of these cover the local news media, the thousands of
newspapers and journals across the land, which often carry news
items or interesting articles about birds. It was to fill this void
that a refreshingly different little magazine, the *Bird Watcher's
Digest,* was launched. This book is a selection of some of the
pieces that have appeared in the pages of that publication. They
range from scholarly to light-hearted and joyous.

Bird watching is one of the fastest-growing hobbies, both here
and abroad. It has sparked the environmental movement and in
turn has been caught up in the momentum of that movement.
Its devotees, who now number in the millions, share an en-
lightened awareness of the world's other two-legged creatures.

*Roger Tory Peterson*

# *Preface*

ON a winter's day in early 1978, Elsa and Bill Thompson decided to change their lives. For years they had discussed ways of working and living that would involve their whole family— so that Bill, a vice-president of a midwestern liberal-arts college, could be at home with their two teen-age boys and their young daughter, so that Elsa could make further use of her energy and talents, so that the children could experience directly the working lives of their parents. They wanted a project that all could feel passion and joy about. That February day they came up with the idea of publishing a magazine about a subject both loved: bird watching. Six months later the idea was reality, and the charter issue of *Bird Watcher's Digest* went into the September mails.

Theirs is truly a cottage industry. The editorial, circulation, advertising, and business offices of their magazine still operate out of their home. They began that first month with a clipping service and then progressed to the reading of thousands of stories and to the discovery of hundreds of first-rate (and, as it turned out, cooperative and sympathetic) writers. Working out the mechanics of getting *BWD* into print and into circulation, they have seen their project materialize into what is already the most popular periodical devoted exclusively to the subject of birds and bird watchers.

The Thompsons's faith and the enthusiastic response of those first subscribers have brought *Bird Watcher's Digest* to its third year of publication and to a sense that it has now a life of its own. This book is an outgrowth of the magazine and brings together thirty-eight stories that appeared in *Bird Watcher's Digest* during its initial years.

It has been a privilege and a happiness to have been included in the Thompsons's dream and to have worked with them in making the magazine what it is. And it has also been a rewarding experience to have served as editor to the writers who have appeared in its pages, including those represented here.

*Mary Beacom Bowers*
Marietta, Ohio

# Contents

xviii

# Contents

## V   THE FLIP SIDE

## VI   REFLECTIONS

# STORIES ABOUT BIRDS
# AND BIRD WATCHERS

# I  *A Species Miscellany*

---

*Starlings. Flickers. Quail. Owls. Swans.
Bitterns. Albatrosses. Penguins. Each of
these has its own distinctive character.
But the stories here, about such various
species, have common elements: drama,
news, surprise.*

# In Loco Parentis:
# A Starling Story

FAITH MCNULTY

We have a lot of starlings living around our farmhouse and nesting in our barn. I have ambivalent feelings about them. I know I am supposed to dislike starlings, because they are interlopers rather than native birds, and because there are too many of them. They evict other, gentler birds from nesting places. They flock together, making mess and noise that greatly annoy some people. On the other hand, I like to see them walking across my lawn in phalanxes with a busy, businesslike stride, as they search for Japanese-beetle grubs that I am glad to get rid of. Also, in the spring, when I go out to the barn and hear their nuptial songs, I find them varied and beautiful. This year, the nuptial songs were followed by the cheeping of a multitude of baby starlings—perhaps actually only a dozen, since that's all it takes for baby starlings to sound like a multitude. They are very vocal, and their voices rose and fell in excited choruses, first from one corner of the barn, then from another, as the parents came with food. One of the nests was on a beam high over the doorway. Just when my husband and

I were busiest, getting in hay, I happened to glance down as I went through the door and saw, sitting solemnly on the concrete, an ugly, half-feathered little starling. He must have only just fallen, or one of my voracious cats would have got him. I actually groaned. I looked at him with real chagrin, recognizing him as a gratuitous and unwelcome burden. "I *don't* want a baby starling," I said to myself. "I really don't." Just then, my black panther of a house cat glided innocently out of the shadows. I picked up the starling impatiently—the way a housewife picks up another dirty dish—and carried him into the house and put him in a box in the bathroom. I have a book that gives advice on caring for wild orphans. Its main recommendation for young birds is a diet of dog food. I fed the bird easily enough, but I was so cross about the whole thing that I would barely look at him. Besides, I didn't want him to be, as the ethologists put it, imprinted by me. I wanted him to grow up as a wild starling, with no illusions that I was his mother, so I barely let him glimpse me at each feeding.

For two days, all through the frantic business of getting the hay baled and into the barn, I stopped whatever I was doing every hour or so and went and fed the damned bird. On the third day, when the rush was over, I realized that the stack of baled hay had brought the nest from which the bird had fallen within reach of a ladder. I persuaded my husband to climb up and put him back. When my husband climbed down, he reported that the bird had settled in beside his single nestmate with no fuss. That, I thought with relief, is that. Two more days passed. I crossed the threshold of the barn and chanced to glance down, and there on the concrete waiting for me was my damned bird. The sequence of events was as before: the bird stowed in a box in the bathroom; the hourly duty grudgingly performed. This time, I knew I was stuck with him until he fledged, so I grudgingly gave him a name—Albert Ross,

6

to be pronounced rapidly. Like most of us, I had read about imprinting and how by early experience birds learn to behave in a way appropriate to their species. It occurred to me that there was no use in saving this bird's life if he grew up without knowing how to be a starling, and this he could hardly do shut up in a cardboard box in a silent bathroom. I made a nest of hay inside a bird cage, carried the cage to the barn, and hung it from a rafter—safe from the cats—so that the bird could see and hear the noisy comings and goings of the other starlings. I noticed that between feedings baby starlings, unless they are asleep, keep up a sort of whirring, purring sound, like a human baby crooning in its crib. I guessed that it is designed to remind the mother of her duty. My bird did it, too, of course. When I approached, I could tell by the intensity of the sound how hungry he was. When I kept him waiting too long, the crooning turned to a loud, eloquent, insistent whirr.

I took Albert's cage to the barn each morning and brought it into the bathroom each night. During the day, I made five or six visits to feed him. When I walked into the barn, filled with the crooning of many little birds—a sound that seemed full of confidence that satisfaction would always come—it struck me that the barn was a happy place. It had good vibes, as they used to say. I usually knew when it was feeding time without looking at my watch. This phase lasted about a week. By then, Albert was hopping restlessly around in his cage, and I realized that it was time to think about launching him. I called a biologist I know. I opened by saying that what I had was only a rotten starling, but nevertheless I would appreciate instructions on preparing him for release. The biologist said that first the bird should be allowed to flutter around some safe enclosure and practice flying. A screened porch would be ideal. I have a screened porch, so that was OK. Then I should teach him to eat by himself instead of from my fingers. Then I

7

should put him outdoors for trial flights, allowing him to return to the porch for reassurance and refuge when he wished. When he was ready, he would leave for good. I explained that Albert was hardly tame, since I hadn't allowed him to be imprinted by me. I wondered if I should continue to be careful about this. "Don't worry," the biologist said. "They forget very quickly and go wild." He also said I needn't apologize for raising a starling. "They're great birds," he said. "Good bug catchers, very smart, beautiful song. That's why they were brought here in the first place." Then he added, a bit teasingly, "I bet you love that bird." This suggested to me an image of a sappy woman murmuring baby talk with each offering of dog food, so I said coldly that I found Albert "interesting" and that I was grateful for the advice.

Now I had more contact with Albert. He soon flew around the screened porch competently, but he would eat only from my hand. He quickly became very tame. He spent most of his time perched on a bamboo blind waiting for me. Whenever I appeared, he launched himself at me, to land, chirping and begging, on my arm. I tried every strategy to get him to peck at food. I scattered it at his feet on a bench. I held it before his beak. I secreted it. No dice. This went on for several days. I worried. I called the biologist, who said to let him go hungry all day and then put food before him. That day was hell. Albert was desperate, and I felt awful. At twilight, he still had not pecked a single crumb, so I fed him and, with relief, watched him go contentedly to bed on a perch I had fixed for him in a sheltered corner. The next day, there was a partial breakthrough. I put down a big ashtray full of water. Albert hopped in and took a vigorous bath, during which he sipped some water. I felt like cheering.

By now, I had had Albert about two weeks. He looked quite adult, but not like a starling. He was a soft-gray color, with a

8

pale spot on his chest. His outline was graceful. He was a nice-looking bird. When I went out to the barn, I realized that his class had graduated. The barn was silent, but the lawn was busy. Where the lawnmower had recently passed, I saw mother starlings working intently, followed by gray juveniles who seemed to watch the mother bird and emulate her movements as she probed the sod for grubs. It was clear what I had to do next. Albert and I went outside. I put him on the ground and, squatting down, scratched up the earth with a trowel. Albert watched, whirring insistently for food. A worm appeared. Quick as a flash, Albert seized it. I continued scrabbling, hopping to a new location when the previous one was exhausted. We found all sorts of insects: wireworms, grubs, beetles. Albert was enthusiastic. Finally, he was full and flew to a tree. I felt relief that another hurdle was behind us, but when I returned to the porch Albert cried out and flew in with me. It was just as well. At that moment, one of my cats passed by.

Now we were on the home stretch, but new worries seized me. I was teaching Albert to find food by hunting on the ground, as a starling must, but I was unable to give the warning cry that would teach him to beware of predators. He was foolishly trusting of my dog and would land on the ground right under her nose. I couldn't be with Albert every minute he was outside, and besides, he needed to learn to do his own hunting. For two days, I shut up my cats and left Albert outdoors. It didn't work. In the first place, he did very little searching on his own. He spent most of his time in the tree by the porch door waiting for me to come out, so that we could search for food together. Every time I went out, he would fly down to the ground and hop along after me wherever I went. I usually responded by getting down on all fours and scrabbling through the grass with my fingers while Albert stood by to grab whatever little scurrying things I scared up; then, when I left Albert, he always flew

9

back to his perch in the tree. Inside the house, the cats were furious and frustrated. Maneuvering to get in or out without letting one of them escape was nerve-racking. They waited by the door. I swore and kicked them back. It was all too easy to visualize what would happen if one should get out: my two weeks of hard labor going down the drain as Albert flew trustingly into the jaws of death.

When nothing had changed by the evening of the third day, I knew that the impasse must be broken. I was under too much stress. "I've got to get rid of the damned bird," I told myself. I recalled that there is a bird sanctuary twenty miles from my house. I found that it had a phone number. I asked the man who answered if I could lay a partly fledged starling on him. He said he didn't know much about the job but was willing to try. I put Albert in his cage, covered it with a towel, and drove to the sanctuary. Even muffled by the towel, the bird's voice was penetrating. Albert chirped all the way in apparent bewilderment and alarm. I said, "It's going to be all right, Albert. I promise you it will be all right."

I found the sanctuary headquarters and the caretaker, a friendly young man in jeans with a red beard, who had a degree in invertebrate biology. That was reassuring. He should at least be good at finding insects. I let Albert out of the cage and he sat on my arm. We both admired him. Then I got down on the grass and showed the young man how to rummage about so that Albert could find food. I told him that Albert liked a nice, deep bath. I told the young man that if he would just look after Albert for a few days, helping him to find food and learn his way around, the bird would probably go wild after that. I picked up the towel and cage, and left. As I drove out, I was reassured by the sight of the young man on all fours progressing slowly across the lawn with Albert hopping along beside him. During the silent drive home, I felt relief that

10

anxiety over Albert's safety had been removed. I congratulated myself on such a fine solution. I looked forward to a leisurely drink, with no bird-nurturing duties to perform. A drink would cheer me up.

Around noon the following day, I called the sanctuary. The young man said that when darkness came Albert had split. He had disappeared into the trees, and hadn't been seen since. The young man said he was sorry and hoped the bird would be OK. As soon as I hung up, I realized my mistake. At home, I had put Albert on the porch each night while the cats were let out. Naturally, at bedtime he had gone to look for his accustomed sleeping place. He had probably fluttered in confusion through the dark woods. At daylight, I imagined, he had started out again for home. He would probably stop at the first house he came to. If a person appeared, Albert would land at that startled person's feet and beg. I prayed there would be no cats in the house that Albert found.

I went out to tidy up the porch. I took down Albert's perch and picked up the food dishes and the ashtray bathtub. Outside, the lawn was dotted with starling parents guiding and instructing their young with an air of busy competence. They were a noisy bunch. Each time one of the young birds spoke in a voice like Albert's, there was an involuntary response inside me. I wondered how long it takes for a person who has become imprinted by a bird to get over the illusion that she is its mother.

# Hot as a Flicker's Nest

## MARY LEISTER

$A$ LONG the western slopes of the Allegheny Mountains, in years past, when any countryman spoke of a grossly overheated area, whether heated by stove or sun, he used the ultimate superlative to describe it: "It's hot as a flicker's nest in there!"

How hot, I wondered every time I heard the expression, can a flicker's nest be? And it became a childhood ambition to put my hand into a flicker's nest to learn for myself just how excessive the heat was in there. But the few flicker nests I ever discovered were high up in great old trees whose lowest limbs were well beyond my reach, and, though I did some energetic climbing in nearby trees, I never quite managed to get close enough.

Thus, when, on a certain April morning, I caught the glint of golden underwings from a mated pair of flickers hunting a nesting site among the trees on either side of the shallow creek in my neighbor's marsh, I watched with more than casual interest. Perhaps, after all these years, a nest might be located

12

low enough that, with thermometer in hand, I could find out exactly how hot "as hot as a flicker's nest" is.

The two birds investigated every knothole and hollow and tapped exploratory bills along a hundred interesting limbs and trunks without finding exactly what they wanted. The mustachioed male did cut a few whopping chips from the wild cherry tree on the high bank, making the black bark and the light inner wood fly in all directions, but the female flew at him with scolding cries until he left off his sculpting and followed her on an inspection tour of the sassafras grove on the top of the hill.

From the sassafras grove they flew to the oak and hickory woods that stretched across the lower end of the small valley, searched it for a day and a half, then worked their way back up the marsh until they reached an ancient willow just below the pond in the middle of the valley. And here they stopped. Only eight feet up on the rough-barked trunk they immediately chipped out a circle nearly three inches across and chiseled a hole three or four inches deep straight back from the opening.

Only eight feet up! I could scarcely wait for their nesting to begin. But, after that enterprising opening, the birds suddenly became indolent. They flew about the marsh and the pond on no errands whatever, or sat, tail-braced, on the trunks of neighboring trees and filled the April air with their whickering. Then they found an ant hill in the fence corner across the marsh and spent long hours sprawling about on the great crumbly mound, tucking occasional black-and-red ants under their wings and constantly thrusting their sticky tongues into the ant-hill openings to collect mouthfuls of plump ants. And nearly a week went by before the nesting hole was completed.

But when it was done it was a beautifully carved-out cylinder in the heart of the willow trunk. A dark little cell nearly eighteen inches deep and more than six inches across, it had a

13

round doorway, already polished by their comings and goings, and a few wood chips and a sprinkling of sawdust on the floor to make it more comfortable for the brooding flickers and their eventual babies. The grasses at the foot of the willow were thickly littered with untidy scatterings of large-chiseled wood chips and rough-powdered sawdust.

Finally, quite early on an April morning, when the countryside was shrouded in fog, and a persistent light drizzle fell through it or from it, the female entered her new willow-wood home and settled herself to produce her first egg. The mate pecked around at the bark of the nearby mulberry trees, eating a few insect eggs or new-hatched grubs to pass the time, and every so often he flew over to perch in the willow tree and to talk softly in his throat to his mate hidden away inside their nest.

It was well past the middle of the morning and the mist of rain still fell softly through the gray fog. Suddenly, the valley was filled with vivid streaks of light flashing up, flashing down, from a blazing, quivering lightning high up in the fog, while the air tightened, then rocked apart with intense, explosive sound. The willow tree split from top to bottom, right through the middle of the new flicker nest. Its scorched limbs and charred branches flew through the air, scattering for hundreds of feet along the creek bank and in the marsh.

The male disappeared never to be seen again, nor any trace of him found, but the female still sat on the gray ashes of the wood chips on the bottom of one half of her cylindrical nest, her feathers vanished, her brick-red flesh baked dry to her bones.

In the earlier hours of that morning I stood near the willow watching the course of the flickers' nesting, but at the moment of the lightning strike I was nearly half a mile away, just opening the back door of my own home. I felt the strange sensation which I can only call a "tightening" of the air, saw the wild leapings of light, was enveloped in the unbelievable force of the explosive thunder.

And all that day and all that night the fog and the steady drizzle continued, but there was not another flash of lightning, not another boom of thunder, not even a quiet rumble. I suppose that, just as in a winter snowstorm a charge of electricity is sometimes generated, to be discharged in a surprising flash of lightning and resultant thunder, so, possibly, a charge was built up in the constant drizzle-through-the-fog, to be dramatically discharged on that April day.

One wonders, of course, why in that particular spot? Why that particular willow tree? Did the hollow within that tree, heated by the little flicker body, have anything to do with the electrical attraction? Whatever the reason, one thing I know beyond doubt—for one catastrophic instant that was surely the hottest flicker's nest ever to be known or imagined.

# Desert Rescue:
# Worth a Gambel

CARLA MCCLAIN

THIS was no gentle birth and sheltered childhood. You wouldn't give a lick for their chances of turning out decent. All they had known, from their first conscious moment, was cold, terror, fear, and abandonment. If they survived at all, they would be nothing but trouble.

If they had been ugly or uncute, perhaps they would have been left to die in peace. But they were eight tiny puffs of heart-melting fluff, and so, when the cat raided the nest, mauled the parent, and scattered the family far and wide, the little chicks were scooped up in the spirit of human kindness, with the instinctive and ignorant intent to save their lives. Who could argue with that?

Well, the law argues with it. Because in human possession, newly hatched Gambel's quail chicks are as illegal as whiskey in the hands of a minor. But it's a law easily ignored when orphaned babies are running around in hysterics, with no place to go and no one to turn to. What is one to do, turn a deaf ear and ignore this micro-tragedy? The cold legal structure asks

16

too much when it asks that. So we grab a box or a paper bag and chase frantically here and there capturing the chicks, ensuring their safety and our sanity, at least for now.

The irony of it is that there is not a trained biologist—or professional animal person—around who does not agree with the state law that says to leave those wild things alone, tragedy or no tragedy. And they agree with it simply because they know that the animal's chances are much better if left to nature than when taken into the human world. At the very least, nature will take care that the drama is played out within the highly complicated and interdependent biological scheme designed for such wildlife as quail, whether in life or death.

Well, there had been precious little time for psyching out Mother Nature. And so a bunch of quail babies tripped all over each other in a cardboard box, wet and shivering, making heartrending noises. The only ones more helpless than they were ourselves, as we stared down at their misery.

This is an all-too-common scenario here in Tucson, Arizona, where the natural desert is still close to our ever-urbanizing lives. We bump up against the helpless and the orphaned, and if we don't shoot at them, we are wont to try to save them. In this particular case, the rescuers did the next best thing to not rescuing at all and took the rescuees to the Arizona–Sonora Desert Museum the next morning. The museum is licensed to accept wild animals and will do so when facilities permit.

The timing was bad, however. That spring found the museum under quarantine because of the bird-killing exotic Newcastle's disease reported in the Tucson area. No wild or domestic birds could be accepted by the museum for the rest of the summer. It was May 3, 1977.

With the curator of birds out of town, it fell to several indecisive underlings at the museum to debate the chicks' fate. Overriding all other concerns was to get them away from the

17

museum at once, as they were a potential threat to the museum's entire bird inventory. But to where? Some said just turn them loose in the desert; one suggested making their end quick and painless in the gas chamber. But too many mushballs stood around wailing at the very thought. Finally, the head keeper of birds and mammals, Dagmar Summer, turned to one of these bleeding hearts and said, "Okay, you take them home and raise them. I'll help you." Laden with a large glass aquarium, a heat lamp, some wire mesh, chick starter mash, a bag of dirt, a glass lid, a feather duster, and the chicks, I bounced them by truck back over Gates Pass and home, to set up the nursery.

Despite the odds, there were several strong factors going for us in this venture. First was the nature of the species: Quail are precocial—immediately after hatching they are on their feet and able to run for safety and to feed themselves. The adult quail only show them where the food is and teach them when and from whom to flee. They do not have to catch and bring food to the young, and so neither did I. (Remember, though, that other birds usually have only two or three chicks to care for; I've seen quail parents pass by with as many as twenty-two babies in tow. Papa quail—whose duty is to guard and protect his family—is a very nervous bird during this period.)

So I could provide the food and the water (the latter in a shallow glass lid criss-crossed with tape so they couldn't fall in and catch cold). It would be up to them to eat and drink. What I could not do was brood them during the chill nights, which their mother would naturally do, gathering all her young under her body and wings.

The substitute mama was the feather duster, which they loved to snuggle up against, no doubt as much for emotional as physical warmth. Heat was provided all night long by the heat lamp placed on top of the aquarium. And they invariably slept all over each other—the only natural warmth they had.

The second positive factor was that my home at this time was well outside the city limits and surrounded by natural desert thickly populated with wild quail. This made their chances for return to and survival in the wild much better— and that had to be the real purpose of the whole effort.

The third factor was access to the advice and help of some of the best people in the animal business, at the Desert Museum, where I was then working.

Nevertheless, within hours, I watched one chick become punier and punier, and by 9:00 that night he was dead. It had been a rough start and a bad day, and there was every excuse in the world for dying, but O Lord, I didn't want to sit around and watch them kick off one by one. His stiff little body was placed under a paloverde tree away from the house and was gone by morning. Food for something, filling some ecological need out there, as he was intended to. Probably a snake. Small comfort.

Fortunately, the rest were hardier and hung in there. Two days had gone by, and I had not yet seen them eat or drink. They had great affection for the feather duster, but that was about the only reaction so far. I took to pushing their little beaks into the chick mash and into the water, but this seemed only another lousy indignity they had to endure.

I needn't have fretted so much, but new mothers always do. Gradually they emerged from their feather duster to inspect and peck at the food and eat. The floor of the aquarium was covered in desert dirt, not only to absorb their droppings, but also because this grit is necessary for digestion.

When they eat, from infancy on, they do a kind of two-step, shuffling first one foot, then the other in the dirt, presumably to dredge up the goodies. When adult quail shuffle,

19

they look for all the world like little old ladies learning the cha-cha. Quail are basically comical.

Once these youngsters got the eating and drinking thing together, their growth was very fast. The downy buff-and-brown stripes gave way to feathers almost in the first week. This transition period is a scruffy one; they walked about looking like partially plucked miniature chickens. Their topknots— symbol of the Gambel's quail—were apparent from the start as the tiniest tuft on the top of the head; these grew daily longer and thicker and darker.

Perhaps the headiest thing of all was their imprinting on me. Besides their beloved feather duster, I was the only ma they had, and so they took it, for better or worse. It was odd to think that something so tiny could grasp, or take in, something so monstrous as I, but they did. It was not too long before they would follow me whenever I got up to move about the house. Here they would come, all seven in a row, pitter-pattering behind me on the hardwood floors, trying to keep up. Luckily for them it was a one-room cabin we all lived in, and so they were not likely to lose sight.

It is precisely this phenomenon of imprinting, however, that is most dangerous for young captive birds, because it just about negates their chances of returning to and surviving in the wild. They have picked the very worst role model, for lack of a better one. It is one reason why the law is so firm about not taking in wild animals.

Quite by accident one day, I whistled at the chicks while they were out on the floor, just to capture their attention. Their reaction was startling. Every one of them stopped dead in his tracks and flattened to the ground for several long seconds. When no whistle followed, they gradually and timidly resumed an upright position and went about their business. This sharp whistle is a well-known alarm signal to wild quail;

the interesting thing was the instinctive reaction. Obviously no parent quail had taught these birds to do what they did. It must be programmed into their psyches at birth.

Many of my working hours at the museum were spent tapping curators' and keepers' brains about how to return these birds to the wild and what their survival chances would be. No one was very optimistic. The best suggestion came from Chuck Hanson, then curator of birds and mammals. He said to take the youngsters outside in a wire cage with no bottom in it and put them in the shade. When a wild pair of quail with chicks came by, he suggested that I lift the cage and release the chicks and that they would join up and be accepted by the passing quail family, even if the young were of different ages. If done right, this is the one sure way to give orphaned birds a good chance to get back to the wild.

Well, I tried it and turned a good idea into disaster. I managed to get six of the chicks out of their aquarium and into the wire cage outside. But the last one wiggled out of my cupped hands and into the air and thence to the ground and then took off a-runnin'. I panicked and did the very worst thing I could have done, which was to run after it. I chased the little squirt—and he could run—all over the damned desert, under cactus, into mesquite thickets, down into the wash, everywhere. I lost sight but could keep track of him by his panicky peeping. I ran both him and me ragged, a big mistake. Finally, much later, I gave up and in my own panic went back to the house to move the other chicks inside to safety. Then I sat on the porch steps and bawled and tried to think.

I went out again several times looking, because I could still hear the peeping from time to time. No luck. Night was falling, and I had to give up completely in the dark. I went inside and lay down, with no dinner, and proceeded to spend one long, sleepless night, listening to the cold and terrorized little thing peeping all over the desert. All night long. All I knew was that he hadn't been eaten yet.

Dawn came and with it the first sane thought I had had since I lost him. I put the six chicks back outside, rigged up a cardboard box next to them, propped it up on a stick and attached a string which I held in my hand. I sat on the porch a good distance away and waited. Sure enough, in not too long a time, the little renegade heard his siblings and came back to the cage, running all around it trying to get inside with them. I couldn't believe my eyes or my stupidity. When he was positioned under the box, I pulled the string, the stick collapsed, and the box fell. I had him.

Very carefully I transferred the whole batch back inside once again and put the wayward one in with his family. A bad day passed. The little guy was dying. From exhaustion, from cold, from stress, I didn't know what. It took him all day to die, but he did, by nightfall. Another stiff little body under the paloverde. Another meal for something. The memory of that little one running all night in terror still haunts me. It was a lousy way to die.

As if that weren't enough, one of the other chicks cashed it in the very next day, and I thought, "Well, now you're being punished, but good, for breaking the law. This is what happens to bad people." I about lost heart for the whole thing.

So I waited the next few days for the mass death, and it didn't happen. Five chicks were left now, and to avoid depressing you further, they all made it. No more tragedies.

They were flying now, and that is a whole new chapter in a one-room cabin. Usually if one flew they all flew, and for a few minutes the room would be a blur of whooshing wings and streaking bodies until they all found a perch. Their favorite spots were in the plants, where they would eat the leaves and kick all the dirt out onto the floor, and on the high exposed beams near the pitched ceiling. And in my hair.

*Desert Rescue: Worth a Gambel*

The night routine changed after they learned to fly. Instead of huddling together in a heap in their enclosure, they took to flying up to high places—usually on the ceiling beams or hanging plants, roosting exactly at sunset. It was uncanny how they tracked that sun. No matter what they were doing, at sunset they flew up high and settled down to sleep. Electric lights and human noise made no impact.

One thing they were mercilessly good at was catching spiders. Any spider attempting to make it across the floor while they were out was a goner. Which was fine with me. Summertime was spider city in that place.

It was mid-June, and they were maybe half grown by now. Bigger, too, was the mess they made. And they grew more and more defiant toward their cage, yelling nonstop when confined. The whole thing was getting out of hand. They were also becoming more and more adapted to human ways and house living. This only meant trouble, in the long run.

Right about this time, black faces began to appear on three of them. I had three boys and two girls. A nice family, it was. The house was a mess.

So one very hot June Saturday afternoon, I got an old bedspread, a bunch of old brooms, some lumber, some chicken wire, wire cutters, and a hammer and nails and decided to build an outdoor enclosure—kind of like the aviary at the Desert Museum, only on a smaller scale. You know, with rocks and trees and all sorts of natural things to get them used to the wild.

Four hours later I gave up, furious, hot, and grumpy. I'm no builder. I went back into the house to lie down amid the bird poop to ponder this. I fleetingly considered forgetting the whole thing and fattening them up for Thanksgiving before my tantrum passed.

By Sunday morning I had decided that there was nothing else to do but open the door and take them outside. There just was no gentle way to make the transition. I could only hope their imprint on me would hold until they got used to the real world. It did.

I hooked the screen door open and walked outside. All in a row they followed me onto the open porch. There they looked around in what seemed to be shock and disbelief. They were scared. A bird flew up in front of us, and they beat a very hasty and noisy retreat back inside, where they fell to discussing the matter with great energy. I had to laugh. At least they didn't fly off to L.A.

For a few days we practiced going in and out, getting used to the porch and the great outdoors. It took only one of them to wreak havoc—if one freaked, they all freaked, squawking their heads off at they didn't know what. Gradually they ventured into the desert, never wandering out of sight.

They displayed an innocent curiosity toward other birds and often got hassled by the thrashers and flickers for their nosiness. Discouraging was their utter naïveté, which led one of them to march right up to a coyote to inspect it. Not smart. A loud whistle prevented a bloody confrontation, but I would not be around to whistle in the future.

Their outside time increased. They were now spending almost entire days outside, and I didn't always have to be right there. They would come up to the screen door when they got hot, and they faithfully asked to be let inside at sunset. Desert training seemed to have reached a stalemate. They had accepted and become comfortable in the out-of-doors, but they were not street-smart enough to survive there.

Then an incredible thing happened to solve the whole prob lem. A lone, wild, unmated adult male quail (there are always a few unmated each spring and summer, and their lonely, mournful call is a tear-jerker) one day spied the two juvenile females and decided that his prayers had been answered. In that instant, so had mine.

*Desert Rescue: Worth a Gambel*

Greatly excited by this unclaimed female flesh, he began to make advances to them—very timid at first and from a distance, because the wild bird was shy of anything to do with the house. He would stand some distance from the chicks and call to them and run toward them and then retreat. Ever so slowly his libido beat back his fear, and he moved closer and closer. The chicks were not nearly so turned on by him, but neither were they afraid. They tolerated his presence, perhaps not even realizing they were the same animal.

This little dance went on for several days. In the evenings, when the youngsters would come inside for the night, the wild male would walk off toward the wash, slowly, dejectedly, wailing as if his heart would break. And every morning he would be waiting for them at the edge of the wash, just watching for the screen door to open and for the young girls to sashay out into the sunlight.

Of course he was interested only in the females. The boys were allowed to tag along, which they did, but he did not want to fuss with them. According to Tucson naturalist Linwood Smith, the adult could have mated the females at this stage, but it is doubtful that they would have let him, and certainly fertilization was impossible. So it is assumed the male had to settle for a platonic relationship and bide his time till the next year, when there would be more action.

This adult quail took over the whole burden of desert training, and the chicks finally had a teacher who knew what he was doing. They now spent the whole day with him—he showed them what to eat, and he taught them avian communication and what to be scared of. He took them down into the wash under the mesquite trees for shade during the hottest part of the day. He did it all.

This is perhaps not so strange as it might seem. Both male and female parent quail raise their young together, but it is known that if something happens to the female, the father

25

coming; soon the large coveys would form, and I knew then I would lose track of them forever.

In late September I happened to be sitting outside one afternoon, doing nothing, and a group of quail passed by not too far from me. I called to them, and one of the males stopped. I knew then. I kept calling, and he walked slowly, very slowly, toward me, leaving the rest of the group. I called again, and after a long time he came up on the porch step and jumped up on my knee. His beauty startled me. He was in full feather now—all his colors glistening, his eyes bright and healthy. I could see every marking on him—he looked as if someone had very carefully painted the perfect lines and colors on his face and body. We silently said hello to each other. And then he jumped off my knee and went down the steps and back to the desert. It was our last encounter.

# The Unkindest Cut of Owl

## DOTTI SANBORN

THE owls have taken to hooting again. I often sleep right through it, but my husband, Andrew, wakes sometimes while it is still dark and eavesdrops on their dialogue. He says that two of them are currently working on an arrangement from "A Tree to Dream In," with variations on the variations. That means they are barred owls. A barred owl can't ask a simple question nor sing a straight declarative sentence without modifying it with arpeggios and double-tonguing the punctuation.

He says one of them seems to be fairly close-by down here in our woods in Bridgton, Maine, and the other out on the island. This week he says they have been engaged in some kind of a vocal *pas de deux:* One has a solo, then the other. After that they both sing at the same time, although it isn't exactly a duet. It doesn't, moreover, seem to come off quite as the score has been written but more as the result of both of them singing so fortissimo that neither can hear anything outside his own head. That's a barred owl's idea of music, of course.

## The Unkindest Cut of Owl

The horned owl spoke from the trees by the north wall before we went to sleep last night, and he was in good form, too. He was so close we could hear him warming up with deep breaths and throat clearings before he went into his first aria. Somewhere up near the Ridge Hall one answered him. They spoke back and forth at suitable intervals for about half an hour, and then ours had to stop and do his homework.

He's taking a course in screech owl and has got the general idea fairly well. He starts way up at the top and comes down from high C to low G without missing a note. It is adequate, but not brilliant. He seems to lack a facility with the black keys. When a genuine, goose-bump screech owl descends the chromatic scale, it has the brilliance of a falling star in stereophonic sound. It brings you standing up out of bed, if you're in bed, and raises the hair on the back of your neck if you aren't.

One of the newer neighbors up here on the ridge asked recently if anyone ever gets to see the owls we hear at night. The answer is that we don't often, and when we do it's real cause for excitement. Some years ago at dusk I was lucky enough to glance toward the western sky at just such an important moment. Silhouetted against the waning sky-glow, a great horned owl was perched on the very top of a tall pine at the edge of our woods. It balanced there for several seconds, then drifted effortlessly and soundlessly down in a wide-wheeling glide and disappeared into the gloom of the tree shadows. We have not actually seen him since that time, although we sometimes hear his voice.

I was also fortunate to get a look at a tiny saw-whet owl one night a while back. At that time we had a front porch over a flagged walk. Our bird feeder hung out there, and food often fell to the stone floor. As a result, a variety of wildlife visitors was attracted to the spot after dark. We never knew what

to expect, so we got into the habit of turning on the porch
light at any time of night that we passed the front door.
Sometimes there would be a couple of raccoons or a skunk.
Once there was a hedgehog chewing quietly on the front step,
and one night there was a neighborhood horse which had
mistaken the porch for his stall after a midnight stroll.

Late one night when I flipped the light switch, a tiny owl
was perched on the feeder shelf. I quickly woke Andrew, and
he identified it as a saw-whet. Probably carried away with its
soft feathers and dainty size, I said I did wish I could touch
the cute little thing. Andrew said he was glad he couldn't. He
said he'd had an encounter with one of the cute little things
once, and it was going to last him the rest of his life.

He said it had been many years before, when he was young,
chivalrous, and romantic. He and his father had just finished
milking one summer night when they realized that something
was beating and fluttering at the inside of a window high up at
the top of the barn. Andrew said he knew right off it was his
duty to climb up over the haymow and rescue the helpless little
feathered thing.

When he got up close he could see it was a saw-whet owl.
As he reached out for it, he had an idea. He would take it
down to the lake where the summer cottages were and become
a hero to the glamorous young lady visitors. Not more than
three seconds later he'd abandoned the plan.

He put his hand out for the tiny whirlwind, and as he did so
it extended eight newly honed switchblades and seized his
reaching fingers. It was at this point that he decided he wanted
no part of the helpless little feathered creature, but the decision was no longer his. It sank all talons directly to the bone
for a firmer grip and took the added precaution of seizing the
end of his thumb in its beak. Andrew said he slid and slithered
down over the haymow as fast as he could, while it kept shift-

30

ing its clutch on his bloody fingers and clinging even tighter on the rough spots.

In the agony of the descent Andrew recalled a horsehide glove down in the harness room, and through blinding tears of pain he lurched in through the door, snatched it, and worked it onto his free hand. With it he seized his embattled companion, who obligingly gave up its grip on the first hand and seized the new horsehide perch.

Andrew said he'd drawn but half a breath of relief when the poor defenseless little thing closed its knives on the gloved fist and cut straight through to the meat again. He said it was no longer a question of making an impression on beautiful young ladies but of how he could leave the scene of battle with anything beyond his wrist to eat supper with.

When he finally managed to ease himself free and toss the little defenseless creature out into the summer night, he said he swore he'd never go near an owl again. No, he said, he didn't want to step out onto the porch and touch this one.

He's never changed his mind. Back in March, a nature column in our Sunday paper was about owls. The author said that some were already nesting and that it was a good time of year to go owling if anyone wanted to get a glimpse of one. He suggested waiting until after dark some evening and then, armed with a long-beamed flashlight, stepping quietly through the woods, calling out as realistically as possible, "WHOO WHOO whoo whoo." He said if you were lucky, you would presently see something light-colored drifting through the trees toward you, and you would hear its answering "WHOO WHOO whoo whoo."

I said I thought it sounded like fun, and I'd like to go. Andrew said not if he knew it. He said he didn't know who this writer was or where he'd come from but that around these parts tiptoeing through the slash and blowdown at night with a long-beamed flashlight was looked upon with suspicion and went by a different name than owl hunting. He said it would be just his luck to go "WHOO WHOO whoo whoo" and have a voice close at hand answer, "The game warden, brother, that's who."

# Spring Passage:
# The Whistling Swan

## MARY LEISTER

E x c e p t as high and usually noisy wedges moving across
the equinoctial skies, migrating water birds are not much a part
of my outdoors world. Their main flyways lie well to the east
of my home in Maryland, and it is only the flocks off course, or
the adventuresome flocks exploring back country, whose flights
I see.

There are enough of these eccentrics, though, that I always
know when the Canada geese are leaving the bay, or returning
to it, for their honking, dog-barking voices override all other
country sounds as their dark skeins sweep over, every bird seeming to jockey for place, argue the route, or generally rouse a
commotion in the flock.

Snow geese I saw but once. A silent skein of round, white
bodies balanced between enamel-black wingtips, high against
the blue of a bright March sky, and never forgotten.

And swans. Whistling swans. Those great, graceful, snow-
white birds whose long necks point their black bills to the far
horizon like compass needles to be followed without fear or

deviation; those splendid birds whose northward flights fill me with a yearning excitement I can scarcely contain and cannot explain, even to myself—those birds I have seen only several times in a dozen years. And I remember every flight.

One springtime morning, my dog, Kela, and I walked along the ridge of the pasture hills, soft grass and soft earth beneath our feet, the air filled with the o-kra-leeing of redwings from the marshes, and a wedge of whistling swans flying from the south with the light of the rising sun on their snow-feathered bodies.

They were flying so low that I could see the black bills tipping the lines of outstretched necks, the dark feet tucked up against arcs of spread white tails, almost feel the lift and the pull of every curving wing. Twenty-five birds forming a perfect wedge, twelve birds to each side, and their leader making the point.

They flew in trim formation without the usual hue and cry of swan voices. Only their leader, at the apex of their flight, fluted a constant musical note.

A flock of seasoned birds, I assumed, all well known to one another, and settled down, now, for a long and steady pull to the north. Flying in confidence and purpose, headed for the coasts and islands of the Arctic seas, where in a month or six weeks each mated pair would find a nesting site on the borders of a marsh and set about building with reeds and grasses and cushions of moss.

The female warms the half-dozen white eggs for the five or so weeks necessary to develop and hatch the down-covered cygnets; but the male feeds her and stands guard over her and over their nest.

For swans are truly family birds. Both male and female feed and train their little ones, and the cygnets run with equal assurance to father or to mother, often climbing upon their backs and riding in safety between partially uplifted wings.

34

But those parental wings cannot lift them into the air, for the parent birds molt all their flight feathers at this time and no one in the family can fly. By the time new flight feathers grow in, the cygnets will also be well feathered, and they will all take to the air together. They strengthen their wing muscles and learn to fly in proper wedge formation so that when autumn comes to the northland, they can join forces with other local families and all fly south together.

The family stays pretty much together through the first winter in the south, but when the restlessness of northerly migration time stirs through the flocks, the cygnets leave their parents and take off with their peers on adventures of their own.

But the parent birds never separate. They mate in their first or second year and stay together in unquestioned faithfulness for however long they both shall live. And forever after. For swans of a mated pair are strictly monogamous. Not slightly so, or partially so, but completely so. This is a situation neither moral nor rigorous but simply the way things are. When one dies, even in the first year of mating, the other goes on alone to the end of his life, though that time may stretch on for years.

These thoughts took only a flash of time to think—though minutes to tell—and while I planned the season ahead for these swans, the flock drew abreast of us, flying above the farm pond that silvered the foot of the hill where we stood.

At this exact moment, the bird at the end of the western leg of the wedge uttered a strange, ringing cry that sent surprising chills of apprehension rippling over my body. He left his place in line and flew steadily up its outer edge, passing so close to his fellows that their beating wing tips nearly touched. He crossed the path of the formation leader and swung down the eastern leg of the V so that he looked each of these flyers in the face as he passed. When he reached the last bird in line, his voice rang again in a cry of such utter desolation that pain twisted in the pit of my stomach.

35

He turned about, sped swiftly up the eastern leg, crossed again in front of the leader, and flew down the western leg, looking, now, into the faces of these.

When he came to the end of the line, he did not call again, nor pause, but flew straight on without a falter, back toward the south. While the unruffled flock pulled steadily northward, one lone white figure beat its way to the south against the immense blue of the sky.

Three days later, one whistling swan came gliding in to float gracefully on the rippling surface of the farm pond. There was nothing to distinguish this swan from any other of his kind, yet I knew, even as he dropped from the sky, that it was the same bird I had seen desert his northward flight above this very pond, days before.

I watched him as I could for the next five days while he floated in silence on the center of the pond. He did not eat. He did not move, except as the current moved him. He sat on the water craning his neck and scanning the skies hour after hour after hour.

Late in the afternoon of the fifth day, with a gray haze obscuring the horizon hills and a thunderstorm grumbling in the south, the lone swan lifted himself from the pond and headed into the north. His white wings beat the heavy air as he strained for altitude. His single cry rang down the misted valley and careened between the hills. It echoes there still.

# The Enduring Bittern

## LAURA RILEY

A friend who lives down the road from our New Jersey farm remembers a bird from her girlhood in Vermont which she swears was an American bittern, and which she says had unusual musical talents.

It was on a remote lake where her family used to spend summers, and what she remembers most is going out every evening to the boathouse where the children in the family had a play-room; there she would put records on the Victrola and then, she says, the bittern would beat time to the music, while marching up and down the beach.

Close questioning cannot shake her from this story.

"I was only about twenty or twenty-five feet from him," she says. "He appeared to enjoy the music—it was mostly fox-trots, which were my favorites at the time. He would be out there wandering around in an aimless sort of way, getting his dinner, I suppose, and when I would play the records he would fall right in with the rhythm and pace of it while tromping up and down the beach."

This would be notable in any bird; in the bittern, whose social graces are next to nil and whose utterances are some of the
strangest and most unmusical in the ornithological world, it is
all but preternatural. ("Not at all inconsistent," said my friend,
reading this. "I can't sing a note but I can certainly tap my foot
in time to music!")

Except for this uncommon and otherwise unreported characteristic, she seems to know her bitterns.

"We only saw him at dusk," she says. "Beyond our beach
was a knoll, then a cove with lots of swampy, marshy ground
with cattails and pickerelweed, an ideal place for him, with a
little brook trickling down. I think he must have spent most of
his time there, except when he would come out and march up
and down to the records. We would hear him calling, that odd
sound that is exactly like someone hammering a stake into the
ground."

An odd sound indeed; it has been called the most peculiar
bird call in the world—and especially the most peculiar *love* call.

But then, the bittern is an odd bird—so solitary and secretive
by habit pattern and camouflage technique that he is often
unseen even when present.

"Time and again I have tried to point one out to bird
watchers," said the noted ornithologist Alexander Sprunt, Jr.,
"and could not, though the bird sat only a few feet away." Another able observer, J. Clinton Andrews, told me recently that
his experience on the Nantucket marshes has been much the
same: "You can see one in the air sometimes," he said, "but
then a bittern doesn't just land in the ordinary sense; it disappears!"

"Not a bird," complained Witmer Stone in his *Bird Studies
in Old Cape May*, "that offers us many opportunities for study."

In a way, though, while not observing the bird at all they
have seen it most clearly—for if there is one essential character-

38

istic that pulses like a tidal current through the bittern's nature, infusing his life's every aspect, it is what amounts to a primal passion for secrecy.

For this reason (that is, the combination of his strange sounds and his ability literally to vanish as if magically before one's eyes) it was a number of years after men had grown quite accustomed to hearing the somewhat ghostly but penetrating calls before the mystery of their source was cleared up.

Before that, it was usually decided that a woodman must be about—sometimes a phantom woodman—cutting trees, splitting logs, or actually driving stakes, and sometimes, as a variation, vigorously operating an old wooden hand pump to get a drink of water. Because this is what his two alternate calls sound like—not just a *little* like, but *exactly* like—giving him the alternate nicknames "Stake-Driver" and "Thunder-Pumper."

One naturalist reported he slogged around for what seemed hours and many miles through sloughs and wooded swampland in a determined search for the woodman he was certain must be in the neighborhood, before giving up and only learning later what it must have been that he heard.

"The bittern is pumping in the fen," wrote Thoreau on learning what it was, but even Thoreau had few more intimate glimpses to offer of this wetland hermit.

Of those who have seen the bittern, none has ever described him as fancy-looking, but his subdued feathered garb suits his retiring personality (a tragic irony were such a one suddenly to sprout a peacock's tail!): medium height and build, twenty-four to thirty-four inches from end to end, the soft, fluffy plumage streaked yellow-brown and buffy on the neck and breast and shading to solid dark brown on the back and slatey on the crown. His sharp-pointed bill is yellowish-green and longer than his head, and his short legs are greenish-yellow and trail behind when he takes flight.

His outstanding feature, if he could be said to have one, is a pair of sparkling golden eyes, placed unusually low down on his head, with penetrating black irises.

But against his usual background it is not only difficult to distinguish his individual physical characteristics, it is almost impossible to see him at all, so identical are his streaked markings both in hue and dimension to the reeds and marsh grass against which he is almost always standing.

The extent to which this is true is hard to imagine; it is, more than anything else, like one of those trick visual puzzles in which you are told to find objects concealed in a picture by confusing lines that seem to delineate several things simultaneously.

I once saw a bittern in our own yard, in a spot where the grass had been allowed to grow tall near a pond. There had been much rain that year, and the area was almost like a marsh. I went by the front door, and something made me stop—I did not know what at first. I stared and stared and finally got out my binoculars and stared some more and still could not figure it out. I only knew, with the certainty of one who has observed a place so long it is known as well as the back of one's hand, that something was different from the last time I had looked out at it.

At last, going over the area minutely with my glasses, I saw what it was—a narrow clump of grass that had not been there yesterday and had not grown there overnight: the American bittern, bill pointed skyward, body narrowed and held absolutely motionless, his striping precisely matching his surroundings, while those two bright-gold eyes—eyes which are set so exceptionally low in his head that he has in his defense posture binocular vision, able to see straight ahead, on the ground, and in a considerable arc all around him—stared back and waited to see what I would do.

40

I called my husband, and we both watched, both of us hoping to see him break the visual pattern and move away.

But we never did.

Few persons even if so inclined have the time and patience to outlast a bittern in this situation, and we did not that day. We resumed other occupations and tried to look out whenever we could. But he was always there, still poised as we had seen him first.

Then suddenly, between glances out the door, he simply disappeared; we looked out and that tall clump of grass that had grown up overnight was gone.

At first it hardly seemed possible, so we looked for a long time, thinking we might have misplaced him somewhere in our visual field. But he was really gone (I think!)—and then somehow it hardly seemed as if he had been there at all, as if the whole experience had been some kind of imagined illusion—a feeling that has been noted by others who have seen him, and then seen him disappear, "leaving," as one writer said, "no spot in the vision, so much had the bird been a part of the marsh and the sedges, the sun and the shadow."

Oh, the quiet bittern has his moments which are neither quiet nor entirely solitary—but they are private moments reserved for sharing with a few chosen intimates, a practice not without charm and merit.

Concealed beneath that subdued coat of streaked brown and buff on the chest and shoulders are two patches of white feathers capable of expanding and fanning straight out from the shoulders like two extra snowy wings; and when he believes himself alone and unobserved except by his mate (or sometimes a rival) he can display them with as much ardor and abandon as any courting male.

Back and forth he will go, parading himself in his finery, his pure-white "wings" pointing sometimes directly skyward, some-

41

times at right angles to each other as if he might be contemplating using them to take off in flight; turning them as he turns his body so they will appear their largest and most impressive to the object of his emotions.

He may crouch, then take off occasionally in a spirited leap that will take him six or even twelve feet directly up in the air —and if it is in conflict with another male, the two may leap simultaneously at each other and grapple briefly but fiercely in midair, a conflict usually settled without bloodshed, however, despite the daggerlike weapons available in their sharp beaks. Several tilts like this and all bitterns involved usually retire to their corners for a rest.

The "wildest love song in the world," as it has been called— the "thunder-pumping" or "stake-driving" depending on which version he is giving that day—may or may not accompany this visual display. But it, too, is dependent on a special physical adaptation that comes over the bittern at breeding season, and as befits this generally undemonstrative bird, this too is largely an interior alteration. As the breeding time approaches, the male bittern's neck and chest thicken and enlarge, the result of the inside growth of extra reinforcing muscular and gelatinous tissues attached to the gullet, so that when the spirit moves him to bellow forth his feelings, his physical being is ready to obey.

And, seeing the bittern screw himself up to sound forth these "weird, wild love notes," as Arthur Cleveland Bent called them, is to understand why they sound unlike any other bird, and also why they can sometimes be heard for perhaps several miles on a clear night, for his method is similar to that of the tiny spring peeper tree frog whose clarion calls ring out for similar distances on a spring evening.

First he jerks his head forward as if to stretch and enlarge his throat capacity, at the same time taking in a large swallow of air which he forces down his esophagus with a great gulp, closing his bill with a click so the air cannot escape; that done, he repeats the process, apparently with a greater effort as his capacity fills, and repeats it again and again until his throat is so distended it must ache, and even with great effort he can take in no more.

Then from this throat that has formed literally a giant bellows he lets go with violent, abrupt contortions of the head and neck, "suggestive," said one observer, "of a person horribly afflicted with nausea," and belches out the sounds which have been variously written down as "pump-er-lunk," "oong-ka-choonk," and "plum pudd'n," depending on the auditor; but the aptest description by far is their likeness to the pump handle and stake driver.

All this effort is worthwhile, of course, if it sufficiently inspires a female bittern to set about building an ingenious nest of reeds and rushes—not only a sturdy nest platform but one, again befitting the nature of this bird, with secret entrances and exits.

Typically the nest itself is located in a fresh or brackish marsh and built of last year's dead grasses and rushes, which are broken off and laid in a mat until they form a platform a foot or so across, either on the ground or an inch or so above, sometimes loosely connected to surrounding rushes as a kind of adjustable floating anchor, should surrounding waters flood or recede.

Then she picks her way silently, slowly, through the surrounding rushes, breaking off grasses as she goes and laying them down in a path, actually a secret tunnel-like runway of deliberately broken and trampled vegetation perhaps a dozen or as much as twenty-five feet long—and perhaps several of these—undiscernible from the outside but sturdy enough for her to traverse quickly if necessary.

At last she retires to the nest platform, lays three to seven slightly glossy olive to buffy eggs, and begins to incubate them for some twenty-eight days—and usually, if her timing is right, the new rushes begin to sprout and grow on just about this date, so that by the time she is well into incubation, the new growth has come up and leaned over her, tentlike, from both sides, entirely completing her concealment.

So well hidden is the bittern nest that neither Audubon nor the great ornithologist Alexander Wilson ever saw one in their lifelong investigations.

Should a stranger pass by, however, she will of course assume her cryptic defense posture—feathers and body and neck tightened and contracted and bill pointed skyward until she becomes perhaps twice her usual height but so reedlike in appearance she is all but undetectable—and with even a further astonishing adaptation: Should an errant breeze cause the surrounding vegetation to sway, the bittern will immediately start to sway also with the precise motion and speed of the grasses around her, quickening and subsiding as the grasses do in response to the air currents, so that an unmoving stance will not betray her presence amid the suddenly moving background.

The bittern young have this same adaptive ability almost as soon as they are out of the egg. One observer reported seeing what he and a companion supposed were four stakes, the remains of a shooting blind, until closer examination showed the "stakes" were the motionless necks and bills of four young bitterns still in their natal down. When approached closely they reacted as do their parents when occasionally forced to abandon their sham, by snapping their tiny bills and emitting a faint hissing snarl—rather admirable, considering their leverage in the situation.

The young are fed the same organisms they will hunt as adults—all kinds of marsh animals, lizards, fish, snakes, eels, mollusks, mice, and especially frogs, the apparent favorites—for the bittern feeds freely, even gluttonously, on all the marsh offers. These are partly predigested and regurgitated by the parents when they return to the nest, and the young seize their bills and shake them until they spill out the contents of their upper digestive systems.

The bittern hunts as he lives: slowly, deliberately, and successfully, with an apparent irreducible minimum of waste motion. He approaches a fishing ground with stealth and almost imperceptible movements—his speed has been likened to the hands of a clock. Watching him, it is hard to see that he is moving at all, except that some minutes later he is in a different spot.

Once in place, he waits until soon the frogs and others are cavorting about as if entirely unaware of his presence. Then when one comes in range, the bill shoots out and seizes or spears the prey, after which he will retire to a different spot to digest and wait again, and perhaps to ruminate.

What does he ruminate about? What does he ponder there, on the edge of the slough, his rolling eyeballs turning now to the fenny bog below, now to the grassy far shore?

It is difficult to say; but there has been a surprising amount of speculation, for, like many a solitary eccentric, the bittern's personal outlook on life has attracted a degree of interest and puzzled scrutiny far beyond the usual routine cataloguing of pertinent vital statistics.

The poet Shelley, for example, wrote a dedication describing a future time when much of that with which we are presently familiar will have changed, even disappeared:

"St. Paul and Westminster shall stand shapeless and nameless ruins in the midst of an unpeopled marsh," he said; "the piers of Waterloo Bridge shall become the nuclei of islets and reeds and osiers, and cast the jagged shadows of their broken arches on the solitary stream. . . .

"And London," he said, "shall be a habitation of bitterns."

Perhaps this, or something quite a lot like this, is what the contemplative bittern may have in mind.

45

# The Wandering Albatross

## GEORGE CLARK

*And I had done a hellish thing*
*And it would work 'em woe:*
*For all averred I had killed the bird*
*That made the breeze to blow.*
*Ah wretch! said they, the bird to slay*
*That made the breeze to blow!*
—FROM COLERIDGE'S "THE RIME
OF THE ANCIENT MARINER"

I T is no great wonder that the albatross—and the wandering albatross in particular—has become closely linked with the sea and sailing legends. No bird is closer kin to the seafarer in its life-style and habits. Pelagic, awkward and uncomfortable on land, its true elements are the wind and sea. A perennial wanderer, circling the globe year after year, like the sailor it seems to have no real home. It thrives on wind and boisterous seas and languishes in calms. On land it appears foolish; at sea it is a monarch—dignified, graceful, and regal.

*Diomedea exulans*—Zeus-taught exile—is the Latin name Linnaeus gave it. That he chose a name describing the wandering albatross's solitary life rather than one noting its great size pointedly draws attention to the extreme singularity of its ways.

Alone the vast majority of its life, the wandering albatross presents a strikingly lonely appearance to sailors far at sea. And when it takes up its silent vigil crisscrossing the ship's wake, almost as though to assuage such loneliness, it more than completes the image of a lost and aimless exile. This is far from the truth. A wandering albatross is very much at home in its wind-swept solitary existence, and rather than expire of loneliness will probably live to a ripe old age of seventy or eighty.

The world's largest living flying bird, with a wingspan sometimes reaching fifteen feet, the wandering albatross is rivaled in size only by its close cousin the royal albatross. Both birds come from a family of some eighteen species, members of which range the oceans over both hemispheres.

The range of the wandering albatross, however, is restricted to the high southern latitudes. Only rarely has it been discovered straying north of 40°S. To the south it travels as far as Antarctica, and in longitude it circles the world, riding the strong westerlies of the roaring 40s, 50s, and 60s. In the course of its long life each bird will circumnavigate many times, flying hundreds of thousands of miles.

The environment of the wandering albatross is one of almost constant winds, vast stretches of empty ocean, and very little land. The land that does exist is in the form of small rocky islands, barren except for all but the heartiest of life's species. And the winds, blowing almost continuously out of the west, over endless fetch, build seas of mammoth proportions, capable of rolling a ship under, or, with a small boat, of pitching her end over end. Adapting almost perfectly to this windy, sea-tossed band of earth, the wandering albatross has specialized in the ability to manipulate wind currents and to make long, effortless flights.

For hundreds of years sailors have marveled at the ability of the wandering albatross to follow a ship for hours without once flapping its wings. For days and even weeks the same bird might follow. Did it never rest? they wondered. Did it never sleep? What the wondering seamen did not realize was that even as they marveled at its endless motion, the wandering albatross was essentially at rest; that with its vast wings fully extended it is capable of locking them open, much as a horse locks its legs to remain standing while it is asleep. Direction and altitude may then be controlled with trim alone, an activity requiring slight effort. Its wings thus set, its course determined, it lets the vertical variations in windspeed carry it along swiftly.

Windspeed just above the sea's surface is slowed by friction with the waves. It increases significantly only a few feet up (as every sailor can attest), and continues to increase up to about fifty feet. Utilizing this windspeed variation, the typical flight pattern of the wandering albatross is to glide down with the wind on the leeward leg, gaining speed and momentum, then to wheel back into it at the sea's surface, rise on the increasing vertical windspeed, and, after regaining altitude, to repeat the cycle. Moving down or across the wind, the bird may travel many miles this way, trimming its wings as the pattern demands, but without real exertion.

The birds are ordinarily alone on their long patrols, but ship-following is one of the few activities that may bring two or more wandering albatrosses together at sea. Another is to feast on a dead whale or other large creature. Well-developed olfactory organs permit the birds to smell ship's garbage, oily meat, or blubber for many miles.

While the dynamics of the wandering albatross's flight were especially marveled at by early sailors, naturalists had still further questions, such as the extent of its range, the significance of its elaborate mating dance, and the frequency of its brooding. And mild controversy often surfaced among the naturalists over the purpose of the oily, evil-smelling liquid wandering albatrosses would sometimes spray from their tubelike nostrils. Some people claimed it was a defensive weapon, others that it was used in grooming, or sprayed on the sea in gales to quiet the

48

waves. These and other questions, kept open largely by the difficulty of banding and following individual birds, have provided sailors and scientists with countless hours of imaginative speculation. Recent studies have produced some of the answers. Others, however, such as where the wandering albatross disappears in the height of gales, remain elusive.

The life of the wandering albatross typically begins on one of the rocky, windswept islands above the south 30 latitudes—on South Georgia, perhaps, or one of the tiny Crozet group far off the southeast tip of Africa. The eggs, laid one to a nest, hatch in early March, which corresponds to our early fall. Several months earlier, however, the parent birds have gathered on the island to mate and either put one of last year's nests in order or build a new one.

When the chick emerges from its shell it weighs about twelve ounces and is covered with thick brown down. Weak, helpless, and in danger from marauding skuas, it is possessed of a voracious appetite. Therefore, one parent must remain at the nest while the other goes off to feed and bring back food for the chick. Returning to the nest with its gullet full of fish and cuttlefish, the parent opens its beak and regurgitates a half-digested meal down the throat of the offspring. The parents then trade places, and the other goes off to fish. At the end of a month the chick will weigh 6½ pounds and be out of danger from the skuas. The parents may then go off to sea to fish together.

The days, meanwhile, are growing shorter and colder. Fall is slipping into winter, and much of the body weight that the chick has been gaining is in the form of a thick layer of fat to protect and sustain it through the coming months.

In June, the beginning of the Antarctic winter, the parent birds leave the chick to wait out the long season alone, except for the similarly helpless company of the other chicks. And then, wrapped in its cocoon of body fat and thick down, and

49

huddled deep in its nest, the chick slips into a semiconscious state approaching hibernation. Its rate of metabolism declines sharply, and drawing slowly from its thick layer of body fat for heat and energy, it survives the gales and freezing temperatures with reserves to spare. It will need these reserves, as its parents will not be returning with the warm weather to continue feeding it. For its next meal it must go to sea itself, which means it must first learn to fly, a lengthy and taxing enterprise.

Winters, as a rule, are severe in the rookeries. Blizzards blast out of the west repeatedly, but their very strength prevents them from piling the snow in drifts much higher than the nest tops. Facing into these onslaughts, the young bird sleeps away the winter, waiting for spring and carefully husbanding its strength. Meanwhile, beneath its thick down, it's developing its first coat of true feathers.

With the first days of spring the chick stirs out of its sleep and begins to stretch and exercise its wings. They are still covered with down, but this soon begins sloughing off, and by November glistening brown feathers have replaced the down completely. The young bird is now in its fledgling stage and ready to learn to fly. The first problem is how to become airborne.

Because the wandering albatross's long, thin wings are specialized for sustained flight, taking off is sometimes a problem, even for practiced adult birds. Lacking sufficient wind to lift them from a standing jump, the birds have to run along the surface of the ground or water to gain airspeed. For a bird with short, underdeveloped legs, this is no piece of cake; for a fledgling it is altogether impossible. Instead, it must find a low cliff to leap from. Or, if none of these is in the area, then at least a hill to run down.

Selecting from what's available, the fledgling begins struggling up laboriously, with frequent rests, until it reaches the top. There it sits down for another rest. Finally, its nerve and strength gathered for the attempt, it rises, faces the edge, flaps its wings a few seconds, and jumps.

Whether it runs downhill or jumps off cliffs, its first attempts at flight are invariably short and laughably amateurish. Its landings are still worse. From all appearances it must be a painful and discouraging experience. There is no giving up, however. Instinct and growing hunger drive it to struggle up the hill again and again. Days and weeks pass, and gradually its short flights become longer—from a few feet to a few yards —and at last all the way to the bottom of the hill. In a month, the fledgling will be able to sustain flight, and shortly thereafter take its first meal from the sea.

By then it will be summer again. The old males begin to arrive once more to breed. When the fledglings leave with them, at the onset of winter, they all will be accomplished fliers.

Surviving the agile skuas and the other hazards of their first year and having left the rookery, the majority of young wandering albatrosses can look forward to a long life. The next seven to eight years are their period of adolescence, during which they will circle the globe almost constantly, rarely, if ever, touching land. At the end of this time, sexually mature, they will return to land and take up the brooding chores of adulthood. If they successfully mate and brood a chick, they will skip a year before returning to breed again. This alternate-year breeding pattern helps explain the presence of adult wandering albatrosses found far at sea throughout the breeding season.

Although it is still a mystery where wandering albatrosses go in the height of gales—perhaps they soar above the winds, or ride them out on the sea's surface, obscured in the maelstroms of waves and spindrift—there is no question of where they go in the rare calms. Deprived of lifting air currents, and unadapted for prolonged flights without them, the birds glide down to the sea's surface and wait out the doldrums as becalmed as any sailor. With the return of the wind, they spread their wings and ascend once more into their true element.

# *Penguins*

## ROGER TORY PETERSON

"Comical"—"adorable"—"the little fellow in the dress suit"—it is tempting to be anthropomorphic about penguins. Using human comparisons, it is easy to think of them as little clowns, the ridiculous dwarfs that enliven the circus, waddling with baggy pants across the arena for our amusement.

They are far from that; they are not little people dressed in feathers. They are highly specialized birds dedicated to penguinism, a life molded by the cold impersonal sea, harsh climate, and the crowded colonies in which they reproduce. No other birds are so superbly adapted for an aquatic or submarine life. The water is their element. The air is for the petrels, shearwaters, and albatrosses.

Although the popular concept is that there is just one kind of penguin, stereotyped by the Adélie, there are actually seventeen species. These are divided into six genera, easily grouped by their head patterns:

• the *Spheniscus* (latinized Greek for "little wedge"), including the jackass or black-footed penguin of Africa and the

53

Magellanic, Peruvian, and Galápagos penguins of South America;

• the *Pygoscelis* (loosely translated from the Greek, it means "rump-legged"), including the Adélie, the chinstrap, and the gentoo;

• the *Eudyptes* (Greek for "good diver"), the six crested penguins—the rockhopper, macaroni, royal, erect-crested, fiordland, and Snares;

• the *Aptenodytes* ("featherless diver"), the biggest and most colorful penguins, the emperor and the king;

• the *Megadyptes* (Greek for "large diver") or yellow-eyed penguin, assigned its own genus;

• the *Eudyptula* ("good little diver"), the little blue (or fairy) penguin and the white-flippered penguin, of New Zealand and southern Australia.

I have seen and photographed them all in the course of more than a dozen expeditions to the Antarctic and the Subantarctic in as many years.

Just what is the penguin environment? I confess that I cannot define it precisely, nor can I suggest a common denominator—other than the obvious fact that penguins are confined to the cooler sea currents of the Southern Hemisphere. Of the seventeen species, only four—the emperor, Adélie, chinstrap, and gentoo—live on the Antarctic continent. The rest inhabit more temperate latitudes, and one actually reaches the equator. Thus, the penguin environment varies from the eternally frozen slopes and sea ice of Antarctica to such diverse habitats as the tussock-covered hills of Macquarie, the green pastures of the Falklands, the ferny dells of the Aucklands, the forested fiords of New Zealand, the scrub of coastal Australia, and the parched lava flows and cacti of the Galápagos.

A penguin colony invites comparison with a crowded city. The Adélie rookery at Esperanza (Hope Bay), near the tip of the Antarctic Peninsula, has a population of perhaps 200,000 birds, roughly the same as the human population of Mecca, or of Syracuse, New York. The great assemblage of Magellanic penguins at Punta Tombo on the coast of Patagonia exceeds one million, equal to the number of human inhabitants of Baltimore or Brussels.

I have spent many intensely active days in both of these megacolonies, but the penguin city I know best is the Adélie metropolis at Cape Crozier in the New Zealand sector of the Antarctic. This colony, by latest figures, numbers somewhat more than 100,000 pairs. If we assume that most couples fledge at least one youngster, the total midsummer population is on the order of 300,000, about that of Rochester, New York.

At the invitation of the National Science Foundation, I spent a month at Cape Crozier in November and December 1965, helping Dr. William Sladen of Johns Hopkins University with his banding studies. I also was asked to observe some of the problems related to wildlife conservation in the Antarctic.

It was early November when the helicopter from McMurdo put me down near the hut on the hill above the penguin colony where I joined Dr. Sladen. He told me that practically all of the males had already arrived and were holding or disputing territory. The first to come had trudged with short waddling steps across several miles of sea ice to reach the rubble-strewn slopes where they congregated for reproduction. At Cape Crozier the distance from the open sea is not as great as it is at some other colonies, where penguins may be compelled to walk as much as sixty miles to reach home base.

A few males, not yet joined by their look-alike mates (or perhaps they were first-time hopefuls), stood erect, with chests out and bills pointed skyward, while they fanned their flippers rhythmically. Their hoarse voices rolled to a resounding *gug-gug-gug-gug-gaaaaa*—their "ecstatic display."

55

Each day, additional females arrived. Established pairs reaffirmed their devotion by raucous demonstrations. Facing each other, toe to toe, with flippers at their sides, they wagged their uplifted heads to and fro, climaxing the performance with bills pointed to the zenith. This posturing, called "mutual display," was repeated every few minutes. It helps to keep the pair bond strong, at least for that season.

Dr. Richard Penney, the behaviorist, who marked a large number of birds at Wilkes, found that a majority—about 83 percent of those that had been paired the year before and had survived—resumed marital relations. Returning to the very spot where they had nested before, they instantly recognized each other by voice. Dr. Penney determined this by means of tape recordings. Some whose mates had come to grief during the months at sea were forced to find new partners. A few switched partners, particularly those birds whose nesting attempts the year before had been failures.

Based on this evidence, the divorce and remarriage rate of Adélies from year to year is about 17 percent. This is comparable to the divorce rate of yellow-eyed penguins, which varies from 13 to 18 percent yearly, as determined by the investigations of Dr. Richdale in New Zealand.

In the frozen terrain of Antarctica, devoid of grass and sticks, the only nesting materials available to Adélies are pebbles and small stones. These the birds gather energetically, often walking a hundred yards or more to some spot outside the colony that has not been depleted of suitable stones. Selecting one of just the right size, two to three centimeters or about an inch in diameter, the bird trots back to the nest site as fast as its stubby legs will carry it, flippers stiffly outstretched for balance. Laying the treasure at the feet of its loved one, it elicits the noisy mutual display that seems to be *de rigueur* for the occasion.

56

*Penguins*

Whereas some individuals work hard and honestly for their stones, others are addicted to stealing. While the homesteader has its back turned, a neighbor may slyly amble over, snatch a pebble, and deposit it in its own nest. Should it be confronted by the owner before it can grab the stone, it may stop in its tracks and look blankly innocent as though to say, "Who, me?" One experimenter who furnished a supply of colored pebbles found that they held a special attraction to pilfering penguins, who eventually distributed them from nest to nest throughout the colony.

A homecoming Adélie trying to make its way through the crowded colony runs the risk of a poke or a jab from every bird within reach. Sometimes a serious fight breaks out, or a less dominant bird is chased and soundly thrashed. At first glance, life in a penguin community would seem to be chaotic, but there is a pattern, a kind of order.

Only a highly specialized ethologist would attempt to explain the behavior and mannerisms of an Adélie or any other species of penguin. A penguin, on the other hand, must have an innate understanding of the body language of its neighbors.

Besides the "ecstatic" and "mutual" displays, all sorts of gestures are meaningful to them. They may bump each other with their chests or chase, peck, and paddle each other with their stiff flippers, actions that obviously are aggressive.

But what is meant when they roll their eyes, exposing the whites? What is the message when the bill is pointed into the wingpit, or when they bow to each other, sometimes shallowly, sometimes deeply? What is the meaning of the sideways stare, the pointing posture, the crouching gape, and the fluffed or raised feathers on the crown?

Even such ethologists as Sladen, J. Sapin-Jaloustre, Penney, E. B. Spurr, and D. G. Ainley may differ somewhat in their interpretations of these actions. But to be a successful penguin,

57

it is imperative to know this language of recognition, pair bonding, aggression, appeasement, escape, play, and frustration, as well as a number of other things less obvious to the human observer.

Within a matter of days after my arrival at Cape Crozier, the first eggs were laid. On each bed of stones, a chalky greenish-white egg appeared, followed about three days later by a slightly smaller one. Then the males took over the incubation. The temperature had risen above the melt point, and reddish mud stained the white bellies of the females, who filed down to the sea to renew their depleted energies. During courtship and laying they had fasted for about three weeks, losing 20 percent of their weight. Many of them showed dirty tread marks on their backs, mementos left by the muddy feet of copulating males.

The traffic of soiled females waddling downhill coalesced into straggling lines. Some birds, in a greater hurry, flopped forward on their bellies and, propelled by flailing feet and flippers, tobogganed speedily down the slopes. Reaching the ice lip, they congregated by the hundreds, awaiting the propitious moment for a mass departure. If leopard seals were patrolling offshore, the penguins might wait at the edge of the open water for as much as two days, building up to a concentration of many thousands.

On days when the tides brought the sea ice right up to the shore, they were less hesitant; they ventured forth on foot, forming long black lines across the white ice. Each penguin took its cue from the bird ahead, and when the lead bird stopped, they all stopped to rest or even to sleep a little. Then onward again, perchance in a difference direction. They might stand or mill around by the hundreds, until the pressure building up from behind made it imperative for some to leave.

I witnessed a late-spring blizzard a week after the females

had laid their eggs and had made their exodus. The snow-laden winds swept down the slopes of Mount Terror with gale force, confining us to our creaking hut for nearly two days. When the skies cleared, Dr. Sladen and I ventured forth to find that those penguins that had occupied the merest depressions were half buried in the snow or encased almost completely, with naught but their heads or the tips of their bills showing above the crusted surface.

None of the males abandoned his charges. I suspect that occasionally the hard-packed snow might become a tomb. However, a male Adélie is able to go without food for as much as five or six weeks, from the time it leaves the sea, makes the trek ashore, takes up territory, mates, and incubates, until its partner, who has been away fourteen to seventeen days, returns from the sea. During this period males may lose as much as one-third of their weight, dropping from twelve or fourteen pounds to eight or nine.

When the females return for the changeover, they must run the gauntlet of leopard seals, but most of them are experienced at evading this dreaded predator. In ice-free water, they can probably outswim a leopard seal, but when negotiating slush ice, they run a much greater risk.

When the male, famished and emaciated after his six-week fast, goes to sea, he stays away for about fourteen days, gorging on krill before returning for a final session on the eggs. Less than a week later, the first egg hatches, then the following day, the second. The blessed event takes place about five weeks after the eggs are laid.

The downy newborn Adélie chick is silvery gray with a dark head. This baby coat is superseded within ten days by a longer, woollier down. The chick is then dull sooty brown or blackish all over, not nearly as attractive as the bicolored babies of the chinstrap or the gentoo.

The chicks are very vulnerable at first, and one parent must act as baby-sitter while the other is fishing for krill. If the temperature drops, the chicks must be brooded. They must be guarded against skuas, kelp gulls, and giant fulmars. Not for a moment can vigilance be relaxed; at Paradise Bay on the Antarctic Peninsula, I saw an opportunistic sheathbill peck the eyes out of a penguin chick when its parent was distracted by a neighbor.

The brooding period in Adélies may last from three weeks to a month; then the fur-coated young, growing fast, start to move around a bit. They join the youngsters of neighboring families until a crèche, or nursery, is formed.

Why these huddles? Are they formed for mere togetherness, for warmth (as must be the case with emperors), or are they for mutual protection against predators? The latter offers the most likely advantage.

During this period both parents may be at sea much of the time, trying to satisfy the insatiable appetites of their babies, but usually one or more guards—"aunties"—are about. It has been suggested that these may not be parents of chicks in the crèche but simply unemployed birds. If a skua hovers overhead looking for the main chance, it is threatened with a lacerating beak.

When an adult returns with a crawful of euphausiids, it does not feed just any chick in the crèche. It finds its own, identifying it by voice. Although one penguin may sound exactly like another to our ears, penguins are as sensitive to nuances of sound between themselves as human beings are. Parents undoubtedly learn to know the voices of their progeny during the first few hours of life.

When an adult arrives at the crèche, it sounds off. The chick, recognizing the familiar voice, rushes out and identifies itself (a strange chick would be rebuffed). It then begins to nibble

60

at its parent's bill to stimulate the feeding response. With its own bill wedged crosswise in its parent's, it gobbles up the half-processed krill that the parent regurgitates. After several such feedings, when the supply is gone, the potbellied youngster may still beg frantically for more. This eventually causes the beleaguered Adélie to flee with its bumbling child in hot pursuit, stumbling over rocks and bumping into other penguins. These food chases are as amusing to watch as an old Mack Sennett comedy.

But what of the chick whose parent is killed at sea by a leopard seal, or, worse, who has lost both of its parents? While other babies around it are well fed, it grows weaker and weaker. Unable to put up a defense, or perhaps wandering from the crèche in desperation, it eventually falls prey to the skua or the giant fulmar. These predators are less likely to take healthy, well-guarded chicks.

Mortality is high in Adélie colonies. Eggs and chicks suffer a loss that may vary from 40 to 80 percent. And yet some Adélies manage to raise both of their young. The related chinstrap more often than not succeeds in fledging both of its bicolored chicks.

To me, watching penguins has been a moving, thought-provoking experience. Although they may look a bit like little brothers nattily dressed in feathers, they respond to life rhythms quite alien to our own. They are dedicated to being penguins, and they are good at it. Because of their great numbers and the simplified ecosystems in which they live, we can readily observe cause and effect, some of the basic principles of survival —and life.

# II  *Discovering the World of Birds*

*Some are born birders, some achieve birding, and some have birding thrust upon them. But whether the interest in birds develops early or late, it is often inspired either by a book or by the impassioned example of others. In any case, most bird watchers, like those in the following accounts, come to feel that they are in the best of company.*

# It Happened One Night

## KAY MCCRACKEN

P E O P L E often ask me how I happened to get interested in birds. "Happened" is a good way to put it, for in the beginning, twenty-six years ago, I had no intention of taking birds seriously. I merely wanted to learn the difference between a gull and a tern and a few other little items.

It happened at Christmastime. I was a reporter on the *Times*, here in Corpus Christi, Texas, and periodically was sent to interview some visiting VIP from the bird world: presidents and other officials of National Audubon, authors of bird books—people like that. They gave me good stories because they were experts with the press as well as with birds, but I always had the feeling that my questions were inane and that the stories would have been much better had I known just a little bit about the subject.

And I kept wondering why these important people, mostly from big eastern cities, kept coming down to my part of Texas. Finally, I asked one what brought him here. He looked at me with some amusement and some pity and said, "Because the birds are here."

It made me realize that I must be missing something. Then I found that a fellow reporter, Mary Gene Kelly, had a similar inkling, but we didn't know how to begin.

Shortly before that Christmas, Mary Gene and I were shopping (probably on office time) in a bookstore, and there on the counter lay two new Audubon bird guides, one to the land birds, one to the water birds. The pictures were fascinating.

We decided on the two volumes, one for each of us, for Christmas gifts and turned our backs while they were wrapped so we'd be "surprised" come Christmas. We planned to swap books later, quite sure that those two contained all we wished to know.

I worked the late shift that Christmas Eve and well remember writing fifteen or twenty obituaries; it seemed as if everyone in South Texas was dying that night. Church bells chimed midnight carols as I drove home in the moonlight. I lighted my tree, made a cup of eggnog, and sat down in solo festivity to open my presents, saving the book until last. I cannot now recall the contents of any other package.

Mine was the land-bird book—orioles, grosbeaks, buntings, thrushes, warblers, hundreds of birds. And so colorful! (I am still partial to the land birds, and Mary Gene to the water birds in her book.) I took the guide to bed with me and, reading, was overwhelmed to find that most of those birds could be seen in Corpus Christi in the course of a year. But I had never seen them! Had I been blind? It was nearly five o'clock on Christmas morning when I turned out my light. But a door to a new world had opened.

Mary Gene was equally excited. Our next paychecks were invested in binoculars, and thereafter we were no longer seen in all the old familiar places: We spent our time at the beach, in parks and cemeteries, touring country lanes, and hiking fence rows. My bridge game fell off so badly that former partners refused to play with me.

*It Happened One Night*

Nobody could have started with less bird background than I. The scissor-tail I remembered from childhood but didn't know it was a flycatcher, and the brown pelican, then prominent on the bayfront, I knew. An Eagle Scout identified a mockingbird for me—it had lived in my yard for years. Soon others came to share our interest, and some friends who went with us to watch the bird watchers (they said we were very funny) ended up watching birds too.

One great irony of it all is that before coming to the *Caller-Times* I had worked in Rockport and counted Connie Hagar, even then making ornithological history on the Texas coast, among my good friends. But I never asked her one question about birds. What an opportunity missed! Needless to say, that oversight has since been corrected.

That first bird guide, so thumbed and worn it must be handled with care, has a place of honor among many bird books now occupying some fifteen feet of shelves, not to mention volumes on wild flowers, butterflies and other insects, shells, snakes, mammals, frogs, stars. For one area of natural history inevitably leads to others. And I've only begun. I could fill another five-foot shelf with my want list.

Just knowing so many birds is enough, but knowing them also enhances other activities, especially travel. And "because the birds are here" I have come to know hundreds of interesting people from elsewhere, bird friends from all around the globe.

I sometimes wonder how it would have been had Mary Gene given me something else that Christmas instead of a bird book. Would I never have discovered the birds? The thought is suffocating.

# Discovering the World of Birds

BENNIE BENGTSON

W HEN I was about ten my mother gave me a book—
Albert Field Gilmore's *Birds Through the Year*—that had a
greater influence on my life and that has since given me more
enjoyment and satisfaction than any one other book that came
into my hands during my boyhood. Where she obtained it I
cannot now recall, if I ever knew, but it certainly wasn't locally,
for at the time there couldn't have been a bookstore within
four hundred miles.

The book lies in front of me on the table as I write; its well-
worn dark-brown cover shows wild geese in flight against a
background of cumulus clouds, and no better or more apt
design could possibly have been used. I had often seen and
heard wild geese going over in the spring and fall, their flying
Vs and wild honking awakening in me a yearning I could not
explain. The book was equally fascinating, opening doors that
I hadn't been aware of before.

The wild geese sailed off into mysterious and romantic
regions I knew nothing of and had no way of reaching. The

book did exactly the opposite. It showed me a marvelous world in the commonplace that I had at my very elbow, and which I hadn't seen before. All I had to do was open my eyes and look.

The author, who lived in Maine (which has a climate quite similar to the part of Minnesota where I lived), described the birds he saw through the year—spring, summer, fall, and winter. The book was written for juvenile readers, slanted perhaps for the middle teens, but I had at ten read some books my parents were reading and was able to understand at least in part what these were about. All of the illustrations were in black and white, but the brief biography of each bird described it succinctly and told when and where to look for it. I learned about migrants that were only seen in spring and fall as they passed through, about birds that were summer residents and nested here, and about birds, only a handful, that remained with us all the year around. For the most part only the common birds were included—a few others but not many.

Other bird books followed. The first of these—Chester A. Reed's *Bird Guide: Land Birds East of the Rockies*—I found in a Sears, Roebuck catalog. It had the birds in color, reproduced from paintings, and was helpful, though in some instances the color reproduction was not too accurate. It was pocket-size, and I slipped it into my pocket when I went looking for birds. I still have it, worn almost to tatters, ink-stained and falling apart at the seams.

About this time too, or possibly a few years later, the old Minneapolis *Journal*, the daily paper my father read, started running a column on the back page, the same page the cartoons were on, called "Nature Notes." It was edited by the famous naturalist and author John Burroughs, and in it he answered questions sent in by readers. It concerned birds, flowers, trees, insects, but most of the queries were about birds, that apparently being a primary interest of his followers. I cannot recall that I wrote in and asked any questions, but I read it avidly.

There were several creeks in our vicinity, three of them converging just northeast of our barn into one larger stream. All of them had their sources in the swamp that lay east of our home, and until they flowed out on the prairie a mile or two to the west, they were fringed by trees and brush. Aspen, elm, ash, oak, balm of Gilead, and box elder were the principal trees, with an understory of several kinds of willows, wild plums, Juneberry, red osier dogwood, red and black haws, wild roses, and other shrubs and bushes.

This was ideal habitat for songbirds. I spent hours prowling the "coulees," as we call them, looking for birds. The spring migration was an especially exciting time. I still remember the thrill of identifying my first white-throated sparrow one late April day as I focused a small telescope I had bought from a mail-order house. Then I bought a pair of field glasses that I used for years.

For several summers I hunted birds' nests assiduously, once a week searching every creek bottom and thicket in the vicinity for nests, besides watching birds in localities where they were apt to be nesting. I learned quite a bit about them in this way, where the different species were likely to build, what materials they used in construction, how they reacted to my presence, even what they were feeding their young. I heard their songs and call notes and picked up sundry bits of information about them.

In the spring I heard the booming of the prairie chickens coming from the cow pasture. On mild mornings in late March the sound rose and fell on a light breeze, a rolling melodious murmur that I loved to listen to. We likened it to the words "O-o-o-ld Mul-d-o-o-o-n-n," held and accented on the first and last syllables. The pasture had a growth of brush along one

70

side, some small willows and red osier dogwood, but mostly dwarf birch, and I crawled as close to the edge of this as I could through the grass and patches of snow, to where I could get a good view of the birds through the glasses.

Back and forth the males strutted, dragging their wings on the ground and puffing out the air sacs on the sides of their necks. The females trotted about, picking up seeds here and there, to all appearances not at all impressed by Papa's showing off. I watched until they wandered off, or until I got so cold I called off the vigil and went home to warm up by the kitchen stove, a cup of coffee and a doughnut speeding up the process from the inside. Later in the summer I found these birds' nests when I rounded up the cows for the morning and evening milkings.

Several species of ducks nested in the vicinity—mallards, blue-winged teal, gadwalls, pintails. Often I found the nests on high land, at some distance from water. The mudhens, or coots, and the pied-billed grebes, however, always floated their raftlike nests of dried reeds and rushes on the waters of a spring-fed slough at the end of our pasture, the grebes covering their eggs with grass when they left to feed, to keep them hidden from sharp-eyed crows.

Red-winged and yellow-headed blackbirds hung their nests, woven of dried grasses and lined with duck feathers, in the tall rushes, quite often roofing them over completely. The eggs were curiously scrawled with purplish brown on a light bluish-gray background, as if some mischievous boy had been scribbling on them with an indelible pencil. Long-billed marsh wrens, too, nested in the slough, also suspending their globes of dried grass in the tall reeds. They were so industrious that for every nest that was occupied there were two or three dummies.

The slough was one of the most intriguing places on the

71

farm. In the spring wild ducks by the score stopped off to rest, some of them to stay for the summer. Migrating shorebirds such as sandpipers, killdeer, phalaropes, several species of plovers, dowitchers, yellowlegs, two species of godwits, and others waded its shallows and fed. Often of a summer evening we were entertained by the frogs chorusing from the slough, their weird croaking pulsating rhythmically. Now and then the hollow booming of a bittern, or the tinkling, bell-like notes of a sora rail, or the cackling of a mudhen rose above the frog concert. It was especially appealing and had an aura all its own, in the quiet of a summer evening, or all through the night for that matter.

The bird books soon suggested others, and I sent for pocket guides to the wild flowers, trees, butterflies, and mammals. As I became a little older, into the middle and late teens, I obtained books by the two Johns, Burroughs and Muir, Thoreau's *Walden*, books by W. H. Hudson and David Grayson, and Darwin's *Voyage of the Beagle*. On the subject of natural history I read everything I could get my hands on. It is still a major interest in my reading.

I suppose nature as I saw it around the farm had stirred my curiosity and attention to some degree even in my preschool days. But it was the little book *Birds Through the Year*, more than any other or anything else, that stimulated me to learn more about a world I had at my very elbows.

It is a door open to anyone living in a rural region, wherever that may be. Edwin Way Teale found it on his grandfather's farm in Indiana, as he tells us in *Dune Boy*. W. H. Hudson discovered it on the pampas of Argentina, and his account of his boyhood there, as told in *Far Away and Long Ago*, is still absorbing reading.

It isn't closed to city dwellers either. I even suspect that many who grow up and live on farms miss it altogether, because it seems so commonplace and ordinary. It looks trivial and unimportant. But it is surprising how many wonderful things may be found by simply plowing the furrow of the commonplace and the everyday.

# The First Prothonotary Warbler

## JUDITH A. TOUPS

T H E first spring migrant that I ever identified was a prothonotary warbler. I found him in a roadside ditch. He was a hot citron spark among decaying leaves, a burst of brilliance above still water.

I let the world go by while I watched the golden bird turn the ugly, odorous ditch into an enchanted place. He was busy, too busy to know or care that I stood above that little universe of his. He threaded his tiny body through a lacework of leaves and inspected the dank recesses of the mudbank. He scrambled up and down, in and out, between the new-green stalks of "elephant ears"; once he disappeared beneath a fallen willow branch and turned up atop an ancient cypress stump; he never stopped probing, scrutinizing, inch by inch, as if to him had fallen the task of sleuthing out all that lived and grew or had ever lived and grown in that insignificant place.

For several days I returned each morning to watch him. He was in many ways a magical bird. He made a bird watcher out of me. He made me a lover of swamps and a believer in mys-

74

tical ditches. He became symbolic of spring, like the lilacs and forsythia of my New England growing-up; like the azaleas and wisteria of March in the South. Eventually he sang for me in that assertive, no-frills, ascending series of notes that breathes life into the swamps and river bottoms and insignificant ditches of eastern North America.

Each year when March begins, I wait for him to signal the start of the great northward pilgrimage. No matter that the Louisiana water thrush traditionally arrives earlier, or that northern parulas are already making hammocks in the Spanish moss. I must wait for the first prothonotary, the torchbearer of spring, and I have great expectations.

The first prothonotary was late this year. I searched the ditches and swamps for a glimpse of his burning yellow plumage, and listened for the ring of his song. It was March 12 before I found him; he lay lifeless on a dewy woodland floor, smaller in death than he looked in life. His delicate body was still warm; every feather was still smoothly in place, as if at any moment life would return, and all would be well for him, and for me.

I cupped him in the palms of my hands and realized that he weighed less than a camellia blossom. He was longer than my ring finger. I knew he was a male by the brightness of his head and breast.

I couldn't guess how old he was—perhaps he was a bird of the year who had never really lived at all. Or maybe he had lived beyond his prime. For so small a bird, that prime might have been three or four years at best.

He would have spent the first dozen days of his life in an insistent clamor for food—spiders, insects, and small, plump, green caterpillars—and at home in a nest of moss tucked discreetly into an old chickadee hole or in a natural cavity in a fallen limb. Between the warmth of that nest and the cool

75

forest floor of the Gulf Coast, he would have traveled a long way.

Somehow he had survived the ordeal of the fledging, so he must have been one of the fittest, for a time, at least, favored by nature. By mid-October of last year, he had left the swamp behind to join other warblers in the southward migration. Strong wings and favorable weather would have carried him across the Gulf of Mexico to the Yucatan Peninsula, an incredible over-water journey of more than five hundred miles.

He may have traveled even farther south, to the mangroves of Sevillano or the fresh swamps of Cienaga in Colombia, to spend the winter in habitat so much like that in which he fledged.

Sometime during February, a restless stirring arose in his heart, so persistent that he moved up from the swamp forest, away from the mangroves. He responded to an ancient instinct that drives all birds back to ancestral breeding grounds. It was preordained that he should soon attempt a long exhausting flight back to the place of his beginning, where he would battle his rivals, win his mate, and with inbred solicitude, feed her on the nest and bring insects to the young, until the cycle was complete.

In that day before he began his last flight across the Gulf of Mexico, he ate, and grew stronger, building up reserves of energy and fat, enough to sustain him for more than thirty hours of day-and-night flying. He made it to the shore of Waveland, Mississippi, and fell to earth just a fraction of a mile from the gulf.

I scooped a little hollow in the earth, lined it with pine needles and Spanish moss, and laid spring's first prothonotary in its grave.

# Foray for Birds

## BOB TEETS

T H E Y get up at 4:00 A.M.—rain or shine—wade into swamps, shiver in the cold, tramp through brier patches, stab their hands into cold ponds to snatch water snakes, become the target of a sharp-shinned hawk's talons, stay up until well past dark trying to catch a wayward woodcock, and fumble around in the darkness while attempting to latch onto an assortment of creatures that go hoot, hiss, or howl in the night.

And they love it—so much so, in fact, that each of them shells out money to take part in it. They come from all walks of life and join together in a voluntary effort to study, record, assess, and project the pulse of nature. In the end, the enormous amount of information gathered by these folks benefits hunters, fishermen, environmentalists, scientists, nature lovers—and the community as a whole. And the only payment they receive is the satisfaction of knowing that they helped make our lives more compatible with nature. They are the magnificent—if obsessed—people of the Brooks Bird Club. And even after they wrap up their annual June foray and go home, their influence remains.

The Brooks Bird Club, with headquarters in Wheeling, West Virginia, has 570 members in thirty-six states and eight foreign countries. It conducts land-acquisition and sanctuary programs, birdbanding and hawk-counting operations, and year-round ornithological activities. But it is the June foray that stirs members' passions. It stirred mine too.

Camp Galilee, in West Virginia's Preston County, had the look of a carnival as the BBC'ers staked out colorful tents, parked shiny RVs, and took residence in Galilee's cabins. And even though they ate and slept at the camp, the real carnival took place on the hills and in the valleys of Preston County. Their obsession for completing the job of taking a census of nature—and for getting the job done right—led me to believe that there must be more at stake than met the eye. As a result, I traveled with some of the members for a couple of days to find out what it was that made them so dedicated. In the end I shared their obsession.

The frantic pace they kept would shame Spectacular Bid. As they scoured Preston's landscape in search of various species, their energies easily eclipsed my own and nearly put me on the endangered list. Many times I found myself stopping for a breath while sixty-nine-year-old Chuck Conrad charged with the rest of his troops up one hill, then another. And when I wasn't running to catch up with someone, I was madly trying to absorb the waterfall of information that swept out of this remarkable group of people.

On one occasion, Wild Bill Wylie, a West Virginia University associate professor who is trying to save the Terra Alta Biological Station, conducted a walk around the Terra Alta Lake and put on a show to remember. He carefully orchestrated the bird songs we were hearing and, like the finest maestro, used his knowledge to turn the raw sound into a symphony. His ability to make us tune in our ears to nature was simply unbelievable.

78

And he was assisted by one of Preston's own rare species, the flaming red-haired Garbart. Frances Garbart, a Kingwood, West Virginia, resident and avid BBC member, attended every session of the foray during the first week. Her obsession for birding was truly infectious, and I soon found myself lurking around in the underbrush, trying to sneak up on a swamp sparrow or a veery for a closer look.

I couldn't believe what a charge I was getting out of learning to identify birds and their songs. It was easily as exciting as hooking a giant bass. Abashed, I remembered the unkind, stereotyped view I had once held about birders in particular and nature studiers in general.

And then, early one morning (5:30), I discovered what the BBC obsession was all about. Glen Phillips, Ellen Snyder, and I were silently walking along the Pine Run Road where one of the BBC study areas was located. Phillips, with twenty-five years of birding experience, was teaching Snyder, the newcomer, how to "run the line." Their purpose was to plot on a complicated graph the various singing perches of every bird they could hear in the study area. The information they were gathering would someday be used by environmentalists and others all over the country.

Glen Phillips's art is an exacting one that requires the finest ear and the utmost knowledge of birds. And it demands an uncanny ability to sense all of one's surroundings while still being able to zero in on one particular part of it. Phillips was a wizard.

"Grid one," he said, indicating to Snyder the exact point on the graph, "a black-throated blue warbler at a hundred feet that way." Snyder never questioned his estimate of the distance away from us that the bird was singing. She knew she didn't need to: "He never misses," she said. Dutifully, she inscribed "BTBW" at the point on the graph which he had indicated.

79

And so it went as Phillips happily, exuberantly, shared his experience with us. He joyfully unfolded many of nature's secrets and—although he had already seen those secrets before —took as much delight in seeing them again as we did in discovering them for the first time. It was a marvelous experience. And the most important aspect of the whole morning was realizing that his attitude was the key to what the foray was all about.

The joy of discovery, the absolute happiness of sharing knowledge, the benefits to all of us of their work, and the sublime excitement of seeing nature at its best—these are the reasons that brought these schoolteachers, housewives, business executives, sales clerks, doctors, writers, miners, and others together to stage a voluntary effort to understand, appreciate, and protect the environment around us.

That morning on Pine Run made a bird watcher out of me.

# Birding California-Style

## RON NAVEEN

*Welcome to the birder's California*
*Such a crazy place,*
*Such a frantic pace.*
*Plenty of room at the birders'*
*California,*
*Any time of day,*
*You can list away. . . .*

*I've been rocked by the waves,*
*Scorched by the sun,*
*I'm sick to my stomach, and*
*My mind's gone numb,*
*But I'm still birdin'. . . .*
                    —VERSES FROM TWO CALIFORNIA
                    BIRDING SONGS

THESE verses signify the very special birding mania that exists in California, where hard-core birding has gone far beyond the game of listing. If there is a frantic pace, it is because of the California birders who push their field-identification skills to the brink. Nowhere else are so many people pursing field excellence with so much energy and passion. I talked recently to Terry Clark, a young woman who began birding in California several years ago.

Q: How did you get started in birding?

81

A: I got dragged into it. My husband, Barry, had discovered the pleasures of bird watching when he was in his teens, but lost sight of his interest until he started writing nature documentaries. I was a totally urban person with absolutely no interest in the outdoors. Getting up before 8:00 A.M. offended my sensibilities. Occasionally, I would enjoy seeing a bright spring warbler, but more often than not, I felt bored and imposed upon.

When Barry signed us up for the Malibu Christmas Count in 1975, I was not at all pleased. But all my negativism changed at the midday compilation, when I noticed a group of young birders, the likes of which I had never seen on any field trip. The fraternity between them seemed defined by a common denominator of expertise, confidence, and energy. I think that I intuitively recognized this "energy" as passion, and it wasn't very often I met anyone whose life was enriched by a passion for anything. The people whom I knew were driven by desperation rather than passion—a big difference in my mind. Anyway, what I saw at the Malibu count stirred my imagination and my enthusiasm.

Q: Initially, though, your interest was journalistic, not participatory, wasn't it?

A: Yes. My first fascination was that of an observer's, just peeking in on it. I didn't anticipate getting sucked right into the current. I had worked as a television writer, but two TV writers in one family was too much, so I went into a peaceful retirement. I thought that I might try my hand at journalism, and birding appealed to me as an attractive subject. One of my first efforts was the *Western Tanager* piece on the 1976 Big Day in California.

As editor of the *Western Tanager*, Barry had frequent con-

82

tact with Jon Dunn. One night over dinner, Jon started telling us about vagrant-chasing. Big Days, weekends in Death Valley. It all seemed to parallel Jack Kerouac's *On the Road*, except this was now. I became absolutely fascinated by hard-core birding as a sociological phenomenon; its spontaneity really appealed to me.

Q: Tell me about your first birding trip.

A: I told Jon that I wanted to write an article, but didn't want the birders to know so they wouldn't feel self-conscious. In order to get acquainted with the personae of the upcoming Big Day, Jon suggested that I go on the northern cardinal expedition to the Colorado River. At that time I had no idea just how notable an all-star cast was participating in the search for an "organic" cardinal: Jon, Louis Bevier, Guy McCaskie, Paul Lehman, and Van Remsen.

I didn't know what to expect. Jon arranged for Paul and Louis to pick me up on their way out from Santa Barbara; we would rendezvous with Van in Riverside. Because Jon would be leaving with Guy from San Diego, I would be with total strangers until the next morning. It was a very quiet drive out to Riverside; no one talked to me. When Van joined us, however, the bird talk never stopped among the three of them: recent sightings, county lists, year lists, anecdotes. On and on. I was hearing a new language.

We spent the night sleeping near a major truck intersection. Between the noise and the discomfort of not sleeping in a bed, I suffered acutely. By the end of the weekend, I had aching muscles, unbrushed teeth, unrepaired makeup, an overdose of fast-food carbohydrates, and a natural high.

I had no idea that the sport of birding could be played so well. Eyes, ears, memory, and logic were always in use. Something would blur across the road, and, instantly, someone would call out, "Crissal thrasher." It all seemed so magical. And there was a refreshing disregard for day-to-day order, creating a nice kind of anarchy among six people in the middle of the desert totally oblivious to everything but birds. Whether we were eating or traveling from place to place the concern was birds, birds, birds. We were outsiders, not weighed down with any of the realities shared by the residents of Parker or Indio or distant L.A.

Passing Palm Springs on the way home, I actually felt sorry for all those perfectly tanned and dry-cleaned people returning from two days by the pool and an overpriced dinner at Ruby's Dunes. I felt a kind of deliverance.

Q: When did you get serious about listing, keeping field notes, etc.?

A: I started "studying" birds after the '76 Big Day—late June, early July. Up to that point I was interested only in passerines. Gulls, ducks, and shorebirds might as well have been in another class of vertebrates. But Jon's enthusiastic coaxing finally got to me. Suddenly, I was no longer drawn just to bright colors and high contrasts. I found that I really enjoyed the challenge of subtleties. Now my favorite birds are immature fall females.

Q: What is it about hard-core birding and sorting out the difficult groups of birds that has interested you so much?

A: It's pushing my senses beyond their limits and liberating myself from expectations. It's chasing a bird, driving all night to see it or miss it, and dropping everything for the chance. It's learning to be flexible. The phone rings, someone tells me there's a snowy owl in Eureka, and I don't say that I've got a dental appointment or something else going on—I go to Eureka.

Q: Has Barry been supportive?

A: Very supportive. He gets many vicarious thrills from my birding. He's not interested in chasing; he's more involved in the distribution and speciation of birds—and on a global scale. But I can come home and completely share my highs with him. Our separate birding interests complement each other perfectly. If his passion were identical to mine, we'd both suffer every time he couldn't get away to chase after a state bird. Another advantage of having different interests is that I have had the opportunity to develop my own identity in the birding family, which is no small accomplishment, since I spent a period as "Barry Clark's wife."

Q: I'd like to discuss elitism and prejudice among birders. For example, many easterners are perceived as being more concerned about checking off birds on lists than making accurate identifications and developing accurate identification skills. Also, I've noticed quite a bit of prejudice against women back East. Any comment?

A: Well, there's an elitism here too, but it's primarily a prejudice against incompetence. The people out here have extremely high standards and an obsession with accuracy. If you try to pass yourself off as being better than you are, they'll nail you. They'll mop the floor with you. But everyone recognizes that it takes a lot of hard work to develop good skills. As long as you have a sincere enthusiasm, you'll get all the support needed. You've just got to show a love for the sport and a willingness to learn, and that means admitting your mistakes. But everybody makes mistakes. The better a birder, the more gracefully a mistake is admitted.

There is no prejudice against women birders per se. I know how much encouragement and instruction I've received. On the other hand, there has never been a woman on the California Rarities Committee. But look at it this way: The top birders in California started peering through binoculars at a very early age. Birding has caught the public's attention only recently.

Q: What lists do you keep and what do you think about listing?

A: Lists serve useful purposes, but if they become the only goal, then a lot is lost. For one thing, a list is a kind of reward, as well as a motivation. And when the alarm goes off at 2:00 A.M., you need all the motivation that you can get. Lists—month lists, county lists, spot lists—can help a birder learn distribution. I keep only a state list and an L.A. County list. No, I don't have a life list. Oh yes, I forgot my California warbler list: I've seen thirty-nine species.

As a not-too-advanced birder, I hate to check off a bird that I can't instantly get a good mental picture of. For example, I've had three goshawks pointed out, but I'm still not comfortable with counting the species. As a group, the pelagics pose a real listing problem for me.

Q: I'm interested in what I call "gestalt birding," getting to know as much as you can about every species. My ultimate goal is not listing the bird; it's getting to know it well.

A: Out here the word "gestalt" comes up a lot in discussions of immature gulls. To me, identifying a bird on gestalt—being in touch with a whole that is greater than the sum of its parts— is the highest high.

To me birding is like a form of yoga, a way of keeping my senses in shape. Because I gather information about my environment through my senses, then the sharper my senses, the better my grasp on reality. The illusion of being on top of things is preferable to feeling like a confused victim of life.

86

Reality may be governed by randomness, but by attuning my senses to an optimal efficiency, I can maximize my ability to convert chaos into order. And the less confusion in my mind, the better!

Birders can be very contemptuous of people who go through life with blinders on. There must be so much unfulfillment for people who climb out of their car, look around, and say, "Oh, I guess we're here. So this is Yosemite." Then they take a couple of pictures and climb back into the car. How much have they absorbed? How far have they really ventured beyond the narrow confines of their private lives?

q: Like looking at Van Gogh's *Sunflowers* and not seeing the whole, just seeing that it's a painting.

a: Right, just seeing something literally rather than seeing the forms, the patterns—the gestalt, if you will. Birding is deciphering patterns: field marks, vocalizations, behavior, distribution, probability. What does the entire pattern tell you? You've got to get past "What does it resemble in the field guide?" Like the folks with blinders looking at abstract art. They want everything to be visually recognizable and literal. They ask, "What am I supposed to see?" rather than "What do I see?"

You're out in the field. Birds are all about—chipping, singing, flitting—and the world seems chaotic. But, using your senses and your knowledge, you can get in touch with the natural order. And when you can pick out the anomalies, the vagrants, it gives you an exhilarated sense of being on top of life, not overwhelmed by it.

Birding is also an antidote for anonymity. Even in this vast morass known as southern California, I've developed a spiritual bond with many people who've become close friends. That's a very satisfying feeling.

Q: Birding is to some extent removed from the dog-eat-dog, economically oriented society in which we live. Certainly, there are birders who bear any expense to list almost every vagrant, wherever it is found in the U.S. But they seem to be a bit of an exception. Birding is a means of getting outside, enjoying that which you've never seen before. And you don't need to spend much money or do much traveling to get that satisfaction.

A: Sure. Birding and many other outdoor activities are becoming popular because people are redefining themselves. There is more to life than just being a consumer. The American dream is tarnished, if not altogether corroded. A successful career can have limited benefits, and spiritual rewards are too often elsewhere.

Initially, going birding caused me anxieties. I'd go birding thinking that my life would be a shambles when I returned, simply because birding was keeping me from my daily rituals. But my daily rituals had developed as a way of warding off imagined consequences.

Birding is an indulgence that contributes considerably to the quality of my life. Although it doesn't seem very "sensible," I can't help thinking that birding is a beneficial kind of irrational behavior. It provides a particular kind of adventure and stimulation which I don't get any other way. And why narrow my range of experience by always acting sensibly?

I mean, driving all night to see a bird, then turning around and heading home—that's totally irrational to most people's way of thinking. But I think of birding as good mental hygiene, for even if I miss the bird, I will have had the pleasure of anticipation. We think in terms of physical well-being, but we're so ill equipped to take care of ourselves psychologically and emotionally. Birding really helps.

Birding creates healthy tensions. You want to do better, you

88

want to improve, to tell the difference between all those chip notes. You're pushing yourself to learn more and more. Birding helps me keep a perspective on the rest of my life. It may sometimes strain our bank account, but what does that indicate about emotional or psychological well-being? I can't think of a better way to spend money than on bird books and airline tickets!

Bob Hines

# III  *In Pursuit of Birds—Almost Anywhere*

*If birds may be found in the wilds of our big cities, they may be found almost anywhere. The birds themselves fascinate. But of equal fascination is the mere fact of their existence: amidst macadam and neon, above freeways, in our own back yards, over the open sea, on the continent of Antarctica.*

# Our Own Wildlife Sanctuary

## LAURA RILEY

I f one has held an idea in mind for a very long time, it is sometimes hard to trace its beginning. Where did we get the idea we wanted to make an old farm in the country into a wildlife sanctuary, one that would attract the birds and beasts of our New Jersey countryside?

I don't know, but I think it may have started with the phoebe nest under the porch of a house we were renting. We watched while the phoebe built it of mud and grasses, decorated it with cool green moss, incubated five small white eggs, and finally hatched out five youngsters, which grew so quickly. Just when it seemed they would topple over if they piled up any more, with a rush of wings they were gone. We missed them—that most appealing sight, a bird feeding its young on the nest— and the excitement of watching their daily struggle to survive. Indeed, it may be at least partly this, the fight for existence, along with the extraordinary beauty of most natural life, that many persons today find so fascinating, persons whom civilization has largely relieved of these burdens.

That nest of phoebes was the start of two interests. First, we wanted a home of our own, with room around it to accommodate wild creatures such as the phoebe, and as many others as possible. Our primary motivation was a desire to see more and more, at as close range as possible, of the beauty and drama we had come to find in the daily lives of animals.

The second interest was really an outgrowth of the first, the desire to see our surroundings, not in a generalized way, but in sufficient detail to really study and know what was going on. Yet many of nature's sights are so evanescent—a barn swallow, swooping in with a beakful of insects for its young. How long does it stay at the nest? A millisecond, we discovered, before it is off and flying again, seeking more insects. How could we capture these sights and see them for more than a millisecond, see them again and again, if we wished? Photography, of course. Our photographic attempts with the phoebe had been disappointing, to put it mildly. But we knew if we practiced and kept trying, we could learn.

First we had to find the land. We did not have much money. My husband, Bill, had just completed two years in the Army as a private; I had helped support us, and we had just made it financially, with no nest egg. But we started looking. The first problem surprised us. We wanted a house that was isolated, with some acreage around it, and water—a pond, or a place to put a pond. The problem was in communicating to the real-estate agents what we meant by isolated. Again and again we would be assured of isolation, only to be taken to a house built next to a main road, or in a development.

One day an agent told us he had found something. The house needed repair, he said, but otherwise fit our expectations. And so it did—even the financial requirements. The house, which had an old barn and chicken house, was in the center of forty acres of alfalfa farmland and faced on a natural basin. The basin was an ideal spot for a pond, fed by a spring under the house. The water from the spring was of such high quality that it was widely known as the purest in Hunterdon County; it was to be our entire source of water. The spring had never gone dry, and during Prohibition it provided the base for all the illegally made gin in the area.

That first winter (we took possession on January 1), we put out birdseed on a picnic table, and no one came—no one at all. The seeds remained there all winter. Heavy snows fell, and the white icy coating was pristine until the melt in March.

Nowadays, by noon after a winter snowfall, the ground within an acre of the house is trampled with literally thousands of footprints. Only a few of them are human ones, the result of our daily circuit of the house and pond.

We have counted 164 species of birds within view of the house itself (of which at least 54 are nesters), more than two dozen mammals, and hundreds of fascinating insects and reptiles and wild plants and flowers. There are many dozens of individuals of each species. Once we counted 70 pheasants at one time from the windows of the house; 186 Canada geese stopped over one afternoon while in migration. A dozen stately great egrets explored the pond and island for all of one Saturday. Another time, 46 deer passed in beautiful procession on a slope in back of the house, silhouetted against a setting sun.

We didn't really know what to do at first to attract wildlife, and only gradually learned, mainly by trial and error. We also did much reading (librarians are helpful in directing such research) and observing, and tried not to be discouraged when our efforts were not fruitful.

Ideas came from odd places. We visited the Doris Duke estate with its famous gardens and greenhouses near Somerville, New Jersey, and there saw a wooden trough that was put out to furnish grain for wild birds and animals. We copied it and

95

later modified it for better drainage. We visited the Middleton Place, one of the oldest estates in America, near Charleston, South Carolina; there we saw mallard ducks nesting in a structure shaped like an orange crate turned on its side. We came back and put one of those in our pond; it proved a great success. A newspaper article told of wood duck houses that were being put up at the Great Swamp National Wildlife Refuge; we sent for their plans and duplicated them. We constructed four wood duck houses, installing them in winter, as was suggested; it gives the houses a chance to weather a little before making them available for occupancy, and the installation is easier then. You can stand on the ice and hammer the galvanized-iron-base poles first through the ice, then on down into the pond bottom, and attach the house while still on a fairly firm footing.

The wood duck houses were successful, too, though we were prepared to be philosophical if they did not work out at all. But what a wonderful surprise to have them all occupied the very first year by those spectacular birds, justifiably called the world's most beautiful ducks.

We did not have four wood duck families the year after that, however (though it was sometimes hard to be sure; these lovely birds are so wary that it is necessary to post a nonstop vigil to be certain of their presence). We didn't know why they were avoiding the fourth house until we looked out late one afternoon and saw three woolly-headed young screech owls peering out of their appropriated home.

Food, water, and cover habitat are the important ingredients in making an area hospitable for wildlife, and often what furnishes one of these will provide at least one of the others as well (for instance, seed-bearing plants, in addition to food, provide cover and nest sites).

The first and most important improvement we made on our

property was the pond, and of great help in this was the Soil Conservation Service. In fact, I cannot overstate the help that various state and federal, as well as county and local, agencies can be in finding out the answer to almost any question that might arise. In this case Jesse Denton of the SCS came out and looked over our land and with his staff drew up exact plans for the pond. Then, together, we modified it to suit our special desires—an irregular rather than perfectly round shape; a dock from which we could swim and that would cover the pipe that would handle the overflow; and an island in the middle, where we hoped birds would come to rest and nest (as Canada geese have been doing for six years now).

Putting in that pond required considerable faith on all sides, for at the time we were going through a severe drought and even our famous spring was down to a trickle. (I remember Jesse Denton referring, rather derisively we thought, to the joining of our spring overflow to another feeble trickle that was coming down from the field in back as "harnessing the Tigris and the Euphrates.")

For a while that winter the pond was a peculiar-looking cavity indeed—a doughnut-shaped half-acre excavation, with the island like a tiny inactive volcano in the middle. But one night in late February we got a tremendous cloudburst. The drought had broken, and the pond filled up in a matter of hours, fed by the brooks and melting snow from the surrounding hills.

The pond has been wonderful. Here again the Soil Conservation Service helped out by giving us fingerling fish to put in it. We now have bass and a few trout, some of which are two feet in length. They seem to be in a natural balance, their population stable from year to year. Perhaps a few are taken from time to time by such as the handsome osprey I once watched dive, come up with one of the larger specimens, and fly off with it. Great blue herons and little green herons fish from the sides, and kingfishers from the air, spearing some of the smaller ones and on occasional frog or large water insect.

From the state agriculture department we obtained, free, seedling pine trees—nine hundred of them—some of which are now many feet tall, and autumn olive and Tartarian honeysuckle bushes, both of which grow quickly and bear abundant fruit in spring and fall. Dozens of species of colorful birds are attracted to the fruit of these plants.

We have largely allowed the grounds to develop naturally. Beyond the pond are woods that have grown up around old orchards; they are filled with apples of various kinds (most are unwormy even though we do not spray), along with many volunteer walnut and cedar trees, and an undergrowth of barberry and spicebush. We have marked walking trails through the woods, and along the larger brook, which bounds the lower property beyond the pond, we have put up a large hammock. This accommodates two persons, and is an idyllic place for watching spring warblers; it is cool and serene on the warmest day, with the brook babbling by. In fact, it is so soothing it is sometimes hard to stay awake.

We have a lawn area around the house and pond, and where it meets the woods, birds and other small creatures flourish. Even the lawn is largely natural; although we keep it mowed, we do nothing to eliminate the plantain and dandelions that sprout in it. As a result, rabbits and woodchucks prefer to work on these large-leaved plants and leave unmolested the flower beds we plant along the old stone walls. And the dandelions are such a lovely sight, both their blooms and their seed heads. They support sometimes dozens of bright goldfinches clinging to their heads in the breeze.

In addition to the special food plants mentioned, we supply food in feeders: sunflower seeds at a large bedroom-window feeder and a log feeder in the yard; suet, dispensed in two ways —stuffed in holes in a large four-by-six piece of lumber hung from a telephone guy wire, and in a covered galvanized-wire milk-bottle container mounted atop a post with a squirrel guard (raccoons or squirrels would devour the suet in a minute); and fine-ground chick scratch, ordered from the farmfeed store and put about in the troughs, to bring various small birds as well as pheasants and deer. For waterfowl we throw a few handfuls of cracked corn under the water, where they can duck down for it.

We have two rules we follow: We do not put out enough food to provide the sole sustenance of any of our wild visitors, and we do not attempt to make friends with any of them. Tempting as this may be, it is a cruel trick when the next human they meet may not wish them well as we do.

Our general outlook may be expressed in the words of the popular song "Let It Be." Let it be, and nature will provide for its own. On one fall day we counted eighteen different kinds of fruits and berries about the place, all volunteers, producing in abundance for the birds and animals. We also have jewelweed blossoms feeding the hummingbirds, dozens of kinds of weed seeds in the fields, and uncounted other food sources at other seasons of the year. Of these the elderberries alone are known to attract 120 different species of birds, according to the government pamphlet on the subject. (Government pamphlets are available on plantings for wildlife, houses for birds, and an almost infinite number of related topics.)

Although many of the food plants provide shelter as well, we also investigated nest boxes and how to install them. It has been our plan gradually to put up and provide nest arrangements for every creature that might possibly accept them, and a great help in this is the government pamphlet called "Homes for Birds" (available from the Government Printing Office,

Washington, D.C. 20402). It gives the standard measurements for boxes for all birds in the United States that are known to use them.

Of course, the birds don't always know, or, apparently, care whether a house is precisely the right dimensions. We have had sparrow hawks in wood duck houses, flickers in sparrow hawk houses, tree swallows in bluebird houses, and many other birds making choices quite independently of the charts, but still with satisfactory results. (We always put up houses on galvanized iron poles with metal squirrel-guard discs to keep off predators. Birdhouse gourds, which we grow ourselves, we hang from porch eaves.)

All the houses we have put out, dozens of them now, have been used. The most exciting visit of all (or is it just that it is the most recent?) was this year, when we put a box built to barn owl specifications on the third floor of the barn, with an eight-inch hole to the outside. A beautiful barn owl arrived shortly after and proceeded to bring around a mate, lay eggs, and raise a family. We watched daily through a small peephole in the top of the box. They are still with us, arriving and calling every evening at dusk, and helping us maintain our total sanctuary by keeping the small rodents in balance.

The barn has been hospitable as well to barn swallows and phoebes—and sometimes birds find their own odd places. A Carolina wren built a nest this past spring in an old coffeepot hanging in the little chicken house, now a potting shed. A robin this fall had its third successful nesting atop a house floodlight—a queer location, perhaps, but a practical one: Through the most torrential rainstorm she was dry and snug under the overhanging eave.

Our photography has progressed, and we have learned much more about blinds, telephoto lenses, lights, and remote-release cords. We thought at first it would be interesting to see how many different species of living things we could photograph within a small area (about two hundred feet) of the house, but the number seems to be endless. Like the great entomologist Jean Fabré, who spent much of his long life observing a plot of 2.47 acres in France, we have learned that even a small parcel of land holds more beauties and mysteries than can be plumbed in many years.

Is all this worth the trouble? Obviously, to many it would not be. When I try to explain why it is to us, my mind comes up not with words of explanation but with a flood of sights and sounds.

A Canada goose incubates her eggs during a late-night sleet storm, her back shining, under the light, with a thick coating of ice. She stays, unmoving, protecting the precious eggs, until the sun melts her glassy coat in the morning.

A doe struggles in the field across the brook during a spring thunderstorm. We watch from our window, wondering if we can and should try to help her. After a great paroxysm she lies still for just a moment, then leaps up—and straggling behind her in the tall grass is a newborn fawn.

A sparrow hawk swoops down on our bedroom-window feeder and carries off a gold-and-black evening grosbeak, dead the instant the hawk's talons sank through its feathers. A goshawk is less lucky or less skillful, perhaps because it is immature, in its efforts to capture a gray squirrel in the cherry tree beside the same window.

We hear the snowy tree cricket in the fall, and count the number of chirps per minute, divide by four, and add thirty-seven—an accurate gauge of the outdoor temperature.

Barn swallows play toss with a feather, passing it from bird to bird while they display their stunning aerial skill swooping back and forth.

A tree swallow defends her nest box against me as I try to

photograph her. It is a moving display as the tiny creature dives again and again, snapping her bill in my face, knowing but not caring that I am so much bigger than she, until I leave—not because I must but out of respect for her concern and her bravery.

Young animals play games preparing for adulthood. Orioles just out of the nest weave bits of fiber; next year they will construct intricate nest hammocks. Young bucks play at butting one another, behavior that will become deadly serious in the next rutting season.

There are so many new things to see and questions to ask that many lifetimes could be consumed, on our farm alone, seeking to understand.

# A Back-Yard Diary:
# Rufous Hummingbird in Minnesota

## NEL MARIE MELVILLE

I first saw the rufous hummingbird at my back-yard feeder in Bemidji, Minnesota, at 1:30 P.M. on September 6, 1978. It was a warm sunny day. My formula was one part sugar and four parts water and no food coloring. The hummer flew up to the windows of my home several times. I have some horizontal windows, and it flew between the opened window and the screen and hovered in front for several seconds.

As I later discovered, this was a very rare sighting, as rufous hummingbirds had been recorded in Minnesota only once before (August 1974, at Grand Rapids in Itasca County). In the autumn of 1978, in addition to my (now official) sighting, the rufous was also reported at Hastings, with another possible sighting reported at Lake Ada, in Cass County.

When the ruby-throated hummingbirds were at the feeder, the rufous gave way to them. This surprised me, because I had read that the rufous is among the most pugnacious of the hummers. When the hornets were at the feeder, the rufous would repeat a "tzik, tzik" sound and try to avoid them. The sex of the bird has not been positively determined, but I shall refer to it in the masculine gender.

On September 8 I called Dr. Harold Peters, professor of biology at Bemidji State University, and he confirmed my finding. On September 9 and 10 I was out of town. September 11 was my last sighting of the ruby-throated. I was then out of town intermittently through most of September.

I had assumed the rufous had migrated with the ruby throats. For some unknown reason I had left the feeder out. On September 30 at 1:30, a glorious fall day, in zoomed the rufous. I was stunned. I called Dr. Peters and Dr. A. S. (Laddie) Elwell, and we decided to remove the feeder. We thought that perhaps a source of food was keeping him from leaving, and after he fed well, I took the feeder down. He returned twice within the next five minutes to the feeder area, and from there he flew and fed on the fuchsia, nasturtium, lobelia, and hollyhock blossoms. We had not yet had a killing frost, and there were many flowers still in blossom in my garden. He also hovered around some dried day lily blossoms.

The following week I was away Tuesday, Wednesday, and Thursday. The weather was cold and blustery, but by the weekend it was sunny and warmer. At 3:00 P.M. on Sunday, October 8, there zoomed in my rufous, straight at the feeder area. He hovered there for a second and then flew and fed on lobelia, petunia, and hollyhock blossoms. Again I called Laddie, and we decided to put the feeder out again. It was now so late in the season we felt we might as well feed him until nature took its course. But, the more I thought about it, the more I wanted to try to save this hummer.

On Monday, October 9, I called the Minnesota Bird Alert, stated my plight, and asked for help. Little did I know what excitement this would create in the bird world. I talked with Bob Janssen Monday evening, and he also suggested putting the feeder out again and asked me to watch for the rufous. That evening I also attended the meeting of the Mississippi Headwaters Chapter of the Audubon Society and asked the members for suggestions on how to save the bird.

Tuesday, October 10, the hummer appeared at the feeder thirty-two times between 11:20 and 6:45! Laddie Elwell, Jim Mattsson, and several others observed and photographed it. Needless to say, I was wild with excitement in reporting this great news to Bob Janssen Tuesday evening. Unfortunately I had to be away, but I was informed that Bob Janssen, Dr. Peters, Laddie Elwell, and others observed the rufous on Wednesday, October 11. I understand the rufous even perched for twenty-five minutes.

I was home on the weekend of October 21 and 22. Saturday, October 21, dawned a beautiful fall day. From 10:16 A.M. until I had to leave for the evening at 5:10 P.M., the rufous was observed twenty-three times. Dr. and Mrs. Peters again observed him, and Lloyd Paynter of Aitkin, Minnesota, spent the better part of the afternoon photographing him.

An interesting thing occurred at my first sighting this particular Saturday. I was having a cup of coffee on the deck and was wearing a brilliant Chinese-red robe. The rufous zoomed in to within three feet of me and hovered, looking at me. I believe that he was attracted by the color of my robe. He then flew to the feeder, which was four feet from where I was sitting, and turned his back to me as he fed. I had not seen him do this before. Previously he would feed facing me or else he would peek at me from behind the feeder.

I wanted somehow to save this rare visitor. I placed a custard cup with my formula in it on a table on the deck and floated one of the red plastic "flowers" removed from my first feeder. I also hung another feeder right next to my house and under the roof overhang. Then I placed a fourth feeder inside of my house, hoping to lure him into the house. I thought perhaps the greenhouse of Bemidji State University could then be the home of the rufous for the winter. I just had to try to do something to save him. I am a sentimentalist, not a biologist.

At 11:55 I again observed unusual behavior. A red squirrel was stretched out on a limb of a tree by the deck. The hummer zoomed in and perched on a limb of an adjacent tree—just several feet away. Then the hummer zoomed to within twelve inches of the squirrel and hovered for several seconds, just observing the squirrel. He then flew to Feeder No. 1 and fed. By 1:00 P.M. a front had moved in, and it began to get cold, windy, and cloudy. The hummer was having difficulty perching at Feeder No. 1 because it was swaying in the breeze. He still did not feed at the two other feeders.

According to Karen A. and Verne Grant in *The Humming-birds and Their Flowers*, the northernmost distribution of the rufous is southeastern Alaska; there is one brood in late spring; by August they begin their migration; and the rufous is the hardiest of the hummers and can tolerate cool weather quite well. The Grants also report that "on migration through Ranch Santa Ana Botanic Gardens, the rufous, which passes through in early spring, is usually seen feeding on flowers growing in the deep shade of tall trees." My home is situated amid tall Norway and white pine trees, and the yard is quite shaded. I have wondered if that attracted the rufous to my feeder.

Sunday, October 22, was very cold and very windy—in the low 30° range all day. My first observation was at 9:00 A.M. From Feeder No. 1 the hummer flew and hovered in front of an orange ceramic owl I have hanging on the house. At 9:20 he hovered around Feeder No. 3 (under the roof overhang and right next to the house). This feeder was out of the wind. At 10:02 he again looked at this feeder after much difficulty in trying to perch and feed at Feeder No. 1.

## A Back-Yard Diary: Rufous Hummingbird in Minnesota

At 10:12 he again looked over Feeder No. 3 and then flew around the corner to the front of my house and down to where some nasturtiums were. The blossoms had frozen during the night. He flew up to my living-room windows and hovered for a few seconds and then flew around the corner to my glass sliding doors and again hovered in front of the door. At 11:05 he flew into my flower garden—the flowers were mostly frozen here too—then around my bird bath in the middle of the flower garden and up to my winter bird feeder that contained sunflower seeds. Ordinarily he would feed and perch or feed and zoom away and be out of sight in a second. Between 9:00 A.M. and 11:30 there were nineteen observations. Mr. and Mrs. Byron Bratlie of Blaine, Minnesota, were now observing and photographing the rufous, and several times I commented upon his erratic behavior.

At 11:25 A.M. the rufous fed from Feeder No. 3 for the first time. It was getting colder outdoors, so I opened full wide the sliding glass doors directly across from Feeder No. 1. We would be sheltered but still be able to observe him. Mr. Bratlie observed the hummer perched on a brush pile by my garage— about fifty feet from the house. From the brush pile he flew to Feeder No. 1 and on to hover in front of the open door and then into the house.

I closed the sliding door, and the hummer began beating against the window. I then closed the draperies, and he was caught on the loose weave of the fabric. I got my butterfly net and carefully put it over him and then gently took him in my hand. I held him while my son and Mr. and Mrs. Bratlie, on instructions from Laddie Elwell, made up a perch in a box. While they were doing this, twice I took the hummer to Feeder No. 1 and twice he fed. He did not appear hurt. All this occurred at 11:30 A.M.

We placed some fine netting over the top of the box, and over that some aluminum foil to darken the box. While my son drove me into town I forced the tube of the feeder through the netting and again fed the hummer. He readily took food, and he was on his perch. He was beating his wings, so I knew he had not injured them beating against my windows. He appeared alert and chipper.

I turned him over to Laddie. We thought perhaps the Minnesota Zoological Gardens could winter him. She called, but they did not have the facilities for so tiny a bird. The next step was to contact an airline and have him flown to South Texas.

Sunday, Laddie fed him a formula of a milk protein/carbohydrate solution, which included sweetened condensed milk, and he took this formula well. Laddie made perches for the rufous about her house, and he flew about freely. By Monday she saw a change in him. He would feed when hand-held, but when not held, he tended to slip backward on his perch. By Tuesday it was obvious to her that he was failing. He fed very little, if any. On Wednesday, October 25, he took no food essentially, only flicking his tongue into the feeder tube a couple of times when hand-held. Wednesday evening Laddie took him with her (to force-feed him) to the State Audubon Council. There she tried to force-feed him, but he died at 6:00 P.M.

The study skin was prepared by Diane M. Morris, Dr. A. S. Elwell, and Jim Mattsson. The rufous was probably a male. A growth was discovered on the neck, dorsal to the vertebral column. Laddie said that this growth could perhaps have blocked his esophagus and prevented him from feeding. In any case, it is doubtful that the rufous could have survived the cold weather of that late-October weekend in Minnesota.

# Flash: Top Priority—UFO

## PETER DUNNE

L u c k , I have been assured, is the collision of opportunity and preparation. All birders know the knuckle-biting anguish of opportunity lost—opportunity cloaked in feathers, offering a profile that could only be discerned, without binoculars, by an avian wizard. Never one to learn anything from less than a dozen mistakes, I now stow a pair of Bausch and Lomb 9 × 35s under the front seat of the car and a vintage pair on top of the desk. A trip outdoors, for whatever reason, is accompanied by a pair of Leitz 8 × 40s. This long-winded windup, by the way, paves the way for the disclosure that follows. Some people might wonder how it came to be that the Cape May Bird Observatory's naturalist director was wearing binoculars on April 24—while taking out the garbage.

My attention to the bird loping across Lake Lily was a simple conditioned reflex. No mysticism, no empathetic encounter. A laughing gull would have aroused as much or as little curiosity. The bird, closing from the far side of the lake, was not a laughing gull. In fact, it really didn't fall into any of the top-drawer categories.

Now, the front steps at the observatory headquarters are irregularly spaced, hard, and unkind to inattentiveness in people who carry out garbage. Because of this, and because the bird was approaching on a near-intercept course, field identification points were quickly noted, arranged in order of importance, and run through the mental data bank marked: "Field Identification, Code 1." The rest of my mind busied itself with the pressing task of surviving the steps.

Possible identifications were considered and discarded like so many ill-fitting garments. The bird just didn't seem to fall into any of the regular categories. Curiosity gave way to mild puzzlement.

The bird was closer. I chanced another quick visual scan at 20/20, and fed the fresh readings into the data bank marked: "Field Identification, Code 2, Broad Categorization." All observed field points were weighed against known field points. When all the reasonable possibilities had sifted through the fine mesh of experience and probability, there wasn't anything left in the pan.

At this point, several things occurred. The sighting immediately became a "Code 3," and 82.144 percent of all neurons used for deductive reasoning and 66.012 percent of those concerned with motor control were shifted over to the task at hand. Close scrutiny of a "Code 3" bird is mandatory. Sensor readings on the avian projectile disclosed a slim, long-pointed-winged, long-tailed bird with a slow, regular loping wingbeat and an utterly graceful fluidity of motion. At 170 yards, the contrasting coloration, dark above and light below, was easily discerned despite the day's gray overcast. A tentative identification flashed on the screen: BROAD CLASSIFICATION: RAPTOR. . . . POSSIBLE IDENTIFICATION: NORTHERN HARRIER. ADULT. MALE.

I continued to navigate the steps, garbage in tow.

With a possible identification in hand, the mind downshifts to "Code 1 level" functioning, releasing most motor-control units for navigation. The hypothetical identification (in this case, harrier) is fed into the proper slot and the well-lubricated gears of the bird-watching mind pass the amassed data through a series of relays marked: "Raptors, Flight Identification."

In .000720 seconds, every red light on the panel flashed. The energy drain halted all motor drive function. The visual read-out board sprang to life. Emblazoned in letters of Univers 18 point Bold was this ominous message: NOT A MARSH HAWK . . . NOT A MARSH HAWK. . . . BIRD SUFFICIENTLY CLOSE TO PERMIT ACCURATE IDENTIFICATION OF ALL REGULARLY OCCURRING MEDIUM-SIZED RAPTOR SPECIES. . . . SPECIES UNIDENTIFIED . . . UNIDENTIFIED. . . . POSSIBLE EXTRALIMITAL OCCURRENCE. . . . CODE 5 PRIORITY. . . .

At "Code 5 Priority," all actions are automatic. Three things happened rather quickly as all impulse power shifted to backup auxiliary data banks. Motor control to all parts of the unit not associated with sight identification were cut off; both hands went for the binoculars; the garbage went for the street. Identification came a strobe flash ahead of visual confirmation (and a split millisecond behind the bag-muffled sound of Ragu jar meeting macadam). In a pair of 8 × 40s at 110 yards, it's tough to mistake a swallow-tailed kite for anything *less* than that.

# Freeway Birding

## BONNIE HENDERSON

You don't need binoculars and a safari hat to watch birds. You can do it in the privacy of your own car. Best of all, you don't have to plan a gas-consuming, long-distance trip to some far-flung, exotic locale. In fact, you don't even have to plan a special drive. You can, instead, make the most of the driving you're normally required to do. What began as an occasional distraction from the monotony of driving interstates has become for me a passion: I am a freeway bird watcher.

My habit got started on one of many seemingly endless Salem-to-Portland (Oregon) stints at the wheel. The sky was an even, clouded gray, the road an even black, my speed my usual even fifty-five, edging sixty. The novelty of watching for familiar landmarks had begun to wear thin, and my eyes began wandering to hills and flat fields on either side of the road. Occasionally I'd see a crow soaring high over a field or just sitting on a fence post. As I sped by one such post the large bird sitting there suddenly rose into the air with a graceful clapping of brown-and-white wings. I peered more closely and realized, with a start, that the birds I kept seeing weren't all crows.

"That's a hawk!" I shouted to my companion, who turned to me with scorn: "That's the first time you've seen one?"

She, however, was an expert bird watcher, the kind that sees a flash of wings out of the corner of an eye or picks out a bird cry from a mélange of city sounds and knows what it is, genus and species.

But once I realized that I could see hawks from my car window, I started searching them out actively, whenever some obligation drew me back to the freeway. What had always been a monotonous expanse of gray sky above flat green fields was suddenly animated with life, with a whole array of wild birds, different from the more common varieties I saw every day pulling worms from my lawn or settling in a flock in my willow. Hawks and falcons are no worm-pullers; they're what legends are made of, legends and nature movies, and there they were, carrying on their carnivorous, legendary lives right next to the freeway, seemingly oblivious to that steady stream of noise and exhaust.

My interest was piqued. Soon it wasn't enough to know that there were raptors on the fence post; I wanted to know what kind. Red-tailed hawks, I learned, are the most common in the Willamette Valley, but there are others: low-flying, light-colored marsh hawks and, occasionally, Swainson's and rough-legged hawks. Each hawk or pair of hawks, it seems, has an exclusive territory stretching from three to five miles long, though I've seen them at closer intervals than that. My friend theorizes that hawks have adopted the freeway as a territorial boundary. It wouldn't surprise me.

Hawks aren't the only raptors in the valley. There are falcons, too, perched not on fence posts but on top of telephone poles. They tend to fly higher than the hawks, soaring with the whim of air currents that constantly rise and fall above the valley floor. I often watch tiny sparrow hawks, misnamed members of the falcon family, hovering motionless over a field

113

with rapid wings. They'll hover for several seconds, then dive straight down, leveling off like test pilots only at the last second to swoop low over the ground, scanning for mice. Sometimes I see these kestrels alone on telephone wires, heads bobbing up and down like little china dolls.

I've seen several great blue herons along I-5, and their appearance over a freeway interchange always strikes me as strangely anachronistic. With their curiously bent necks and their slow, large, flapping wings, herons more than any other bird seem less a part of the Space Age than the Age of Reptiles. I see them most often in the marshy areas between Corvallis and Salem, the same place I always search out mallards and wood ducks and transient Canada geese.

The smaller birds, the ones I used to assume were all starlings, have begun to interest me as well. Where the freeway passes stands of trees I occasionally see a red-shafted flicker, though it's not easy for a novice to distinguish one in flight from a starling. My expert friend, however, has no trouble: "Starlings look like cigars," she tells me. Stogies, to be exact. In contrast, flickers look like pointed torpedoes, perfectly honed. A flash of red under the wing is the most certain in-flight identification. More common and more distinct are the red-winged blackbirds that crowd the roadside cattail marshes, characterized by a red patch on the shoulder.

Sometimes in the fields I'll see a pheasant rise and glide off, triangular, solitary. Or quail in twos and threes, rising together and flapping away rapidly on an even plane to some lonelier corner. Tiny black-and-white killdeer free-lance the fields for insects and worms, occasionally flying haltingly across the road, or walking stiff-legged on the road shoulder.

Once, only once, the unmistakable sight of a golden eagle pulled me immediately off the freeway to sit idling, straining through my windshield for a closer look before it left its telephone-pole perch to wing off regally toward the Coburg Hills.

That single sighting caused more interest in those skies than all the hawks and falcons I'd seen. It has in fact tempted me into some hasty but mistaken identifications of several far-off crows.

What fascinates me most about these birds, though, isn't so much their identification as merely their existence, among the cloverleaf interchanges and truck-stop billboards, apparently unruffled by the steady stream of semis and sports cars and four-door sedans. Traveling the freeway tends to be a very insulating experience: Everything the driver needs is available within a few hundred feet of the road. It's easy to get the feeling that the Willamette Valley is the freeway, the spreading fields and wood lots to either side being merely a scenic backdrop.

Not long ago I hiked to the top of Spencer's Butte in Eugene. On that rare clear day I had to search to locate I-5. From my butte-top perspective, it wasn't much more than a tiny thread, thinner even than the still-small Willamette River. It must look something like that to the hawks, circling high over the fields, searching for mice where hawks have searched for mice since long before asphalt was even a word. They're not the backdrop to my play; I am a guest in their house, temporarily, jetting in and out of their territory, part of a thin, ever-moving stream of vehicles that apparently means little more to a hawk than a convenient boundary line.

One Sunday morning a couple of weeks ago, on a drive to Portland, I noticed a familiar-looking form on a fence post ahead, and strained to identify it before I sped by. As I passed, I saw it was a redtail, sitting with feathers puffed up in the cold mist. It seemed strange that a hawk would be facing the road and not the fields, singling out tiny rodents for pursuit. Then I realized that this hawk wasn't, at that moment, any more interested in food than I was. He was simply watching the traffic. Watching, in fact, me.

# Someday My Hawk Will Come...
# Riding on a Cold Front

PETER DUNNE

I don't think that there is any such thing as a typical hawk watcher. The only thing held in common is an interest in birds of prey that borders on obsession and at times transcends it. One hawk watcher I know starts the season in Duluth, Minnesota, to catch September broad-winged hawks. The latter part of the month finds him in Cape May for accipiters and falcons and the closing days of October and November at Hawk Mountain in Pennsylvania for buteos and eagles. Another hawk-watching couple religiously drive from their Manhattan apartment to their favorite Kittatinny Ridge lookout and back, every Saturday and every Sunday, the first weekend in September through the last weekend in November.

There are hawk watchers who have earned their forty-year-merit badge, and hawk watchers of but a single season. There are hawk watchers who live on independent means, and hawk watchers who are merely independent. Most consider themselves to be birders, but some only during "off season," and a few have given up birding all together. It interferes with hawk watching, they insist.

116

I met one hard-core hawk watcher who scornfully asserted that he could put a name to anything with feathers and wings. He proved it. A fall warbler dropped into a bush as quick as a fall warbler dropping into a bush. His identification was a half a wingbeat behind. "Sharp-shinned food," he exclaimed, without even lifting his binoculars. Awed, I pointed to a distant flock of peep. "Peregrine food," he noted, after a few seconds. I was, needless to say, suitably impressed, and it occurs to me now that I had witnessed the ultimate expression of lumping syndrome.

Hawk watchers are also gifted with boundless optimism. If the autumn wind is blowing from the southwest, it will turn. If it's raining, it will clear. If the nearest cold front is in the Aleutians, it will arrive. Viewing the horizon through rose-colored binoculars would not be an asset were all days on the hawk watch bountiful ones. I have noted that the conversation of the not-so-good days follows a fairly predictable pattern. (On the good days, there isn't time for conversation.)

Early-morning discussion is dominated by references to the anticipated excellent hawk flight, lavished with the reinforcing half-truths needed to support such a notion. If all the facts belie optimism, accounts of days which began with everything stacked against them and then became red-letter entries are retold, embellished, or fabricated.

After three hours, the count stands at 3.5 sharp-shinneds, .5 Cooper's hawks, 1 flock of something that might have been geese, 3 local turkey vultures, and 1 unidentified buteo recorded simultaneously at Sunrise Mountain and Montclair Quarry. The first dawning awareness that the day might not live up to earlier expectations heralds a shift in the conversation. The causal factors which are at the bottom of the not-so-over-whelming flight are examined. Those most often heard include: Excuse No. 23A, "The wind isn't right"; Excuse No. 294, "There isn't enough cloud cover" (see also Excuse No. 294B,

"Too much cloud cover"); Excuse No. 70B, "There aren't any thermals"; and Excuse No. 14A, "They are going over too high," or Excuse No. 14B, "They are going by too low." If it's September, someone is sure to mention Excuse No. 111A, "It's too early in the season"; and conversely, in November, Excuse No. 111B, "It's too late in the season."

By 10:30, conversation has turned to whether or not the Kansas City Chiefs can do it again, whether crushed graham crackers or vanilla wafers make a better cheesecake crust, whether the oil in the crankcase should be changed at three thousand or five thousand miles, or whether predestination precludes free will. Lunch begins at 11:00, and by 1:00 the leaves that need raking or the storm windows that need hanging begin to weigh on mind and soul. Good-bys are said, punctuated by the traditional "Well, now that I'm leaving, the eagle will come," and singly or in small groups (and with many a backward glance), the watch is vacated. Most of the crowd will be back tomorrow because the front *could* come through, and the birds that have been held up for so long *have* to move!

. . . And it does, and they do.

The relationship between meteorological happenstance and hawk migration is acute. With the possible exception of sailors, pilots, and umbrella salesmen, there is no group of human beings more weather-conscious than hawk watchers. Hawk-watching conversation is littered with references to "fronts," "highs," "lows," "occlusions," "backwash," and "thermals." At the Cape May Bird Observatory's raptor banding headquarters, banders gather at day's end to total up the scores, compare notes, and recount the day's events. At 5:23 P.M., all conversation stops! It does not lower a few decibels. It does not trail off. It stops. All eyes turn toward the TV weatherman with the intensity of the accused facing the jury.

The words that everyone waits to hear are "cold front."

118

Where? How fast? Is it moving? When will it arrive? A cold front is to a hawk watcher what six inches of fresh powder is to a skier. It is Christmas, the Mardi Gras, the Fourth of July, VE Day, and the Coronation of the Queen all rolled into one. Cold fronts mean northwest winds, and northwest winds mean hawks in Cape May just as they mean hawks along the ridges. More often than not, a quick glance at the weather map behind the smiling face on the TV screen is enough to tell the tale. Either the speaker's words will be drowned out in a flood of rebel cheers, or the fatal utterances of "occluded front" or "stalled over the Midwest" will fall into sullen silence.

The alarm rings hard and cold in the predawn darkness, and sleep-dulled senses strain to catch some hint of the day's judgment. Sand hisses against the west window, and the street light dancing on weakened supports sends flickers of light through the drawn blind. Cold front! Outside, the stars glitter like shards of ice, and above the wind the rising and falling bark of snow geese can be heard far off. Sounds of hurried rising drift in from the next room. Muffled snatches of conversation and the smell of coffee indicate that the banding crew at the Cape May Bird Observatory is up and about. The air is electric with excitement.

Morning light softens the eastern sky, silhouetting kestrels and sharp-shinneds. Cold-numbed fingers work the counter in my pocket, and a dozen birds are recorded on the short walk from the parking area at the Cape May Point State Park to the hawk watch. Other hawk watchers arrive, both regulars and newcomers, and high anticipation counters the bite of the chill autumn air.

Sharp-shinned hawks emerge from the gray dawn: three, four, a dozen, more! A small, dark falcon courses along the

woods' edge, accelerates suddenly, and disappears into a bay-
berry thicket, which explodes a millisecond later with scattering
yellow-rumps. Merlin. Someone (Jerry? . . . Harold?) picks up
a bird, "over the town . . . dropping now . . . up again, over
the dunes approaching the bunker . . . *Now!* It's a, it's a . . ."
"Peregrine," shouts another voice. "Peregrine," echoes another.
*Peregrine!*

On the ridges, buteos and accipiters are moving beak to tail.
New arrivals of watchers (between gasps) ask to be filled in on
the morning's flight. The cries of "goshawk" and "red-shouldered" are heard simultaneously, and two of New Jersey's *most*
veteran hawk watchers square off . . . again. "Look at the tail,
the tail . . . accipiters have long tails; page 42 of your Peterson's, remember?" tutors the goshawk proponent, with exaggerated patience and a heavy dose of irony. "I can see the tail,
but even a person with your mean experience should be able
to recognize a buteo when it's pointed out to him," chides the
red-shouldered advocate. The verbal duel is as much a tradition
at this hawk watch as the 4:00 eagle at Hawk Mountain. With
great reluctance, a neutral party points out that the two friends
and antagonists are looking in opposite directions.

A lull ushers in lunch. Thermoses are cracked, sandwiches
unwrapped, and mouthfuls snatched between binocular scans.
Everyone is well into his second half and reaching for the
thermos when the rustle of cellophane is broken by the frantic
cry of "ghouldon eeeghoul." Half the remaining lunches are
trampled in the ensuing melee, as hawk watchers scramble to
the north side of the ridge, frantically clearing mayonnaise
from their binocular lenses.

Back at the Cape, the accipiter flight has dwindled, and the
afternoon belongs to the falcon tribe. The merlin count is inch-
ing toward the 50 mark as the afternoon sun is edging toward
the horizon. A dozen hold-over merlins are cutting around the

marsh, engaging in their favorite pastime, deviling sharp-shinned hawks.

A steel-blue jack arcs across the horizon, checks his speed momentarily, then throws on the afterburners and heads for the Delaware side. That makes 50! The attainment of the goal seems to signal the day's end. Good-bys are said, interrupted only by the passage of merlins number 51 and 52.

Memories of seasons past are as much a part of hawk watching as the anticipation of seasons to come. They are purchased by perseverance and skill (heavily subsidized by lavish amounts of blind luck), and they are hoarded jealously, as is befitting something which cannot be priced.

But this is September now, and anticipation leaves little time for conjuring up past glories. It's time to intercept memories, so that the conjuring will be better come next December.

# Sea-Bound Blues

## JOHN PANCAKE

Pelagic bird-watching trips, a social psychologist will one day conclude, are the ultimate in masochism.

"Pelagic" is a word that describes the open ocean, far out of sight of land. What occurs on a pelagic bird-watching trip is that forty or so bird watchers pile onto a chartered fishing boat. This boat, with a mildly amused captain, chugs as far as sixty miles out to sea. If the bird watchers are lucky they may see a rare sea bird—a fulmar, an Audubon's shearwater, a red phalarope, storm petrels, a parasitic jaeger, or even an artic tern.

If the boat is plowing through heavy seas, many of the forty bird watchers may engage in an activity politely known as "chumming." The only positive thing that can be said for this is that it sometimes draws birds. A Maryland ornithologist reported that for three years the first sightings of the rare skua, northern fulmar, common puffin, and yellow-nosed albatross were all attracted in this manner.

For reasons we have since forgotten, my wife and I made reservations on such a trip a couple of years ago at twenty-five dollars apiece. We were to show up at a pier in Virginia Beach at 4:00 A.M. on Sunday, May 28. Here are my notes from the weekend:

Saturday, May 27

6:00 A.M.—Telephone rings. It is the Warbler Wizard. An avid mountain bird watcher, the Wizard made reservations for the pelagic trip the same time we did. Now he has been overcome by a fit of sanity.

The Wizard, who might be able to get seasick in a bathtub if he worked at it, decides for some reason that it is not worth driving all the way to Norfolk so he can blow lunch in the North Atlantic.

7:45 A.M.—Pull out of driveway. The weatherman is talking about a beautiful Memorial Day weekend.

11:00 A.M.—Suffolk. It appears this is not a weekend the weatherman will want to remember. The beautiful weekend has turned into small-craft warnings. A weather front has crept down the Atlantic coast and taken a seat on top of Tidewater Virginia.

1:30 P.M.—Portsmouth. Stop at Craney Island—the man-made peninsula in Hampton Roads where the muck dredged from the harbor channel is dumped. It is one of the best birding places in Virginia.

On our tour around the edge of the island we find avocets (big black-and-white wading birds with upturned bills); several kinds of sandpipers (white-rumped, semi-palmated, dunlin, short-billed dowitchers); a score of snaky-necked cormorants; several piping plovers (small, light-colored versions of the killdeer that is common in our area); and seven northern phalaropes.

Also find George Stubbs of Franklin County. The clouds are hanging low over Craney, and the wind is beating whitecaps out of the harbor.

"Hello," I say.

"Expletive deleted," says George. George has come down for the pelagic trip, too.

George's record on pelagic trips being weathered out is two for four.

"I think I'm a Jonah," he says.

It looks very much like George will be two for five when the weekend is over.

6:30 P.M.—Reach the Norfolk home of Bob Ake, the organizer of the trip. Bob has offered to let folks sleep on his floor, and about twelve birders take him up on it. Anne Ake somehow accepts having twelve bodies in sleeping bags on her floor as if it happened every day.

9:30 P.M.—Go to sleep.

9:32 P.M.—Bob wakes me up. Says it is 2:30 A.M.—time to get up.

9:33 P.M.—It *is* 2:30! Why am I getting up in the middle of the night to go out in the fog and wind and rain so I can throw up in the presence of some birds that have never seen me before? Why am I a bird watcher? Stamp collectors don't have to get up in the middle of the night to buy stamps.

3:00 A.M.—Have had three cups of coffee. Still planning to drop birding and take up stamp collecting.

3:55 A.M.—Arrive at *Big D*'s slip on Lynnhaven inlet. *Big D* is the boat we have chartered. Ake says it is sixty-five feet long. It looks like it is sixteen. Ake says the *Big D* and her captain are pretty good, but in describing *Big D*'s path through the water he uses words like "yaw," "pitch," and "roll." These, I gather, have to do with the way it bounces up and down. They do not sound like friendly words.

The pier is cloaked in fog and drizzle. Winds are supposed to get up to twenty-five miles an hour. Forty bird watchers are huddled on the dock.

Ake and *Big D*'s captain begin delicate negotiations.

Despite the weather, Ake hates the thought of not going out.

He figures the storm must have brought in some pretty good birds. But Ake (who gets seasick on about one pelagic trip in two, according to his wife) knows how uncomfortable it can be in a small boat on rough seas.

The captain does not say he will go and does not say he won't. He just says things like:

"There might be eight-foot swells out there. I'd just about be willing to bet my salary on six."

And:

"It was plenty rough out there yesterday, and the wind hasn't dropped enough to let it die down overnight."

And:

"We had a woman on board the other day who got very seasick when we were out on the bay—not even the open ocean. She was too weak to make it to the toilet to vomit. We had to carry her in there."

The eerie screams of least terns and laughing gulls fill the night. Ake, a veteran of this sort of encounter, is not to be stampeded. He spends about five minutes listening to the winds and discussing the weather report. If he decides not to go and the weather turns clear, he is a goat. If he decides to go, everybody who gets seasick will blame him. Very few people are offering any advice. Finally, Ake holds up his hand:

"OK, everybody. A decision has been made. We're not going out."

I can already hear the Warbler Wizard laughing.

4:50 A.M.—Several of us pile into cars and head for Back Bay, a wildlife refuge south of Virginia Beach, hoping to make the best of a bad situation.

I am riding with Bob Paxton, a Lexington native who now lives in Manhattan. He is fighting drowsiness brought on by the Dramamine he swallowed earlier in hopes of escaping the Revenge of the Bounding Main.

5:15 A.M.—First robin sings.

5:20 A.M.—Thunder. Lightning. Downpour. Despair.

7:30 A.M.—Finally emerge from automobile. Sprint for picnic shelter near the beach at Back Bay. Spend next three hours standing on picnic table under shelter trying to see over the sand dunes. Finally catch glimpses of a gannet, several sooty shearwaters, a handful of Wilson's storm petrels, and a common scoter out on the brawling sea. The petrel and shearwater are birds we had hoped to see on the pelagic trip. Their appearance makes the weather a little easier to swallow.

11:00 A.M.—After checking a few other hot spots, we pile twelve people into a van to go out on the Chesapeake Bay Bridge–Tunnel. The man-made islands at the ends of the tunnels are fine places to spot sea birds. Unfortunately, the toll is seven dollars. It is not so bad when you split it twelve ways.

3:00 P.M.—Return to Lynnhaven inlet to look for the rare Arctic tern. Terns are the small, black-capped gull-like birds often found on the coast. A very good bird watcher reported seeing an Arctic tern in the area the day before.

There has never been an authenticated record for an Arctic tern in Virginia, though there have been several reports. To be backed up, the bird must either be collected (shot and taken to a museum), or a very good photograph must be taken. The bird looks very much like the common tern found in this area. There have been cases when ornithologists have staked their reputations on a bird's being an Arctic tern, only to find when the bird was collected that it was a common tern.

We have not been on the sand flats long when Ake spots a bird with a long, red bill and a grayish breast. A possible Arctic tern. Most bird watchers might be better off not trying to distinguish an Arctic tern from a common tern, but there are some experienced hands in our party.

Ake is one of the top birders on the East Coast. Paxton is a New York regional editor for *American Birds*. David

Hughes, also on hand, is president of the Cape Henry Audubon Society. While Hughes and Paxton use high-powered cameras to photograph the bird, Ake goes over every field mark like a diamond cutter checking a jewel.

Everyone else seems satisfied it is an Arctic tern except Ake and Paxton, perhaps the two most experienced bird watchers present. Then the bird flies over, showing a characteristic pattern in the wing tip that separates it from the common tern.

"I'm impressed," says Paxton.

"As far as I'm concerned, it's an Arctic tern," says Ake.

It is a very fine moment, and I decide to forget about stamp collecting and stick with bird watching.

# Cruising in the Antarctic

## OLIN SEWALL PETTINGILL, JR.

C RUISING in the Antarctic? Any such idea was unthinkable when I entered college in 1926. The South Pole had been reached for the first time only fifteen years earlier. To most of us, Antarctica was a vast, icebound realm, as forbidding as it was remote.

Then in the late 1920s, soon after Lindbergh's historic flight across the Atlantic, came Richard E. Byrd's first Antarctic expedition, drawing attention to "the bottom of the world" as never before. After Byrd's later expeditions in the 1930s, Antarctica became a well-known entity, though still remote and accessible only by specially organized—and costly—expeditions.

My interest in the Antarctic might have been no greater than the average American's had it not been for a happy coincidence in 1936 when I took a teaching position at Carleton College in Minnesota. On the faculty was none other than Laurence McKinley Gould, professor of geology, who had been second in command of the first Byrd Antarctic expedition. In the course of our friendship his enthusiasm for the Antarctic rubbed off on me. Already a professional ornithologist, I visualized opportunities for studying and photographing Antarctic birds, so little known at the time and practically begging for attention. My getting there was a problem.

It might always have been a problem had it not been for the genius of Lars-Eric Lindblad, a Swedish-born entrepreneur with a flair for adventure cruising. Experimenting first with various ships available in the 1960s, Lindblad and his associates designed a small rugged vessel, capable of ice-working as well as sailing in some of the most tempestuous seas in the world. The result was the M.S. *Lindblad Explorer*, built in Finland, sailing under Panamanian registry, and catering largely to Americans.

In no sense a luxury liner, the *Explorer* measures 250 feet from stem to stern with a displacement of only 2,500 tons and a draft of no more than 15 feet. Among her other attributes are twin engines able to generate 3,800 horsepower, sufficient to break through pack ice up to a meter thick, and a bow thruster that enables her to turn around in her own length. She has fifty cabins, all on the outside, carries ninety-two passengers and a crew of sixty, and is a no-class ship with public rooms, including an auditorium—the Penguin Room—for films and lectures.

As an ornithologist, I was invited to join the scientific staff aboard the *Explorer* on her maiden voyage to Antarctica in 1970. Also invited to join the staff were persons authoritative in the fields of marine biology, oceanography, glaciology, and other scientific disciplines. Our presence was clearly an indication of the cruise's primary objective: to develop among the passengers a lasting appreciation of Antarctica's unique environment and its abundant wildlife.

How did we achieve this objective in so vast an area as Antarctica, fifth in size among the six continents, the highest

129

(average elevation six thousand feet), coldest, and windiest, and harboring easily 90 percent of the world's glacial ice? Fortunately, birds and seals, which constitute all of Antarctica's wildlife, can be readily observed on the coast or adjacent islands where they breed or rest, never far from the sea in which their food resides. Fortunately, too, the *Explorer*, designed as she is, can maneuver close to shore where her passengers can disembark in her rubber motorized boats called zodiacs and, within a few minutes, be on shore watching and photographing penguins, petrels, skuas, sheathbills, cormorants, seals—whichever happen to be present at the particular landing site.

Since 1970 the *Lindblad Explorer* has sailed every year to the Antarctic. I was aboard her in 1974 and again in 1979 on her tenth-anniversary cruise. Here is a brief idea of what these cruises, promoted as *adventure* cruises, are like.

Each cruise usually takes about two weeks in December and/ or January—late spring and/or early summer in the Southern Hemisphere—departing from a far southern South American port where the passengers arrive by air. Our destination, after three or four days in the Falkland Islands, some three hundred miles east of the tip of South America, is southward for eight hundred miles across Drake Passage to the Antarctic Peninsula. This requires two days—and exciting days they are, generally with strong winds, sometimes at gale force, and rough seas.

Albatrosses, shearwaters, fulmars, and petrels we regularly see from the decks. Indeed, there is never a time when some of these birds are not in view. If something unusual shows up, for example, a wandering albatross (the largest seabird that flies) or a pod of killer whales, it is announced from the bridge into the intercom, alerting everyone throughout the ship. Result: a rush to the decks.

The first iceberg sighted from the bridge also brings an excited voice through the intercom. It will be the most photo-graphed iceberg on the cruise; icebergs soon will be common-place. Toward evening on the second day snowy mountains begin looming ahead. They are really high islands just north of the Antarctic Peninsula.

For five or six days the *Explorer* sails south on the west side of the peninsula through channels between coast and islands. Daylight becomes practically continuous; the sun dips below the horizon more briefly each day, for four hours, then three hours, and so on as we proceed south.

Our daily routine on this climactic part of the cruise begins after breakfast with a briefing in the Penguin Room on the day's program ashore. It may be an inspection of one of the penguin colonies, or taking a zodiac tour of ice formation in some sheltered bay, or visiting one of the scientific stations operated by the United States, Russia, Britain, or Argentina. We may entertain staff from one of these stations at dinner, preceded by the usual recap in the lounge of the day's observa-tions and followed by a film in the Penguin Room—for those passengers not exhausted by all the events of the day.

Air temperatures during these days are steadily cold. On the sunniest days the thermometer commonly ranges in the 30s F. On cloudy days with wind, the thermometer may not read much lower, but the air nonetheless seems much colder.

If there is one aspect of this Antarctic sojourn that passen-gers enjoy more than any other, it is the time spent watching and photographing penguins in their colonies. Caricatures of ourselves, tame and winsome, penguins enthrall everyone, even the urbanite who has never watched birds before, much less cared about them. Although penguins occasionally show inter-est in us, more often than not they go about their affairs as though we didn't exist. We see how they cope with their environment, including their natural enemies; how they come

131

out of the frigid sea while ever watchful for leopard seals ready
to catch them; how they care for their eggs and chicks in fair
weather or severe and guard them against attacks by skuas,
gull-like birds with hawklike habits.

By the time the *Lindblad Explorer* turns back north, after
coming as close to the Antarctic Circle as ice conditions will
allow, her passengers have gained a lasting appreciation of
Antarctica's unique environment and associated wildlife. I
feel confident that every passenger returns home a champion
of Antarctica's preservation.

Bob Hines

# IV  *Stop, Look, and List*

---

*We are a record-keeping species, and the birder, like the golfer, the ball player, the mountain climber, is no exception. Most bird watchers keep one or more lists: day lists, year lists, life lists, yard lists, state lists, county lists, or whatever other lists the imagination can devise. Some limit themselves to their own area, while others charter planes, abandon sickbeds, miss anniversaries, forsake spouses—all to chase the elusive rarity. Many participate in the annual Christmas Bird Counts and Breeding Bird Surveys, and the lists compiled on these occasions have scientific value. For the rest, birders readily admit that the meaning is for themselves.*

# The Birder as Lister

## ROBERT J. CONNOR

U NDER the date of July 22, 1942, and over the notation "These birds were seen on a hike along the Wallkill River; these birds are also the first birds I ever recorded," there is a list of twelve species of birds. The thin black notebook in which that list is recorded was filled by May 16, 1943. Piled in front of me as I write is a collection of various sorts of record books that I filled in the ensuing years. For with that first scrawled list I became an inveterate "lister," the species of birder who painstakingly records the bird species he sees.

I could write an autobiography from these records. There are lists from Washington, where I spent my service time, and from an ocean voyage (maneuvers) from Washington to southern California. There are lists from most of the western national parks that I hitchhiked to after my discharge. There are lists from Maryland, where I went to college (although these are the sparsest of lists, as birding temporarily yielded to studies and social life). There is a list for thirty-four species that I saw as my wife, Marty, and I drove to Tennessee on our honey-

137

moon. There are lists from all over the country and the world as I traveled on business. There are lists from all of our family vacations.

There are two life lists (U.S., 425; World, 536), and the thirty-sixth year list is still being added to (best year, 1972, 272). There are state lists (New York, 243; California, 208; New Jersey, 301) and a list for Rockland County, New York (214). There is a yard list for our first home in West Nyack, New York (131), and one for our current home in New City (96). And there are area lists for frequently birded places like Brigantine (193), Cape May (221), and Tuckerton, New Jersey (127), and for special places like Nova Scotia (65) and Cape Ann/Newburyport (84).

Browsing through those record books I can relive hundreds upon hundreds of days in the field, some good, some bad, some great, some miserable.

January 23, 1944—bitter cold, freezing rain, gusty winds from 7:45 until 1:15—until we found the evening grosbeaks that had been reported in Paramus, New Jersey (then mostly farmland). My record book tells me that there were three males and four females and that they were flying, perching, calling, and feeding in a lowland area.

May 1, 1954—a twenty-hour "Big Day," over four hundred miles from ocean to desert to mountains in the Los Angeles area. I was with Bob Smart and Arnold Small, both of whom later made the ABA's 600 Club. I listed 145 species on my list (they had 6 more that I missed), including 12 life birds. The next day Bob took me to Sespe Canyon and showed me four California condors.

My records show that on February 12, 1945, the temperature ranged from 31° to 36°, the barometer was 30.1, winds were 15 to 25 mph, cirrocumulus clouds provided .3 to .7 sky cover, and the tide was high at 7:00 A.M. Birding the North Jersey

138

shore from 7:30 A.M. to 5:30 P.M. (door-to-door, 6:30 to 8:10) produced 4,332 individuals of twenty-four species, ten of them life birds. One of the latter, listed as a Holboell's grebe, is found on today's lists as a red-necked grebe.

January 30, 1976, was my only "blitz" trip, when I journeyed with two others from Albany to Boston to see the ivory gull. This record never fails to give me regrets that I hadn't earlier "blitzed" the Ross's or later done the smew.

There is a list for August 9–26, 1972, listing 116 species but including notations of sightings of moose, caribou, fox, porcupine, snowshoe hare, chipmunks, groundhog, and red squirrel—all seen in Gaspescie, Quebec. Earlier that year there was the May 5–8 trip to Shad's Landing, Maryland, and Chincoteague, Virginia, with 164 species total.

There are the Cape May lists, sixteen trips over twenty-five years, fifty-one days of the best possible birding, totaling 221 species. On these lists there are the great days of arrival of a migrating "wave" (the best of them producing 128 species) when there were too many birds to look at. On these lists too are some of my best rarities—cattle egret when they had first arrived in the country (what a difference now!), Greenland wheatear, and many others.

And so it goes. There are lists from the Grand Canyon and Yosemite; from Fiji, Japan, and Australia; from England, Italy, and Norway. There are lists for most New Year's Days for our back porch and for a trip to Nova Scotia on the *Bluenose* (long-tailed jaeger, a life bird). There is even a list of eleven species that I have been watching just outside my window as I write this.

Yes, even at this moment I am making a list, and I'm certain that no matter where I am or what I'm doing I'll go right on keeping these lists: day lists, year lists, life lists, state lists, and special area lists. And there will be new special area counts as time passes (like the one I keep now for the thruway from Rockland to Albany). There is no question but that the lists, at least from a scientific point of view, are worthless. Still, part of the excitement of birding is coming in from the cold, the rain, and the sleet and making the list. And the bonus is to look them over years later and vicariously relive the trip. Birding is a lot of fun; listing makes it more fun and makes the fun last longer.

Once a person becomes an active field birder and begins making lists of birds seen, it is inevitable that other lists are soon kept. Some are kept in books, so that along with a life list of birds, there will soon be found life lists of trees, reptiles, ferns, insects, mammals, and so forth.

Some aren't kept in books, not being suitable for listing, but form instead a mental list. For one cannot seek out, and list, species of birds, animals, trees, and wild flowers without also seeing the whole. Yet you would not list that you had seen a salt marsh, a freshwater lake, a spruce forest, a wood edge, a tidal flat, or the myriad of ecological niches that you pass through.

Nor do you keep a list that records an evening sitting quietly on an ocean beach watching the phragmites by the bayside turn rosy with the lowering sun, while dunlins and dowitchers dart through the last ripples of a receding tide for a final snack before the night's rest. Nor is there a list that tells about the same beach on a winter's day when a frigid spray blew in from the ocean and the marsh grass was plated with a sparkling coat of ice. And while the day's lists record the Ipswich sparrows (there was once such a bird) and snowy owl whose presence tempted you to this insane expedition, they won't record at all the burning sensation on nasal membranes from inhaling frigid air, or the remarkable geometry of the unsupported ice anchored above the emptying tide pools.

No list records that most marvelous trick of nature that re-

140

quires sound to sense absolute silence—that special silence observed at a twilight lakeside, when peepers sing and from across the pond a bullfrog croaks, or when in the evening summer woods a single wood thrush sings in the distance. All these records are not written, but they are felt and so they are remembered. And you look for them again.

You won't always find them. That beach is nearly gone. Block upon block of frame houses reach almost to the tip, and snowy owls don't visit there any more. A woods I visited almost every day in boyhood years is a park now, the low wet spots filled and graded, the underbrush cleared so that there is a limited variety of flora and fauna. The riverbanks along the same daily bike route are built up right to the edge— paved for a parking lot here, fenced for an industrial building there, and the remaining spot that looks as if it might be still wild displays, on closer approach, piles of discarded mattresses and other debris of our consuming society.

The best pond I knew to find gallinules on is now beneath a power plant, and the field for bobolinks is the site of a housing development. My warbling vireo spot became an auto wrecker's lot, and the little marsh that always had resident marsh wrens is more than half gone now, the wrens replaced by a sign that says "Clean Fill Wanted" and another that reads "Industrial Acreage Available."

And so the birder becomes an environmentalist. Not just for those missed memories, but because it will be a lesser life for all if every beach is built upon and every woods cleared for development. Children and grandchildren and theirs must know those special silences. There must be sense in our use of resources—there is a limit to how long we can denude one place to supply us, while filling another place with our debris— else we will eventually all be crammed between the desert and the dump.

Clean air and pure water are part of a heritage. The public

can no longer be deprived of them for the limited benefits to a few. Toxic wastes concentrate as they go upward through the food cycle—a hazard to health that cannot be tolerated.

In my own recollection, over the past three and a half decades, birders were the first environmentalists: the first to know the sense of loss when woods were wasted for a super-highway, even if at first the only impact was on the length of the bird list that could be kept; the first to note ducks that couldn't fly because they were drenched in oil. It was natural, then, that they were in the vanguard of the environmental movement.

# Keeping a Clean List

## JUDITH TOUPS

I used to scoff at bird listing. Keeping records requires both an orderly mind and self-discipline—reasons enough for me to reject the idea. After years devoted to reaching a pinnacle of organized chaos, I looked upon listing as a threat to my way of life, a life in which the most routine chores were spiced with uncertainty and adventure.

Take the income tax, for example. For me, half the challenge lay in the week-long search through drawers, under beds, and through unlabeled brown paper bags for the tenuous proof that Uncle Sam owed us $65.84, followed by the race to the post office just seconds short of the deadline. My sense of accomplishment was greater for having overcome the obstacles of self-imposed confusion. That philosophy extended to my sightings of birds: Dozens of names, dates, and places were committed to naught but memory.

Then I revealed myself as a birder, and naturally someone asked to see my life list. Woe! I was unable to produce one shred of written evidence that I had seen a western kingbird in

August of 1966, and I wilted under the arched eyebrow and ill-concealed sneer of my inquisitor, whose own list, he claimed, was as pure as the driven snow.

If I wanted a place in the birding fraternity, I realized then that I would have to temper my laissez-faire philosophy with some common sense. Spurred on by a merciless probationer, I gritted teeth and thought vile thoughts while waiting for a legitimate western kingbird to replace the one of my nonlisting days. But victory was sweet, and my list is now "clean."

Keeping a clean list is done on the honor system. It involves personal ethics and integrity, and it helps to have birding associates who will periodically inspect your list, free of charge. I herewith claim that my own list is clean and can stand the scrutiny of the FBI, the CIA, the NKVD, and the AOU. On the other hand, there are those who still regard it as slightly sullied, and they have threatened to bring down the full wrath of the ABA upon me.

The dispute stems from my refusal to remove the burrowing owl from my Mississippi list. Now this owl spent the night at my house; I was its benefactor, nurse, keeper, chauffeur, and general all-around patsy for twenty-four hours. It perched on my typewriter while eating chicken liver and later rewarded me by dropping a pellet on my desk. As if further proof were needed, I took the bird to the offices of the *Daily Herald* in Gulfport, where numerous pictures were taken. (The wire photo subsequently was carried in dozens of southeastern newspapers.)

On the following day, Larry Gates, Gerry Morgan, and I escorted the owl to a place forty miles away and released it. Nearly four hours later we found it again, "in the wild," whereupon we checked the burrowing owl off on various and assorted lists. Larry found the owl again several weeks later on the Jackson County Christmas Bird Count (nobody has yet suggested that it was an obvious plant), and this fortuitous encounter removed Larry from the list of suspects who don't keep clean lists. On that occasion I couldn't claim to have seen anything more than a blur in the sky.

My twenty-four hours of intimacy with the owl have been ruled upon by our friend Wayne Weber, whose list actually squeaks. Wayne suggests that since the ABA says twenty-four hours must elapse before a released bird can be added to one's list, I should remove the burrowing owl or live out the rest of my birding life in disgrace.

My answer: "You keep your list, and I'll keep mine."

# Tracking a Lifer

## THOMAS C. SOUTHERLAND, JR.

I T was just starting to drizzle. I glanced at my watch and noticed it was about 10:45 P.M. We were far enough north that it had been dark for only about an hour. "Damn!" I muttered to my wife, Margot. "The rain could really hurt our chances of seeing it."

The motel where our two girls were asleep seemed miles behind us as we sped down the road in our camper, yet we had been gone only some twenty minutes. We had passed the last small village and were entering one of the most vast expanses of marshes along the Atlantic Seaboard. We were north of the small village of Middle Sackville in New Brunswick, near the Nova Scotia line, and we wanted to be near an isolated railroad bridge by 11:00. We knew what the bridge looked like because we had made a dry run in the afternoon.

As we slowed down to approach the bridge, headlights suddenly appeared from behind. The surprise was enough to take away my forthcoming comments of relief that the rain had stopped and some stars were in evidence. We stopped at the bridge, expecting the car to pass us and continue onward. The car did pass but pulled to a stop twenty feet in front of us. It was a Beetle with New York license plates.

Out of the car jumped two men. The taller of the two wore a poncho and an old porkpie hat, brim pulled down partially covering his face. Despite the heat, the other wore a heavy jacket and ski cap. Both had several days' growth of beard. We recognized one as Davis W. Finch, maritime reporter for the National Audubon's *American Birds*. His companion was Dennis J. Abbott III, nationally known birder and records chairman, as well as the editor of the *New Hampshire Audubon Quarterly*.

We had actually met Finch three weeks earlier in Nova Scotia at Kejimkujik National Park, where he had given us much helpful information in our quest to see birds in Newfoundland. We had met Abbott two years before on a bird trip in search of oceanic birds on the S.S. *Bluenose*, a ferry that sails between Bar Harbor, Maine, and Yarmouth, Nova Scotia.

When we got out of the car, we realized why their hats had been pulled so far down. The mosquitoes were unbelievable. It was as if we had landed in the midst of a mosquito convention, and we were to be their first banquet. The conditions couldn't have been more favorable for them. It had just rained, it was almost the middle of July, and the location was their prime habitat, a marsh.

All four of us had converged at this spot to try to see the yellow rail, a North American wading bird only five inches in length from the tip of the bill to the tip of the tail. It is extremely shy. Its clicking call is not too unlike the sound made by tapping two small pebbles against each other in alternating groups of two and three. The bird is heard far more than it is seen, and few have ever seen it.

The American Birding Association (ABA) asked its members what forty birds they would most like to see in North America. The results of the poll, published in 1970 in *Birding*,

IV STOP, LOOK, AND LIST

the ABA's bimonthly magazine, showed the yellow rail to be
in fourth place. In a later polling, it moved into second place,
passing the ivory-billed woodpecker, the giant woodpecker
of southern primeval forests and a bird that may already be
extinct. Only the Bachman's warbler, a bird of southern swamps
in danger of extinction, remained ahead of it. Even now the
yellow rail remains among the ten most wanted birds. The
yellow rail is not yet considered to be in any danger of extinction by the U.S. Fish and Wildlife Service, in spite of man's
widespread elimination of marsh habitat. Because the bird is so
elusive, making a census difficult if not impossible, the bird
guides all list its status as "rare."

Like other members of the rail family, it has a narrowly compressed body enabling it to slip between dense blades of marsh
grass and reeds without being noticed—thus the origin of the
expression "thin as a rail." The yellowish plumage helps camouflage the bird and perhaps explains why it is also sometimes
known to inhabit certain meadows and grain fields. The best
place to locate it, however, is in salt marsh grass, where it likes
to feed on small snails. According to the *Audubon Water Bird
Guide*, "This bird is more of a mystery than any other North
American species of comparable distribution."

Most of the few people who have been fortunate enough
to flush the skulking yellow rail only catch an unsatisfactory
glimpse of the bird taking off very quickly and flying a short
distance before disappearing in more marsh grass. "As they are
virtually impossible to flush and seem to avoid open places,
they are seldom detected except by their notes," the *Guide*
points out, adding that they are "loath to fly." To locate a yellow rail, the book suggests using a trained dog. Another way
to success might be "through mowing or beating down a long
lane in the grass and driving the rails across it." Some unthink-
ing bird watchers, in the attempt to see the rails, commit

destructive acts such as starting fires, operating grass cutters, and even setting off explosive devices. Roger Tory Peterson, the oracle of all bird watchers and originator of the popular field guides, also suggests the services of a bird dog, because these rails "are so mouselike."

Margot and I came as listers. Like a growing number of bird watchers, we were working on our North American list with the hope of becoming members of the 600 Club. At the time, our North American list was a little past 500, helped by the recent addition of ten new species in Nova Scotia and Newfoundland.

A phone call to Dr. David S. Christie, of the New Brunswick Museum in St. John, had alerted us to the bird. We had called about a northern three-toed woodpecker that had been observed nesting the previous year near the Bay of Fundy. We had seen its close relative of north coniferous woods, the black-backed three-toed woodpecker, in Newfoundland a week earlier. No, Dr. Christie had not seen the bird this year, but suggested that we might like to try for a yellow rail that he had seen two weeks earlier with Davis Finch and several others.

Margot and I had been instructed simply to park just beyond the railroad bridge and from there to proceed by foot to the thirteenth telephone pole and listen for the clicking sound of the yellow rail. We had brought a strong four-cell flashlight and tape recorder, and we hoped that we would be able to lure one into close range. We had a number of tapes of birds with us but not one of the yellow rail. We would just have to try to record its call and play it back with the hope that a rail would respond and move into closer range. Unfortunately, we had no parabolic microphone, the highly directional electronic instrument used by TV cameramen for high-fidelity recording at great distances. Basically, this device consists of a dish-shaped parabola with a microphone in the center.

149

With Davis Finch and Dennis Abbott, we knew we were in good hands, for Finch knew the area, was obviously familiar with the bird, and, moreover, had the parabolic microphone we lacked. Finch had even pinpointed the "magic" pole with a yellow marker. But there was no sound of a rail calling. We heard a barred owl in the distance and also a whippoorwill, but no rail. We kept walking back and forth. Nothing. Finally, Finch suggested we all drive to another location where he had also had some luck.

Meanwhile, we did everything in our power to keep the mosquitoes from bodily carrying us away. Covered from head to toe with clothing, we were downright hot. But we chose to be hot rather than fodder for the buzzing, howling pests. Margot pulled her ski hat down over her neck and forehead. I had a rain hood tied tightly around my face, and, for the small amounts of exposed skin around our eyes, noses, and mouths, we all were using combinations of lotions.

We got into our cars and sped in close caravan several miles along the dirt road through the marshes, until our cars spooked up a short-eared owl which had been resting in the center of the road. We slammed on our brakes and quickly leaped out of the cars to glimpse the owl flying away.

After the excitement had died down, and we were about to resume our trip, Finch cried out, "Listen, there it is!" I thought he was talking about the owl, but no, he was definitely hearing the rail. The rest of us then strained to hear the sound, but to no avail. Only mosquitoes. We tried cupping hands behind ears and moving our heads from side to side. The hand cupping gives the ears more surface area to catch sound. But still no luck. So we drove onward.

Margot wondered if Finch was really hearing it or just putting us on. We drove a few more minutes, not knowing where we were, conscious only of the fact that it was dark outside, that the stars were out by now in full force, and that the marsh was even bigger than we had originally thought. Finally, we stopped again and got out to listen. Abbott could now hear its call, but we still could not—a call that is only as loud as the clicks of two pebbles or, as Finch remarked, more like a *tick-tick* sound.

We resumed driving a few more minutes and repeated the procedure of stopping and listening. Margot eventually joined the ranks of hearers, those jokers Abbott and Finch. On our last stop, even I could hear it. No mistake about it, a yellow rail was calling.

We walked some hundred yards down a narrow dirt lane perpendicular to the road where our cars were parked. By now the rail seemed as if it were walking in the marsh alongside us. Finch recommended that we head directly into the marsh. This meant first descending a steep bank, crossing a two-foot stream, then going up another bank and into the tall grass itself. Of course it had to be done quietly, without benefit of lights and ignoring the ever-present mosquitoes as well as the heat.

Once in the marsh, the only sounds to be heard were the frequent sucking of water reluctantly breaking contact with rubber boots and the incessant call of the rail. *Tick-tick, tick-tick.* It would also change its pitch. The sound was not unlike the clickers children play with, at least until parents have had enough. Every ten yards or so we would come to a complete halt, all huddled together, while platoon leader Finch recorded the call, using his sensitive parabolic microphone. And at every stop Margot fought off the twin temptations of letting out a yell, as the victim of a mosquito, and trying to slap one of the pests off her face and hands.

At last Finch felt we were in a good position to play back the rail's call. Instead of one set of clickings, there were now two. It was difficult to tell which belonged to what. Then

the order came to open fire with our lights in the direction
Davis pointed—about five feet ahead. The whole area was suddenly awash with light. The grasses shook, and instantly the
bird flushed and in a split second dropped. Our hearts sank.
The brief sighting was certainly not good enough to add the
bird to our life list. This cat-and-mouse approach could go on
all evening. One good field mark of a yellow rail flying is a
white patch on each wing, and although we strained for a
glimpse of the patches, we didn't come close. All we saw was
whirling wings.

Shaken but still hopeful, once more under cover of darkness,
we walked a few more feet and again tried the recorder. A few
minutes later word came to shine the lights. We had heard
the clicking, seemingly louder than before, but try as we could
with moving heads, we just couldn't locate the bird.

Suddenly, I saw it—right at my feet. I could see a little
yellowish bird with a small bill through the transparent plastic
parabola dish held in front of me by Finch. I couldn't believe
what I saw. Here was a bird I never dreamed would be on our
list, much less this close. Apprenhensive that the rail might
instantly take flight, I whispered to Margot to notice the dark
striping on its back, a diagnostic field mark. Incredible as it
seemed, the bird did not appear anxious to fly. Finch handed
me the parabola, then slowly bent down and quickly grasped
the rail with both hands. It was now ours. It had some slight
streaks on the head and a dark line from the bill through and
beyond its eye. We gently spread its wing to see the bright
wing patches. The complete underneath surface of the wing
was a soft white, almost like mother-of-pearl. Amazingly, the
bird seemed completely unperturbed by such body handling.
We sang out the field marks as if we were performing a pre-
flight checkout of an airplane.

It was then that Abbott produced one of the most elaborate

cameras we had ever seen. It came equipped with all sorts of gadgets and lenses. "What a picture," we thought. Magazines surely would vie for the honor of having such a photograph.

While the bird was still being held, Abbott quickly and expertly made all the camera settings, aimed the camera, and pressed the shutter. There was no flash. A hurried check, another press of the shutter—still no flash.

Abbott was disappointed, to be sure, but by no means distraught. For want of a small pen-sized battery that could be purchased in many drugstores, he could not get a single picture. But just having this bird in the hand was its own reward, and that would have to do. Finch and Abbott would go out the next evening with the hope of a repeat performance for photographic purposes but would have no luck.

Meanwhile, we released the yellow rail, and it flew a short distance. This time we went on talking in normal, if excited, tones. For no other reason except to see what would happen, we decided to play the tape again. This time we were cavalier about the whole situation and kept the lights on. Lo and behold we looked out ahead of us and to our surprise saw the bantam rail striding toward us. Fearless, it came right for us. As we squatted down to get a closer view, it proceeded to walk up Finch's arm and to give the recorder a peck. "Take that," it seemed to say to the intruder-recorder, which was still tickticking away. Finch stopped the recorder, shook his arm, and the rail was gone. For a few seconds, we were numb. The encore had been just too much.

The mosquitoes no longer seemed to be biting. Back at the cars, Margot and I produced two cans of beer and split them four ways in celebration. I looked at my watch. It was 2:30 A.M., on cloud nine.

153

# In Quest of Number 689

## JAMES A. VARDAMAN

[*Jim Vardaman, of Jackson, Mississippi, attempted to see 700 species of birds in North America during 1979. He came very close to doing so, listing 699 species for the year and breaking the old Big Year record of 657.*

*On May 17 he flew to Attu, in the Aleutian Islands, for a planned two-week tour with a party led by Davis Finch. The group was quartered in an unheated twenty-foot-square quonset hut abandoned after World War II. The first week was highly successful and included sightings of a greenshank, a rustic bunting, an Indian tree pipit, a common sandpiper, a spotted redshank, a Temminck's stint, and a green sandpiper (the first verified North American sighting). The following firsthand account picks up the story at midpoint during the Attu tour.*]

A steady south wind at 10 mph brought clouds and fog May 24, but no new birds and no weekly plane. We hoped that this wouldn't happen May 31, the day we were scheduled to fly back to Anchorage for a bath and the day the variety and quantity of our food would drop off sharply.

On such a day, when all migrants have gone and only breeding birds are left, birding on Attu yields a very small list. The common land birds are the snow bunting and Lapland longspur, and you will probably see the gray-crowned rosy finch and snowy owl. On the shore and sea the common birds are common eiders, red-faced and pelagic cormorants, rock sandpipers, and glaucous-winged gulls. We walked and rode about ten miles and found little else.

May 25 was almost a repeat performance. With a gentle east wind and several periods of sunshine, the temperature climbed to 60°, and birds were scarce again. It was a hard day physically. We made the eight-mile trip out to Aleksei Point, riding bikes when snow and road conditions permitted, walked several miles over the beaches and abandoned runways, returned the same eight miles, searched the beaches and ruined building at Navy Town, and wound up with another three miles along the main runway and the beach south of it. We traveled over twenty miles, half of it on foot, and I got only one new species, the horned puffin. Four other birding teams working all other accessible parts of the island had the same lack of success.

May 26 was much worse. It rained all day with a south wind of 10–15 mph. Nobody went birding. Although the rain decreased to a drizzle May 27, we found nothing in a six-mile trip to Murder Point. The only progress was the sighting of a pair of parasitic jaegers flying directly overhead about noon. The gentle south wind continued.

The same gentle, unproductive south wind held all day May 28, and a steady rain joined it to make matters worse. A birding group led by Larry Balch lightened our spirits by inviting all birders over for lunch. It was good to eat slices of regular white bread again, and I also had a treat wholly unexpected on Attu: a cold can of beer. The gloom soon set in again, however, even though the rain ceased, for most of us had not seen a new

bird since about noon May 23. Bored and discouraged, we got
ready for bed early.

Soon after 9:00 P.M., we heard a distant shout, "Get on the
radio." The only fully dressed man rushed outside with the
radio; the rest of us began to throw on clothes in feverish haste,
certain that any news would be exciting news. It was. Thede
Tobish broadcast, "I've found a Siberian rubythroat near the
east end of the little runway. It was singing and hopping around
the big pile of old barrels." The gold rush was on again, with
birders rushing from every direction toward the bird, a drab
thing about 5½ inches long with an incredibly brilliant red
throat visible only when it faces you. It was Number 688 on my
probable Big Year list, and was seen by everyone before 10:00
P.M. The little straggler lifted the gloom immediately, for it
showed up in spite of unfavorable conditions, and we joked
and told funny stories until nearly midnight.

There was good visibility, no rain, and no wind May 29, and
the ocean and bays were like glass. From the shore at Navy
Town, particularly with a Questar telescope, we got Kittlitz's
murrelet, often hard to find. We spent late morning and early
afternoon in a three-mile walking sweep of the marshes off
Massacre Bay and turned up nothing exciting and very few
birds of any kind. Things changed in a flash about 4:30 P.M.,
when Jeff Basham broadcast, "I've got an eye-browed thrush
on the bluffs south of Kingfisher Creek," a spot some three
miles from us. All thirty-four birders got to the bird, including
two men who first heard about it when they were eight miles
away on the road to Aleksei Point.

The next morning there was a 25-mph wind and intermittent
fog and drizzle, and everyone spent the morning looking out
the front door and talking about birds. The weather was too
miserable to do otherwise. On the 1:30 P.M. broadcast two
birders reported a Mongolian plover at Aleksei Point. I groaned.

The thought of making that tough fifteen-mile round trip, the first half of it straight into the wind, made me want to stay by the stove. But I came up here to see such birds, and Terry Hall agreed to go with me, so off we went. By the time we arrived, the drizzle had changed to steady rain, the wind velocity had increased by 10 mph, and the plover was gone. This was the seventh or eighth time I had chased and missed the Mongolian plover at Attu. I did get a consolation prize, however; on one of the old runways Terry and I flushed a ruff, and I was glad to get this bird out of the way.

May 31 was torture by frustration, boredom, and helplessness. The Coast Guard instructed us to have our baggage on the runway by 1:00 P.M. for the departure on Reeve Aleutian Airways. Everyone was eager to get back to the comforts of civilization, so we got up early, boxed and stored all the camping gear, treated the bicycles with WD-40, boxed all the food we could take with us, and assembled on the runway to watch the fog drift about in the still air.

Then the rumor came from the CG station that the plane had left Anchorage two hours late and was supposed to arrive about 3:30. When this time came and went, we got a report that the plane was on the ground in Adak with mechanical trouble. Thirty minutes later, after we had become thoroughly worried about mechanical trouble, we got a report that the plane was fifteen minutes out of Shemya, that Shemya was completely fogged in, and that it would have to circle in hopes of finding an opening. An hour and a half later the plane reportedly landed. Soon after 6:00 P.M. we were notified that the plane had left Shemya for Anchorage and that the next flight was June 4.

I could have cried. I hated the prospect of going back to the quonset hut and our living conditions on Attu, but I mainly worried that the migration had passed Attu, that the action

157

was now taking place on St. Lawrence Island, and that, being stuck on Attu, I was missing for good several indispensable species by not being at Gambell. All thirty-four birders here felt as I did.

We lugged all our gear back to the hut and undid all the work of the morning. Then we divided the remaining food. My share consisted of fourteen assorted Granola bars, one pound of cheese made into twenty-four individually wrapped slices, two cans of sardines and one of kippered herring, six small boxes of raisins, three packets of hot cocoa mix, and one chocolate bar. There remained some undivided food: large amounts of powdered milk, instant oatmeal, coffee, and dry salami, moderate amounts of pilot bread and instant soup, and small amounts of peanut butter, jam, and mayonnaise. I wondered how long it would last—until the plane of June 4 or June 7 or June 11?

I became fifty-eight years old June 1 and was able to reach my wife, Virginia, by phone (June 1 is her birthday too) to find out the situation at home and to report my status. It was wonderful to be in touch again and also the only rewarding event of the day. Our group made the Aleksei Point grind again and found nothing new. June 2 brought the best weather of the whole trip (blue sky, gentle south wind, and a temperature near 60°), but no new birds; we continued birding but got nothing more than exercise.

After spending the morning of June 3 unsuccessfully looking for albatrosses over the ocean off Murder Point, we walked a long way up Henderson Marsh and headed home for supper when it began to rain. Near the bay John Keenleyside and I flushed five ducks—four red-breasted mergansers and another that, as they flew by in poor light and at a distance, we decided was a female greater scaup. I didn't give the bird a second thought. At 8:30 P.M. Mack Smith returned to the hut with news that he, Davis Finch, and Larry Peavler, who were following John and me, had spotted four red-breasted mergansers and a female common pochard, a bird that all of us thought we had missed. I could have kicked myself. I had actually seen an essential bird, but couldn't count it because I had missed an identification. The gold rush was on again, this time in the rain and with less than two hours of daylight remaining. We were on the hills above the marsh at 9:00, located a small and very distant flock of mergansers by 9:30, and had the female common pochard in all the telescopes at 10:05. It was the only bird I added during the four days of enforced delay.

The Reeve plane made it to Attu on June 4, and I finished this report on the flight to Anchorage and my first bath in eighteen days. In spite of the canceled flight from Attu, my trip was successful. I got thirty-nine new species for an actual total of 581 and eleven rarities for a probable total of 689. I added three birds I saw the last afternoon in Anchorage, the boreal owl, boreal chickadee, and rusty blackbird.

One sighting is yet to be decided upon: that of a female spot-billed duck in a marsh next to the big runway a few hours after we arrived. All of us studied it with binoculars and telescopes, but no one got to view it as well as Davis Finch, who had examined it the day before in better light, at closer range, and with a better telescope and who made detailed notes on it. Davis is reasonably sure of the identification, but considering how rare the species is, he wants to study the skins in the American Museum of Natural History before he makes a final decision.

Two miscellaneous items stick in my mind about Attu. First was the quality of the birders. The leaders I mentioned earlier are recognized authorities; two co-leaders, Terry Hall and Thebe Tobish, live in Alaska; five of the eight members of the ABA's 700 Club were there; all other members of my tour group had life lists of more than 650 when they arrived. I may never again have such expert help.

Second was the physical stamina of those present. We traveled from eight to fifteen miles a day, and although I stay in good physical shape, I was very tired every night. And yet one tour group contained two men aged seventy-four and seventy-six and one woman aged seventy-one who had no bicycles and walked every step of the way. In addition, living conditions reminded me of those I endured in combat in Europe in World War II.

# A Day for Counting Birds

## BART EISENBERG

Decembern 1978. Olema Marsh, in Marin County, California, north of San Francisco, is covered with frost; the streams are iced, the trees barren. A large thermos of coffee sits on the roof of a parked car, comfort to those of us who have gathered at dawn to participate in the annual Point Reyes Audubon Christmas Bird Count. From now until dusk, we will leave no bird untallied.

Section leader Rich Stallcup, thirty-four, has been birding "on and off since forever." The rest of us have brought abilities ranging from proficient on down to dabbler, where I rank myself. Rich divides the group into three parts and passes out maps and routes. We are to meet back at the parking lot by noon.

We begin by skirting the marsh. We see white and golden-crowned sparrows, a Bewick's wren. Rich had set up a table with seeds that attract two swamp sparrows—seldom seen in California. He says more of them live here in the marsh than any place else west of the Rockies.

A gull flies off in the distance. "Ring-billed," Rich says. "You can tell by the wing tips. If the bird were older, we'd have to look closer."

Stallcup is a professional birder, one of about twenty in the country making a living giving bird tours. He has two partners on the East Coast and estimates he's on the road about 170 days of the year. Most trips sell out. You have no idea of how refined an art birding is until you go with someone of his caliber. He can tell the sex of some shore birds by bill size, the difference between cormorants by the shape of their heads and slope of their necks.

We walk down a road, the sun higher now. Houses are on one side, the marsh to the other. We look at the houses. "The ornamental gardens make for a wider variety of species. Meanwhile, we're *listening* off that way," he says, pointing to the marsh.

We check out a farm on the outskirts of Olema, then return. But for an ocasional car, nothing sounds but chickens and dogs. "See those two white-faced cows walking toward us? There's a bluebird between them." The bird sits in a field just this side of the Evergreen Trout Farm, which serves as our boundary.

We turn back. "The tide used to come from Tomales Bay down to Olema," Rich says. "Now Papermill Creek is diked, and Olema Creek has been altered. The ground water has been taken for people's use. These fields were on the flood plain at one time, but now they've captured the wild streams and put straight lines on them—managed."

The Christmas Count began at the turn of the century. It was then the tradition among hunters to go out on Christmas Day and shoot anything that moved. In 1900, possibly as a retaliation, twenty-seven observers went out in the field to survey all the birds they could find in a day. The results were published by Dr. Frank Chapman in his magazine, *Bird Lore*.

162

In this, the seventy-ninth count, there were 31,140 participants and 1,269 counts, each encompassing a perfect circle with a fifteen-mile diameter, and each taking place around the latter half of December.

The published counts range from Alaska and Canada to Venezuela and Trinidad, although the editors have received surveys from Africa, Europe, and Kathmandu, Nepal. The tallies fill five hundred pages of the National Audubon Society's July issue of *American Birds*, providing baseline data for studies. An increase or decrease in a species says something about the health of the land.

The journal also captures the count's mix of science and sport. Editors' summaries will chide compilers for accepting impossible birds. The California editor said he was encouraged that no black-chinned hummingbirds or other highly unlikely and undocumented sightings were turned in, but still said there was room for improvement. In the seventy-ninth count, the Atlantic Area Canal Zone count came in with the high of 354 species, while Nanisivik and Pond Inlet, Baffin Island (both in the Northwest Territories), reported one each, for the low. In Corona, Mexico, in 1977, the count was aborted due to political turmoil, barricaded highways, and rain. The leader sent in an apology.

More cars pass now. A single bird on a willow: orange-crowned warbler—by process of elimination. "You can't see the crown, but the chip note is diagnostic. Also, it has no wing bars and is yellow all over—default. I use default a lot. If something seems wrong with the initial gestalt identification, we take a deeper look."

Throughout the count, members of our party make a "pshhhh, pshhhh" sound. The theories of why it attracts birds are mixed. "It simulates the noise small birds make when they are harassing something," Stallcup explains. "It's not an alarm,

163

just a fussing." He also makes a low warble that he says is an imitation of a screech owl. "In Mexico, if you imitate a ferruginous owl, you get swarmed. They don't like predators and will try to chase them away." When he comes to a thicket or group of trees, he will pshhhh and warble and wait until what seems like every bird in the area has at least made an appearance. Inevitably, there are more around than you would suspect.

Distant birds get identified, too. "Right there amongst the cows is a cattle egret."

"How can you tell?"

"It's been there for a week. And besides, the bird is amongst the cattle. Cattle egrets are very tuned in to cattle."

By midmorning we are ready for the main body of the marsh, "the splashy quadrant," as Rich calls it. Pickerelweed covers much of it. A female goldeneye duck flies overhead. Although the creek is still frozen over, the air warms quickly, and we wrap jackets and sweaters around our waists. I'm grateful for my rubber boots. Peter, who makes furniture in Los Gatos, wears a pair of cut-off chest waders, the kind used in fishing for steelhead. He's left them piled in the back of his truck on and off for the past three years, and they now retaliate by leaking.

The rustle of our footsteps mixes with the calls of coots and marsh wrens. Tules and rushes grow tall to each side of the path. A night heron, his red eye visible through the binoculars, sits poised, almost stately, on a willow.

"I just saw a large birdlike object fly into the brush," says Peter. Stallcup thinks it might be a bittern and crawls and cracks his way through the thicket and berry bushes, stepping deep into a cold brook which rushes over the top of his boot. No bittern.

"I do this for the sheer joy of playing in the swamp water," he says later, wringing out his sock while friend Sue rubs his

164

feet. I ask him if he would have tried for the bird were it not for the count. He considers: "It could have been a long-eared owl."

Up the road to the stables, we see more sparrows. At the top is a barn made of sheet metal. Someone calls from inside: "Ain't no birds here, buddy."

Back down the road past the Limantour turnoff, an immature hawk lands in an alder tree. Clearly an accipiter, it is either a goshawk or a Cooper's hawk. From our position the diagnostic features are not visible, so a small group goes into the woods to look at the bird from beneath. "We'll have to go with the Cooper's hawk," says Stallcup, emerging. "The tail size overlaps with the gos, but I couldn't see the unambiguous barring."

At lunchtime, Rich sits at the back of his station wagon, smoking a cigarette and reading off the Marin County bird list. "Marin," it says on the back, "is a hotbed of bird life." The reconvened group munches on sandwiches.

"Black phoebes?"

"Eight."

"Sixteen."

He writes the sum onto the list. "Swallows . . . none? That's a bummer. There were some a week ago. Chestnut-backed chickadees?"

"About a hundred."

"Eighteen."

"And we saw one. A hundred and nineteen. Varied thrush? None? Then what were you doing up in those bay trees—that's a project for this afternoon. Last year was filled with them. Hermit thrush?"

"Well, I heard what I thought was one, but I didn't say anything."

"Robins?"

"I'd say about thirty-two to thirty-eight."

People always ask how exact a count can be with a mass of amateurs turned loose on the countryside. "No one pretends that this is an accurate census," Rich explains. "With some species like the cattle egret, there are so few of them that we can be reasonably certain we've got them all. But with more numerous birds we base a lot on impressions and figure that we are consistent in our margin of error from year to year."

After lunch we head off toward the Point Reyes Park Headquarters, Rich ever pshhhhing at the stand of alders as we pass. Two birds circle off in the distance. We all raise binoculars to see two falcons, a prairie chasing a peregrine. We watch them wheel out of sight. "Almost a lifetime experience," Rich declares. "We should really sit down for a while and consider our place."

The light is already noticeably lower. We wade through grass; Rich continues to pshhhh. A red-shouldered hawk sweeps low. A tree of ruby-crowned kinglets and two Townsend's warblers, patterned a bedazzling yellow, green, and black, are tallied.

The sun is now behind the ridge. The willows form a cloud of rust. "Come on, let's have just one flock of swallows—with all the species."

The final tabulation of our section takes place in dim light and threatening clouds, accompanied by beer and wine. Rich writes while his cigarette burns close to his fingers. At 5:00, the stars already out, we wait for owls.

The Point Reyes circle consistently comes in with such a high diversity of species as to place it within the top five counts in the country. In the 1978–1979 count, its 200 species tied it with San Diego for third place, below Freeport, Texas, with 216 species and Santa Barbara, California, with 214. Cocoa, Florida, was fifth with 194. The Oakland count had the most participants. Point Reyes was second.

166

## A Day for Counting Birds

After slogging through mud and frost all day with but a few compatriots, to walk into a room of 150 fellow sloggers comes as a shock. The red barn in Point Reyes Station is filled with a motley crowd: high school students and retirees, beginners and ornithologists, beards and clean shaves, flannel shirts and down jackets. After a group dinner that could pass for a church social, compiler Jules Evens takes over, reading first the 160 birds that have been seen for the last four years. This is to get the species total—the tallying of individuals sighted goes on for days after.

"Red-tailed hawk?"

"Yes!" replies a chorus of section leaders.

"Mourning dove?"

"Yes."

Then come the rarer birds, those seen only periodically in the past, such as the pileated woodpecker and the whistling swan.

"Black rail?"

"Yeah—one."

"Two here."

Finally, the floor is open to birds not on either list. A rare-bird committee made up of Stallcup, Jon Winter, and Dave De Sante—all ace birders—screens all findings, which must be presented in writing. In order for a bird to be official, two competent watchers must see it.

Someone reports the sound of a poorwill, a nocturnal bird, a half hour before the count began.

"Why didn't you wait?" someone shouts. Everyone laughs.

# A Rare Day in June

## PAT MURPHY

I T is 5:10 on a June morning. You and your companion pull up at an intersection on a country road. The headlights go off; a flashlight goes on. Out come a thermos of coffee, a doughnut hole or two, papers, pencil, thermometer.

You get out of the car and mumble to each other. One of you scribbles things onto the paper. The other one keeps looking at a pocket watch. The timer is set; the writing-by-flashlight is done at a furious pace. Both of you keep looking around. The timer dings. All is put back into the car, and you drive down the road for a half mile. There the routine is repeated, sans coffee and doughnut holes.

Dawn dawns. The tour goes on. And on. Three-minute stops each half mile for twenty-four and a half miles, for fifty stops.

On a day in June, together with one or another of my long-time birding buddies, I will be out on a prescribed country road, parked with the aforementioned equipment. The hour will be, if we are on time this year, ten minutes or so before a half hour before dawn.

We are a part of one of the largest unpaid armies that exist

168

today: an army of bird watchers, located throughout the country, who have been selected by the Migratory Bird Populations Office of the U.S. Interior Department's Fish and Wildlife Service to engage in the annual Breeding Bird Survey. The original survey routes were established at random in 1966 (east of the Mississippi; 1967, west) by state coordinators, who sought as many competent bird watchers as possible to participate. In 1979, for the third consecutive year, more than 1,800 routes were run, with about 1,200 surveyors who took along up to 800 helpers, rounding the army to about 2,000 strong.

Fifty stops, each at half-mile interval, are made on every route. All birds seen and heard during each three-minute stop are listed. The bird census figures are sent to the Patuxent Research Office in Laurel, Maryland, to be computerized and compared.

Over the years it has been the intent of the Breeding Bird Survey to compare the changes in bird population according to both species and numbers. The survey has helped to document the effect on the bird population of changes in land development and use of pesticides and herbicides. Some bird-population trends are cyclic naturally; some are up or down according to whether the winter was mild or severe. But most changes as to species and numbers definitely reflect the hand of human beings on the environment.

To most of us, grueling though these early-hour trips are, the surveys are the highlight of the birding year. There is always the possibility of finding a species new to an area. In the East we carefully watch certain species like purple martins, chimney swifts, grasshopper sparrows, and upland sandpipers, which have never fully recovered from the 1972 fury of Hurricane Agnes. And now, after three severe winters in a row, bobwhite, Carolina wrens, bluebirds, and others are monitored for hoped-for population restoration.

Naturally, fourteen years of doing this survey, covering hundreds of predawn miles, have not passed without all kinds of foul-ups: times when alarm clocks didn't go off (or failed to wake me up); times when a "just fixed" car quit; times when well-meaning, curious people ("Are you in trouble?") made me encounter the worst enemy: delay. And I am always apprehensive about being apprehended by the local constables in those predawn cloak-and-dagger hours.

One year I had to reschedule part of one route because a strip-mining operation had closed a portion of a state highway. Another year my helper and I decided to camp out near the start of our route to avoid the long pre-survey night drive and to gain two hours of sleep. The expected all-night diner for early-morning coffee did not exist. Instead of owls and whippoorwills to lull us to sleep, we weathered a torrential thunderstorm, were eaten alive by mosquitoes, and endured the woes of the worst bed in the world: the reclining seats of a '62 Rambler. We got no sleep at all.

Perhaps the funniest happening occurred when, around a bend on a country road, I was blocked by a bulldozer. Now, I have been delayed by odd things before: an inebriate looking for the nearest pub; traffic hazards and unfriendly dogs; once a shotgun blast at 8:00 on a Sunday morning. But a *bulldozer*? There it was, right in the middle of the road, sitting on its own mountain of dirt, which it had just borrowed from the roadbank. Standing alongside it were a couple of self-appointed superintendents—one with a chaw in his cheek, the other with his hands in his back pockets. And nobody, neither the supers nor the dozer driver, paid me the slightest attention.

Their inattention drove me wild. Not only was my way blocked, but those blockheads weren't even aware of this little lady in tennis shoes, who had turned into an instant virago— shaking her fists and shouting at the top of her lungs some pretty nasty things. (They couldn't hear me.) Finally the driver moved enough of the mountain that I could get through to the next stop. The number of minutes wasted by this encounter were noted by the Patuxent computer.

And what do we do after those long, exacting hauls down country roads in the early-morning light (after getting up at 4:00 in the morning)? We go down the road and go birding some more.

# Keeping a Back-Yard List

## LAWRENCE CUNNINGHAM

T HERE are no street lights in the country. If you choose, the electric cooperative will put up a safety light—a comfort for those living in the boondocks.

As I was reading late one night, our safety light seemed to dim. It didn't actually go out, but it seemed something was blocking it. I rose and went out quietly to investigate. There, sitting on a branch of a dead pine tree between the house and the light, was a great horned owl.

I grabbed the binoculars, called my wife, and for the next thirty minutes we studied the bird, until it finally lifted into the air and slipped silently into the darkness. The owl made such an impression on me that the next day I wrote in an old brown notebook: "Great horned owl—12/30/75." That was the beginning of my back-yard bird list.

It wasn't difficult to make the next few entries. After all, chipping sparrows, ground doves, and blue jays are around the feeder daily. Also, there is the batty mockingbird who dive-bombs his image in the window of the VW, leaving himself in a state of frustration and the car artfully streaked with purple droppings.

As the list began to get a certain size, rules had to be agreed upon. An example: The bird had to be spotted in the yard. That rule presented certain moral distinctions for me. For example, does one include the covey of quail that runs along the fenceline just outside the property? Absolutely not. In a world gone mad with moral relativism, there must be certain basic standards. On the other hand, the pileated woodpecker did make the list, because, even though the tree is outside the wire, he sat on a branch that overhangs the fence.

A second rule: No bird is listed unless positively identified. One day I was on the back porch and a hawk dropped out of the sky intent on a snack of one of my young pullets. Unfortunately (for the hawk) he didn't see the hen yard was totally wired in. When he hit the overhead chicken wire, he fell stunned to the ground. I was dashing for the hen yard when the bird rallied and flew off with a certain wobbly attempt at dignity. Now, I could have written "hawk" in the brown notebook or even "red-tailed hawk," which is what I think it was. My friends would never know. But I would, and the question of standards came up again.

A third rule: Note the reappearance of migratory birds. I'm not compulsive about that, but it is nice to know that for the last two years a ruby-throated hummingbird has come to the pink althea as it bloomed outside the kitchen window, while this year one came a bit earlier to hover in the spray of the garden sprinkler for a prolonged shower. Careful notation helps you decide when the martin house goes up to avoid sparrow nestings that would crowd out those wonderful mosquito-eaters. Somehow I goofed this year, because we have no martins. But there is a great crested flycatcher hatching out a brood in our martin house. I watch it every evening and look for

173

the summer tanager that has a nest over the property line.

Any keeper of back-yard lists waits for the day when a new bird can be entered in the old brown notebook. I noted a doubleheader when slate-colored juncos and eastern bluebirds hit the property on the same day last year. A banner occasion was the arrival of a blue grosbeak that hung around a patch of young dogwoods for an entire week, until the unruly blue jays drove it away. I remember with mixed feelings the morning a flock of cattle egrets marched in solemn procession through the high grass where the septic-tank drainfield is. The sight of those birds so agitated my dog that he tore out of the house to investigate. Unfortunately, he did not use the door. The stately "tickbirds" were gone in a flash. So was a section of the back-porch screening.

Keeping a back-yard list is not dull. You get involved. One day my dog (the same one of cattle egret fame) sniffed up a crippled male cardinal from under a pine tree. I caught it and put it in a cage. A friend told me that if it lived a few days in captivity, there was a good chance that the injured wing would heal itself.

For two weeks I fed it seeds and left water in the cage. I tried not to get close to the cage, except when necessary, because it beat against the bars. One afternoon I hung the cage from the branch of a holly tree and went to work. The cardinal was now fluttering both wings a bit and seemed to be on the road to recovery. I felt good about it—the Albert Schweitzer of Wakulla County, Florida.

When I got home that evening my wife met me in the driveway and told me (rather incoherently) to go out and check the bird cage. With a flashlight I went out to the holly tree. In the bottom of the cage was a well-fed, extremely lumpy oak snake. No cardinal. Not even a feather. Just a snake that was lithe enough to get into the cage but now was too full

174

to get out. I resisted the temptation to kill the snake. Letting it go on the back of the property with a slight prayer that it would eat more mice and fewer birds, I went back into the house feeling, for a second time, like the good Dr. Schweitzer.

Most of my memories are better than that. As I look over the old brown notebook my mind goes back to happy moments. I saw the black-and-white warbler (1/22/77) walking down the side of the oak tree outside my study the same cold morning that my wife called me to see the purple finch in the back yard. The flock of cedar waxwings that got here in April 1977 arrived a month earlier in 1978. The loggerhead shrike seems to favor the young pecan in the front yard. For the last few years it has appeared like a sentinel on top of that tree during January. Robins are common enough, but when you see forty or fifty in the front yard scratching during the cold months, it is an impressive sight.

I've only got some thirty birds on my back-yard list, but it means a lot to me. All you need is a notebook, a bird book, some binoculars, and a set of standards. The last item is important. Standards pay off. Three weeks ago I spied a covey of quail in the yard, not just inside the fenceline. In the yard! Noting that in the book gave me more pleasure than anything else that had happened that week. I waited until after supper, got out the notebook, and wrote: Bobwhite quail—4/5/78, near the roses and the birdbath. A day well spent.

Bob Hines

# V  *The Flip Side*

*Bird watchers are often seen as funny. These stories show just how funny they can be. Watching the watchers develops sharp identification skills and makes for some great field notes.*

# The Spouse's Complaint

## SUZANNE BAILEY

**B**IRDS entered my life as suddenly as a rock thrown
through a window. One day my husband was curious about a
bird he saw in the yard, and the next he bought binoculars.
That was an early warning sign, had I known.

A few days later we were driving down a highway when he
slammed on the brakes. Fortunately the windshield prevented
me from being thrown from the car. I slid onto the floor, clutch-
ing my head, while my husband jumped out and ran across
a field.

"Did you run over someone? Are you sick?"

"It's a black tern," he yelled over his shoulder.

I didn't know which of my questions he had answered, but
it didn't sound good. Later, he explained a tern was a bird, and
eventually I learned it was a tern for the worse.

He soon started talking funny. It seems a bird can be anything, even a noun or a verb. He would say such things as
"Birders like to go birding and bird birds." You have to be a
direct descendant of John James Audubon to understand that
kind of sentence.

Our bookshelves filled with Roger Tory Peterson's field
guides. I noticed he dedicated one book to his wife, who was
described as an "ornithological widow." Lucky lady. My problem was just the opposite. My husband wanted me to join him
in his hobby, even though I had never asked him to do needle-
point with me.

"If I want to see a ruddy duck, I can look it up in one of our
ruddy books," I told him.

"It doesn't look like the picture," he said.

That didn't make sense. But I have lowered my expectations
on how much to expect where a bird is involved. According to
the books, warblers do not warble, and the laughing gull merely
chuckles.

Just because I don't watch birds, my husband presumes I dislike them. That's not true. I don't hate goats either, I just don't
care about looking at them. My husband doesn't understand,
and keeps insisting that I go birding with him. Although I feel
sure A. J. Foyt never makes Mrs. A. J. go along on the Indian-
apolis 500, I finally gave in.

A typical birding expedition is a hike through hill and dale
(mostly hill) with nothing between my foot and the snakes but
a thin boot.

"There's a pretty one," I say, trying to get into the spirit of
things.

"Quit kidding," he says. "You know that's just a blue jay."

Blue jay, blue jay, I repeat silently, hoping I'll remember next
time. The truth is I don't know a blue jay from a jaywalker, a
fact my husband will not accept.

The physical requirements for birding are demanding. You
need the legs of a Swiss Alpine guide, the cunning of a spy, and
the eyes of a counterfeiter. My husband can see birds that I
cannot. My eyes are either very bad or his hallucinations very
good. When he points out a siskin, I see a pine cone with wings.

I try to compensate for my stupidity and blindness by sharing his enthusiasm for new sightings. "A black-bellied plover!" he declares. I'm thrilled he's seen a plover, of whatever-colored belly. I want to make the proper response. "Really?" sounds as if I doubt him. "I'll be darned" could be taken as sarcasm. Finally I make a noise as if I'm strangling on hot porridge.

Bird watching is psychologically addictive. It soon became evident that my husband cannot stop watching. Sometimes I think he'd like to, but he can't help himself. What the world needs is a Birders Anonymous Association—if you should feel a desire to look at birds, a BAA member would come over and drink with you.

Such an organization is needed, because my husband is not alone in his compulsion. All the birders I've met are feather fanatics. Under my husband's wing, I once sneaked into a resort motel which was advertised as being run by birders, for birders. In case I had to talk to someone, I memorized the American bittern's song (oonck-a-tsoonck). I figured that would cover most situations.

I was exposed as an impostor at once. The owner noticed my lack of birder's mask—two pale circles around the eyes where binoculars have prevented tanning. "You are not a birder," she accused. "If you're going to stay here you'll have to do something. Can you do flowers or trees?"

I had never "done" a tree, but I thought this was the time to start. So far as identifying things goes, trees aren't bad. You don't have to tiptoe up on one, and when startled it won't fly away.

The climax of the birding year is the Christmas Count. It is the Super Bowl of the sky, an ornithological orgy. On this day, near Christmas, all serious birders take a flying census. Local bird clubs are competitive about their total sightings and have been known to import superior identifiers to swell their numbers. Last year, an out-of-state club picked up my husband on waivers. He bragged that his group tallied 200,000 brown-headed cowbirds.

"Your lips must be numb from counting, dear."

"No, we put boards under their roost and weighed the droppings to estimate the number." I stuck my fingers in my ears and made "ubala ubala" noises to block out his words. It was the first time I'd refused to listen to a bird story.

His obsession has led us into some embarrassing situations. He once thought he saw a white-breasted nuthatch in a tree next to a supermarket. Caught without binoculars, he tried to sneak up on the bird. Several people gathered to watch him, no doubt wondering what he was doing.

"He's just trying to see that bird," I told the growing crowd. "Wow, that's crazy," said one kid. A little lady came forward. "Let me ask him about a bird I saw. He had a beak like a parrot, but he was robin-sized. He had huge yellow feet and red eyes."

It sounded like a bad hangover to me, but somehow my husband figured it out. The lady went away, believing she was now a bird watcher. Sorry, but it's not that easy. After all, I watch the hummingbirds at our feeders. Three dozen hummers should satisfy anyone, but my husband has high standards and was displeased with our summer flock. "They are just immature males," he said in disgust.

"How can you tell?" I asked. "Do they all have zits?"

Our marriage barely survived that remark. Birders are serious and do not laugh often, even when confronted with birds called marbled godwits and blue-faced boobies.

# Common Varieties of Wild Bird Watchers I Have Known

### GERRY BENNETT

I F there's anything that rivals bird watching for sheer fun, it's watching bird watchers. They come in all shapes and sizes, just like the birds. They feed, preen, chatter, and migrate. But unlike the birds, the females are found in brighter plumages than the males and are much nicer to look at. Most birders dress as though they're afraid of being discovered and shot. Or, as the professionals call it, "collected for the sake of science."

There are many different kinds of birders. My life list of varieties is still growing. Let's review the field marks of some of the commoner ones.

DISDAINFUL DAN. For some reason, there seem to be many more males than females. They are often found in pairs or small groups and are constantly competing for excellence.

Disdainful Dan has seen it all and absolutely never needs (or admits needing) anything you've listed. He handles himself in such a haughty manner that you'd like to shove his checking card down his throat.

You've just found a full-plumaged ruff and want to tell somebody. Along comes Dan. You hurry to tell him, expecting some kind of exuberant reaction. He calmly says, "Good bird. Saw two of them at Bradley's yesterday."

This is deflating enough, but, as he says it, he puts up his binoculars and says, "Lark bunting just dropped down behind that woods."

Naturally, you had your back to the woodlot at the time. By the time you remember that lark buntings aren't found in the woods, he's gone. Just as well. If you had brought up that point, he'd have looked down his nose and said, "I said behind the woods, not in it."

You always end up feeling like a dummy when Dan's around.

ALIBI AL. Poor old Al works as hard as anybody in the group. Although he means well, he hasn't really learned his birds, and he does so want to help. As soon as he's found in error, he has all the answers.

"Here's a cormorant out over the lake!" Al yells. Everyone looks and sees a common merganser flying low out over the water.

"Where's your bird, Al? Where is it from that merganser?"

"Must have landed," he says. "All I see now is a merganser."

There's one small tree in a field. Absolutely nothing else. "Philadelphia vireo in that tree," calls Al. You look at the tree and see an orange-crowned warbler. "Where's your vireo, Al? I can't find it."

"Funny. I only see one bird in the tree now," he says. "Must have flown. Philadelphia, all right. I saw the yellow throat."

"Well, what's that one that's still there?" you ask.

"Holy cow!" he replies. "Is it four o'clock? I told Elsie I'd be home by now. See you!"

Another kind of alibi artist just spent four hours trying to find a rarity recently reported from a steep, tangled ravine. He's just about broken his neck looking for it, but no luck. At least

184

he's not going to try to pretend he saw it. But when his friends call him that night, he says, "Didn't get a chance to do it right. Just took a fast look on my way home from work."

Somehow he thinks he has to say that. Goodness knows why.

**WALLY WANDERSOFF.** Mr. Wandersoff is a pest most birding parties would like to see collected and mounted. Every time you stop the car to spend just five minutes sampling an area, he takes off into the woods and disappears. He seems to think the only way to find birds is to detach himself from the group. His worst habit of all is saying, at the end of the day, "When I was on the other side of that sumac thicket, I saw a blue grosbeak. I forgot to tell you."

I've seen some bitter feelings displayed because of this annoying straggler. All hands are back at the car, right on schedule, ready to get on to the next planned stop. But wayward Wally can't be found. Such language! From bird watchers, yet!

You can't change this laggard. He's either too dull or too thick-skinned to get the message from polite hints or poison-tipped darts. I was part of a group once, on the back roads of the Bruce Peninsula, when two of the party were so incensed they demanded the driver take off and leave this straying offender to find his way home (all 150 miles of it) all by himself. It was a sticky situation.

Actually, that's probably the way to weed out Wally and his ilk. Leave him in the woods with a compass that's been intentionally tampered with so it points in the wrong direction. Then go on with your birding.

Speaking of malfunctioning compasses, I'm told that you can obtain such an instrument from the Corrigan Company. It is called a tates and it always points the wrong way. That's why people say, "He who has a tates is lost."

**PRESTO THE MAGICIAN.** Some birders are quicker on the draw than others. This one is the fastest of them all, and he's almost always right. Every time you stop to look over a brush pile or a bayou, it doesn't matter what, he spots something better and faster than anybody else.

You start the tedious job of looking over a thousand ducks, 90 percent of which are bound to be scaup. You're just nicely started, and he says, "Harlequin duck on the extreme right!" Naturally, you started on the left. Next stop, you start on the right. "Barrow's goldeneye on the left!"

You try to figure out what he's got that you haven't. You decide that when you stop at the next brush pile, you'll look at the field across the road. Surely there'll be something good there. "Harris's sparrow in the brush pile," he yells. You've been one-upped again. As it turned out, there weren't any birds at all in the field, the only field in North America that day with no birds.

You look out from a spit of land. "Here's a red-breasted merganser," you call out. "Two hundred of them on this side," he says. And sure enough, so there are.

There's nothing you can do with this type other than be thankful he, or she, is in your party. Don't try to keep up. Presto is just a very sharp, very intense birder who has studied every phase of the game and knows just where to look for optimum results. While you're watching television, he's studying field marks. He's earned his skill. More power to him!

VIGILANT VIRGIE ( OR VIRGIL ). This bewildered maiden in the game of birding is a turned-on rookie eager to learn everything in one day and instantly catch up to veterans who have birded since the oldsquaw was a coween. Sometimes they move in flocks under the leadership of someone who has been that route many times before. They have to go through the process of "making the team" just as in any other sport. Some make it. Most don't.

Virgie no sooner learns the song of the chipping sparrow than a junco sings a very similar song. After a long period of sorting

186

out those two songs, a pine warbler is heard giving a like rendition. It's just one frustration after another.

Some Virgils have a combination of passion and persistence that can become very bothersome. One of these started clinging to me one day on his first trip afield, checking card and pencil in one hand and guide book in the other. Birds are always shown on checking cards in ornithological order, and because of this, beginners have a tough time locating them. The afternoon went like this:

"I can't find the black-billed cuckoo on the card."

"Second page, right-hand column, halfway down," I'd say.

"Oh, here it is. Why are the cuckoos in with the owls?"

"They're not. They're just ahead of the owls," I'd tell him.

"I can't find the song sparrow. Where is it?"

"Last page, last column, third last bird."

"Why don't they put them in alphabetical order?" he demanded.

"I guess so the bluebirds don't get next to the bobolinks."

"Wouldn't that be all right?" he went on and on.

"Maybe you should make up your own card," I countered, getting a little edgy.

It went like that all afternoon.

"Now that I've finished my card," he said at the end of the day, "what should I do with it?"

I almost told him.

**STATIONARY HARRY.** This birder is the exact opposite of Wally Wandersoff. He hardly ever leaves the car. Or tent, or whatever. While you're combing the woods for an elusive Connecticut warbler he stays put. Usually, a crowd gathers from nowhere and joins him. There they are, telling stories, sharing a thermos of coffee, and generally having a ball while you're doing all the work. You get back to the car, a little touchy, and say, "Well, that was a waste of time. Let's go."

Harry says, "You saw it, didn't you?"

"No, I didn't see it. Did you?"

"Yeah. Funny thing. We were standing around the car, and Betty just happened to spot it under that Virginia creeper. Got a good look at it. A lifer for me."

There's something in the way he says it that's just a little hard to take. You go back for another look, but, of course, the fool bird doesn't show.

Now it's winter. Three of you button up against the cold and proceed to scour a woodlot where a barred owl was found last Sunday. Harry pleads a sore throat and stays with the car. One hour later you're back with no luck.

"Nice going," Harry says. "Kicked it right out in the open."

"Huh. Whazzat?" say three voices in unison.

"Well, you scared the owl out like you intended. Flew right over the car. My first barred owl in four years."

There's nothing more to say.

Curiously, year in and year out, Harry sees just as much as the bush-beaters and field-trampers. I've often thought of adopting his style. Trouble is, I like beating bushes and tramping fields.

# The Big Sit

ROBERT K. MUSIL

B I R D watchers have made it into the big time. Man and woman alike, they are not sissies. Your average birders, in fact, are no longer owlish and sensible-shod. They look more like the Marlboro man or those open-throated smokers on Winston billboards who stare alluringly into your car until you squirm with embarrassment. The motifs are boots, leather, lined faces, windblown hair. Birding has gone sexy.

Like anything exploiting sex these days, birding has become competitive and expensive. There is, of course, the 600 Club; it is reserved for those birders who have seen almost all of the more than 700 species of birds that nest in, fly over, leave droppings on, or come to die in North America. Several winters ago, for instance, a rare Ross's gull, a small, pinkish Siberian sea gull, got lost, or defected, and landed in Newburyport, Massachusetts. Before it could even get its bearings straight, this poor immigrant Russian gull, which sat shivering on some rocks across from the local Coast Guard station, had attracted birders from across the continent. Executives in Lear jets, Defense officials in Air Force fighters, professors in dented Volvo station wagons, retirees in Buick station wagons, all materialized around that gull within days, peering through their spotting scopes, developing that leathery, squinting, sexy Winston look. They were birding's beautiful people—the royalty of the 600 Club.

More proletarian birders have been pushing a new event—the Big Sit—to rival membership in the exclusive 600 Club, or in the elite Big Day, when local birders race like Grand Prix drivers to previously classified locations in order to log the most species in a single day. The Big Sit has been spreading as rapidly as news of someone's sighting an offshore smew. Whereas the elite, the 600 Club and Big Day birders, claim to trace their lineage directly to John James Audubon, who was willing to scramble anywhere around the continent to see a new bird, Big Sitters will not move at all. They prefer to see themselves as descendants of those expert, local observers whose colorful, lyrical, and precise descriptions fill the pages of Arthur Cleveland Bent's *Life Histories*.

Big Sitting takes several forms. The most common involve listing either the most species or the most individual birds seen while at a choice location from which the birder is not allowed to budge for twenty-four hours. Big Sitting's growing popularity may be nipped in the bud, however. A ban on Big Sitting is under consideration at the American Birding Association, since it poses a distinct threat to the birding-industrial complex that churns out Lear jets, down jackets, vans, ferry rides, pelagic trips, mountain climbs, desert treks, and the like for the 600 Club and its minions.

The Big Sit is truly people's birding. It was invented by Elmer T. "Big Sitter" Briggs of Brooklyn, New York, who had been divorced by three wives, declared bankruptcy four times, and had two nervous breakdowns and one heart attack before quitting big-time birding with a mere 563 species. Out strolling to recuperate along the Belt Parkway one winter day, Briggs sat down and began counting sea gulls inhabiting the garbage dumps lining the Brooklyn shore near Jamaica Bay. Before he was done, Briggs had charted 10,148 herring, great black-backed, and other gulls. The Big Sit was born. Although Briggs was hospitalized from overexposure to the elements, garbage, and gull guano, his original Big Sit record of over 10,000 gulls, including one lesser black-backed, still stands today.

As in all birding, controversy over the credibility of some Big Sit records has developed. William C. "Wigeon" Williams of Shreveport, Louisiana, has seen over 341 species from a location somewhere in the Southwest. He refuses, however, to show anyone where it is. Williams's location has been verified by his wife, Miz Lillian, who regularly brings him orange juice, Reese's Peanut Butter Cups, and Southern Comfort during his Big Sits. But she, too, refuses to reveal the exact spot.

The Big Sit champion for pigeons, Herman "Helmet" Sneer, won't reveal his secret either. Sneer is widely detested for his furtiveness, which violates the original openness and spirit of the founder, Elmer "Big Sitter" Briggs, who welcomed challenges to his gull-gazing record along the Belt Parkway. (Four aspirants for the record did perish, however—three in traffic accidents on the Belt Parkway, the other of asphyxiation when a city dump truck dumped.) Wearing only a World War II Nazi helmet ("I refuse to ruin good clothes, even for a Big Sit"), Sneer has seen 48,337 pigeons in a single day. "If I told where my spot is," chuckles Sneer, "no one would believe me. It's here in the United States and far surpasses Trafalgar Square or St. Mark's. It's Shangri-la for pigeon-watchers."

Of course, even the Big Sit is quickly developing an elite. Until recently, most Big Sitters, like other bird listers, counted any bird seen on a separate sighting, whether or not it was the exact same individual. Thus, some ornithologists contend that statistics such as Helmet Sneer's widely touted pigeon record may consist of only about 22,182 or so actual pigeon individuals.

In a quest for greater accuracy, a new breed of Big Sitters only counts separate birds. Interviewed at his lovely home in Darien, Connecticut, the current Big Sit champion for black-capped chickadees, Charles W. "Chick" Atley III, explained, "We are the true birders and often provide new information about species that would otherwise go unnoticed."

Atley, who has seen 738 separate chickadees in a single day at his Darien home, which sports fifty-seven feeders requiring over a hundred pounds of sunflower seeds per day, claims that individual chickadees are best distinguished not by cap or bib size, or even the amount of white streaking in the wings, but by their distinctive voice patterns.

"They're like fingerprints. Unmistakable. Listen," he says, proceeding to imitate some of the 738 chickadees who frequent his lovely home. "Chick-a-dee-dee-dee, chick-a-dee-dee-dee," he intones. "Hear that nasality in that one, the post-glottal stop. . . . Chick-a-dee-dee-dee-dee." The calls are coming from Atley faster now. "Notice the stridency, the abrasiveness, the rather low-class style of this one," he says through his good, rather large, white teeth. "Chick-a-*dee*. Chick-a-dee-dee. There he goes by the window now. Uncouth little fellow. See how he picks through the seeds."

"What do you think of big-time birders, the 600 Club, the Big Day, and all that, Mr. Atley?" I interrupt tentatively as, perched atop his wing-back chair, head snapping back and forth, arms flailing, he demonstrates just how certain lower-class chickadees push into the feeders and hold the seed, rather gauchely, far back in the bill. "Chick-a-dee-dee-dee. Those aren't true birders. They're all insane, literally insane, rushing about the continent like that, wasting precious energy resources, supporting all those tacky tourist agents. Only the Big Sit reveals the true birder. It develops the powers of observation. Just read the descriptions in Bent's *Life Histories*. Those fellows knew how to sit and sit and sit. None of this insane jet-setting. Quick, look! See that black-capped chickadee with the funny accent, a slight limp, and the pearl-gray wing feathers blending into steel-gray and then into light charcoal? That's number 738. He gave me the championship!"

Atley is very excited now. Perhaps this is true birding, after all. "Let me call him for you. You could get a picture! What magazine did you say you're with? Chick-a-dee. Chick-a-dee-dee!"

Atley is hopping about, kissing the back of his hand in a highly agitated manner, alternating high, squeaky kisses with a monotonous, clear, two-note whistle that drops a whole octave. "Teeeet *Zeeee!* Teeeet *Zeeee!*"

I quickly leave Atley hopping about his sun porch. I have one more interview—I have managed to arrange the ultimate, an interview with the current Big Sit champion for acorn woodpeckers. He has kindly invited me to observe an actual Big Sit atop a gigantic cactus whose exact location, just outside Phoenix, is an extremely well-kept secret.

# The Flip Side: Overdosing on Birds

### MARIAN H. MUNDY

T H E big ornithological news around our place is the heron who has decided to make the small muddy pond behind our house his summer place. Officially, he is either the little blue heron or the green heron, but actually he isn't either, or any, of those things. He is rather large and gray all over with yellow legs.

We are lucky to have the heron, I am told—I almost said "by ornithologists," to make it sound good. But the truth is, I don't know any ornithologists. People I know sell bonds or real estate or work for the phone company.

The heron has added a little class to the general run of birds at our house, which in the main are a dismal lot. Mostly small brown and gray things, the civil servants of the bird world. Other people have flashy yellow warblers, purple finches (which aren't purple any more than the heron is green, incidentally), orioles, cardinals, monsignors, and who knows what glamorous types. We have, except for the heron, a dozen catbirds and eighteen kinds of sparrows. Having eighteen kinds of sparrows is like having eighteen kinds of nails. It's not what you would call an accomplishment.

Perhaps we don't have good birds because I don't really encourage them. I probably don't deserve them. For to be honest, my reaction to birds in general is one of intense, acute boredom. It would be nice, in a mildly boring way, to have a Baltimore oriole, or even a whole team, but I'm not going to go out of my way to plant tent caterpillars in trees to attract them.

A number of factors combined to queer me on birds. In my youth I lived with a pusher who forced me to consume large quantities of bird lore. I OD'd on birds at an early age, and I've been on the bird wagon ever since. Which is a shame in a way, because birds in moderation are not harmful. But there are those like me who are especially sensitive. We can never learn to bird-watch normally. We have to stay away from birds, one bird at a time.

When I was a kid, I was made to go on bird walks with my Brownie troop. Talk about a bad trip. We never found any birds. All we did was giggle and shove and try to push each other off the railroad tracks.

Also to blame is the Cornell Laboratory of Ornithology. Back in the 1940s these worthies produced an album of records (78 rpm) called *Bird Calls of Northeastern America,* or some equally catchy title. I used to be made to listen to it.

By far the greater part was scratchy silence. The records went like this: Sssssssssst. Sssssssssst. Sssssssssst. Around and around and around, until you thought there must be some mistake, they forgot to put any sound on this one.

Then, just as you were about to throw something at the Victrola, if your mother wasn't looking, a man's voice came on. In tones that sounded as if he were announcing the death of the President, he said, very slowly and sadly: "The . . . pied . . . billed . . . grebe."

195

The record went Sssssssssst. Sssssssssst. Sssssssssst again, and nothing happened. But just when sleep nearly overcame all those present, something did happen: Oopp. EEEP ooop. Oooop EEEP.

Then came about another minute and a half of silence until the voice announced another important guest at the funeral: "The . . . yellow . . . bellied . . . sap . . . sucker." This was followed by the usual Sssssssssting and finally by Kitchit. Kitchit. Birchit. Birchit. BRRRRRACK. Well, there were three records of this, and each record had two sides.

Later on, I used to have to baby-sit for some little relatives who would beg to hear records. To torture them, I would threaten to haul out *Bird Calls of Northeastern America* until they yelled piteously, "Not *birdie wekkids!* We'll be good."

Actually, I'm not blaming the gang at Cornell. I'm sure they were very sincere. It's just that they could have used a little help. The reason *Bird Calls of N.A.* never made it to the top of the charts was simple. It was never promoted right. They could have hit solid gold—maybe platinum would have been reaching —with a different approach.

First, you hire Robert Stigwood or Lew Grade to manage the group. Remake the movie *The Birds* with a disco sound track, then lift out *Bird Calls of Northeastern America* and release it as a hot new single. Maybe with a backup group of whales. Then a heavy media campaign, personal appearances by guys in bird suits, Don Kirshner and all the deejays.

"Comin' at you now with the great new sounds of that smokin' single by the hottest group in town, the Sapsuckers. This giant smash skyrocketed all the way to number four this week, makin' the Sapsuckers a really flyin' solid-gold winner. These guys came all the way down the Atlantic Flyway from a back yard in upstate New York to make it big in the Apple. So give a listen while we spin *Bird Calls* . . ."

196

Fan magazines would appear with the true life stories of group members Turdus Migratorius, Otus Asio, Bombycilla Cedrorum, and Dumetella Carolinensis. "Is it Splitsville for Otus and his live-in mate? Are Turdus and Dumetella an item these days?"

I would be happy for their success. And if you don't believe bird calls could hit the big time, remember, every Christmas we get that number with the singing dogs.

# Expert in the Fraudest Sense

## JACK SMITH

[A few years ago Jack Smith, a columnist for the Los Angeles Times, reported the sighting of two grackles in his back yard. At the time, grackles were considered nonexistent west of the Mississippi River, and Smith's report was dismissed. He stood by his story—"If there are grackles east of the Mississippi, what is to keep them from flying across it and coming on to Los Angeles?"—and was eventually vindicated when it became apparent that his grackles were merely the first of a number migrating westward. Readers now assume that he is an expert on ornithological matters and besiege him with questions about birds.]

I T is no use. My candid disclaimers of my ill-gained reputation as an expert on birds are not believed, except by those who are bird experts and know a fraud when they meet one.

Only recently I thought I had unmasked myself for good in terms that anyone could understand, by saying that I knew no more about birds than you could learn from owning an airedale. However, the inquiries keep coming in, as if I were John James Audubon himself. These people need help, but in good con-

science I cannot refer all of them to the ornithology staff at the
Natural History Museum. Not only are they already overworked,
but some of the questions I get they couldn't answer anyway.

For example, this one from A. L. Wikholm of Laguna Hills:
"Mr. Edwards of Denton, Montana, once said to me about a
new teller he had in his bank, 'She doesn't know any more about
banking than Elam's ass knew about the Hebrew language.' So
it is with me about birds, and I am writing to you because you
seem to be an expert on birds.

"We live in a condo on a hill overlooking the Saddleback
Mountains. In the evening birds in flocks fly over our place
toward the foothills. I sit here and wonder where they go and
what they do at night. Do they sit in the trees? On the ground?
Do they close their eyes? Do they sleep? Do they make love, lie
on their sides, and roll from side to side? If they sit on a branch
and fall asleep do they fall to the ground? Please tell me."

As you can see, part of my problem is the ambiguity of the
question. Without wishing to embarrass Wikholm, I must point
out that I simply cannot answer his questions in their present
form.

What do they do at night? he asks. What does *who* do? He
has not told me what kind of birds we are talking about. Different birds do different things at night. The nightingale sings,
the owl hoots, the chicken sleeps (with his eyes shut).

Also, how can I say whether they sit in trees at night or on
the ground? Take the kiwi bird. He doesn't sleep at night at all.
He sleeps in the daytime, and neither in trees nor on the
ground, but in burrows. I don't know whether there are any
kiwis in Laguna Hills or not, but in any case this can't be the
bird Wikholm sees flying over his condo at night because kiwis
can't fly. They are unable even to flap their wings, which are
more hairy than feathery. Their eyes are tiny and their legs
stout, and they have disagreeable claws on their toes. It is be-

199

cause they are so ugly that kiwis do not come out in the daytime. They are afraid they will be exterminated like their relative, the moa.

All birds make love; but whether they lie on their sides and roll from side to side I do not know. Again, it depends on what kind of birds we are talking about. In seeking an answer to such a question there is no substitute for field work. I suggest to Wikholm that he spend a night in the foothills of the Saddlebacks and watch. One is advised to wear warm, dry clothing for such an outing, and to be equipped with a pair of night binoculars, a compass, a pup tent in case of rain, and at least one half pint of bourbon whiskey, per person.

One is also cautioned to camouflage oneself and keep still, as most birds will not make love while being observed. In this they are more fastidious than mammals, including contemporary man.

No; birds that sleep in trees do not fall to the ground. Birds may sometimes be found dead under a tree, that is true; but in every such instance autopsies prove that these creatures have frozen to death, or suffered a heart attack while sitting in the tree, and were dead when they fell. (It would be interesting to know whether birds found dead on the ground suffered heart attacks while making love, a hazard not unknown to man.)

Meanwhile, I also have a question from Jan Carmichael of Tarzana: "On either the 18th or 19th of December (in the midst of all the Christmas preparations or I would have advised sooner) I'm sure I saw an egret in an open field of Encino. It was feeding alone, which seemed to me to be unusual. Would it be migrating alone? Curiosity has prevailed since that interesting discovery. Please tell me if it might have been a truly wild bird or simply an escaped pet."

No, there have been no reports of an escaped egret, and this bird does not migrate alone. They fly in corps de ballet. I think there is little doubt that what this reader saw was a common regret that had lost one of its r's. Regrets are especially common toward the end of the year.

By the way, anyone who writes to ask if I can identify a certain bird should first find out what kind of a bird we are talking about. This would help me greatly. The following query from Sheryl Rubinstein of Northridge is typical of those from readers who cannot be discouraged by my lack of credentials:

"Although I am well aware that you are not an ornithologist, I have yet another question about birds. There is a certain bird that has been coming regularly to my brother's window and pecking on it, for at least a year. After trying to discover why it comes, we realized that its visits always occur when my brother is ill, and home from school. It is one of those everyday birds that are found everywhere. I think it is either a sparrow or a wren. I find it very spooky and would appreciate any assistance you could give me as to the cause of its visits."

Fortunately, this is an easy one, and I believe I can dispose of it without bothering Ralph Schreiber at the Natural History Museum. Ms. Rubinstein's brother's bird is either a raven or a house finch. I would have said raven for sure, but Ms. Rubinstein's guess that it is either a wren or a sparrow inclines me to rule the raven out. If it were a raven it would be bad news, as we know from Edgar Allan Poe.

More interesting than the identity of the bird, to me, is Ms. Rubinstein's statement that the bird always comes to her brother's window when he is ill and out of school. Implicit in this is their conclusion that the bird comes because Ms. Rubinstein's brother is ill.

The evidence is not sufficient to support that conclusion. Ms. Rubinstein's brother can easily test it, however, by staying home from school some day when he is not ill. My guess is that the bird will come anyway. It simply wants to play.

Therefore, I believe we can logically conclude that the bird comes because Ms. Rubinstein's brother is home, not because he is ill. This adds weight, by the way, to my guess that the bird is not a raven. A raven would be more likely to come because the boy was ill, and in this case I would advise the Rubinsteins to engage the services of either an exorcist or a witch doctor.

# VI *Reflections*

We human beings have regarded ourselves as the lords of creation, with dominion over every living thing. Now, like it or not, we do indeed dominate the scene—our numbers alone make this true. But we are also a part of nature, and our fate is tied to that of the other species of the earth. In one way or another, the stories here comment upon these realities.

# The Messenger

## FAITH MCNULTY

I T was a bright, sunny day. Snowy fields glittering outside my window. Lots of birds in the bird feeder. The sky perfectly blue, and the air as cold and clear as water in a mountain brook. A lovely interval between the storms we'd been having that January. My phone rang. A friend said she'd heard that a man fishing down at the Narragansett Pier (Rhode Island) had seen a penguin sitting on a rock. I doubted it was a penguin, but I was curious. I got in the car and drove the four or five miles from my farm to the pier.

On the stone fishing jetty, I parked beside a van. A tall young man—mustache, watch cap, denim jacket, blue jeans, binoculars —was looking out at something in the water. He said that it wasn't a penguin—that it was an oil-covered sea bird, probably a murre. Standing on a rock with its wings stuck to its sides, it had looked like a penguin. Now it was back in the water. He couldn't figure out any way to catch it. He had no boat, and even if he did have one the bird could dive and get away. The young man said that his name was Jim Herrmann, and that he was a biologist.

We watched the bird bobbing on the water. There was almost no surf. Sometimes waves roll in here and crash against the sea wall, but on this summer day of winter there were only shiny wavelets lapping the rocks. Herrmann said that the bird wouldn't last long. Another storm was due, and anyway the bird would starve in a few days. The little waves were washing it closer to us. It looked serene and graceful. No distress. It was eerie to see it float without complaint—or any sign that it was doomed. Herrmann felt bad about leaving it there, he said, but he guessed there was nothing he could do. He turned to go. I couldn't leave quite yet. Suddenly, a series of larger waves came along. They washed the bird toward the rocky shore. I called to Herrmann, and he came back. The bird was at the edge of the rocks. A bigger wave came. I don't know if the bird scrambled ashore or was tossed, but it disappeared among the boulders. Herrmann's hopes revived. He said that maybe the bird was wedged in a crevice. If so, he might be able to get it. He climbed down among the boulders and along the shore. I followed. Then the bird reappeared—it had got up on a rock about fifty feet ahead of Herrmann and just a few feet from the water's edge. It stood up straight on the rock with its wings hanging down, looking very much like a penguin. It seemed to be trying to soak up warmth, but, even in the bright sun, the air was icy.

Herrmann dropped behind a rock, so as not to startle the bird back into the water. Then he crept along—slowly, cautiously—stalking it. I followed. It was exciting. Like a kid's game. When the bird turned our way, we stopped dead and waited. The bird hopped and struggled up to a higher rock. That was good. Now there was room for Herrmann to get between it and the water. He took off his jacket and balled it up under one arm. The bird was looking nervous now. Turning its head this way and that. Herrmann moved fast. He reached his goal—the narrow space between the bird and the slippery, weed-covered rocks where the

208

sea lapped. Then he threw his jacket over the bird and dived
after it, like a football player covering a ball. He shouted in
triumph and got to his feet, holding the bird bagged inside his
jacket.

When I got to him, he was grinning. "Gee whiz!" he said. "I
did it. At last, I saved something." The bird was a quiet lump
inside his jacket. We picked our way back to smooth ground.
Herrmann stopped and opened the jacket a little. I saw the
bird's dark-gray head and pale breast, its slender bill. Its bright
bird eye closed and opened, closed and opened. Herrmann said
he would take the bird to the Norman Bird Sanctuary, in Mid-
dletown, to be cleaned. I congratulated him and went back to
the car.

Since it was such a lovely day, I decided to take my dog for a
walk on the beach at the other end of Ocean Road. I drove
under the arch between the Towers, designed by Stanford
White, which are all that remains of Narragansett's heyday as a
watering place. In the nineties, it had a casino and a bathing
pavilion. My grandmother used to come here in a horse-drawn
carriage. The casino and the pavilion have been replaced by
what our town officials consider suitable for a seaside "play-
ground"—parking lots and an apartment-and-shopping "complex." However, the beach is still one of the most beautiful
beaches in the world.

I parked and walked along the sand, and my dog dashed
about in great joy. On the mile-long stretch of beach, half a
dozen other people were walking, with children and dogs racing
around them. A flock of sandpipers mined the sand at the
water's edge. No oil on them, apparently. They flew easily when
I approached. I looked out at the far-stretching flatness of the
sea, which ended in a sharp line at the horizon. It was totally
empty out there. I wondered how far out it was to the place
where a tanker with thirty-eight sailors from Taiwan and eight

million gallons of oil had recently sunk. I heard someone on television surmise that most of the oil would stay solid in the cold depths, like a giant glob of Silly Putty, and roll around for years on the ocean floor. The Chinese sailors, floating peacefully dead, wouldn't last nearly so long. Sailors are more biodegradable. I thought of the rescued bird. It linked me to that scene more compellingly than any of the words I'd read or heard spoken about the disaster. I wondered how many days the bird had swum and floated and endured to reach our shore with its message from way out there.

As I was walking along thinking about this, I heard a roar, and a blue sports car carrying three young men whipped through the gate opening onto the beach. The car zoomed across the frozen sand and roared along, swaying and sashaying. As it passed me, scattering snow and sand, smashing down small dunes, just missing a dog, I saw the young men's faces. They were having a wonderful time. That glimpse told me that the bird had brought its message in vain.

# Hawk and Hare Are One

### WILLIAM A. CALDWELL

T H I S morning the covey of quail exploded. First time this
spring that had happened. As a rule, when the long-tailed shadow swoops across the grass the fourteen quail freeze. Long
neck signifies that overhead is goose, gull, duck, cormorant—
however big, harmless. To quail, at any rate.

The quail that have survived the wintry millenniums are the
offspring of quail that froze or exploded when a silhouette or
shadow served a split second's notice that a hawk or an owl was
prowling, silent on its wide wings, silent on its long tail.

One morning last week, rummaging for seed in the sod under
the pine on the lawn, the quail froze. Now they were scratching
in the grass like the little chickens they are, bobbing their tidy
heads and muttering that the quality of the victuals had gone
way downhill lately; and now, suddenly, they were transfixed,
immobile, just so many ceramic bobwhites in a potter's window.

The great hawk dropped out of the sky and wheeled between
the quail and me, its eyes glaring, its talons unsheathed. It sailed
on, turned back, satisfied itself the quail were indeed ceramic
quail, and went mousing in the fields over the way.

For seventeen minutes the quail held the pose. I wondered whether they had died of fright. At last they scurried away, stumbling drunkenly over invisible hummocks of grass. They don't run very well.

They don't fly very well. This morning the hawk came through on its routine patrol, and the quail panicked, exploded. Two or three in the cluster broke and ran for cover in the rose bushes along the front of the house. Then they fluttered into the air, and the rest of the fourteen scattered into frantic flight outward, radially.

I suppose the dissolution in all directions has as its purpose the confusion of the predator, but how the quail decide who'll go northeast by north and who'll take the southwest exit is too mystical for my simple wits, and it doesn't matter.

What does matter is that two of the quail rocketed headlong against the window inside which I was doing my daily imper- sonation of a naturalist. Two muffled thumps, and there they lay on their sides in the grass, kicking feebly—something coded into their genes was instructing their muscles to keep running.

The hawk had climbed, stalled, and circled, and by the time I had scrambled out it had lighted on the lawn a few feet away and was closing fast on the two casualties. It perceived that I was angry and too big to eat, and got lost.

I took the quail inside to keep them warm, as we are in- structed to do for victims of shock after an accident. Before I set them before the fire in a cage improvised of turkey wire, one fluttered briefly, and the lids closed over its eyes. It was dead.

The other is all right. We saw it later in the day, limping along behind the other twelve. It whistled. One wing seemed to be dragging. It wouldn't have to die.

Not until much later did it occur to me that I ought to won- der why I was so depressed and wrought up over the death of one small bird. Because of a refined horror with respect to any death?

## Hawk and Hare Are One

Uh-uh, William; if you're alive you're a killer, and if you're moved by a quail's breaking its neck, why, O St. Francis of Hackensack, aren't you shamed and revolted by considering the ceremonies antecedent to your sailing into a hamburger, a breakfast of flapjacks with sausages, or a plate of veal scallopini? A calf's eyes are no less innocent and trusting than a quail's. Die it must.

Selective compassion won't do. For maudlin pity Nature has no use, and this goes for the self-pity that takes a form so bizarre as a distaste for the sight of blood and entrails. A decent reverence for life must extend to reverence for the life of the natural predator, doing what it was put on earth to do. Some poet said it better: The hawk, the swoop, and the hare are one.

Well, I decided before I took the limp little body out and gave it fitting burial in a cliff on the far side of the town dump that I was grieving not because a life was destroyed but because the destruction was pointless. Something merry and guiltless had gone out of the world because a big bird had done what it was programmed to do and a small bird had done what it was programmed to do.

And there, I said to myself, going back to the chair by the window to resume tea and yesterday's newspaper where they'd been interrupted, there is the difference between the animal and humankind. The animal has no alternatives. We make choices.

Nothing much new in the paper. An airplane had been hijacked, and the pilot was dead, not because he had done anything punishable but because he was there. Grown women had stoned a bus and shattered glass, had lacerated some faces whose DNA coded their pigmentation black, as once upon a time grown men dynamited a Sunday school to indicate the relative superiority of being coded unblack.

Something merry and guiltless had gone out of the world that morning too. Some bewildered old man had been kidnaped and killed to reinforce some obscure point in political science. On

213

an island far away patriots were blowing the legs off girls who were on the way home from the wrong church. Away in a corner of the Mediterranean, children were being slaughtered in the once holy name of justice. Closer to home was the numbed reiteration of murder for kicks, belly-slitting for kicks.

The bluefish and some kinds of shark are the only other animals I know that kill for the sheer delight of killing, and even they have no choice in the matter. We do. In view of the fact that we are by and large inedible, we have no need for killing each other, and we could stop doing it today, this minute, if we gave a damn.

Next time the long-tailed hawk comes by I shall invite it to settle and hear me apologize. I'll never be able to explain.

# The Very Last Heath Hen on Earth

## DOREEN BUSCEMI

T H E mournful call cut through the morning fog and drifted across the pasture to where James Green was tending to his chores. To the uninitiated, it sounded like the wail of foghorns in nearby Buzzards Bay, but Mr. Green knew better. He hurried to his phone.

Soon four men were speeding down the highway from Edgartown on Martha's Vineyard to the Green farm near West Tisbury. Mr. Green met them at the gate and quietly led them across his pasture. Suddenly a small chickenlike bird materialized out of the mist. This was the bird these four distinguished scientists had been waiting for over a month to see—the very last heath hen on earth. While the five men watched, he spread his wings and flew off into the scrub oaks, never to be seen again.

Although most people are familiar with the passenger pigeon, the whooping crane, and other extinct and vanishing birds, few today have ever heard of New England's lost bird. Yet when the last of these heath hens were clinging perilously to life in the 1920s and 1930s, people all across New England followed their saga as avidly as a radio mystery serial. Countless people went to Martha's Vineyard to see the last heath hens. Front-page headlines reported their ultimate extinction, *Newsweek* noted their passing in its "Transitions" column, and the *Vineyard Gazette* even carried an obituary.

What was the heath hen? Scientists knew them as close relatives of the prairie chicken, a species that still lives today on the Great Plains of the West. To the people of New England, the heath hen was a small, reddish-brown bird, shaped something like a domestic chicken, that was easy to shoot and especially tasty.

When the first colonists arrived in New England, heath hens were amazingly abundant and frequently graced the dinner table. It is even suspected that it was the heath hen, rather than the turkey, that had the place of honor on the dinner table at the first Thanksgiving. The birds were so common around eighteenth-century Boston that many servants stipulated in their contracts that heath hen be served "no oftener than a few times a week."

Heath hens were constantly trapped, netted, and shot. Never noted for their cunning, heath hens were an easy mark, since they stayed close to the ground as they flew slowly away from the hunter. Also, in colonial America, there was no concept of a closed season. Heath hens were frequently killed in the spring when they had young, and as a result two generations would be wiped out.

Not surprisingly, the numbers of this once-abundant bird dwindled rapidly. Although formerly found from New Hampshire south to Virginia, their range gradually constricted until they had disappeared completely from the mainland by 1870. Martha's Vineyard was the only place heath hens could then be found, and there they made their last stand.

The well-known ornithologist William Brewster journeyed to

the Vineyard in 1890 to conduct a census of heath hens. Although he combed every inch of the island, he could turn up only two hundred birds. Six years later, less than a hundred remained, and the heath hen was poised on the brink of extinction.

By this time, the sympathy of the people of Martha's Vineyard, and of Massachusetts generally, had been aroused, and the plight of the heath hen touched the hearts—and the pocketbooks—of the local citizenry. A heath hen preserve was needed to save the birds, and it would take money to establish it. The towns of Tisbury and West Tisbury contributed a total of $2,420 (not a small sum in those days). More than six hundred acres were purchased with money from private donations, and an additional thousand acres were leased by the state of Massachusetts.

At the time the preserve was established, only about fifty heath hens were still alive. Everything possible was done to save the birds. A warden zealously guarded the preserve, and poaching was kept to a bare minimum. Fire stops were built to protect the nesting birds from the ever-present threat of forest fire. Special crops were grown in the summer to feed the heath hens, and additional food was placed out in the winter. Any possible predator—a hawk, an owl, or a feral cat—was shot on sight.

Slowly the tactics began to work, and the heath hen was snatched back from the brink. By 1915 the birds could be found in all parts of Martha's Vineyard with the exception of Gay Head in the extreme western end of the island. Over two thousand heath hens then inhabited the island, and hikers passing the corn and clover plots that provided food for the birds frequently flushed up three hundred or more at a time. Hope began to build that the heath hen might be saved after all.

During this period, people came from all over to see the famous heath hens of Martha's Vineyard. They especially came in the spring, when they could watch the spectacular courtship rites of these birds. The visitors crowded into the blinds built on the edge of the "booming grounds" of the heath hen—places where the male birds had always come in the spring to vie with each other for the favor of the females. With the hens waiting patiently on the sidelines, the cocks would strut, dance, and spar in mock fights. They would then inflate the large orange sacs on each side of their necks, erect the feathers around their necks, and boom (a mournful *whoo-oo-oo* sound). When the spring rites were over, the males retired to the coolness of the scrub oaks for the summer while the females built a nest and raised the young.

Also during this time, when the birds were so abundant, scientists attempted to transplant some heath hens to other areas. The birds failed to adapt, however, and all of the heath hens remained concentrated on Martha's Vineyard. Whenever a species is located in only one area, disaster is often only one short step away. In this case, disaster came quickly.

No one knows how the fire started. It may have been lightning or a careless smoker or hunter. But regardless of how it began, the fire grew rapidly and swept across the barrens, over the fire trails, and into the heath preserve. It was May, and the female heath hens were sitting on their nests on the ground in thick underbrush. Nothing could disturb a sitting heath hen —not a person, a dog, nor a fire. The female heath hens stayed on their nests, protecting their eggs and future young, until the smoke and the flames took their deadly toll.

Not only did the fire destroy the females and their nests but also much of the food and cover that the birds required. That winter was especially severe, and in the midst of it came an unusual influx of goshawks—that fierce hawk of the far north. By the time a census was taken the next spring, only about 150 birds remained—mostly males.

From there, it was a precipitous decline. The excess of males, extensive interbreeding among the small population, and disease

218

continued to kill the birds. In 1920, many birds were found dead or dying. They were victims of the blackhead disease that had been introduced to the Vineyard by domestic turkeys.

By 1927, scientists conducting the survey could find only thirteen heath hens, and eleven of these were males. All but two disappeared during the following year. After December 8, 1928, only one bird could be found, and, although most scientists expected him to die that winter, this remarkable bird clung tenaciously to life for several more years.

Every morning during the next few springs, the last heath hen would go to the traditional "booming grounds" of his species. There, all alone, he would perform the courtship ritual of the heath hen. It was a pathetic sight to see him go through the motions by himself, for there were no other males for him to tussle with, nor were there any females to impress.

One day, while several scientists watched from a blind, the bird flew to the top of a nearby scrub oak where he could be seen (and heard) by every creature in the vicinity. There, in a vain attempt to find others of his own kind, he boomed again and again from his high vantage point. Only the calls of robins and bobwhites answered him.

On numerous occasions, ornithologists tried to interest the last heath hen in female prairie chickens. Since the two birds are so closely related, the scientists hoped they would breed and perpetuate the species in this manner. But the heath hen would have nothing to do with them and continued his solitary existence.

In 1931 the heath hen was trapped and banded. After being turned loose, he was spotted only three more times. Once he was nearly run over by a car traveling down a dirt road through the barrens. He was next seen on February 9, 1932; and then on March 11 of the same year, James Green and the four scientists watched him fly into the mist.

No one knows how he died. But he was never seen again, and

219

in spite of the efforts of the people of Martha's Vineyard and Massachusetts, the heath hens had succumbed. In their obituary in the *Vineyard Gazette*, Henry Beetle Hough wrote: "And so it is that the extinction of the heath hen has taken away part of the magic of the Vineyard. . . . There is a void in the April dawn, there is an expectancy unanswered, there is a tryst not kept."

# *Moving On*

## WILLIAM A. CALDWELL

I t is half past high water. Wind northeast at the sixteen to eighteen knots it takes to blow up the little squads of whitecaps on the bay. Barometer 29.9 and rising. Temperature 60° and ditto. Sky clearing, after last night's mizzling of rain. Peace. The seventeen varieties of silence. A first brushful of color on the hardwood trees. The month: September.

Out toward the end of the pier below the edge of the lawn, a convocation of thirty-four cormorants. They have caucused and agreed it is time to be getting the hell out of here.

They are right, of course. Soon enough the line storms and perhaps a hurricane or so will come thundering ashore, and the Vineyard, which is all shoreline, will be no altogether safe haven for man or garden plot or cormorant, and we know this because we can read a calendar and remember other equinoxes. A cormorant has no memory, no means of calculating time, no haziest notion of what this is that it dreads. All it knows is that it had better be going while the going's good. Now.

I want to know, need to know, how a cormorant knows.

221

Which of them called this meeting? Or did some collective intelligence instruct each of them that the company would be assembling on such a pier at such an hour for the takeoff to Virginia and Florida or the Gulf Coast or maybe Yucatan? And, by the way, what do we mean when we make statements about collective intelligence? The finches whose now came in late August, the migrant gulls whose now won't be along until November, the monarch butterflies that gathered on the pines for the immense journey, the moths that, knowing it was now or never, laid their tiny raft of eggs on the window screens—how do they know?

The cormorants' now is not quite yet, not quite, but you know (how do you know?) it is a matter of minutes away. They are waiting for something or someone. They have positioned themselves on the spiles of the pier, most of them hanging out their wings to dry in the attitude of the Prussian double eagle, a few playing pecking order, or musical chairs. One sails in, circles into the wind, settles toward a spile it has selected—how? The spile is occupied. Its occupant teeters forward, swoops away, circles, and comes to perch on a lower-ranking spile. No contact. No identifiable threat. The evicted tenant knows its place in that society. How?

Cormorant No. 35 comes bustling up—cormorants are always in a hurry—from some last sampling in the Mattakeset herring creek. That completes the roster. It is what the brotherhood has been waiting for. Whenever birds forgather to migrate, you've observed, they loiter about on utility wires or sunny rooftops asking each other where's Charley and why can't certain people ever be on time and shouldn't we teach her a lesson and go without her, and then the latecomer scurries up twittering implausible excuses and apologies, and suddenly the assemblage has attained what physicists call critical mass. It explodes. It spirals into the sky until it gets its bearings (on what landmark in heaven or on earth?), and very suddenly it is gone. Where to, God knows. But the bright packets of water and minerals that we call birds—how do they know?

People with orderly minds tend to resent and reject such silly questions. Meaningless, they tell me, sometimes sharply—as meaningless as the parlor cosmogonist's wondering what was here before the Big Bang in which the universe was created or what will be here five minutes after the last molecule twitches and cools and the universe subsides into death and nothingness. As meaningless as the rocking-chair physiologist's wondering, as he tapes an adhesive bandage on the finger he just ripped on a rose thorn, how his body will know the way to repair the damage layer by layer, tissue by tissue—and then stop, rather than go on growing till the finger is the size of a parsnip, a pineapple, a pumpkin.

Meaningless, yes, at this point in one man's exploring the desert wilderness of his ignorance; but idle, fatuous, infantile? Not quite. Down on the New Jersey coast a professor at the Institute of Animal Behavior at Rutgers University has been studying for a fifteenth summer the conversation of gulls. His name is Colin Beer. He is persuaded that gulls talk to each other in a coherent, articulate language.

Just listening, never having to turn and look, you know what gulls are doing. They utter one cry, not translatable into words or symbols on paper, when they drop a clam on the hardtop road and flutter down to tear it apart. There are cries signifying they are being pursued, they are hungry or bored, they have just found a windrow of scallops in a drift of eelgrass on the beach. Sometimes they mutter curses to themselves, the way commuters mutter about the boss after a bad day at the office. "Certainly gulls have a vocabulary just as we do," Professor Beer says, "in which the same sounds used in different combinations, or voiced differently, have different meanings."

223

But gulls "talk." Cormorants are mute. The question remains. How did the cormorants arrange to meet on this little pier at this hour of this morning to begin a journey over the edge of the earth into some unimaginable destiny? Don't say instinct. That only defers the question.

The cormorants have glistened away, silent, hurrying. The question remains, and so does a single black-backed gull, facing into the wind and croaking, "Holp! Holp! Holp!"

# The Swamp's Talk

## JOSEPHINE JACOBSEN

W<small>E</small> are told that it is the zoo which soon will be the last refuge of wild animal life. Already several endangered species are safest there. With all its warts, the zoo image is an invaluable one: Where else shall an urban generation for whom the animal kingdom is represented by the cat, the dog, and the sparrow watch the huge, ill-fitted, moss-gray hide of the looming elephant or the slanted spring of the giraffe's neck, carrying the long, gentle face, the paintbrush lashes?

The masses of the human majority gather around the cage of the solitary or paired captive. People flow like an uncertain river around the rails and bars, the pits and the ledges, where the wordless minority returns their stares or ignores them.

Most of us live in areas in which the human animal is in such an overwhelming majority that for us the status of minority, of intrusion into a world where we are vastly outnumbered, is almost inconceivable. And yet, there are travelers for whom no museum, no architecture, no shards of history made visible, are so transforming, so curiously liberating, as that exact experience.

The snowy egrets and the scarlet ibis fly home to roost at night in the branches of the mangroves, on islets in the Caroni Swamp, outside Port-of-Spain, Trinidad. Late in the afternoon, a small boat snarls down the long, narrow canal toward the giant swamp. Always the mangroves advance to close in the boat, with a sidelong thrust of their crooked branches, a motion invisible. Past great tumuli, some taller than a tall man—the metropolises of the ants—the boat rips along with a steady droning snarl. Then suddenly you are in the swamp.

It is no swamp at all, but an expanse of shallow lake, no deeper than a foot or so, with canals branching out in a deceptive dozen directions. Small or larger islands of mangroves dot its pale-pewter shimmer. The sun is low now. The boat, its motor shut off, slips in close to an island, knocking softly against the mangrove roots, and there is complete silence, until it is torn by another boat, which drones in and hushes beside a distant island.

No one speaks. The canals stretch out, shining and identical. The sky is still a clear blue, and against it, two white shapes wing in, curve, and drop into the dark confusion of the mangroves. They shine against the leaves' dark, fly up, settle again. Now a flock—twenty? more?—appears, flying fast. They dip, in some preconcerted pattern, rise, dive, and settle. Two mysteriously peel off and sail, zeroing in to a special tree, apart. Now the sky, gradually altering its blue, is full of white wings. The branches of the mangroves grow globes of egrets; one great tree is white with a snowfall of folded wings.

Then suddenly, very high, directly in the slanted sunlight so that they catch fire against the blue, two scarlet ibis are overhead. They are so bright they dazzle.

Into an uninhabited tree, down they drop; and following them, larger and larger flocks, small and dark in the distance; blazing in the low angle of the sun, they fold into mangroves which now look like giant flame trees in bloom.

## The Swamp's Talk

Then, with belated pairs and trios still caught and kindled by the sun, a sound begins—confused, rumorous, coming from no special place.

It is some sort of avian congress; a hoarse, muffled speech, not conveying tranquillity, or its opposite—concerned with matters specifically nonhuman. It swells and spreads, dies and resumes. The human listener is suddenly conscious of eavesdropping—queer species that she represents: present, uninvited and invisible, in a city of organized, social nonhuman life.

All around, the hoarse voices talk, overtaking each other, raucously rising, sinking to a sort of harsh mutter.

Two egrets flash up into the darkening air, find another tree. One cannot say, "A difference of opinion," "A wish for more privacy." This is the inscrutable, blessedly nonverbal world. It is the swamp's talk, the motion and sound of the society of ibis and egret.

All at once, *snarl!* A motorboat has started up. Another, and another, from unseen points close to the tiny islands. It is hard to describe the physical sense of shock. It is like being pitched down the well of centuries. The sun has left the swamp; the pewter-colored water has gone dark. Now we are in a line: back along the canal, between the mangrove fingers. No one wants much to speak.

The dock is waiting and, after the dusty drive, the lights and noises of Port-of-Spain: its carnival preparations, its steel bands and calypso tents. At night, no one is allowed in the swamp, except government boats, patrolling for the poachers who always manage a boatload of still-warm feathers each night, in the swamp's deep reaches.

No one will be there to see the first light, the earliest sun that will start a stirring, a multiple shifting, and the first hoarse, confident voices, the sound spreading and growing; or the first wings lift into the air.

227

# Kwee Kwa: The Way of the Eagle

## MICHAEL MODZELEWSKI

I searched the sky in the United States for twenty-three years and never saw a bald eagle. The day I arrived on a widerness island in the Inside Passage of British Columbia, I saw twenty-three of them. It was the height of summer. A vast school of herring ruffled the sea. Each eagle swooped down to grab its prey. Dropping . . . seven feet of wing . . . dropping . . . fifteen pounds of bird . . . tilting . . . diving . . . then descending like a parachute. *Stab, stab.* A few flaps to gain altitude . . . then wings out, herring wiggling, they rode a thermal up to their pine perches and nests. With wings folded and snow-white heads set between square shoulders, the eagles emanated fierce pride and regal command.

One morning I saw two eagles soaring high above the sea. One dipped under the other, flipped over on its back, and held its legs up. They locked talons. The top eagle swung over; the other tucked its wings and was catapulted straight up. Then they locked talons and flipped over each other, turning cartwheels, and tumbled down to the sea. A few yards from the water, they parted and climbed up to where they had started. They did it again. A nuptial display.

In early spring, eagle couples prepare the nest for the birth of their young. The female usually lays two eggs, and both parents take turns incubating the eggs for five weeks. When two eaglets are hatched, one usually is the aggressor, pecking and scratching the other, encouraged by the parents, who give it extra food. The battered and hungry eaglet either endures the harassment or dies in the nest.

The first flight usually takes place when the eagle is ten weeks old. Eagles have to *learn* to fly. They are guided by instinct, but they have to learn what their feathers can and can't do in the wind. The maiden flights are breathtaking—the young eagles shake, wobble, and roll all over the sky.

The eagle is not intelligent. It is guided by instinct that thunderbolts across an unfurrowed brain. Eagles can live as long as human beings. Seventy years in the wild so finely hones their instincts that the bird *appears* to reason.

While fishing near the island, I saw an immature eagle on a rock close to the sea. I thought it peculiar that the eagle was perched so low. The next day I fished the same spot, and the eagle was still there. I beached the boat, grabbed the salmon landing net, and slowly approached the eagle. She hopped away, dragging her left wing. I cornered her against a boulder. She flapped her good wing, leaned back on her tail, shot out her talons, opened her beak, and hissed. I gently netted her; then into the boat and back to the island.

I released Kwee Kwa (Kwakiutl Indian for "eagle") in the strawberry patch—a long run enclosed in mesh net. Kwee Kwa stood on her injured wing, blinking her eyes. I tossed salmon guts into the run. She stood on the guts and ripped them with her beak. I gazed into her round, yellow eyes—small suns that beamed a brilliance.

At dark I crept into the run and slowly approached her. She seemed blinded by the darkness. I was able to probe the injured wing. Through a gaping hole I saw two broken bones, smaller holes throughout the wing, and clotted blood. A twelve-gauge wound.

I called a doctor in Alert Bay, the nearest town. He said he'd see what he could do. The next morning I put the eagle into a crate and went to the hospital.

The first step was to X-ray the wing. On the floor of the X-ray room, I put Kwee Kwa on her back and grasped her ankles. The technician stretched the injured wing out full-length and took a picture. All the while she was still, except for the wild pounding in her chest. The X-ray showed a broken radius and ulna just above the elbow.

The doctor came in, scanned the X-ray, and said, "If we immobilize the wing in a wrap, the bones might mesh." We wrapped her wing against her torso and then decided to attempt a penicillin shot. I was certain the eagle would hit the ceiling. A nurse held a cloth over Kwee Kwa's eyes. The needle entered a large thigh vein, and the doctor slowly pushed the thick fluid in. She didn't flinch. I put her into the crate, and we went back to the island.

For the next two days, she devoured a big salmon, dashed back and forth, and furiously flapped her good wing at anyone who came near. The weather was extremely hot, and there were many flies in the run. The second night I went in, put Kwee Kwa on her back, and before tightening the wrap I looked at the wound. I was horrified. It percolated with maggots. A quarter of her wing had been eaten away by infection.

I was eyeing my rifle when I remembered that the hospital receptionist had given me the phone number of a man "who's up on eagles." I called him, and he told me about a veterinarian who had successfully treated gunshot wounds and infected eagles.

230

At daybreak I put the eagle into the crate, went to Alert Bay, and arranged for her to be flown to the doctor. While waiting for the plane, I heard thrashing in the crate. I opened the door. A tremor lifted her . . . she came down dead. I walked for miles, feeling rage burn inside. On the screen behind my eyes I kept seeing the eagle soaring, and then falling from the sky—her wing shattered by a gun in the hands of a demented man.

I took a talon and the long bone from Kwee Kwa's good wing. I went out to the spot where I had found her, put her into the sea, and watched as the tide carried her away.

Out of the bone I fashioned a flute.

# List of Contributors

SUZANNE BAILEY lives in the Big Bend National Park in Terlingua, Texas. She and her husband work six months of the year as lookouts in the Tonto National Forest in Arizona.

BENNIE BENGTSON lives in Kennedy, Minnesota, and writes frequently about nature and birds.

GERRY BENNETT is the author of *Wild Bird Watchers I Have Known* and its sequel, *More About Bird Watchers*. He lives in Woodbridge, Ontario.

DOREEN BUSCEMI is a widely published writer who lives in Columbus, Ohio.

WILLIAM A. CALDWELL received a Pulitzer Prize for commentary in 1971. He lives in Edgartown, Massachusetts.

GEORGE CLARK is a free-lance writer from Portland, Oregon. He has served in the U.S. Navy and worked as a white-water guide.

ROBERT J. CONNOR lives in New City, New York. He is a New York State assemblyman.

LAWRENCE CUNNINGHAM is a professor of religion at Florida State University. He lives in Wakulla County, Florida.

PETER DUNNE is the naturalist director of the Cape May Bird Observatory at Cape May Point, New Jersey.

## List of Contributors

BART EISENBERG is an editor and free-lance writer who lives in Mill Valley, California.

BONNIE HENDERSON, a recent Phi Beta Kappa graduate of the University of Oregon, lives in Cannon Beach, Oregon.

JOSEPHINE JACOBSEN is a poet and critic from Baltimore, Maryland. Her most recent book is a collection of short stories, *A Walk with Raschid and Other Stories*.

MARY LEISTER lives in Sykesville, Maryland. Her most recent books are *Wildlings* and *Flying Fur, Fin, and Scale*.

CARLA MCCLAIN is a free-lance writer from Tucson, Arizona.

KAY MCCRACKEN has written a Sunday bird column for the Corpus Christi, Texas, *Caller-Times* for seventeen years. She is a former newspaper reporter.

FAITH MCNULTY is a staff writer for *The New Yorker* and is the author of, among other books, *The Whooping Crane*. Her newest work is being published as *The Wildlife Stories of Faith McNulty*.

NEL MARIE MELVILLE lives in Bemidji, Minnesota, and considers herself "a professional bird lover and an amateur bird watcher."

MICHAEL MODZELEWSKI recently spent eighteen months on a wilderness island in the Inside Passage of British Columbia. He now lives in Napa, California.

MARIAN H. MUNDY's column, "Today's Mundy," appears on Thursdays in a chain of New Jersey weeklies. She lives in Mendham, New Jersey.

PAT MURPHY writes a weekly bird column for the Marietta, Ohio, *Times* and is an associate editor of *Bird Watcher's Digest*.

ROBERT K. MUSIL directs the syndicated radio series "Shadows of the Nuclear Age: American Culture and the Bomb," produced with grants from the National Endowment for the Humanities. He lives in Philadelphia, Pennsylvania.

RON NAVEEN is a marine-mammal attorney with the National Oceanographic and Atmospheric Administration. He lives in Annandale, Virginia.

JOHN PANCAKE is an editor of the Roanoke, Virginia, *Times & World-News*.

ROGER TORY PETERSON is the renowned ornithologist, writer,

233

and artist. His *A Field Guide to the Birds* has just been published in an entirely new version.

OLIN SEWALL PETTINGILL, JR., former director of the Cornell Laboratory of Ornithology, is one of the world's foremost ornithologists. He is revising his *A Guide to Bird Finding West of the Mississippi.*

LAURA RILEY is a widely published nature writer and photographer. Her recent book *Guide to the National Wildlife Refuges* was written with her husband, William Riley.

DOTTI SANBORN lives in Bridgton, Maine, where she writes a weekly bird column.

JACK SMITH is a part-time bird watcher and full-time humorist whose column is a popular feature of the *Los Angeles Times.*

THOMAS C. SOUTHERLAND, JR., is an environmentalist and author. He lives in Princeton, New Jersey.

BOB TEETS is a free-lance writer who lives in Terra Alta, West Virginia.

JUDITH A. TOUPS's column, "Birding along the Gulf Coast," appears regularly in the Gulfport, Mississippi, *Daily Herald.* She is chairman of the Mississippi Gulf Coast Least Tern Project.

JAMES M. VARDAMAN is a forest-management specialist who lives in Jackson, Mississippi. He is issuing a book about his experiences during his 1979 Big Year effort to see 700 North American bird species.

*Mary Beacom Bowers has served as the editor of* Bird Watcher's Digest *since August 1978. She did her undergraduate work in history and economics at the University of North Carolina, and received an M.A. in English from Kent State University where she taught in the Department of English for a number of years. She is also a bird watcher.*

# EXOTIC
# AQUARIUM FISHES

*A Work of General Reference*

By William T. Innes, L.H.D.

Founder of *The Aquarium Magazine*
Editor of *Aquarium Highlights*
Author of *The Modern Aquarium*
        *Goldfish Varieties and Water Gardens*
        and *Your Aquarium*

*Edited and Updated*
By Klaus Woltmann

## 20th EDITION

## METAFRAME CORPORATION
### A Mattel Company
Elmwood Park, New Jersey 07407   •   Compton, California 90220

# FOREWORD TO THE 20TH EDITION

William T. Innes first published his Exotic Aquarium Fishes in 1935 at the suggestion of friends and correspondents from all over the world. Responding to the needs of the time, he devoted a great deal of space to the practical principles of aquarium management, and he presented the subject simply and clearly. The book was an instant success and throughout Innes' lifetime remained the bestseller of the aquarium hobby.

Designed as a work of reference, Exotic Aquarium Fishes listed the families of fishes in their correct scientific order of precedence, from the lowest in the scale of development to the highest. In order to reflect the latest status of the hobby, the earlier editions of the book were revised almost yearly by Dr. Innes himself. From time to time, fishes which had become unpopular or unavailable, were replaced with current species of greater interest. New information was added as a result of increased knowledge of aquarium keeping. By the fifties, the book had become regarded as the "bible" of the aquarium hobby.

In the earlier editions, all photographs had been personally taken by Dr. Innes, including some color photographs of aquarium fishes which were a milestone in the art of naturalist photography.

In 1956, Dr. Innes retired, and the nineteenth edition, and the nineteenth edition, revised, were edited by George S. Myers, A.M., Ph.D., of Stanford University, and Helen Simkatis, Technical Editor of the late Aquarium Magazine respectively.

Dr. Innes died in 1969 at the age of 95. His book will stand not only as a memorial to a great aquarist, but also as a source of information and delight for many aquarists to come.

The 20th edition of Exotic Aquarium Fishes is the first major revision since the book was originally published in 1935. Although the principles of aquarium keeping, as set forth by Dr. Innes, have changed very little, the technical means of maintaining aquariums have experienced major changes. This is reflected in the expanded section on aquarium filtering devices. The most obvious and notable revision, however, is the replacement of all original color plates and black and white photographs with modern color photographs of the highest quality. Our thanks go to both André Roth and Charles B. Cooper, who, during their tenure as staff photographers at Metaframe Corporation, used fishes kept in our own laboratory to produce all the pictures included in this edition.

As was Dr. Innes' custom, fishes not currently obtainable by hobbyists have been dropped from this 20th edition and others, which are now more readily available, have been substituted. A few marginal species had to be omitted because quality adult specimens suitable for photography were unavailable to us.

In revising the text, we felt that some of the "Miscellaneous Information" of former editions, which could be found near the end of the book, should more properly be included in the section on aquarium management. As an example, the controlling of pH and hardness of water certainly is a function of management, and is dealt with under that heading. Similarly, facts about oxygen and chlorine have been incorporated in appropriate opening chapters. Other chapters of former editions have been deleted either because they had become hopelessly obsolete (like the chapter on constructing metal-frame aquariums) or because our knowledge about the subject matter has increased to such an extent that to treat the subject adequately would go beyond the scope of this book—a case in point was the chapter on marine aquariums.

As will be noted, we have changed the layout of the book to a two column page format, which follows the modern trend toward a more easily readable text. In addition, this layout permits a more economical use of paper which, in a time of trying to conserve our natural resources, seems no small matter. We have tried to present the revised as well as the newly added sections of this book in the same easily readable style Dr. Innes so successfully used throughout his book.

Knowing that several generations of hobbyists have enjoyed Exotic Aquarium Fishes, we sincerely hope that the new 20th edition will help many more aquarists enjoy our pleasant hobby. In deference to Dr. Innes, who inspired so many aquarists with his book and his personal advice, we hope we have succeeded.

Klaus Woltmann
January 15, 1979

# CONTENTS

# AQUARIUM PRINCIPLES

## Primary Principles

The principles of correct aquarium management are based on a few easily learned natural laws. It is our hope to explain these laws so simply that all who follow them will succeed.

Except for feeding the fishes, the ideal aquarium is a self-sustaining unit. It will stay in good condition with little care. This is made possible by considering five fundamental factors:

Water Quality
Water Surface
Temperature
Light
Waste Control

Let us discuss each of these five factors in order.

## Water Quality

Most water furnished by the public systems of cities and towns is well suited to our needs. Perhaps the most serious faults from our standpoint are extreme hardness and chlorine, but these are easily corrected.

If the natural water of a community is so hard that it is difficult to make soap suds, this condition is usually corrected either at the pumping station or by private water-softening equipment. Water so treated is fit for aquarium use.

Chlorine is contained in most public water systems. It can be removed by exposing the water to air. Except where fishes are in running water, chlorine can be slowly evaporated off. That is the main reason for "ripening" or "seasoning" tap water for at least twenty-four hours before using it in an aquarium. The process may be greatly shortened by adding a chlorine neutralizer which is readily available in most pet shops.

Aquarium fishes and plants have considerable tolerance to the type of water in which they are kept. Ordinarily the water's quality is the last thing considered when looking for the cause of failure. Nevertheless, with some of the more fussy species, it may be of major importance not only for their breeding but also for keeping them alive.

If failure persists after running down such common causes as overcrowding, temperature, light, or feeding, the difficulty may be the kind of water used for the affected fishes and plants. Occasionally we hear of aquarists who are generally successful, but who fail with specific fishes or plants. Their failure could well be caused by water unsuited to a particular species. As an example, if light and soil conditions are good and most plants prosper but *Vallisneria* habitually turns yellow, the fault is probably the quality of the water. The aquarist then has to decide either to correct the water quality or to give up the troublesome plant or fish species. There are those unusual cases where the water may be totally unsuited for fishes or plants even though it is drinkable. In such extreme cases a different source of water is needed. The local pet shop should be of use here.

There is no evidence that fluorine is injurious to fishes or plants since the standard dilution used is only one part per million. If fluorine hardens the teeth of humans, it might even be beneficial to fishes.

Such complexities of aquarium chemistry as pH and water hardness are dealt with in more detail in the chapter on "Management."

**Water Surface**

At the surface of every inhabited aquarium two seeming miracles are constantly occurring and both are vital to the life of fishes. One is the dissolving of air into the water to replace that extracted by the gills of the fishes. Fishes sustain life by using the oxygen content from the air. The action of oxygen on their body tissues results in the creation of carbon dioxide, a harmful gas, which is then exhaled by the fishes. This gas, not the lack of oxygen, causes suffocation when it becomes too concentrated. Happily the carbon dioxide is carried off at the water's surface. The larger the surface the more rapidly the double action of dissolving oxygen and the releasing of carbon dioxide takes place.

The importance of water-air contact can be strikingly demonstrated: float a sheet of plastic or paper so that it completely covers the water surface. Soon the fishes show signs of distress and in several hours they suffocate. The water surface is truly the "window of the aquarium."

The dissolving of oxygen and the releasing of carbon dioxide is further promoted by mechanical aeration and, to a lesser extent, by plants under good light. Both of these will be considered in detail later.

*Aquarium Proportions*

From what has been said, it is obvious that those aquariums designed with a liberal air surface in relation to water surface are best

for our purposes. Tall narrow tanks for window sills or for special spots in decorative schemes should be populated only on the basis of their water surface. Water depth should be disregarded altogether.

The aquariums shown have equal water surface areas. Without the aid of plants or artificial aeration each can maintain the same number of fishes.

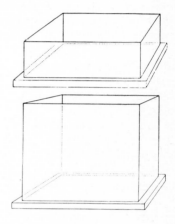

Though it appears that the deeper one could handle more fishes, the initial supply of dissolved oxygen in the water would soon be absorbed by the overcrowded fish. It is only when actively growing plants are kept, or when the aquarium is aerated artificially, that a few additional fishes can be maintained in the deeper tank.

It should also be clear that ordinary "fish globes" must be filled only a little more than half way in order to bring as much water into contact with air as possible.

**Temperature***

The word tropicals places too much emphasis on the idea of high

*Throughout temperatures are given in Fahrenheit unless otherwise noted.

temperature for all exotic fishes. A number of these exotic fishes are not from the tropics and quite a few of them from the tropics do *not* come from particularly warm water. It is true that most of our exotic aquarium fishes cannot stand chill. On the other hand, many of them do not prosper in high temperatures because they may need more oxygen than such water can carry.

The kindhearted aquarist who thinks he is doing his fishes a favor by keeping his tank at 80° or more is actually making them uncomfortable. Nor should one believe that there is an exact degree of heat which is best suited to each species. Most fishes can tolerate at least 10° change and overnight can stand a change of 5° without injury. For example, if a fish has a safe toleration range from 70° to 80°—and most of them have—it would be safe for such a fish to experience a drop from 75° to 70° spread over a period of several hours.

When planning an aquarium the temperature range of each species should be considered. The more tender fishes require warmer, evenly heated tanks; the hardier fishes can be kept in cooler tanks. For each species described in the book an approximate temperature range is given.

A great deal of needless worry and expense is incurred in trying to keep aquariums or aquarium rooms within 2° of a fixed point. Almost nowhere does nature supply such an environment. It has often been observed that fishes are stimulated by a reasonable change in temperature.

Aquarists should not be seriously concerned about the variation between the heat at the top and the bottom of the aquarium. The temperature difference in native waters is often considerable and the fishes negotiate it without trouble. In a modern aquarium, which is usually equipped with a filter or an aerator—often with both—such stratification of temperature does not occur. The circulation in the aquarium insures an even distribution of heat.

Tolerant as fish may be they should never be forced to acclimate themselves to new temperature ranges. Experiments of this sort always result in disaster.

In practice, it comes down to this: the average exotic aquarium fish is perfectly happy at a temperature of 72° to 76°. For short periods the temperature can drop to 68° or rise to 85° without trouble. Even these extremes may be safely passed in aquariums that are in extra fine condition and where the fishes are not crowded. If, through uncontrollable causes, the temperature drops to the extreme danger zone of the low sixties or even the fifties, one should slowly raise it to about 80° and keep it there for twenty-four hours or more.

## Light

Natural daylight is by no means a necessity for the health of aquarium fishes. Artificial light, in fact, has its advantages: it allows one to place the tank in the darkest corner of the room; it can stimulate plant growth without encouraging too much algae since the intensity and duration of the light can be controlled easily. However, if one is going to rely on natural light, several things should be kept in mind about the location of the aquarium.

*Aquarium Location and Natural Light*

With the exception of a few species (top fishes), aquarium fishes do not require light for health and can live satisfactorily in a quite subdued light. On the other hand, plants require light. They should be in a location where one can easily read a newspaper by natural light alone without the aid of artificial light.

For plants of mixed varieties there should be medium light. A position by a window where there is good diffused light and about two hours of direct sun is ideal, but not indispensable. A strong north light without sun is satisfactory. A position by a south window is likely to give too much sun and a certain amount of shading becomes necessary. The great difficulty about excessive light is the growth of too much algae. This results either in green water or a green mossy coating on glass and plants. Too much summer sun is apt to overheat small aquariums. The location of an aquarium presents the interesting problem of securing just enough light to stimulate plant activity, but not so much as to develop other unwanted growth. Given the choice between a location with too much light and one with too little light, it is always better to select the former since one can always shade off the excess illumination.

## Waste Control

Many aquariums, even those without a filter or aerator, often stay fresh and clear for very long periods of time. Such aquariums usually contain only a few fishes, but have a lush growth of various aquatic plants. They receive a proper amount of light (natural or artificial, or a combination of both) and have well-fitting covers to reduce evaporation. Their owners have mastered the art of feeding their fishes the right type and amount of food at the right time. But even though the fishes breathe and produce carbon dioxide, feed and excrete solid and liquid waste materials directly into the water, the aquarium does not become a cesspool, and the fishes do not perish in their own excrement. This is a most amazing fact, and the reason that makes aquarium keeping possible in the first place. How, then, are the waste products removed from the aquarium, especially if the water is not filtered?

We already know that carbon dioxide, which fishes "breathe out" leaves the water at the surface. But it is also used up by plants during the process of photosynthesis. The removal of the other waste products, however, which accumulate through the fishes feces and urine is a little more complicated. It is accomplished by certain bacteria which are found in any aquarium. As soon as fishes or other aquatic animals are present and produce organic waste, these bacteria start to multiply in tremendous numbers, since organic waste is food to them. The most dangerous by-product of animal waste is ammonia, which even in small quantities can be dangerous to fishes. Luckily, it is quickly attacked by these ammonia-loving bacteria, which by their action change ammonia into much less harmful nitrite. Then, as nitrite accumulates, another group of bacteria takes over to change nitrite into nitrate, which is completely harmless to fish. Nitrate does accumulate in the aquarium, but, to our knowledge, no fish has ever died from it. Actually some of the nitrate is discharged from the system into the air by a certain reversed process, again involving bacteria, in which nitrate is changed into nitrogen. In addition, growing plants incorporate some nitrate into their tissue, and if the excess plant growth is periodically removed (as it should be), a certain balance in the nitrogen cycle of an aquarium is achieved.

As we have seen, the ability of an aquarium to almost maintain itself is not dependent upon filters or aerators. Nevertheless, filters and aerators are of great help in maintaining an aquarium. Aerators will speed up the discharge of carbon dioxide and the dissolving of oxygen, and filters will rid the water of suspended solid materials, giving the water the sparkling clear quality which is so much enjoyed by the viewer. In addition, since the bacteria which are so essential to the well-being of the aquarium must settle on some solid surface to be able to do their work properly, the tremendously large surface area of the filter materials provides the perfect place for them. Therefore, biological filtration, as the conversion of waste products is called, can function even better.

In addition to the nitrogen cycle, which has been studied to some extent, there are undoubtedly other chemical processes going on in an aquarium of which we know little. Therefore, we cannot yet set up an aquarium, stock it with the right kind and number of fishes and plants and be absolutely certain that it will

function properly. Occasionally we fail, something goes wrong: a tank may become foul, fishes die for unexplainable reasons. But fortunately, failures have become very infrequent. This is undoubtedly due both to our increased knowledge of the internal workings of an aquarium, and the ability of manufacturers to produce better products that complement the natural functioning of an aquarium.

## MANAGEMENT

A freshly filled aquarium is usually not safe for fishes. Various additives to tap water, in most cases chlorine, are toxic to fishes and have to be removed before the aquarium is stocked. Simply letting the filled tank "age" for a few days will usually make the water suitable. Chlorine will completely evaporate within that time. Even well water, which contains no chlorine, improves with "age." Aeration and filtration will speed up this process considerably.

### Aeration

In this convenient technique, a small electric pump forces the air through a tube connected to a diffuser or an airstone at the bottom of the tank, sending up a spray of small bubbles. It is a common impression that some of this air is *forced* into the water, but such is not the case. All the air is picked up by absorption, some from the bubbles, but most at the water surface. The real value of aeration lies in the fact that the rising column of bubbles sets up a circulation in the aquarium by bringing bottom water to the surface where it is exposed to the air above it. Thus, fresh oxygen is distributed through the whole aquarium.

Aeration is particularly valuable at night for those aquariums that partly depend on day-time oxygen from plants. At night plants give off no oxygen and produce carbon dioxide, a gas that should be eliminated. Aeration is almost indispensable in hot weather, when the oxygen capacity of water is low due to the higher temperature of the water. In addition, where over-crowding of fishes is unavoidable, a stream of air through the water has the effect of practically doubling the fish capacity of the aquarium. At times a cloudy gray (not green) tank can be cleared in a few days by constant aeration.

Usually a thin stream of bubbles is sufficient for ordinary purposes. Small bubbles, using a constant flow of air, are more efficient than large ones.

*Oxygen and Water*

The importance of oxygen to all life and especially to the welfare of fishes has already been explained in general. A more detailed understanding, however, is useful to the aquarist.

Air is composed of approximately four parts nitrogen to one part oxygen. However, when water absorbs air it does not take the two gases in that proportion. It takes two parts of nitrogen to one of oxygen, a ratio of oxygen which is twice as rich as that we breathe. Furthermore, the amount of oxygen that pure water can absorb depends on the temperature of the water as shown by the following table:

At 50° F., 7.8 pts. per 1000 by vol.
" 60° F., 6.9 " " " " "
" 70° F., 6.3 " " " " "
" 80° F., 5.7 " " " " "
" 90° F., 5.0 " " " " "

As the table shows, oxygen content in water rapidly decreases as the temperature increases.

In ordinary aquarium conditions the amount of dissolved oxygen present is about half that shown in the table. This is due to the unavoidable presence of certain gases that displace the oxygen. These are generated mostly by the decomposition of organic matter (aquarium settlings, dead leaves, etc.) and the carbon dioxide from the breathing of the fishes.

While the theoretical capacity of water to hold free oxygen at a temperature of 75° is about 6.0 parts per 1000, as a matter of fact, fishes are fairly comfortable with an oxygen content of 3.3. This is what they get in an ordinary, good aquarium at 75°. Therefore, keeping an aquarium at about this temperature is recommended. With clean water, growing plants in good light (or the use of artificial aeration), and not too many fishes, the dissolved oxygen content can remain between 3.3 and 5.0 parts per 1000 by volume which is good.

Contrary to popular belief, fishes are injured or killed more by an excess of carbon dioxide than by any lack of oxygen. Ample water surface areas and aeration are necessary not only to provide the fishes with oxygen but also to liberate poisonous carbon dioxide.

*Filters*

A number of good aquarium filters are sold commercially. Some fit into the inside corner of a rectangular aquarium, some on the outside. The outside models are usually larger and more easily cleaned and serviced. All inside filters are operated by small electrical air pumps. They are efficient enough for small tanks, but their presence inside the tank greatly detracts from the beauty of plants and fishes. Outside filters, on

via a spillway. The latter type is somewhat easier to operate. It has fewer parts, does not rely on siphon tubes, and consequently does not depend upon a high water level in the aquarium for efficient operation.

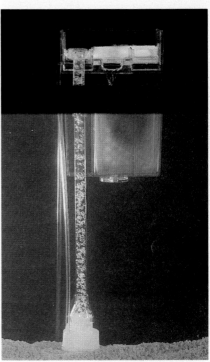

*Air-Operated Inside Filter*

*Air-Operated Outside Filter*

the other hand, can be hung on the back or side of the aquarium. Some of these are operated by airpumps, others by electrical motors. In many models, water from the aquarium is siphoned into the filter tank, circulated through the filter medium, and returned clean to the aquarium either by means of an airlift or by a motor-driven pump mechanism. Other models pump rather than siphon the aquarium water into the filter tank. After the water has passed through the filter material, it returns to the aquarium

*Motor Driven Outside Filter*

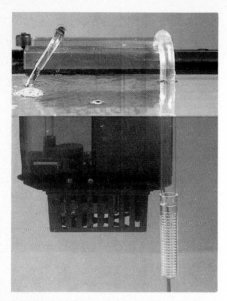

*Motor Driven Outside Filter with Magnetic Drive*

The filter wool removes dirt particles from the water and the carbon adsorbs some dissolved waste products and other pollutants. Changing the filter material periodically is a matter of good housekeeping. Normally, the filter material should be changed every two to three weeks, or whenever it looks dirty. Filters should be cleaned by scrubbing in clean water. No soap or detergents should be used. In severe cases use Clorox and rinse well.

A third type of filter is the under-gravel, sub-sand, or biological filter. Most models have a perforated tray covering the entire bottom of the tank. Gravel, not sand, is placed on top of the filter and an airlift is attached to one corner. Water is filtered through the entire bottom layer of gravel and then airlifted back into the tank proper. Naturally, an airpump is needed to operate this filter. As the water passes through the gravel, certain types of bacteria begin to multiply and colonize the gravel bed. These "good" bacteria convert harmful waste products into less harmful substances and thereby help maintain a biological balance in the aquarium.

An aquarium, whether it be equipped with some type of filter or no filter at all, has its natural filters in the form of plants and bacteria. Plants absorb certain concentrations that are bound to build up where animal life is maintained in a confined space. For that reason alone, an aquarium with healthy plants is better than one without them. Bacteria, by converting fish waste into substances plants can more readily utilize, have an even more important share in maintaining good water conditions. These reactions between fish, bacteria, and plants gave rise to the very good,

*Motor Driven Outside Filter with Magnetic Drive, Using the Overflow Principle*

The best filter medium for inside and outside filters is a layer of filter wool coupled with a layer of activated carbon or bone charcoal.

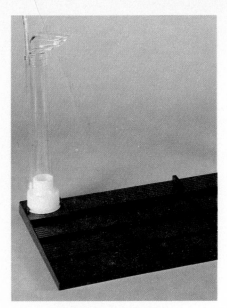

*An Undergravel Filter*

though not quite accurate, expression "balanced aquarium."

There are chemical substances that accumulate in an established aquarium which even the best filter cannot remove. Some of these build up because water lost through evaporation is replaced by water from the tap. Since most waters contain various amounts of dissolved minerals which stay behind as water evaporates, these minerals become more and more concentrated each time water of the same chemical makeup is used to top the tank off. Adding distilled water to compensate for the evaporated water would alleviate the problem, but this is both expensive and unnecessary. A partial change of water, about ten to twenty-five percent, every four to six weeks will help to prevent a dangerous mineral buildup.

There are other little - known substances that may accumulate

through fish waste or other fish secretions. These may cause fishes to grow at a slower rate than normal. Experience has taught us that partial water changes—other conditions being equal—will maintain a good growth rate and improve the well-being of fishes. This advice is in direct contrast to a theory, popular some years ago, that the older the water, the better it is for fishes.

### Green Water

The facts about green water appear to be so simple that its control should be an easy matter. Quite the contrary is true. Unaccountably, green cloudiness arises in the tanks of the ablest aquarists and confounds even those who instruct others on how to keep water clear!

We know that the color is produced by microscopic algal cells that must have food and light in order to develop. By taking away either of these stimulants, or both, we would have no green water. But that is not easy since the plants and fishes present require light themselves and enrich the water by their breathing and by their waste products.

On the other hand, it is perfectly true that there are numberless aquariums that are healthy and clear year after year. It would seem that we should be able to reproduce the same condition at will. To a great extent we can. In such aquariums we nearly always find plenty of strong, growing plants. The reason may be that the plants successfully compete with the green cells (suspended algae) for both food and light.

In these perpetually clear tanks

two other things will be observed. The fishes are not crowded and there is only sufficient light to keep the plants in good condition. That is to say, when the supply of life elements is just enough to keep the plants going and there is practically no excess left, then the green organisms are kept under control.

Many of these green water cells go through periods of activity. If allowed to subside naturally, the water may remain clear for a long time. Then, with only a partial change of aquarium water, they may again become stimulated and start out on a fresh rampage.

The two principal rules to follow to maintain clear water are: (1) have no more fish than the tank can easily support *without aeration,* and (2) use only enough light to keep plants healthy. If necessary, green water can also be reduced in several other ways: by interposing a suitable thickness of paper on the light side of the aquarium; by applying tinted crystal varnish to the outside glass; by using a mantle of floating plants such as Duckweed, Salvinia, or Water Fern. Such a canopy upon the surface of the water will not significantly reduce the dissolving of oxygen and the releasing of carbon dioxide from the water if slight aeration is used.

Remember that green water is not an unmitigated evil. In moderation it is healthy and depleted fishes sometimes improve in it.

Remove some fishes if crowding is suspected. Feed less. Every scrap of food becomes fertilizer. Siphon the bottom frequently.

When green water reaches the "soupy" stage and is very opaque it is dangerous, especially in hot weather. It is liable to decompose suddenly and kill fishes. A change to a slightly yellowish tinge is the danger signal. This calls for an immediate change of water — minutes count!

*Cloudy Water*

Green water is cloudy, but cloudy water is not necessarily green. There is a difference with a distinction. The causes of gray cloudiness are usually decaying food (overfeeding) or too many fishes. The cloudiness is actually a population explosion of bacteria due to the sudden availability of food in the form of decaying organic matter.

Newly set aquariums are particularly prone to gray cloudiness because the plants have not yet begun to function fully. In such aquariums clouding can also come from sand that has not been well cleaned. For these and other reasons, it is best to have an aquarium planted and in a favorable light a week before the fishes are introduced. Even then, the aquarium should not be taxed immediately to its full limit of fishes. Start with a few fishes and add more from time to time.

*Clearing Water*

The best way to clear up cloudy water is to correct one or more of its underlying causes. However, there are ways in which clearing can be accelerated. Gray cloudiness can be reduced in a few days by constant aeration. If fishes are temporarily removed from a green-water aquarium, the water can be cleared by introducing live Daphnia. These small crustaceans feed on suspended algal cells, thereby cleaning the water. After the water has

*Hinged Glass Cover*

*Motor Driven Outside Filter With Special Insert for Diatomaceous Earth Filtration.*

cleared, the fishes can be returned to the tank to feast on the Daphnia.

Normal filtering apparatus will remove neither suspended algae nor cloudy-water bacteria, since both are too small to be retained by filter wool and charcoal. There are, however, a few specialized filters on the market which use diatomaceous earth as the filter medium. They are designed to filter out minute particles and are an excellent tool for clearing cloudy water. As a permanent filter they are useless, since larger debris causes them to clog very quickly.

There are also a few chemical products available which are useful in clearing cloudy tanks. Read the label and follow the instructions. However, if the underlying causes are not corrected, the tank will become cloudy again no matter what method is used.

## Water Contaminants

Water absorbs not only beneficial oxygen but also injurious gases and fumes. Fumes from varnishes, varnish removers, paints, turpentine, shellac, insecticides, or anything containing wood alcohol are all injurious to aquarium water and often they are fatal. An excess of tobacco smoke can be hazardous too.

With the advent of the all-glass aquarium, metal contamination is much less likely to occur. However, troublesome condensation can collect on defectively plated or aluminum top reflectors and run into the tank. Be sure to place a glass cover between the water surface and the fixture or use an enclosed reflector. A glass cover keeps room dust from falling into the water, cuts down evaporation, and prevents the fishes from leaping out.

## Algae on Glass

A green film of algae on glass is one of the aquarist's greatest griefs. It is bound to occur at one time or another. It can be removed easily in a few moments with an aquarium scraper. Many fishes, especially Mollies, Swordtails, Kissing Gouramies, and some Catfishes are extremely fond of algae which is undoubtedly beneficial as food. Two species of fish in particular are sold in pet shops for the purpose of

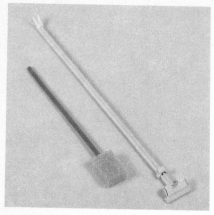

**Aquarium Glass Cleaners and
Planting Stick**

and easily wiped off. Only Goldfish, Tadpoles, and the South American Characin *Prochilodus* eat such algae.

Long, hard, hairy types of algae sometimes take over a tank. These algae cannot be rubbed from plants. The sole remedy is to remove the fishes, destroy the plants, disinfect the aquarium with a wash of weak ammonia, clorox or strong salt, and start again with clean plants—and hope for the best.

### Scum on Water

The cause of scum on water, a disagreeable condition, is often puzzling. It may come from decomposing vegetation, oily food, atmospheric settling, or from domestic frying or greasy cooking. Persistent removal by drawing a paper over the surface may overcome it. Covering the tank with glass helps. Mechanical aeration of the water dispels it.

### Scavengers

Many aquarists, especially beginners, ask too much of so-called scavengers. It is unreasonably to expect any creature to take all undesirable matter out of an aquarium and utterly destroy it or to keep the glass cleaner than the aquarist would.

The original aquarium scavengers were Freshwater Snails. Other important assistants are Weatherfishes, Armored Catfishes, Tadpoles, Freshwater Mussels, and Freshwater Shrimp. All, except the Mussels, hunt out and eat particles of food that have been missed or rejected by the other occupants of the aquarium. This is a very important service for it prevents the evil chain

keeping glass and plants free of algae: the South American "suckermouth catfish" (*Plecostomus* species) and the "Indian algae eater" (*Gyrinocheilus*). These fishes do much toward keeping the glass and plants clear. *Plecostomus,* however, is apt to grow unpleasantly large for the average aquarium and two of them will often fight with each other. Though not very hardy, the little *Otocinclus* is the best plant cleaner for it works both sides of the leaves.

It should be remembered that algae are not an unmixed evil. They are active oxygenators and when they form on the light side of the aquarium create a shield against too much sun. In this respect algae have a tendency to keep the water clear. Judgment should be used in the removal of such algae.

Rusty brown algae are obnoxious and hard to eliminate. They usually grow in tanks which are dimly lit. Equally hard to eliminate are the smelly blue-green algae that sometimes infest tanks kept at tropical temperatures. If left alone, they create a mantle over everything and suffocate the plants. They are soft

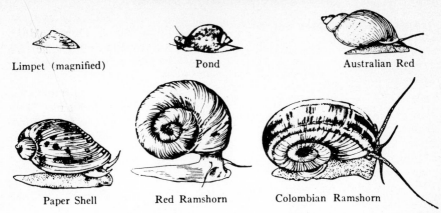

Limpet (magnified)    Pond    Australian Red

Paper Shell    Red Ramshorn    Colombian Ramshorn

## Popular Aquarium Snails

of conditions and events that are caused by the decomposition of such food. It has been argued that scavengers only convert this food into humus. But that is precisely the service they render: the humus they produce (their droppings) is far less harmful than the decomposing food. Unfortunately, scavengers are often added after the aquarium is fully stocked with other fishes. This practice overcrowds the tank. Scavengers should be counted as part of the entire fish population. Some snails keep down the film of green algae from glass and plants, but none of them get *all* of it. They cannot, unassisted, make a polished plate-glass parlor of the aquarium.

Many fishes kill small snails. Big "Mystery Snails" fare better. Snails eat fish spawn, but never attack live fishes even very small ones. This makes them valuable in cleaning up uneaten food in the aquarium nursery.

### Snails

The popular European Red Ramshorn Snail (*Planorbis corneus*) continues to hold interest. Bright red ones, free from chippings or blemishes, are always in demand and their breeding is a matter of some commercial value. In order to get them clear red, they must be grown rapidly, and to be grown quickly they must have plenty of room, warmth, and food, together with slightly alkaline water. The preferred foods are spinach, lettuce, and boiled oatmeal containing powdered shrimp. They should be fed as much as they can possibly eat. This has a tendency to foul the water which, in turn, produces erosion of the shells. Therefore, the bottom of the tank should be siphoned off frequently and fresh water added. Daphnia tends to clear the water and to prosper at the job. The flat, amber egg-masses appear freely in the early spring. If properly raised, snails will be ready for the market in October, although the demand is greater in midwinter. The eggs hatch in anywhere from ten to forty days, according to temperature. Nearly all fishes destroy newly hatched Red Ramshorn Snails.

Freshwater Limpets are very small snails completely covered by translucent shells, like low parasols, rather oval in outline, usually about ⅛ inch across. They are really miniature scavengers and quite harmless. They appear unaccountably, often coming in with aquarium plants.

Pond Snails (*Physa*) are the best of all, in the writer's opinion. Their clear, jelly-like spawn brings forth young that are too hard for most small fishes to eat. Some consider this snail a pest since it multiplies so freely.

Colombian Striped Ramshorn (*Marisa rotula*), reaching a diameter of 1½ inches, is the best of several South American introductions. It is very handsome but eats the softer plants.

The Australian Red Snail is a most prolific breeder outdoors and a handsome creature with a yellowish red body.

The handsome and once popular Paper-shelled Snail dislikes warm water. It breeds rapidly but lives only a year. Like the native snails, such as *Physa* and *Lymnae,* it survives winter outdoors if not actually encased in ice.

The Apple Snails are the big, round "four-horned" *Ampullaria* from South America and Florida. All except one are ravenous plant eaters. They are sometimes known as "infusoria snails" for the reason explained under the heading "Cultivation of Infusoria." The exception is *Ampullaria cuprina,* for some mysterious reason known in the trade as the "Mystery Snail." It does not eat living plants and is a fair scavenger. If not getting enough pick-ups, it should have some boiled spinach.

It may be distinguished from the destructive Ampullaria by the depressed channel around the turns of its rather high spiral. The destructive Ampullaria (*paludosa*) has a low spiral and no channel. All these snails spawn great masses of eggs above the water, generally at night. The young fall into water as they hatch. Hatching in about two weeks requires a warm, moist atmosphere.

The Japanese Live-bearing Snail, like Goldfish, prefers cool water and is therefore popular mainly among Goldfish fanciers. Being large and meaty, these snails are also relished in Japan as food. The young, about the size of a pea, are born alive and fully formed. The right horn of the male is slightly shorter and serves as a sex indication. Once impregnated, a female appears to be fertile for life. Identification of species is by the high spiral and slightly raised keels on the big turn. The so-called American Potomac Snail, sometimes sold as the Japanese species, is generally similar but has no keels. It is sluggish spending most of its time buried in the sand.

One other species of snail has become popular in recent years. It is the Malaysian Burrowing Snail (*Melania tuberculata*) a very effective scavenger. This snail spends much of its time foraging through the gravel bed where it cleans up much of the decomposing matter. It is a prolific breeder.

Mussels remove suspended green algae from the water to some extent, but they require checking to see if they are alive. We are inclined not to recommend mussels, especially since heat does not agree with them. The risk is hardly worth the doubtful benefits.

Several species of fishes called *Corydoras* are generally considered the best aquarium scavengers. They belong to the Armored Catfishes and are illustrated and described later under their own headings. They are popular as well as effective in cleaning up leftovers. Their rooting activities tend to stir up sediment which the filter can then remove from the water.

### Changing the Water

The most popular question put by the beginner is, "How often must I change the water?" As stated earlier, a partial change of water (replacing of ten to twenty-five percent of aquarium water every four to six weeks with seasoned tap water) is a good practice. With good management and sensible feeding practices no other water changes are required.

There are two main qualities in water to be considered: acid-alkaline and hard-soft. These characteristics are not related to each other (except that hard-alkaline and soft-acid conditions often go together) and require different tests for detection.

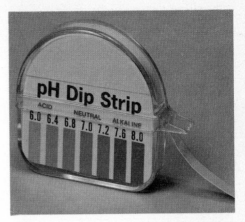

*pH Test Strip Paper in Easy Dispenser*

### What is pH?

Under usual conditions water is either acid or alkaline, seldom exactly neutral. The term of *p*H has reference to those opposite factors and their degree of intensity. A scale has been set up by chemists in which 7.0 represents neutral. Higher figures are alkaline, lower figures are acid. The accompanying scale indicates the degrees of intensity.

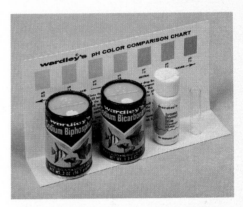

*pH Test Kit with Adjustment Chemicals*

| Acid | Neutral | Alkaline |
|---|---|---|
| ← | | → |
| 6.0, 6.2, 6.4, 6.6, 6.8 | 7.0 | 7.2, 7.4, 7.6 |

Readings are arrived at by taking a small specimen of the water to be tested and placing in it a few drops of a sensitive dye called indicator solution. The color to which the specimen turns is compared with a standard comparison scale consisting of several numbered shades. Readings are determined by finding the shade most nearly matching the water into which the dye was placed. Testing sets are sold by aquarium dealers and by scientific instrument firms. Those sets in which the matching shades are on printed cards should be kept out of long exposure to light, especially daylight. Very accurate, but very expensive, electronic *p*H meters are available to the modern hobbyist. But is is questionable whether that degree of accuracy is really important enough to warrant the high price.

Chemicals for pH adjustments are sold in pet shops. However, such adjustments in established aquariums are of temporary value only. The water usually returns to the original pH in a matter of days. Most well-managed tanks "settle in" at a pH of 6 to about 7.5, which is fine for almost all fishes.

## Hardness

The degree of hardness of tap water is usually determined by the ease or difficulty with which soap suds form in it. Hardness is mainly caused by compounds of calcium and magnesium. Unlike pH, there is no neutral point between hard and soft water. It is simply a question of how much of the hardening minerals are present. From 0 to 50 parts per million is considered soft. From 50 to 100, moderately hard. From 100 to 200, hard. Above 200, very hard. (One grain per gallon equals 17 parts per million.)

Contact with limestone formations is the main cause of hardness. Deep wells have higher hardness content than open streams in the same locality.

Similar fishes are found prospering in either moderately hard or moderately soft water. However, hardness has certain effects on both fishes and plants. It has been found that some of the hard-to-spawn fishes are stimulated to breed when changed from hard to soft water. This seems to carry out what happens in nature. A long dry season concentrates the mineral content of the water, thus making it hard. Spawning often comes with the rainy season and consequent softening of the water.

The addition of distilled or clean rainwater will correct too much hardness. There are also filter materials which reduce hardness as long as they are not overworked. Nature's waters, such as those of the dark cedar streams of New Jersey and elsewhere, are used in whole or part by some breeders for fishes that require specific water conditions.

There are hardness testing sets that can be purchased in aquarium stores. Boiling removes some hardness, however boiled water should be thoroughly aerated before use.

Due to concentration by evaporation, hardness increases in an aquarium over a period of months if no water is drawn off. As pointed out earlier, it is occasionally advisable to siphon away about ten to twenty-five percent of the water and replace it with fully aged water.

Hardness is increased by the presence of a large number of shells from dead snails as well as by sand or gravel containing much lime. Although they have no place in the freshwater aquarium, pieces of coral and empty sea shells are sometimes used as decorative items. These pieces contribute greatly to hardness of the water and should be avoided.

## Heaters

Most heaters on the market today are thermostatically controlled. They consist of a partially submerged tube in which there is an electric coil. The coil is usually placed at the lower end of the tube in order to contact the cooler strata of water and thus produce circulation in the tank. The upper end of the tube houses the thermostat with a knob to set the heater for any desired temperature. Heaters are made in different wattages, most commonly from twenty-five watts to two hundred fifty watts. The best rule for selecting the proper heater is to allow five watts for every gallon of water. Thus, for a ten-gallon tank, a fifty-watt heater should be used.

Most fishes will do well at a temperature between 70° and 82°. Since no heater is made with a built-in thermometer, a separate thermometer is needed to check the temperature. There are many models available and most of them are accurate enough for our purposes. A heated tank should also be filtered or aerated to insure an even distribution of temperature.

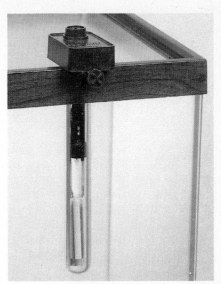

*Thermostatically Controlled*
*Aquarium Heater*

*Sudden Changes of Temperature*

While most fishes can tolerate a slow change of temperature over a range of 10° to 15°, changing fishes from a tank at one temperature to another having a different temperature of several degrees, either up or down, is one of the things that absolutely *must not be done*. Bad results may not be apparent at once, but they are seldom escaped. The fishes usually get the "shakes" or "shimmies," *Ichthyophtirius* ("ick"), fungus, or generally decline. Changes should be made within 2° of the same original temperature.

*Reflectors and Hoods*

The ordinary artificial illumination of a living room, even though it penetrates into the aquarium, is worthless for plants. Electric light to be of value to plants must be *very close, preferably overhead*. Various devices are manufactured for holding bulbs in position over aquariums. The reflectors sold for aquariums are generally rather narrow covering only part of the tank. Hoods are complete covers with a light fixture built in.

Either incandescent or fluorescent bulbs are used, but occasionally a full hood incorporates both types. It should be kept in mind that incandescent light produces a warm light, generates heat, and that the bulbs burn out quickly. Fluorescent light, on the other hand, produces practically no heat, consumes less electricity, and the bulbs have a long life. However, it is more expensive to install. When selecting fluorescent light, the "warm white" tube gives the best illumination.

Special bulbs, which have been developed for growing potted plants, can also be used for the aquarium. These tend to exaggerate the colors of fishes, making them appear more brilliant.

How much light and how long it should be kept on during the day depends upon the availability of daylight. However, a tank receiving very little daylight (one not close to a window) should be lighted for about ten to 12 hours daily. When using fluorescent light there is no choice about the wattage of the tube. The length of the tank determines the length of the bulb and therefore its wattage. With incandescent bulbs, care should be taken not to overheat the tank. Two twenty-five-watt bulbs are the maximum for a ten-gallon tank. A larger tank may require forty watt bulbs. No tank needs stronger bulbs provided they are placed in a reflector directly above the tank.

*Glass Cover and Strip Reflector*

Along with the petty cruelties to fishes that might be mentioned is the thoughtless practice of suddenly placing them in powerful light when they have gotten used to darkness. If the aquarium is in a darkened room, the room lights should be switched on a few minutes before the aquarium light is turned on. The fish give every evidence of experiencing the same distress we would feel under like circumstances. A little care in this matter is a kindness that is not misspent.

*A Full Hood*

## Covers

Tanks should be covered both to keep the fish in and the dust out. A cover also reduces evaporation. Care should be taken so that spray does not wet the electrical fixtures of a hood or reflector.

## Number of Fishes per Aquarium

If you have a well-proportioned tank with liberal water surface, you can make a rough calculation of the number of fish it will support from the following example for a ten-gallon tank:

*Small fishes* (1 to 1½ inches long), such as Guppies, Zebras, Neons—about twenty fishes per tank.

*Medium fishes* (2 to 3 inches long), such as Swordtails, Mollies, Platies—ten to twelve fishes per tank.

*Large fishes* (4 to 5 inches long), such as grown Clown Barbs, Angelfish—two to four fishes per tank.

## Selecting and Buying Fishes

Look for fishes with fins that stay erect most of the time. They should swim in a relaxed manner, not jerkily or with nervous dashes.

The belly outline is also a good indication of a fish's condition. Good specimens have a rounded belly outline; poor specimens have sunken-in stomachs. This is especially important when buying some of the live-bearing fishes, such as Mollies, Platies, Swordtails, and Guppies.

Don't buy out of a tank where fishes "shimmy," that is, go through violent shaking and swimming motions while standing still.

Make sure fins are intact. The fins should not be split or frayed and the body should show no marks or injuries.

Avoid fishes with small white spots or blotches on body and fins.

Fishes should be alert and actively avoid the net when being caught.

## Introducing Fishes

Before the trip to the store, the tank should be fully prepared with the water properly aged and the temperature set. The container—plastic cup, paper cup, or plastic bag—with the fishes should then be "floated" in the tank to equalize the temperature of the two waters gradually. Slowly mix the waters and let the fish swim out.

This procedure is usually sufficient since most fishes are able to withstand gradual changes. In cases where waters are known to be very different in temperature, hardness, or $pH$, the change should be made more slowly.

## Catching Fishes

Approach the task of catching fishes with confidence but not conceit; with determination not to lose patience nor ruin the plants. Any fish can be outwitted and outwaited by man. Each species has its peculiarities, but initially captured, all individuals of that species can be caught by the same method.

Many species yield to very slow movement. This is the first thing to try. When a fish seems nearly caught by the slow-motion method, it is almost sure to dash away if the net accidentally taps the glass. This is often difficult to avoid, but should be kept in mind. A net in each hand often helps—a large one for a catcher and a small one for a persuader.

Very small, newly hatched fishes had best not be handled at all. But, if necessary, a good way is to raise them near the surface with a fine net and then dip out fishes and a little water in a spoon.

## Nets

Except for use in globes, all nets should have straight edges. Suitable nylon netting is preferable to knotted threads. Nets should be hung up when not in use. It is a good practice to rinse all nets in clear water before drying. Every aquarist loses fishes by having them leap from a net while being transferred. We can only suggest to take extreme care at this moment. A net should be deep enough so that the free hand can form a little bag to close off the fishes. A net should not be so deep as to entangle the fishes and tear their fins when they struggle. Small nets, up to about three-by-four-inch frames, should be as deep as they are wide. Larger nets can be proportionately shallower.

With large aquariums a large net is almost indispensable. Professionals, who must catch their fishes without wasting much time, often have a square net nearly the full width and depth of the tank. With this the fishes are raised to the surface and then removed by a smaller net.

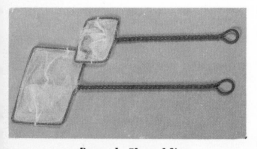

*Properly Shaped Nets*

## Emergency Aquarium

Though it is hard to resist filling a well-planted emergency aquarium with fishes, it will pay off in the long run to exercise restraint. By placing new arrivals in an emergency tank, no matter how clean their bill of health may seem, one can avoid the mournful tale of the aquarium that was once a paradise until a diseased fish or plant was introduced. Strangers ought to have at least two-weeks' probation.

A healthy aquarium balanced with plants and free of other fishes, is the very best place to put an individual fish that is out of condition or that has been bullied. An emergency tank also serves for the female live-bearer needing protection and rest after delivery of her young.

## Tapping on Glass

There seems to be about as much sense to tapping an aquarium glass to gain the attention of the fishes as there is in speaking in a loud tone of voice to someone who does not understand our language. The result is the same—fear and confusion.

## Bullies

Sometimes an individual fish, possibly of a peaceful species, learns that other fishes will flee if chased. This becomes a sport with that fish, to the misery of its fellows and the discomfit of its owner. It should either be disposed of, partitioned off (perhaps in a corner like a dunce), or placed in another aquarium with larger fishes. There, among strangers, it may reform. Like the rooster taken out of its own barnyard, it will not fight so well.

## Comparison of Temperature and Measurement Scales

In practically all aquarium literature, except that written in English, Centigrade measurements (often abbreviated as C.) are used to designate temperature. Centigrade measurements translate into these Fahrenheit equivalents:

It will be noticed that Centigrade zero is the freezing point, 32° in Fahrenheit. On the higher part of the scale, not shown, the Centigrade boiling point at 100° equals Fahrenheit 212°.

In most foreign aquarium literature we find measurements expressed in the metric system, which is gradually coming into general use. For those who have not been reared to think in those terms, we give a few of the most important equivalents. There are three principal measurements of this kind which foreign aquarists use.

Two of the measurements met with most often in foreign publica-

tions are the *centimeter* and the *cubic centimeter,* abbreviated respectively as cm. and cc. For all practical purposes there are five centimeters to two inches, as shown on the accompanying parallel scale. The ten subdivisions to be seen in the centimeters are *millimeters.* These are universally used by scientists to designate the lengths of the smaller fishes, such as we keep in our aquariums and of small objects, such as fish eggs.

The third measurement we often read is the *liter.* It expresses capacity and is just a trifle over a quart. It comprises 1000 cubic centimeters and is the same as a cubic decimeter.

The great advantage of the metric system is that it is based on the decimal system. The denominations are in multiples of ten so that multiplication or division, within the range of those multiples, is accomplished by merely moving the decimal point forward or backward.

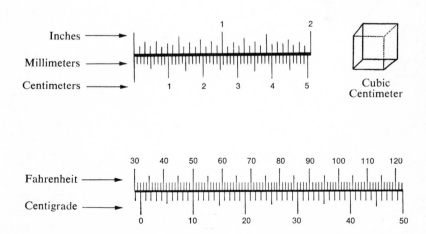

# FEEDING

*How* fishes are fed is just as important as *what* they are fed. A poor food properly handled may give better results than an excellent one used without judgment.

## How Often to Feed

Temperature and oxygen directly influence the amount of food a fish can properly consume. The life processes (metabolism) of all cold-blooded animals are very much affected by temperature. The warmer they are, within their own established limits, the faster they breathe, digest, eliminate, and grow. Such animals as frogs, turtles, and alligators offer extreme examples of this law. With a few degrees deficiency in temperature they will refuse food for months on end. Lizards, lightning fast in the sun, are torpid in the cool of the morning and can be picked up. A warm water aquarium fish has an indifferent appetite at 67°, a good one at 72°, and a ravenous one at 77°. It does not increase above 80° because of the diminished oxygen content of the water at the higher temperature. Appetite and digestion are twins and both require oxygen as well as warmth.

It is well to keep in mind that exotic fishes, mostly from tropical countries, normally lead a life that is speeded up and need a fair supply of fuel delivered frequently. In practical terms this means fishes should be fed at least twice daily instead of once. Such a practice not only doubles the pleasure of aquarists, who usually like to feed their charges, but also increases the sales of the food manufacturers and makes fishes bigger, better, and happier.

Regardless of all other rules, theories, practices, or printed instructions, the aquarist should stick tenaciously to this one: *Feed only enough prepared food at one time so that practically ALL of it is consumed within five minutes.* The rigid application of this rule will prevent many mysterious ills, as well as much clouding of water.

If it is impossible to feed more than once daily, the morning is the best time, especially if the aquarium contains healthy growing plants. The oxygen the plants develop during the day aids the digestion of the fishes. At night, the plants give off carbon dioxide which inhibits digestion. In addition, any left-over food particle is likely to be consumed during the day while the fishes can find it. At night, it would only decay.

## Care During Absence

If one must be away for a few days, it is safer to let the fishes go hungry rather than entrust their feeding to someone without experience. It is quite extraordinary what a number of things can go wrong when aquariums are in unfamiliar hands. In leaving the fishes unfed, it may relieve the mind to remember that when fishes are shipped and are on the road several days they arrive without signs of starvation. Should the aquarist be away two weeks or more and finds it is necessary to call in a substitute, let that person first do an actual feeding with instructions and under supervision.

Substitute caretakers should tend towards *underfeeding* and be most particular to replace glass covers.

A very good plan is to leave with the novice caretaker a set of one-meal packets of food designating the aquarium in which each is to be used.

When fishes must be kept without food for several days, it is better to maintain them at a temperature of 70° rather than at a higher temperature range.

## Fish Foods

It is generally conceded that living foods produce the best results and it is, therefore, the ideal of every amateur or professional maker of prepared foods to produce a compound that will be approximately as satisfactory as a living food, such as Daphnia and Brine Shrimp. This is a fine ambition as a prepared food that is perfect would answer every aquarist's prayer. Each manufacturer of food believes his own to be the best, but as yet no impartial, competent comparison has ever been made. Aquarists, bewildered by a chorus of claims, often use several brands, hoping to combine the merits of all. Not a bad idea, if one has no time to make

systematic tests. The fishes surely give evidence of enjoying a change, so why not let them have it?

## Prepared Foods

Prepared foods come in many forms: granular, flake, pelleted, paste, and freeze-dried (irregular lumps). When selecting a prepared food one should keep in mind whether it sinks or floats. Granular, pelleted, and paste foods often sink rapidly and get lodged in gravel where they can quickly cloud water. Great care should be taken when using them.

Flake foods float much longer and, if not eaten immediately, cloud water less. It is also easier to judge the amount eaten by fish when using flake foods.

Lumps of freeze-dried foods, especially Brine Shrimp, are ideal for larger fishes.

A splendid moist food, though a bit of trouble to make, and suited to all but very small fishes, is made as follows:

One pound of beef or calf liver, finely chopped and put through a Waring Blender twice. Strain

*Freeze Dried Brine Shrimp*

*Flake Food*

through fine wire sieve. Add one level tablespoon of salt. Mix with Gerber's (or other) junior baby-size spinach. Add fourteen level tablespoons of Pablum and six of wheat germ. Stir well, pack in small screw-top jars. Pasteurize thirty minutes. Cool and store in refrigerator. This is known as the "Gordon formula," named after Dr. Myron Gordon, who used it while he was a geneticist at the New York Aquarium. He used mostly Platies and Swordtails in his research and produced many of the now common color varieties of these fishes.

## Frozen Foods

Pet shops offer more than twenty varieties of frozen fish foods among which are Brine Shrimp, Daphnia, Blood Worms, and Tubifex Worms. Like frozen food for human consumption, these foods should be kept frozen all the time. Any thawed-out portion not used at once should be thrown out.

To feed frozen foods, it is best to break off a piece of appropriate size, thaw out in a jar of water, stir, let food particles settle, pour discolored water off, and then feed.

## Live Foods

### Daphnia

Except in a few cases, live foods are not indispensable, but they are always desirable. They are important to baby fishes and they round out a needed ingredient which few, if any, prepared fish foods possess.

Daphnia are the best known of the living foods. They are of almost universal distribution. However, one can not go to any body of water anywhere and get what the fish might describe as a delicious dish of Daphnia. It is not as easy as that.

While it is true that this little aquatic crustacean (about the size and general shape of a flea) occurs in fresh water almost everywhere, it only appears in concentrated numbers in a comparatively few places—rather unpleasant places as a rule. At the margins of pools in city dumping grounds we sometimes find the true "fish fan" enveloped in a cloud of mosquitoes, patiently swirling a net through evil-looking water, hoping to land a few million of the "bugs." What none but the initiated can understand is that the "fish fan" likes to do it.

### Cyclops

Cyclops are found in Daphnia ponds. They are a slight, small animal with one central eye which moves rapidly in a straight line through a series of jumps. Sometimes there is a double tab on the end of the body; this is the female's egg pouch and soon drops off. It is nearly impossible to gather enough Cyclops to make a substantial food, but for fishes that catch them on their own they make a good food.

*Frozen Brine Shrimp*

## Flies

Houseflies freshly swatted, are very fine food for larger species. Once fishes become used to them, they are always on the lookout for their owner to give them a few as a special treat.

## Live Brine Shrimp

The live food most often stocked by pet shops is adult Brine Shrimp. Slightly larger than Daphnia, they are nevertheless relished by as small a fish as the Neon Tetra. Brine Shrimp are collected daily in the shallow salt ponds of the San Francisco Bay Area and shipped via air freight to most dealers in the United States. Being sea creatures, they need to be kept in salt water of a rather high density (four to six ounces of salt per gallon of water). For feeding, therefore, they must absolutely be strained through a net instead of poured into the tank. Adult Brine Shrimp are able to live in fresh water for two or more hours.

Store in refrigerator or with aeration.

*Live Adult Brine Shrimp*

## Brine Shrimp Eggs

Dried eggs of the Brine Shrimp (*Artemia salina*) are now sold by most dealers and are a Godsend to all breeders of aquarium fishes. About the size of ground pepper, they are sprinkled on salted water (six ounces of non-iodized salt to the gallon). After a day or two at temperatures between 70° and 80°, they bring forth thousands of tiny visible Brine Shrimp Nauplii, tidbits of food for baby fishes and those up to and over one inch long.

No serious breeder can be successful without newly hatched Baby Brine Shrimp. They are the first food for almost all egg-laying and live-bearing fishes. Even full-grown fishes such as Swordtails gorge themselves on them.

The best eggs come from California. Various devices are now on the market for hatching them.

*Brine Shrimp Hatching Device*

## Tubifex Worms

Sometimes in Daphnia pools one finds a rusty edge around the shore that looks hopefully like Daphnia but turns out to be a mass of wriggling, threadlike worms called Tubifex. When they are alarmed they become quiet and draw back for a short time into their cases.

It is quite impractical to either collect or propagate Tubifex Worms, nor is there usually a need since they are obtainable the year round from professionals.

The best way to store these worms for use is to place them in a pail under a small stream of water from the tap. The worms remain in a mass at the bottom of the container. Occasionally one should break up the mass using a strong stream in order to wash away the dead worms. The colder the water, the longer they last. They can also be stored in the refrigerator in a shallow pan without water.

Sometimes these worms infest the soil of aquariums. A few of them do no harm; in fact, they provide fishes with an occasional home-grown and quite wholesome snack. Heavy infestations, however, consume oxygen.

Some of the "gravel-eating" Cichlids (*Geophagus*), many of the Armored Catfishes and most Loaches rout them from the gravel bed.

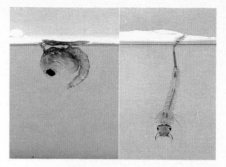

*Mosquito Larva*
*Left, Pupa, Right, Larva*

*Live Tubifex Worms*

## Mosquito Larvae

Here we consider a living food that is often present in Daphnia pools and in many other pools as well. In season it is found in almost any pool that is free of fishes, especially in water containing decaying vegetation, such as old leaves. In many instances mosquitoes place their eggs in rain puddles. This is the reason we have more mosquitoes in rainy seasons. The eggs hatch in a few days and become "wrigglers." They are usually dark and straight; they have a big head at one end and a Y-shaped ending at the other. In length they average perhaps ¼ inch when fully developed. When not eating they congregate in masses to breathe at the surface of the water, but are ready to wriggle to the bottom when alarmed. For this reason it is necessary to approach them rather carefully and make one quick sweep with the net. They can be carried in water in a crowded state and need no ice. Mosquito Larvae are good for fishes large enough to swallow them readily. Fishes about an inch in length have been known to strangle and larger ones to overeat on them. Vessels containing stored Mosquito Larvae should be covered with gauze to prevent escape of the flying pests. Their egg "rafts" look like ⅛ inch bits of floating soot. It is well to learn to recognize and collect them, for on water they hatch into numerous very small larvae that make splendid food for any fishes the size of newly born live-bearers.

When larvae are collected from suspiciously foul pools it is just as well to give them a rinsing in fresh water before feeding or storing.

*Glass Worm*

## Glass Worms

In many lakes and ponds throughout the land one may break the ice in midwinter and net out a liberal supply of live food called Glass Worms. They are the larvae of a fly, are about half an inch in length and are nearly transparent. From a top view they look something like a miniature pike. Although popularly called worms, they are not worm-like in appearance. They last remarkably well in crowded conditions and will keep for weeks in cool water. Food value, fair. They have been known to eat fish spawn and newly hatched fry.

*Blood Worms*

## Blood Worms

Often in Daphnia ponds and other bodies of water one sees deep red, jointed worms, about half an inch long, wriggling awkwardly through the water. They are Blood Worms, the larvae of Chironomus midges. Wild fishes eat them ravenously and they are an extremely nourishing food for all except the smaller varieties of aquarium fishes.

## White Worms

White Worms, little relatives of the Earth Worm, are about an inch long. They are cultivated; cultures may be had commercially. Under proper conditions they may be multiplied rapidly. Keep in covered, damp soil that is spongy and contains plenty of leaf mold or similar matter. Every two days stir in as much dry Pablum or oatmeal as they will consume in that time. Or they may be fed a variety of foods placed in holes in the soil and covered over. Mashed potatoes, cheese, bread wet with milk, or shelled boiled lima beans are some of the offerings they like and prosper on. Overfeeding sours the soil. Mite-like creatures usually accompany them, but do no particular harm, nor are they related. The principal enemies of White Worms, or *Enchytraeids,* are ants, mice, and heat. They like a temperature of about 60°. It is difficult to keep them over the summer. Most amateurs buy a new culture each fall. Pet shops can usually order starting cultures for hobbyists, or they can be purchased directly from mail order houses which specialize in aquarium supplies. There are many methods of getting the worms out for feeding purposes. A pair of tweezers dipped into a mass of the

worms seems to be about as good
as any. As worms in general are
hosts to various parasites, it is good
practice to cleanse and purge them
in clear water for an hour or more
before using. They won't drown.

*Earthworms*

Known also as the Garden Worm,
Rain Worm, and Fishing Worm,
the Earthworm is nature's gift to
fishes and man cannot improve on
it. Even vegetarian fishes take it
with relish. Game fishes probably
suspect the hook but cannot resist
the worm.

Not much need be said about collecting this choice food. That is a
matter of local experience. The one
thing to avoid is taking the evil-
smelling Dung Worm, usually inhabiting manure piles and exuding
a disgusting yellow secretion. Even
wild fishes will not touch them.

Small worms are more tender and
generally preferable. Most aquarium fishes require them chopped
up, although some the size of
large Cichlids can take them whole.
A pair of old scissors does the job
very well. These worms are fine for
putting fishes into breeding condition. Gather a big supply of them
in the fall for winter use. Keep in
damp earth, but not wet. Feed
lightly on mashed potatoes, corn
meal, or rolled oats. They may be
cleansed by keeping for a week in
moist sphagnum moss, or for a day
in water. They won't drown. For
safety one can scald them. Most
live-bait stores sell Earthworms.

*Gammarus*

Gammarus is a widely-distributed,
hard, shrimp-like creature, sometimes arriving with the plants. It

hovers about the bottom of the
aquarium, plowing through sand,
sometimes loosening leaves of Val-
lisnaria, etc., but it is otherwise
harmless. Multiplies rapidly. Too
tough for small fishes, but is eaten
by Cichlids.

*Infusoria*

To the fish breeder the word "Infusoria" means almost any aquatic
animal organism that is of a suitable size to feed young fishes before
they are large enough to negotiate
small Daphnia or Brine Shrimp
Nauplii. Many of these little
animals, such as the important
group of Rotifers, are not Infusoria
at all, but we aquarists are used to
making scientific blunders without
embarrassment, so without apology
we are going to use the word in its
popular sense. "Animalcules" would
be correct and inclusive.

There are a number of ways to
cultivate Infusoria. One is to set up
a mild decomposition in water and
wait for Infusoria spores from the
air to settle on the water and multiply on the products of decay. A
handful of crumpled lettuce placed
in a quart of water produces results
in about four days. So does chopped
hay. One of the best mediums we
know is dried Anacharis sprinkled
on the water, but many organic substances may also be used. A tank
containing those lettuce-devouring
snails, *Ampullaria paludosa* ("Infusoria snails"), soon brings forth
Infusoria that prosper on the
snails' half-digested droppings. Cultures depending on decay should
be started in rotation every few days
if a continuous supply is needed.
Aeration freshens such cultures and
prolongs their life.

A second method is to prepare a

boiled and cooled culture medium and then inoculate it with selected organisms, usually Paramecia. These organisms are commonly found in old aquarium water, in barnyard drainage, or they can be purchased at biological laboratories. Only a little is needed. Boiled cultures do not foul and last well. Rice, chopped hay, canned pea or black bean soup, and dried lettuce leaves are among many suitable stocks for boiling. Use about three tablespoons of mixed ingredients to a quart of water. This may be kept covered as stock and further diluted with water when poured into culture vessels (preferably shallow trays) for inoculating.

A new Frings method, now popular, has dried skim milk as a culture medium, about two pinches to a pint of boiled and cooled water. The milk and the seed micro-organisms should be put in at the same time. A rich growth takes about four days. A pinch of milk powder added every three or four days keeps the culture going. We have also used liquid skim milk, a teaspoon to a quart of water. "Infusoria tablets," too, have their advocates. They are standard items in aquarium stores and provide the cleanest and easiest method for cultivation of Infusoria. Do not place these tablets with the fishes. Make culture water and dip as needed. A liquid formulation is also available.

The "Slipper Animalcule" or Paramecium (pronounced Para-mee'see-um), is the commonest organism produced in the artificial culture of Infusoria. It thrives on the products of organic decomposition and can live in either foul or good water.

Well-established aquariums with old settlings contain Infusoria, but only enough to give the fish a start. A separate rich supply is needed. It is impossible to specify exact feedings; three tablespoons daily of good culture to a five-gallon aquarium with fifty fry would be conservative. The nursery needs a constant supply, to be determined by magnifying a drop of its surface water. Youngsters are kept on this diet until they have about doubled in size. Infusoria are too small for live-bearer or Cichlid fry. These, as well as the fry of many other species, are able to use newly hatched Brine Shrimp as a first food.

How to judge the ripeness of a culture is one of the most difficult (and important) things to impart to the inexperienced. The organisms usually seek the top surface towards the light. Touch the tip of the finger there and place a drop on a piece of glass. Hold glass over something dark, and with the light coming across the drop, examine with a magnifying glass, preferably a folding "thread-counter." If it is swarming with life, the culture is ready. Or the water may be examined in one of those thin pill phials. This slightly magnifies the contents so that a sharp pair of eyes can detect life moving about like particles of fine dust. Or, use a microscope magnifying not over fifty times.

## "Mikro" Worms

These tiny worms (*Panagrellus silusiae*), barely visible to the naked eye, were originally found in beer felts in the presence of yeast fermentation. They serve the same purpose as newly hatched Brine Shrimp in feeding baby fishes that have outgrown the need for Infusoria. They nicely supply the next step upward in size and are far less expensive. A constant supply is easily kept. Many dealers sell them. The growing culture is usually four parts of Pablum (or boiled oatmeal) to one part of yeast, either in granulated or paste form. This is diluted with water to the consistency of thin paste, and kept about ¼ to ½ inch deep in a covered glass container. Temperature, 70° to 80°. The worms are live-bearing and multiply fast, once well started. They creep up the sides of the glass, or will cover blocks of water-logged wood which are thick enough to stand just above the level of the liquid. From there they are easily rinsed off into the aquarium water. As they sink rapidly, it is advisable to drop them into a small net suspended just under the surface of the water. Nylon with openings of suitable size does nicely. Through this the worms escape gradually and are eaten as they fall. These worms are also well suited as a *first* food for the larger fry, such as Cichlids, the Live-bearers and Goldfish.

Even a fresh culture has a mild odor of yeast sourness, but if it becomes offensive, save a portion with which to seed a new batch and discard the remainder. Life remains in the culture, even though the appearance is bad.

## Other Live Foods

While there are many good live foods other than those we have described, such as Asellus, Freshwater Shrimp, Fairy Shrimp, Mayfly Larvae and others, they only amount to interesting conversation for aquarists when other subjects give out—if they ever do. They cannot ordinarily be gathered in quantity.

Brown Meal Worms, such as those sold in pet stores for feeding birds, are good food for strong-jawed fishes like Cichlids. Since it is not practical to cut them, they should be used whole, but only fed to larger fishes. If placed in plenty of bran in a large covered tin box and allowed to go through their natural beetle stage, they will multiply greatly in a few months. Brown Meal Worms serve as a good food especially in winter when other live foods are less available.

During the winter one can also gather bottom scrapings from ponds which, when carried home and brought up to house temperature, yield an amazing amount of life of many kinds. The surface of decaying wood is particularly likely to produce a harvest of Blood Worms. After the worms are revived in this way, the same care must be exercised as in summer for the exclusion of fish enemies; if present, the enemies are easily discovered when the water life awakes. Blood Worms keep best in cotton rags in a cup in a refrigerator, using only a little water to keep the rags wet.

Of course, for those who do not have the time or desire to procure or propagate their own live foods, Brine Shrimp and Tubifex Worms, which are two excellent live foods, are available the year round from pet shops.

## Raw and Boiled Meats

However excellent any dried food may be, fishes should have an occasional change, especially in the long winter months when live food is less obtainable. With very little trouble fish can be served chopped raw fish, shrimp, crab, or clam—all fine foods that can also be boiled.

Mincing them in the hand with scissors is easily done. Blot up clam or oyster juices before feeding. Minced raw chicken liver or beef liver is a good change.

One of the standbys is fresh, frozen, or canned shrimp. Practically all aquarium fishes like it and it agrees with them. For use, cut the shrimp into thin slices with scissors, cutting across the grain.

A boiled, lightly scored shrimp suspended on a string hanging from a light stick across the aquarium gives the fishes sport and exercise. Leave the suspended shrimp in the tank as long as the fishes enthuse over it and consume the fallen bits.

# ENEMIES

Fortunately there are few serious enemies of fishes in the aquarium. The three outstanding ones all smuggle themselves in with your supply of live foods. Since one of these enemies is far more destructive than all others combined, we will give it first consideration.

## Water Tiger

A sleek, spindle-shaped creature, the Water Tiger, is the larval form of a large Water Beetle (*Dytiscus*), which itself is also a powerful enemy of fishes. There are several species, but in effect, as far as the aquarist is concerned, they are all one. The pincers, or mandibles, are hollow, and through these Water Tigers rapidly suck the blood of their victims. Growth is rapid and they soon attain a size where they attack tadpoles, fishes, or any living thing into which they can bury their strong blood-suckers.

Vigilance is the only protection against them. Large, hard-mouthed fishes will eat them. Destroying them gives double pleasure to parent Cichlids while tending their flocks of young.

The Water Tiger breathes air through its rear end and, therefore, must occasionally come to the surface.

## Dragon Fly Larvae

Although not nearly so deadly as Water Tigers, Dragon Fly Larvae have a more widely heralded reputation as killers. Their disadvantage is that they have to lie in wait for their victims and seize them from below with a much smaller and less effective pair of pincers. These pincers are located on the end of a "mask," which is a contrivance having hinged joints. These normally lie contracted just below the head, but are ready to be extended in an instant when within striking distance of a victim.

Although there are more Dragon Fly Larvae than Water Tigers, they are less likely to be collected with Daphnia, for they usually lie half concealed in the mud, whereas the Water Tigers are swimming about.

Damsel Flies are about half the size of the Dragon Fly, and when at rest the wings lie parallel to the body. Their larvae are proportionately smaller and more slender, but they are also killers. They may be identified by three long bristle-like gills at the rear end of the body.

The flies themselves have their uses to man. Dragon Flies (Devil's Darning Needles) devour mosquitoes while flying. Damsel Flies also creep along plants eating plant lice (Aphis) as they go.

## Hydra

Hydra are low forms of life and are enemies of any small water creature that can be caught by their peculiar method of stinging their victims. So far as the aquarist is concerned, Hydra catch baby fishes up to a size of 3/16 of an inch. They also devour Daphnia and Brine Shrimp Nauplii.

Their shapes are extremely variable. They can contract themselves almost to the point of invisibility so that it is impossible to detect them in a can of Daphnia. Even worse, any broken bit of a Hydra soon regenerates into a new complete individual.

Colonies of Hydra usually appear like pendant, slowly swaying gray or green hairs, about ½ inch long or less. From the main thread are from three to seven tentacles, spread starlike. They are usually found attached to the glass and plants. It is rather surprising to find that they can move about, using alternately their tentacles and their suction foot in a clumsy kind of locomotion. Eventually they arrive.

The body and the tentacles contain many sharp barbs filled with a numbing poison. As a prospect brushes against a tentacle, the apparently inert Hydra springs into action. It injects a "shot" into its victim, draws the victim into a mouth from which the tentacles radiate, digests it and presently discharges the undigested portions from the same opening. When business is brisk, a Hydra may have a Daphnia or a young fish held by each tentacle, to be swallowed at leisure.

Immediately following a "strike," the creature undergoes a marked change in form, becoming much more compact. Multiplication usually takes place by budding, and, under the influence of plenty of food, is rapid.

The larger live-bearers, like Mollies, are a little too big for Hydra to negotiate. Their favorites are the babies of the different egg-laying species. In either case they compete seriously with young fishes for live foods, especially for Baby Brine Shrimp and Daphnia.

The easiest and safest way to get rid of this rather interesting pest is by introducing into the aquarium several, Three-spot, Blue or Pearl Gouramies. Give them no other food and they will soon devour the Hydra. A complete change to fresh water from the tap usually puts an end to them in a day. Remove all fishes during treatment. Some of the available fish medications containing copper are probably effective as well.

*Other Enemies*

Two questionable intruders that sometimes enter with Daphnia are Water Boatmen (Corixidae) and Back-Swimmers (Notonectidae). They may be introduced while very small or they may slip in unnoticed in larger sizes. Though they are commonly believed to be enemies of young fishes, our experiments indicate a "not guilty" verdict. Dr. G. C. Embody, a noted fish culturist, says that Back-Swimmers are dangerous, but that Water Boatmen are harmless. Both swim with a rowing motion of their two long oar-like legs.

*Beetles*

Most Water Beetles live on other insects or animals. They seldom get into the aquarium, but should be immediately removed when discovered.

*Fish Lice* (Argulus)

These are free-swimming, translucent, tenacious, wafer-like parasites that become fatally epidemic mostly in Goldfish pools from July to October. Argulus are about 3/16 of an inch across and may attack exotic fishes. To get rid of them catch fish in net, lift out of tank for a minute or two. Fish lice will usually leave their host when out of water. A new chemical marketed under the names of "Dylox" and "Masoten"* has recently been introduced as being effective against Argulus.

### Anchor Worm

While in the small free-swimming stage the Anchor Worm, a parasite, embeds itself in the flesh of Goldfish and some exotics. It develops a big anchor foot in order to attach its 5/8 inch long, thread-like body to the host. The body is so tough that it does not break when given a hard yank. A drop of formaldehyde on the infested area usually kills it. "Dylox" as recommended against fish lice, is also said to be effective against Anchor Worm.

### Planaria or Flatworms

These pale little creatures, growing up to ½ inch long and gliding like snails, sometimes distress aquarists by appearing on the glass sides of tanks. They are carnivorous and live on various fish foods, including live Tubifex Worms as well as dead fish and snails. They may fairly be rated as scavengers. Placed in clean water they starve and in an immaculate aquarium they do not last long. They do no harm and will not overpopulate an aquarium, provided good housekeeping is practiced.

### Leeches

Reports of leeches found in aquariums are not rare. Aquarists do not always recognize them. While there are other animals that travel like the measuring worm, it

*Dimethyl (2, 2 ,2-trichloro-1-hydroxyethyl) phosphonate

is a good guess that anything in the water travelling that way is a leech, especially if it has the ability to contract and extend its length. In North America there are about fifteen genera, divided into thirty species. Only a few attack fishes. Most of them are parasitic on snails or consume small worms, etc. Some prey on each other.

It is rare to see one attached to an aquarium fish, but it is a possibility. Therefore it is good policy to get rid of any such suspicious characters. They are extremely tough. No known chemical affects them that may not also kill the plants. They hate salt; also nicotine. If things become too unpleasant for them, they climb out of the water.

After a meal and at night, they seek a dark spot, such as under a stone. If an inverted saucer is placed loosely on the bottom of an aquarium, and leeches are present, they will likely be found in the morning, clinging to the dark side. Destroy them and continue until no more appear. Most leeches carry their young on the underside of their bodies, but the species most often encountered in aquariums lays eggs. Under-gravel filters are the best breeding grounds for these leeches. Their egg cases, usually containing two developing larvae, are about 3/16 of an inch long, oval in shape, and light brown. They are often attached to the filter plate and inside the tubes of an underground filter.

Most often they are introduced as eggs on plants or as young leeches among Tubifex Worms. They do not attack fishes.

# DISEASES

Fortunately, far fewer diseases and parasites attack fishes in the aquarium than they do in nature. This is probably because the aquarium does not furnish favorable conditions for the life cycles which many of them undergo.

## Ichthyophtirius

The only very common disease which gives us much concern is popularly called "Ick," being short for *Ichthyophthirius,* the name of the parasitic protozoan causing the trouble. The malady is aptly called by some the "pepper and salt disease," because in its advanced stage there are small white specks on the fins and body of the victim which resemble seasoning. At first only a few specks are seen: unless treatment is given these specks multiply rapidly until the body and fins are almost completely covered. A coating of fungus appears and death soon follows the fungus.

The cause of attacks of Ichthyophthirius is usually chill or exposure to the parasite. An affected new fish can wreak havoc in an entire tank. Chill works against the fish in two ways: (1) its own resistance is reduced and (2) the vitality of the parasite is increased at lower temperatures.

The organism that causes the trouble is one of the low forms of animal life, a simple cell covered with swimming hairs. It burrows just below the outer skin of the fish, the irritation causes a tiny pimple. In this pimple the parasite prospers on the fluids and tissues of its host, causing an itching which is evidenced in the early stages by the efforts of the fish to scratch itself against objects in the aquarium.

In a few days the parasite reaches its maximum size of one millimeter, leaves the fish, drops to the bottom of the aquarium, forms a cyst, and breaks up into from 500 to twelve hundred young. Not all these young succeed in reaching a host, but enough do so that the progress of the disease sweeps on "like wildfire."

The important thing, of course, in checking the parasite is to break into its life cycle at the weakest point. This is in the early free-swimming stage. Several methods have been developed. Most methods call for heat of about 85°, either with or without medication. Some aquarists hold the extreme view that simple heat is the best and the only effective remedy. Most aquarists, however, believe in the value of other aids. An old and popular treatment is to raise the temperature to about 85° and add three or four drops of 2% Mercurochrome to each gallon of water. A growing supicion has developed that this drug has a delayed bad after-effect on the fishes. It does not harm plants.

Methylene Blue, two drops of 5% aqueous solution to the gallon, has no such reaction, but it is deadly to plants. Therefore treatment with this dye should be in a bare container. It is one of the best remedies.

The use of quinine at a proper strength has neither of those disadvantages and can be used without high temperature. A half grain of quinine sulphate to each gallon of aquarium water is approximately correct. Place the required amount of powder in a cup, add a few drops of water, and with the point of a spoon mix it into a thin paste. Add warm water to fill the cup. A short stirring will then fully dissolve the powder. Empty into the aquarium and stir gently.

The quinine treatment, which originated in Germany and is generally accepted there as being the best method, has its critics as to its reaction on both plants and fishes. Perhaps it has been used in too strong concentrations. A strength of one grain to the gallon is highly effective, but may injure some plants.

Acid water of 5.8 readings is said to make life hard for the parasites. Sea salt, one heaping teaspoonful to the gallon of water, is also recommended in conjunction with high temperature. Fishes of the Gourami family (Anabantidae) can be treated in a unique way. These fishes possess an auxiliary breathing apparatus, the labyrinth, which permits them to "breathe" atmospheric air at the surface, thus they can survive in water of very low oxygen content while the parasite cannot. If kept in a small aquarium without aeration and filtration at a temperature of 85°, the fishes will be completely cured in a few days without further medication.

The germs of this organism are not carried through the air as are the spores of fungus or of greenwater algae. In an absolutely sterilized aquarium, fishes will die of chill without developing Ichthyophthirius, but in ordinary practice it is difficult to produce or to maintain water in that condition. Biologists state that the microscopic young die in sixty hours if they fail to find a host. If this is true there must be some unknown way in which the life of the organism can be indefinitely suspended, for an epidemic has often been produced by chilling an aquarium that had been subject to no recent contamination and which for a long preceding period had not been attacked. In any case, all aquarium implements should be well sterilized and water splashings into other tanks should be avoided when handling an afflicted fish.

Aquarists are often puzzled as to why in a tank of mixed species only certain kinds may be affected by "Ick." There are several reasons: the parasites prefer certain hosts; some fishes withstand chill better than others, and certain fishes in an aquarium will be in better health than their companions. Several species of Ichthyophthirius exist, this probably accounts for variable results in treatment.

It should be remembered that it is by no means a sure indication of "Ick" if fishes scratch or rub themselves against objects. It could very well be "Flukes" or some other parasitic disease. Treatment for Ichthyophthirius should not be given unless the little white spots are observed. When these are seen, no time should be lost.

Occasionally, fishes will scratch or rub themselves against plants, stones, or gravel as if they were infected with "Ick", but no white spots develop. This is usually not a cause for alarm. If the scratching persists, it is probably caused by numerous microorganisms which have developed from too many settlings and uneaten decaying food in the aquarium. Siphon the bottom, draw off about half the water, and replace with clear conditioned water.

## Dropsy

One of the strangest of fish diseases is dropsy. It is also one of the most unpleasant in appearance. The fish becomes puffed and the scales stand out at an angle to the body. Sometimes the eyes have a tendency to bulge. The puzzling thing about the malady is the unaccountable way in which it singles out individual fishes. Although some aquarists believe that the trouble arises from faults in diet, the fact remains that it strikes without apparent regard to what the fish has been fed and it is just as likely as not to single out a fish in a pool where the conditions seem to be perfect.

Some species seem to be more subject to dropsy than others. *Colisa lalia, Danio malabaricus,* and *Brachydanio rerio* are among the more susceptible.

The disease is fatal in from one to three weeks.

There is no reliable cure for this disease. Since it is usually not very contagious in the aquarium, the removal of the infected fish will prevent an epidemic in most cases.

## Flukes

A malady not often attacking aquarium fishes is "Flukes." It is caused by parasitic animals called *Gyrodactylus* and *Dactylogyrus* which lodge in the skin and gills. The fish dashes wildly about and then when exhausted comes to a sudden stop. There are other maladies which cause fishes to act in this way, but since we know little or nothing about them, the treatments described here may as well be applied. Highly contagious.

Treatment is twenty drops of formaldehyde to a gallon of water.

Leave the fish in this bath until it shows signs of exhaustion, usually in from five to ten minutes. If necessary, repeat in a day or two.

## Fungus

There is a white slimy coating on fishes that usually follows the first stages of Ichthyophthirius but that sometimes appears independently. In either case, it is caused by a fungus called Saprolegnia. Four level teaspoons of salt per gallon of water is the best treatment.

Fishes are made susceptible to Fungus by bruises, attacks of other fishes, sudden temperature change, chill, overfeeding, and poor general conditions.

## Mouth Fungus

A wicked disease, of which we know little, is Mouth Fungus. A light-colored fluff appears at the lips, gets into the mouth, and soon starts eating the jaws away. Unless action is taken very quickly, it is likely to kill all the fishes that have been exposed to it. It is highly contagious. Gouramis, Barbs, and Livebearers are particularly subject to Mouth Fungus. For long no remedy was known, today many antibiotics cure the disease. Among the best are chloromycetin, aureomycin, and terramycin.

Dosage, fifty milligrams to each gallon of water. Follow dissolving procedure described under "Ick" for dissolving quinine. Cure is usually effected in a few days. At specified strength this will not harm plants or fishes. Expensive but effective.

## Fin Rot

Fins sometimes become frayed without having been bitten by other fishes. Treatment is the same as for Fungus. If the entire fins start to rot away (not just the membrane between the fin rays), the treatment described for Mouth Fungus should be used.

### "Velvet"

A comparatively new disease among domesticated fishes is "Velvet." It mostly affects labyrinth fishes and members of the Carp family, such as White Clouds, *Brachydanios,* Barbs, and the live-bearing Tooth Carps. It first shows as a yellowish brown patchy film usually beginning on the body near the dorsal fin. If untreated, this spreads quickly and develops into a series of small raised circular crusts. Fry usually succumb before the disease is detected. The trouble is caused by a protozoan parasite (probably *Oodinium limneticum*) which has a free-swimming stage before becoming parasitic.

The best remedy for this ailment is one containing copper sulphate and salt. Since copper sulphate is highly toxic in unskilled hands, it is advisable to purchase a ready-made solution in an aquarium shop. Many brands are available, most for use in marine aquariums, but all are suited for freshwater fishes as well. Use as directed for marine fishes, but add four *level* teaspoonfuls of salt per gallon of water to be treated.

### Shakes or "Shimmies"

A description of Shakes or "Shimmies" is not easily made, but most aquarists have seen it. Once seen, it is always remembered. The fish usually stays stationary, wobbling its body from side to side in a slow, clumsy motion. It is like

swimming without getting anywhere. There are several causes. The principal cause is chill. Many aquarists declare their fishes to have been afflicted in this way without having been chilled, but they are probably mistaken. A short drop in temperature may do it and the effect lasts long.

Fishes with Ichthyophthirius are apt to "shimmy." This shaking is merely a manifestation of trouble and is not a definite disease in itself, any more than chills are with people. Aside from treating the disease causing "shimmies," the usual successful treatment is a persistently applied temperature of about 78-80.

Indigestion is, no doubt, another cause. There is reason to believe that an overly dirty aquarium gives rise to quantities of microscopic organisms which cause the fish to act in this way. Cases have often been instantly cured merely by a complete change of water. The new water, of course, should be duly seasoned,

### Wasting

Like "Shimmies," wasting is not a disease, but a symptom. However, it may be caused by internal parasites. In any case, there is little or no hope for a hollow-bellied fish with a big head and shrunken body. Usual causes are lack of fresh or living food, infrequent and too small feedings, over-crowding, and continuous cool water. The trouble may be old age.

What ever the cause, an emaciated fish seldom survives, although it may last for some time.

### Swim-Bladder Trouble

The great majority of fishes are equipped with a very wonderful mechanism which enables them to remain balanced, almost without effort, in any reasonable depth of water. It is a flexible bladder, filled, not with air, but with gas generated by the fish. For this balancing system to be effective, the amount of internal pressure must be precisely right. With too little gas the fish sinks; with too much it floats. Sometimes floating is temporarily caused by intestinal gases. Usually floating or sinking is caused by some derangement of the swim bladder and is incurable.

## Wounds

Nothing seems to be better for wounds than touching them with 2% Mercurochrome, or with 10% Neo-silvol or Argyrol. Repetition may be necessary.

## Crooked Bodies

It is probable that deformed spines in fishes sometimes result from constitutional or tubercular weakness similar to rickets in man and are just about as incurable. Malnutrition and vitamin deficiency are contributing causes. The body often assumes a crescent shape. It may accompany swim-bladder or other internal disturbance. In many years of experience we have never seen or heard of a recovery from any of these deformities and death is usually not far off.

## Other Troubles

There is a list of rare troubles of which aquarists know little or nothing. Cysts, lumps on fishes, blindness, partial paralysis, worms eating through from the inside, sudden death with no outward sign of dis-

ease—all things we hear of and hope some day to learn more about. No doubt there are internal parasites which defy treatment. Many of them must have free-swimming stages in which they can be killed.

## Sudden Deaths

Occasionally, a fish in apparently perfect health is found dead in an aquarium that seems to be in ideal condition and in which other fishes are in good health. This *could* be the result of a "stroke." Man is not the only creature subject to that malady, nor to the sudden results of over-eating. Unless this little tragedy is repeated too often, it seems best to file it under "unsolved mysteries."

## Salt

Salt is nature's remedy for many ills. It is effective in most troubles of freshwater fishes, has no bad actions, and is safe to try on obscure cases or when in doubt. Its one fault is that when strong enough to check disease, it is too concentrated for plants. Place fishes in a bare tank or enamel receptacle in seasoned water containing two level teaspoons of salt to the gallon. Gradually over twenty-four hours build it up to four measures. If no improvement appears by the third day go to six measures if the fish shows no signs of distress. Species vary. Guppies and Mollies can stand eight. Aeration helps. At end of treatment, before returning fish to aquarium, slowly add fresh water until the salt content is low.

Sea water is still better than salt crystals. One part to five of fresh is a good strength, about equal to three level teaspoonsful of crystals to the gallon.

*Check-ups*

It not infrequently happens that aquarium conditions seem to be ideal, the aquarist has been careful about feeding and temperature, yet the fishes are low in vitality or otherwise ailing. All conditions have their causes however obscure they may be. Sometimes these causes are beyond the range of our knowledge, but there are several important points on which a re-check can be made.

Is there a possibility of dead fish or snails?

Has the water an unpleasant smell? If so, it should be partially changed and aerated, either by pump or hand pouring. A sprinkling pot serves temporarily. If the cover is down tight, raise it a little.

Is there enough light for the plants? Have they a good green color? Are they growing? Are there plenty of them? Plants which are not prospering are a detriment.

Is there any chipping away of nickel or chromium plating at any point in direct or indirect contact with the water? This is poisonous.

Unsuspected overcrowding is the commonest trouble. Re-read our paragraph (page 19) on "Number of Fish per Aquarium." When in doubt, use fewer fish.

Has the water been thickly green and then turned yellow? In that case it should be changed, the microscopic suspended plant life is dying.

Have the fishes been chilled within a month or are they being kept at 68° or a little lower?

On the other hand, there are heat fanatics who never let the aquarium water drop below 80°. If and when the fishes weaken in this tropical temperature, try something about 74°-76°.

What about insecticide sprays, paint fumes, or even excessive tobacco smoke?

Has the water become too acid or too alkaline? Has it become too hard by adding water from the original source to make up for evaporation without ever actually changing water? If this is suspected, remove half the water and use soft water, such as distilled, clean rain or melted snow that has not been in contact with metal or new wood to refill the tank. In industrial and urban areas where air pollution is a problem, rainwater may also be unsafe to use, unless it is collected after the air has been "cleaned" by a long steady rain.

One of the commonest of mysterious troubles is caused by the use of new copper boilers and piping in residences. Let standing water run out of pipes before using water for the aquarium, or try water from some source not so contaminated.

# PLANTS AND PLANTING

We now come to the point of considering plants not only as renewers of life but also as purifiers and beautifiers. As it is with garden flowers, a few old friends are the ones we find to be best. In over one hundred years of organized aquarium study, about a dozen kinds of plants (with their variations) have come into general use. Several other good plants are growing in popularity but are not yet universally available. Finally, many authentic looking, artificial plants are available.

## Vallisneria spiralis

(*Eel Grass, Tape Grass*)

Perhaps the author allows himself the pleasure of personal preference in heading the list with this beautiful plant. Its tall, graceful, grass-like form with narrow, silken, light-green leaves, rises vertically in undulating lines. The plant in moderately good light multiplies rapidly and forms a dense but not impenetrable thicket or screen. It is one of the very best oxygenators and its roots tend to purify the soil.

Propagation is principally by runners. The plants are male and female and, peculiarly enough, the plants from runners are all the same sex as the parents. Nearly all of them are female. Their little floating, white cup-shaped flowers are on the ends of long thin spirals, rising from the crown of the plant. The word *spiralis* refers to the shape of these flower stems. The flowers of the rare male plants are close to the crown. Pollen rises from them and fertilizes the floating female flowers. The seeds from these fertilized flowers may produce both male and female plants, but very few of the seeds ever germinate. In planting Vallisneria care should be taken to keep the crown just at the surface of the sand.

A giant species with leaves about five-eighths of an inch wide and several feet long with bristly edges is propagated in Florida. It is splendid for aquariums that are at least eighteen inches high.

*Jungle Vallisneria (Vallisneria americana)*

An attractive mutation from the tall *Vallisneria spiralis*, but instead of growing from fifteen to twenty inches and sprawling on the water surface of small tanks, its charmingly twisted leaves average only seven to twelve inches. Very popular. Prefers hard water and fairly strong light.

*Corkscrew Vallisneria (Vallisneria spiralis)*

## Sagittaria

### (Arrowhead)

This famous old aquarium plant is another one having grass-like form. It comes in many more species than Vallisneria, most of them being bog plants rather than pure aquatics. Their barb- or arrow-shaped aerial leaves, common along watery borders almost everywhere, are responsible for the naming of the plant after the mythological Sagittarius, the Archer.

About half a dozen species, some of them of doubtful identity, are being successfully used as aquarium plants. The three most important are *Sagittaria gigantea* (believed to be a cultivated form of *Sagittaria sinensis*), *Sagittaria natans,* and *Sagittaria subulata.*

The strong green leaves of *Sagittaria gigantea* are ½ inch or more wide, and from seven to eighteen inches in length. They are rather firm and withstand a fair amount of buffeting by nets once they are well rooted. As their roots are eventually quite vigorous, they should be planted in sand about two inches deep. The plant is a comparatively slow grower in the aquarium, but aquarium-grown specimens are best. These are easily distinguished by a large mass of yellowish roots, whereas those grown in ponds have fewer, shorter, and white roots. It takes about a year to get pond-grown plants acclimated to the aquarium.

*Sagittaria natans.* This is the original Sagittaria of the aquarium and was at one time very popular, especially in the early days of the fancy Goldfish. In the Goldfish tank it was largely replaced by *Sagittaria gigantea* which was better for that purpose. Since the advent of "tropicals" it has again come into its own, for it has advantages that make it welcome in the small aquarium. The main point is that it does not grow very long and, therefore, does not easily get into a tangle. The six- to twelve-inch leaves are tough and the plant is a very good oxygenator.

*Sagittaria species (Probably S. subulata)*

*Sagittaria subulata.* This is a species that has become very popular in recent years. It is different from the two foregoing kinds in two respects: the leaves are narrower and thicker, they are straighter and of a darker green. Under favorable conditions this plant propagates rapidly. The leaves are from five to ten inches long and are rather wiry.

**Hygrophila polysperma.
Young Cuttings**

While not quite as beautiful or as long as Vallisneria, we believe, all things considered, it is the most valuable plant for use in the average household aquarium. Among its other merits, it is long-lived.

**"Micro" Sagittaria**

A vigorous two-inch *Sagittaria* "microfolia" has its appropriate uses.

All these truly aquatic species of Sagittaria throw up summer stalks which develop long, lance-like leaves above the water. Flower stems bear trusses of pretty cup-shaped white flowers with a yellow ball in the center. Sagittaria and Vallisneria are rivals. They seldom prosper together.

## Hygrophila polysperma

This popular and comparatively new addition to aquarium plants is one of the most important. It adapts remarkably well to a wide variety of conditions, especially to weak light either natural or artificial. Propagates easily from rooted cuttings. It is the only aquatic member of an otherwise terrestrial genus. Introduced from India to aquarists through the late Joe Johannigman, Jr.

**Temple Plant (Nomaphila stricta),
a close relative of H. polysperma, but
not as easily grown.**

## Cabomba

### (*Washington Plant, Fanwort, Watershield*)

While we by no means claim this to be the best of aquarium plants, it is most largely sold and has its good points. It fell out of fashion in the Goldfish aquarium because it is brittle and those husky fishes picked it to pieces. Very few exotics munch on plants and that objection to *Cabomba* is thus removed. Certainly when in good condition, it is one of the brightest and most beautiful of aquarium plants. It is used chiefly for its attractiveness and for

*Milfoil, or Foxtail (Myriophyllum species)*

*Cabomba (Cabomba caroliniana)*

the fact that it is always in supply.
The fan-shaped, light-green leaves on a running stem form good refuge for young fishes, but they are not sufficiently dense to make a satisfactory spawning plant. *Cabomba* is apt to become long and stringy unless kept in a strong light.

## Myriophyllum

### (Water Milfoil)

A plant of delicate beauty, its fine leaves make a perfect maze for catching the adhesive eggs of egg-dropping fishes or a wonderful refuge for newly hatched fish babies. Broken or cut-off bits of its feathery leaves precisely suit the needs of those fishes which entwine a bit of such material into their nests (Dwarf Gouramies, for example). It is beautiful in the aquarium but requires strong light to avoid becoming thin and leggy. Long a popular

favorite, it is generally in good supply. Rinsing well under a tap of water removes most of the possible fish enemies from wild stock.

Sold bunched, it should be separated unless used as a spawn-receiver.

## Anacharis

### (Elodea, Ditch Moss)

Early dealers claimed that *Anacharis* was the best of oxygenators. This was generally accepted and has become something of a tradition, although the claim is open to question. It is probably based on the undoubted fact that it is the most rapid-growing of all aquarium plants—an inch a day for a long strand is not unusual. However, growth and oxygenating power bear little, if any, relationship to each other. Rapid stem growth occurs in poor light, producing plants lacking vigor.

It is the author's observation that *Anacharis* is only at its best in outdoor ponds that are partially protected from the full light of the sun. In the aquarium it gradually becomes stringy and pale. Some aquarists claim that a good supply of it clears green water.

*Pool-grown Anacharis, left & Aquarium grown Anacharis (Elodea (Egeria) densa), right*

## Ceratophyllum

Ceratophyllum, or Hornwort, has a decided beauty that would make it one of our standard aquarium plants, but for two fatal faults. It is brittle and it has no roots. It is like a thinned-out Myriophyllum. Placed in a concrete pool in summer, where it will receive about three hours of sunshine per day, it grows in magnificent scrolls floating just below the surface. It is excellent in breeding and rearing tanks which generally contain no gravel.

## Ambulia

This plant roughly resembles *Cabomba,* but is a little smaller, is a lighter shade of green, and does better in the aquarium. The life-like drawings of sections of the two plants show the difference in leaf formation and arrangement. The alternating pairs of fan-like leaves

*Hornwort (Ceratophyllum demersum)*

*Ambulia*          *Cabomba*

*Ambulia (Limnophila sessiliflora)*

of *Cabomba* form only a semi circle, the cylindrical effect of the plant being produced by the next and opposite pair. *Ambulia* completes its leafy circle from one point.

Imported from India in 1932, *Ambulia* has grown steadily in favor and as it easily multiplies from cuttings, it seems sure to join the surprisingly small circle of best sellers. Sold bunched. Separate the strands when planting.

Correct name, *Limnophila*.

## Water Sprite

### (*Ceratopteris thalictroides*)

Possibly dependent on the species, the leaves are sometimes much broader than shown here, although we have seen both broad and narrow leaves on the same plant. The genus occurs in the tropics around the world and is most variable.

If left to itself and untrimmed, it spreads to the surface where the baby plants, formed on the old leaves, assume the floating form. In a warm moist atmosphere, they pile up into veritable islands.

*Water Sprite (Ceratopteris thalictroides)*

Another peculiarity is the stiff, narrow, aerial leaves that adult submerged specimens sometimes produce. With age the parent plant becomes soft and should be replaced. Snails attack soft plants.

## Amazon Sword Plant

### (*Echinodorus species*)

The *Amazon Swordplant* seems to be nature's special gift to aquarists as a centerpiece for a fifteen to twenty-nine gallon tank or it will suitably colonize a more massive container with a family of giants. Runners from the crown (a king's crown indeed) are free and far reaching. Press runners into sand at points where new plants develop. Do not cut them off until well started.

Several other aquatics with large leaves have long stems making them rather rangy, but the Sword Plant has short stems that give a compact sturdy effect. When the plant appeared here in 1937 it was a truly valuable acquisition for the artistic aquarist. It is now well established.

It likes a good but not powerful light. A moderate amount of daylight suits it very well.

## Melon Swordplant

Here we have a recent introduction of great merit having a marked individual character and unusual toughness of texture.

It reproduces in the same manner as the other members of the family.

Comparatively slow of propagation, it took some time to build a commercial supply. That desired end has now been reached and while not widely offered, it is not difficult to secure from leading specialists.

Some aquarists rank it as the handsomest of the Swordplants.

*Amazon Swordplant (Echinodorus species)*

*Melon Swordplant*

*Pigmy Chain Swordplant*

## Pigmy Chain Swordplant

This plant, one of the latest introductions among the numerous *Echinodorus* family, has several points of value. It is a first-class addition to the low-growing plants of which we have few. It only reaches from three to four inches in height according to conditions.

Reproduction from runners is rapid. In a big aquarium it virtually carpets the floor in a few months. Runners should be pressed just below the surface of the soil.

Perhaps its greatest value is in small tanks (one to five gallons), as there are few rooted plants that do not get too tall for them. If used as a centerpiece in a small aquarium the runners should be pinched off, forcing it into a bushy fountain-shaped miniature Swordplant.

It gets along well in subdued daylight or under good electric illumination from a standard reflector over the aquarium.

**Aponogeton undulatum** (incorrectly *A. crispus*) The somewhat translucent leaves of this striking plant look like green swords with rippled edges. Heights, six to eighteen inches, depending on strong or weak light. In the taller plants the leaves do not broaden in proportion, thus making them more strap-like. Mostly grown from seed, but bulbs are often available in pet shops. They have a resting period in December. The plant has a shepherd's crook flower stem above the waterline bearing small white flowers.

## Madagascar Lace-leaf Plant

*(Aponogeton madagascariensis)*

Although the Lace-leaf Plant is one of the earliest used by aquarists, and many rivals have appeared that are really better aquarium plants, this aristocrat somehow continues to be "the classiest" of them all. Its very high price, its slowness of

*Aponogeton undulatum*

*Madagascar Lace Plant (Aponogeton Madagascariensis)*

The plant is tricky, either succeeding or failing for reasons that are not clear. It does well in the alkaline waters of California, but poorly in the acid conditions of New England—yet at the Botanical Gardens of the University of Pennsylvania, it flourished in half-casks of oak, which certainly ought to be acid. It does prefer soft water.

A moderate light is best. New plants occasionally appear at the root. Recently imported bulbs produce good plants.

### Spatterdock

One of the forms of this plant from the southeastern United States makes a striking centerpiece in the aquarium. The large, long leaves are of a delicate translucent, light green. Propagation is from a heavy, trunk-like rootbase called a rhizome. Unfortunately, when broken off, decay may set in and finally

propagation, and its unique beauty easily account for the distinction it maintains. The illustration clearly indicates the peculiar skeleton structure of the leaves. Surprisingly, they are rather tough. The photograph scarcely does the plant justice.

destroy the rhizome. The break heals better if planted in soil.

Seedlings from northern Spatterdocks produce smaller plants with much more rounded leaves. While the parent stocks of most of those seedlings have aerial leaves which are seen by the millions along the edges of rivers, they seldom, if ever, become sufficiently robust in the aquarium to reach that stage of development. Usually they are pretty little submerged plants not over six inches in height.

## Dwarf Lily

A new dwarf lily from Southeast Asia has been introduced under the name of *Nymphea stellata*. It is a hardy, fast-growing plant, but has not bloomed under aquarium conditions so far.

## Cryptocoryne

Cryptocoryne, long-lived Asiatic plants, were once rarities, but their valuable special uses together with intensified commercial production have brought them into popular demand and fairly good supply. Besides an attractive individuality different from all other true aquatics, they have the great merit of thriving in situations where the light is rather weak. This obliging characteristic should not be pushed too far. They come from well-shaded jungle streams, but need a reasonably strong diffused light. Where an aquarium contains a variety of plants, it may not be possible to give all of them light ideally suited to their natures. With Cryptocorynes in the picture, it is well to place them out of the full glare of strong light.

*Cape Fear Spatterdock (Nuphar sagittifolium)*

*Dwarf Lily (Nymphaea stellata)*

While there is fascination (especially among beginners) about decorating aquariums with a wide variety of plants, there is also a simple, pleasing, and, perhaps, more successful scheme in which only one or, at most, two kinds are used in one tank. Cryptocorynes adapt themselves well to this treatment. They are all long-lived.

*One of the Many Cryptocoryne Species (probably C. wendti)*

## Hair Grass

Growing along the edges of many ponds and streams in the eastern and southern parts of North America are short, hair-like grasses suited to aquarium culture. The majority of them propagate from runners, but the one shown here divides on the leaves and sends down rootlets.

Plants of this character offer not only interesting variety in contrast with other aquarium vegetation, but also make perfect thickets for harboring baby fishes finding themselves in a dangerous world.

*Cryptocoryne affinis*

## Ludwigia

Ludwigia is not a true aquatic, but a bog plant which does fairly well under water. It never completely forgets its habit of having some leaves above the waterline. There are about twenty-five species in North America usually growing at the shallow edges of ponds and streams. Ludwigia is somewhat similar to Watercress, but, unlike that plant, it does not require cool water. A very beautiful red strain of this species is cultivated in Florida where conditions exactly suit it, but elsewhere it soon loses most of its peculiar character.

For best results Ludwigia should be rooted in earth and placed in

*Eleocharis vivipara*

strong light. Otherwise the leaves drop prematurely. It is easily propagated from end cuttings. Nurserymen stick these in small pots containing earth and a top layer of sand. This is not done under water, but on trays of saturated sand or ashes. As soon as growth starts, the pot may be placed in the aquarium—this is a most satisfactory method.

**Ludwigia species**
*A bog or semi-aquatic plant, long used by aquarists.*

**Cardamine lyrata**
*A beautiful light-green plant from northern Europe and America.*

**Moneywort (Lysimachia nummularia)**
*A common creeping terrestrial, sold in quantity to aquarists. Does fairly well under water.*

**Baby Tears**
*Often used by florists in moist terraria. Submerged, its tiny, light-green leaves make a novel and pleasing effect.*

*Willow Moss*
*(Fontinalis gracilis)*

## Fontinalis or Willowmoss

A dark green plant, native to small, cool, clear swift streams. Usually attached to a stone or a bit of water-logged wood, it does moderately well in the aquarium, especially if settlings are regularly knocked off or the whole plant rinsed. The small leaves on a firm stem in nature conceal an infinite variety of tiny crustacea, etc., mostly fishfoods. Useful as a spawn receiver, especially for fishes breeding near the bottom. Some dealers carry it.

## Najas

*Najas species*

Aquarists receiving shipments of plants from our southern states sometimes find masses of the above used as packing material. Of a pleasant translucent green color, like a small Potamogeton. Grows into masses useful to fish breeders. It may take hold in a pool with soil bottom. Grows wild from Florida to Labrador.

*Nitella flexilis*

*Riccia fluitans*

## Nitella

This is one of our native plants, distributed largely throughout temperate North America. There are several species closely resembling this one, which is *N. gracilis*. It is interesting in several ways. Classified for years as one of the algae, there is now considerable doubt on this point.

It has a great deal of sap for so slender a plant, and through its beautiful, translucent, pale green walls the flow of protoplasm is easily seen with the aid of a microscope of moderate power. Used extensively in classrooms and for scientific research. There are no roots.

Young live-bearers among a loose mass of Nitella nearly filling an aquarium need no other protection from hungry parents.

Some fishes, especially *Scatophagus,* greedily eat large amounts of it.

Growth in a sunny situation (in neutral to alkaline water) is rapid.

## Floating Plants

### Riccia

To the breeder of aquarium fishes, Riccia is one of the most valuable plants. Its green, crystal-like formation produces masses which are compact enough to catch and hold the spawn of the surface egg-layers, yet open enough for new baby live-bearing species to use as a perfect refuge. When it is desirable to produce top shade in an aquarium, we can depend upon Riccia to do it in any desired degree.

For some aquarists it grows tremendously, but the surplus never should be thrown away as there are always those in need of it. When a mass grows over an inch thick so that the sun can not force light through it, a thinning is necessary so it will not turn yellow and soft and pollute the water.

Under the influence of sun these little plants are enormous oxygenators. Large bubbles of that precious gas become imprisoned among the massed leaves and stay there until absorbed by the water. This takes several hours and favorably affects the fishes long after sunset.

The great enemies of Riccia are algae which get among the leaves and choke it. A plentiful supply of small snails usually keeps it clean. When used for spawning purposes, no snails should be present.

While Riccia is native to the fresh waters of the middle and southern Atlantic States, it appears to grow better in a well-lighted aquarium than it does outdoors. All-day sun seems to shrivel it.

While Riccia naturally floats just below the surface of the water, beautiful effects can be obtained by anchoring small bunches at a depth where they will not be disturbed and where good light penetrates. Under these conditions Riccia develops into gorgeous green masses, even up to six inches across.

There are few fishes that eat Ricca, but *Scatophagus argus* is extremely fond of it. This seems strange as nothing even distantly resembles this plant in its native salt and brackish waters.

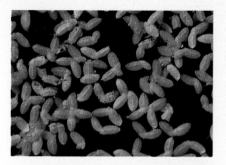

*Duckweed (Lemna minor)*

*Water Lettuce (Pistia stratiotes)*

## Duckweed

A despised pest in Daphnia ponds, but not without its use in the aquarium. Some fishes like to eat it and it is a good producer of shade where a tank gets too much top light. No fear need be entertained about introducing it in aquariums where it can be kept under control, but in large containers and lily pools it is apt to gain too much headway and getting rid of it proves difficult. A native plant of almost universal distribution. For so small a floating leaf it develops quite long roots if they are not nibbled by fishes. Dried Duckweed is a good producer of infusoria.

*Salvinia species*

## Water Lettuce

A beautiful floating plant about four inches in diameter, having fluted, velvety, light green leaves and long roots. Requires warm, moist atmosphere and diffused light.

Propagation is by runners. Does exceptionally well in shallow water (three to five inches) with roots dragging in earthy soil.

# Planting

### Sand or Pebbles?

Coarse sand is best, or a mixture of sand and small pebbles, such as Jersey gravel. Washed building sand is satisfactory. Fine sand packs too hard for the roots to penetrate easily and allows no beneficial circulation of water.

Pebbles, stones, shells, or marbles alone are bad because they have open spaces which catch and hold fishfood where no scavengers can reach, thus causing the water to turn foul. Large and small stones, well selected, may be very ornamental and natural in an aquarium, but they should be set in sand for the reason given.

### Depth of Sand

This is a more important subject than is generally recognized. The planting medium should be only deep enough to be certain of holding down the rooted plants. Vallisneria and the smaller Sagittarias need only about 1½ inches, while Giant Sagittaria requires two inches or more. It is a good plan to root the larger plants in deeper sand in the back of the aquarium and then let the level slope lower towards the front. This serves the double purpose of giving the smaller plants a place in the light and of working the aquarium sediment forward where it is more easily removed. Some aquarists place a glass bar or other stop about an inch wide between the front edge of the sand and the front glass of the aquarium, making an inch trench the entire length. An excellent dirt trap. The stop may also be made of well selected small stones placed in the form of a semicircle.

### Use Earth?

No. Theoretically it might be a good idea to provide soil substance in the form of a sub-stratum for plants, but in practice it does not work out well. It is apt to become foul and any accidental stirring clouds up the aquarium. Besides, we expect the plants to get their sustenance by absorbing the waste products of the fishes. This they do. Professional growers use garden soil below the sand. Some earth benefits potted aquarium plants.

### How to Plant

Enough has been said as to the characteristics of available plants for the aquarium, so that here we are concerned with the mechanics of the job.

The first thing is to make sure that the plants are kept moist while the work is being carefully done. A half-drying may set them back for weeks. If they are laid in water or covered with a wet newspaper, there will be no danger.

The water in the aquarium should be about five or six inches deep while most of the work is being done. If the sand is fairly clean, the water can be kept clear by placing a piece of paper over it while filling. Pour on the paper. When rockwork is to be used, it should be placed before the plants are set. The only real difficulty is in arranging the grasses that have spreading roots, but it is not very troublesome when the water is shallow. Spread the roots of Sagittaria and Vallisneria as widely as possible and cover them well with sand, be careful not to bury the leaves. If there are tall, stiff leaves, partly in the air, be sure to sprinkle them often during the balance of the work. Sometimes a large plant is so buoyant that it is necessary to place a small stone or two on the sand over the roots, or to wrap the base of the plant with a plant weight. Each rooted plant like Sagittaria or Vallisneria should have sufficient space so that there will be room for new runners to expand.

The smaller plants and those with long strands like Anacharis should be placed last. Old yellowish leaves should be removed before planting.

### Planting sticks

If plants must be added after the aquarium is filled, or if any of them ride up, a planting stick is most useful. Many algae scrapers are designed for use as planting sticks. The end of the handle is notched which makes them very handy tools.

### Bunched Plants

Plants in wired bundles look very attractive and one is tempted to plant them in the way they are received. They never grow that way naturally and should not be planted in that way. Stemmed plants, like *Anacharis, Cabomba,* and *Myriophyllum,* ought to be slightly separated so that water and light may pass between the stems at the base.

### Fertilizing Plants

This is a "noble experiment," but a dangerous one. It belongs in the same category as placing a layer of soil under the sand, only it is a few degrees more dangerous. It has been proven many times that *fish fertilize plants.* If there are enough fish present, the combined effects of their breathing and their droppings give the plants all the chemical stimulation they need. The author

has seen many well-planted aquariums degenerate without the presence of fish life, and to revive beautifully upon the reintroduction of fishes. However, if any readers feel that their plants are in need of added stimulation, any of the plant foods available in pet shops can be tried. These fertilizers were developed especially for aquarium plants.

### Selecting Plants

As in other branches of horticulture, it is best to select young or half-grown plants rather than fully developed specimens that have arrived at the zenith of perfection. The young adapt themselves better and last longer. Avoid plants covered with algae or "moss." It chokes the plants and spreads through the aquarium.

### Cleaning Plants

It is, of course, desirable to have new plants free of germs and "bugs." Any known treatment fully accomplishing this would sicken or kill the plants. New plants should first be rinsed and then placed for a day in a shallow, white tray for observation. Perhaps some unwanted snails or leeches will appear, although inspection of the tanks is necessary to detect snail eggs which look like small gelatinous clumps filled with numerous poppy seed sized eggs. Plants like Vallisneria, Sagittaria, Swordplants, and Crytocorynes are often infested with egg cases of certain leeches. These are light brown, oval shaped, about 1/4 inch long and are often attached at the base of the leaves near the roots. Both snail eggs and the egg cases should be removed by gently scraping the leaves with a dull knife.

# CLASSIFICATION OF FISHES

The pleasure of aquarium study can be doubled by organizing it. The following explanation has been prepared in the hope that it will clear up, in the beginning, a number of simple facts that aquarists ought to know. These are facts that have not previously been reduced in plain enough terms for popular use; here they are brought together within the compass of a few pages.

These pages may be skipped without regret (but not without loss) by those who are science-shy.

Anyone who is familiar with the ordinary run of aquarium fishes, if asked whether the Red Tetra from Rio is a Characin or a Cichlid, will not hesitate to say it is a Characin. But if you ask him why, he is likely to tell you that it is similar to other Characins, that it has an adipose fin— and stop right there. Very probably he has never considered what other differences there are between a Cichlid and a Characin; *he has learned to recognize the two families by sight* without attempting to analyze the whys and wherefores. In this particular he is just like the professional ichthyologist who can place most fishes in their proper families by sight, without recourse to books.

There is more to the subject than this, however, and since we have decided to present, for the first time, the different families of aquarium fishes in their correct ichthyological order-of-precedence, a brief explanation of why this has been done should prove helpful.

## Identification by Anatomy

Under each family heading throughout the book there are a few sentences calling attention to some of the external features that will help the aquarist recognize a member of that group. To understand *why* the families are placed in the order in which they stand, something else is required. This is supplied by the bird's-eye-view of fish classification given in this chapter. Before this classification or the notes under the families can become intelligible, we must learn a few simple names for certain parts of a fish's anatomy, especially the fins. Every aquarist ought to be familiar with these few terms, for they are used continually in describing the form and color of all fishes.

The great majority of fishes have seven fins. Of these seven, four are *paired*, that is, there is one on each side of the body opposite its mate. The first or forward paired fins are the *pectoral* or *breast fins,* one on each side of the body just behind the head. These correspond to the forelegs of land animals or the arms of a human being. The second paired fins are the *ventral* or *pelvic fins,* placed close beside each other on the underside of the fish, either before, directly below, or behind the pectoral pair. Aquarists frequently misname these the breast fins. The ventral fins correspond to the hind legs of land animals and the legs of man. The remaining three fins are unpaired or single. They are placed exactly on the midline of the fish as viewed from the top or front. The most important of the unpaired fins is the caudal or tail fin. With most fishes it is the caudal fin that provides the chief propelling power in swimming. It may be forked as in most swift-swimming fishes, cut off straight,

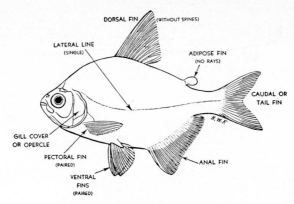

OUTLINE DRAWING OF A CHARACIN
It will be seen that there are no fin spines, and that
the ventral fins are *behind* the pectoral fins.

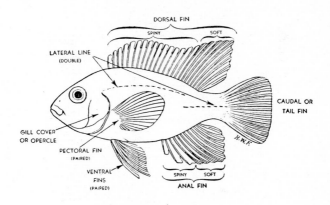

OUTLINE DRAWING OF A CICHLID
Note presence of 2 sets of fin spines, and the forward
position of the ventral fins, *under* the pectoral fins.

rounded at the end, or pointed. On the back of the fish is the dorsal or back fin and on the underside behind the vent is the anal fin.

These fins are formed of a delicate *fin membrane* supported by fairly stiff but jointed *fin rays* that usually branch somewhat as they approach the outer edge of the fin. In certain fishes the front rays of some of the fins are bony, unjointed, and sharp. These bony rays are called *fin spines* and in groups like the Cichlids these spines may make up more than half of the rays of the dorsal and anal fins. In such

cases it is usual to refer to the two parts of the dorsal fin as the *spiny dorsal* and the *soft dorsal*. Fishes that have several spines in the dorsal and anal fins form a group called the *spiny-rayed fishes*. In the Gobies, the Silversides, and some other families, the spiny dorsal has become completely separated from the soft dorsal so that there are two entirely separate dorsal fins, the first spiny, the second soft.

Other fishes, notably most Characins and Catfishes as well as Salmon and Trout, have another small fin on the back. It is behind the dorsal and near the tail fin. This, the *adipose fin*, is unlike the other fins in that it is not usually supported by rays, but consists of fatty or adipose tissue. In the Armored Cat-fishes the adipose fin is supported by one stiff spine.

The similarities and differences in these fins as well as in other, mostly internal, characteristics are utilized by ichthyologists to classify fishes. In some groups the teeth are important in classification.

## How Fishes Are Classified and Presented in This Book

All the fishes in this book, with the exception of the Stingray, *Paratrygon,* belong to the great class of bony fishes, Osteichthyes, which is split up into a great number of *orders,* the orders into *families,* the families into *genera* (singular form, *genus*), and the genera into *species.* There are good reasons for this arrangement, and the aquarist who takes a little time in spying out the similarities in his fishes can easily find out much about fish classification for himself.

The order in which the species and families are treated follows rather closely that in which the ichthyologist places fishes. Those families that resemble most closely the primitive types of fishes of by-gone ages, as revealed by the study of fossils, are placed first; the rest are arranged in an ascending order determined by the advancing degree of complexity of their structure. This complexity is shown externally chiefly by the greater number of spines in the dorsal and anal fins and the more forward position of the ventral fins. For instance, a Characin has no spiny dorsal fin and there are never any spines in the anal fin. Furthermore, the ven-

tral fins are set well back along the belly of the fish. These are relatively "primitive" fishes and belong well towards the beginning of the series. On the other hand, the Cichlids have well-developed spiny dorsal and anal fins and their ventrals are placed well forward, under the pectoral fins. The Cichlids are highly developed "spiny-rayed" fishes. The Killifishes (egg-laying tooth-carps) and *Poeciliidae* (live-bearing tooth-carps) are about midway between the Characins and the Cichlids in their make-up. They have not developed any spines in their fins, but their mouth structure and other points show that they are measurably nearer the end of the series than are the Characins.

We now proceed with a few notes on the orders, in which the families in this book are placed.

The Herring-like fishes (order *Clupeiformes)* are "primitive" bony fishes, lacking fin spines, and having the ventral fins well back. Only a few species are included in this book: the Butterfly-fish, *Pantodon;* the Arowana, *Osteoglossum bicirrhosum;* the Feather-backs, *Notopterus;* and the Elephant-nosed fish, *Gnathonemus.*

The true freshwater fishes (order *Cypriniformes)* include probably three-fourths of all freshwater fishes throughout the world. The Characins, the South American Gymnotid Eels, the Carps and Minnows, the Loaches, and the Catfishes all belong to this order. As a group they resemble the Herring-like fishes. They differ from them and from all other fishes, however, since they have a complicated series of bones (the Weberian ossicles) that connect the air bladder with the inner ear. The exact function of this complex organ is not known with certainty, but it is probably of use as an accessory organ of hearing or in detecting differences in water pressure.

The egg-laying Killifishes and live-bearing *Poeciliidae,* together with some lesser families, are placed in the order *Cyprinodontiformes,* generally known as the Cyprinodonts. These are much like the *Beloniformes* in the fins, but differ in the mouth and other points.

The order *Perciformes,* or Perchlike fishes, includes the majority of spiny-rayed fishes. Among our aquarium fishes, the Cichlids, the Perches, the Sunfishes, the Theraponids, the Nandids, the Monodactylids, the Archer Fishes, and the "Scats" all belong here. All of them have well-developed spiny dorsal and anal fins and ventral fins placed forward under the pectorals.

The Labyrinth fishes are now usually placed with the above families in the *Perciformes,* but are often relegated to a suborder *(Anabantoidei).* They differ in having a chamber above the gills with which they breathe atmospheric air. They are Old World freshwater fishes.

Another group often separated from the *Perciformes* but usually included in that group as a suborder *(Gobioidei)* are the Gobies. This suborder includes the true Gobies and the Eleotrids or Sleeper Gobies, and a few little-known families, peculiar fishes found on the coasts of all the continents. A few inhabit fresh water. The spiny and soft dorsal fins are separate, giving the appearance of a double dorsal; the ventrals are far forward, either set very close together or united into a sucking disk.

The order *Mastacembeliformes,* or Spiny Eels, includes elongated, long-snouted freshwater fishes of the Old World with a great many free spines in front of the dorsal. The only fish in the book belonging to this order is *Mastacembelus.*

Finally, we have the order *Tetraodontiformes* which includes the Puffers and Trigger-fishes. Many of them have the teeth fused together into a beak with which they can give a bad nip. Nearly all are saltwater fishes, but a few of the smaller puffers come up into freshwater streams. A few are used as aquarium fishes.

*Using Scientific Names*

If the reader has scanned the foregoing with care, he will see at once that the terms "order," "family," "genus," and "species," all mean something definite in fish classification. The term "family" is the one most frequently misused by aquarists. We see many references to the "Panchax family," the "egg-laying family" or the "live-bearing family." Such uses of the term family have no meaning and will not be followed by the careful aquarist. Instead of the *"Barbus* family" one should say the "genus *Barbus"* (which belongs to the Carp family). Further, all live-bearers do not belong to one family.

The first word in the name of a fish is the genus to which it belongs. The second word is the species and ordinarily is the last subdivision. However, at times a less important peculiarity is taken into account and made into a subspecies, race, or variety: *Xiphophorus maculatus, var. ruber,* for instance. "Variety" should never be used in any other sense. It is always *within* a species.

When no specific name is given a fish, but the word "species" is used, it means that we know the genus to which it belongs, but not the species. An example would be *"Corydoras species"* or *"spec.,"* as it is often written.

It should also be noted that the singular of species is species, not "specie." The plural of genus is genera.

Sometimes after a fish has just been referred to by its full scientific name, the generic name is abbreviated on following repetitions, such as *Scatophagus argus* being repeated as *S. argus.*

## Changes in Scientific Names

Changes in scientific names present a constant problem to the scientist and aquarist. We can only say on this point that names do change in accordance with the progress of ichthyological research. The chief source of confusion has been the hurry and carelessness of some aquarists in sticking any name on a newly imported fish before it has been carefully identified. Later study usually shows such names to be erroneous. Often modern research has made changes necessary, but when the job has been done

well, we may expect relative permanence before a particular group is again subjected to revision.

## Names of People Discovering Species

In the main heading for each fish the name of the scientist who first described it is given. This is in accord with universal practice. There is one point in connection with this that is not always understood. It will be noticed that sometimes this name is in parentheses. This means that there have been developments since the original naming which require that the fish be moved into some other genus (the first name) instead of that in which it was originally placed. When this is done, the original describer is retained, but his name is placed in parentheses.

Aquarists wishing to have rare or other fishes identified should preserve them in rubbing alcohol. Send them to some large scientific institution with a department of fishes; and give the location from which they were collected, as nearly as possible.

# FISHES

All fishes in this book are arranged in family groups. At the start of each family its general characteristics and breeding habits, when known are described. These are not usually repeated for the species comprising the group because most of them follow the same life pattern. Special traits, if any, of species, however, are covered on their individual pages.

## THE STINGRAYS

### Family Dasyatidae

Most stingrays are strictly marine fishes, but a few enter the brackish water of estuarine river systems. As far as we know, only two species exist in freshwater. Both are found in South America and are occasionally imported. They are often difficult to keep in an aquarium, but once acclimated, make very interesting objects to study.

### *Paratrygon species*

*Popular name:* Freshwater Stingray

*Length:* to 15 inches

Northern and Central South America

Stingrays are fascinating fishes, but they need an aquarium properly set up for their mode of life. A large aquarium of at least 30 inches in length and 12 inches in width is necessary. Instead of coarse gravel, a layer of sand should be used, since rays spend much time resting on the bottom half buried in sand. But, they also need plenty of swimming space. While lying on the bottom, they breathe through special openings, called spiracles, which are equipped with valves and are located on the upper side of the head, just behind the eyes. This is a marvelous adaptation, since normal breathing through the mouth would inevitably result in sand and other foreign

*Paratrygon species*

matter to be inhaled and irritate the gills.

Their feeding habits are equally interesting. Although newly acquired specimens are often very reluctant feeders, hardly any can resist the temptation of a meal of live ghost or grass shrimps. These shrimps are often sold as scavengers in pet shops. If live shrimps are not available, frozen ones often are and should be tried instead. Rays capture their prey by literally "pouncing" on it with the whole body. Once they are feeding well on their preferred food, other, more readily available foods can be substituted. Earthworms, bloodworms, tubifex worms and pieces of fish and shrimp are among the most likely foods to be accepted. Temperature, 72° to 82°.

# THE BICHIRS

## Family Polypteridae

The Bichirs are a small family of primitive African fishes. All are carnivorous and, with the exception of the reedfish, *Calamoichthys,* are better kept with fishes of their own size. Few species of *Polypterus* are imported, but *Calamoichthys* is usually available. None of the Bichirs have been bred in captivity.

### Calamoichthys calabaricus
(SMITH)

*Popular name:* African Reedfish, Rope Fish

*Meaning of name:* Calamoichthys, reed-like fish; calabaricus, from Calabar

*Length:* about 20 inches

Western Africa

The dorsal fin of this odd-looking fish consists of a series of small, one-rayed finlets set about one-half inch apart and starting about midway between head and tail. The scales are quite prominent, hard, and rhomboid in shape. They are fairly quiet fishes and only occasionally swim about with eel-like motions. They do not bury themselves as true eels sometimes do and, therefore, do not dislodge plants. Food is hunted at the bottom. Pieces of fish, beef heart, shrimp, tubifex worms, frozen, adult brine shrimp; and live or frozen blood worms are some of the foods they will take. Dried foods are not accepted. Smaller fish are safe with them. Though they are sluggish fish, their tank should be covered; when frightened, especially at first introduction to the tank, they are quite nervous and many a Reedfish has met its untimely death by slipping out of the tank unnoticed.

Reedfishes have gills like other fishes, but also possess lungs of sorts. These enable them to survive in fairly stagnant water by occasionally taking gulps of atmospheric air. The fish has not been bred in captivity, but secondary sex characteristics are present, the male showing a peculiar thickness in the anal fin. Temperature, 75° to 82°.

### *Polypterus species*

*Popular name:* Bichir

*Meaning of Name:* Polypterus, with many fins

*Length:* 15 inches

Central Africa

A rather secretive fish which should be provided with adequate hiding places. Once acclimated to

*Calamoichthys calabaricus*

*Polypterus spec.*

aquarium conditions, looses much of its original shyness. Bichirs have large mouths, and cannot be trusted with fishes of platy size and smaller. The fish prefers to feed near the bottom on small earthworms, blood worms, brine shrimp and other larger types of live food. Rarely accepts prepared food. Temp. 72° to 85°.

## THE FEATHERBACKS
## Family Notopteridae

This is a small, specialized family of fishes widely distributed throughout Southeast Asia and Africa. The small, featherlike dorsal fin is characteristic of the family, although in one species, *Xenomystus nigri,* the fin is absent. All have a long anal fin which is continuous with the small tail.

Wavy motions of this fin can propel them forward as well as backward.

### *Notopterus chitala*
(BUCHANAN-HAMILTON)

*Popular name:* Featherback Knife Fish, Clown Knife Fish

*Meaning of name:* Notopterus, with feather-like fin; chitala, a native name

*Length:* Up to about 30 inches in nature

Southeast Asia, India

Featherbacks spend most of their time in the lower half of the tank, although they rise to the surface periodically for a gulp of atmospheric air. They are omniverous when young, but usually change to a diet of live fish and shrimp as they mature. Among themselves they are somewhat quarrelsome, but are peaceful towards other fishes of comparable size. Only the large specimens have to be kept alone in a tank.

They are not bred in the aquarium. In the wild, eggs are deposited on smooth, hard surfaces, such as stones or logs, and are guarded by the males. There is no apparent sexual dimorphism. Temperature, 72° to 85°.

*Notopterus chitala*

## *Xenomystus nigri*

GUENTHER

*Popular name:* African Knife Fish

*Meaning of name:* Xenomystus, with strange mustache; nigri, black

*Length:* about 8 inches

West and Central Africa

Although these fishes resemble the South American Knife Fishes in form and finnage, they are not at all related to them. Their mode of locomotion is much more eel-like, and their bodies appear to be more flexible than the somewhat rigid body of the South American Knife Fishes. In the aquarium, they move about at a fairly sluggish pace.

They are generally peaceful towards other fishes, but often quarrelsome among themselves and, therefore, should be kept in large tanks. Various live and frozen foods should be offered; dried foods are only reluctantly eaten. One should provide sufficient hiding places for these Knife Fishes, not because they like to stay hidden most of the time, but because they are much more at home in such an environment. Occasionally they surface to take gulps of air.

The fishes have no known secondary sex characteristics, and no information exists about their breeding habits.

Temperature, 70° to 82°.

## THE BONY-TONGUES

## Family Osteoglossidae

Only five species of this ancient family of herring-like freshwater fishes still exist: *Scleropages leichardti* in Queensland, Australia,

*Xenomystus nigri*

and New Guinea; *S. formosus* in S. E. Asia, Borneo and Sumatra; *Clupisudis niloticus* in tropical Africa; and three in northern South America: *Arapaima gigas, Osteoglossum bicirrhosum,* and *O. ferreira.* All grow to two feet or more in length, the Pirarucú of the Amazon (*Arapaima*) growing to about eight feet. All are voracious and have sharp teeth, all have notably large scales, and all seem to be mouthbrooders.

***Black Arowana (Osteoglossum ferreira)***

## *Osteoglossum bicirrhosum*
### (VANDELLI) SPIX AND AGASSIZ

*Popular name:* Aruana or Arowana

*Meaning of name:* Osteoglossum, bony tongue, bicirrhosum, with two cirri or barbels

*Length:* To over 3 feet

Amazon River and Guyana

Young Aruana are sometimes imported and make interesting and striking aquarium pets if kept alone or with fishes too large to be swallowed by their capacious mouths. They are probably the most graceful, smooth-flowing swimmers of our aquarium fishes. The two forward-projecting barbels which are leaf-like though narrow, the large alert eyes, and the continuous graceful motion make this fish unique. The Aruana likes live food and pre-

*Osteoglossum bicirrhosum*

*Arapaima gigas*

fers to take it off the surface. Most of the time, young three- to four-inch specimens that have just absorbed their yolk sacks are imported. Small insects (flies, etc.); mosquito larvae; and live, adult brine shrimp are the foods most likely to be accepted in the beginning. Later, meal worms can be offered as well as lumps of freeze-dried brine shrimp, for which some specimens develop a particular liking. Temperature, 75° to 80°.

## *Arapaima gigas*      CUVIER

*Meaning of name:* Gigas, giant like

*Length:* Up to 8 feet

Northern and Central South America

As is obvious from the adult size of this fish, only very young individuals can be kept in the average home aquarium. They are seldom imported, and command a high price. Young Arapaimas are very active, extremely graceful swimmers, spending much time in mid-water. Occasionally, they take a gulp of air. They feed almost exclusively on live fishes. Arapaimas that outgrow a hobbyist's tank should be donated to the nearest public aquarium. There they will be much appreciated since they make excellent show fishes. Temperature 70° to 82°.

## THE AFRICAN FRESHWATER FLYING FISH

### FAMILY PANTODONTIDAE

This family includes only one species, the Butterfly-fish of the aquarist, which comes from West Africa. Its nearest relatives are the members of the Osteoglossidae, a family of large fishes, which includes the Arapaima of the Amazon, one of the largest of freshwater

*Pantodon buchholzi*

fishes. The chief distinguishing features of *Pantodon* lie in the teeth and certain peculiarities in the skeleton.

### *Pantodon buchholzi*     PETERS

*Popular name:* Butterfly-fish

*Meaning of name:* Pantodon, with teeth everywhere (in the mouth); buchholzi, after the naturalist, Buchholz

*Length:* 5 inches

West Africa

No finely drawn description of this bizarre fish is needed to help the reader single it out from close relatives, for it has none. However, when we see the picture of so extraordinary a fish, we wish to know something of its peculiarities and the uses for its fantastic fins.

In reality, this is a freshwater flying fish, the immense pectoral fins being even larger and more ex-tended than a side illustration can show. The fish spends much time at the surface of the water, and is said to skim along it for at least six feet at a leap.

The fish is strictly a surface feeder and can be trained to take food from the finger, such as chunks of freeze-dried brine shrimp; strips of lean, raw beef; meal worms; inch-long live fish; or bigger earth worms.

Breeding Butterfly-fish is a rare achievement. Males are slimmer and have bigger "wings" in proportion, also longer anal fins. Very large floating eggs hatch in a week at 75°. Young look like little tadpoles. They remain at the surface, therefore, must have newly hatched mosquito larvae or else a sufficiently large supply of food, like smallest, sifted daphnia so that much of it reaches the top of the water. Lowering the water level about two inches helps to bring the baby fish and food together. The young can presently be weaned to taking some dry food that floats. The species is naturally long-lived, but often comes to an untimely end by leaping out when a forgetful aquarist fails to quickly replace the cover on the tank (which should be fifteen gallon size or larger). They snatch and swallow small surface fishes that come too close.

*Gnathonemus petersi*

## THE MORMYRIDS OR ELEPHANT-FISHES

### FAMILY MORMYRIDAE

These curious-looking freshwater fishes are found only in tropical Africa. Some kinds have the jaws short and blunt, some have the lower lip extended, while others have a long, down-curved snout. All have weak electric organs, probably used as an alert system against potential aggressors. Finally, they have the largest brain for their size of any known fishes. Several species have been imported since 1954, of which perhaps the best known is the following.

### *Gnathonemus petersi* GUENTHER

*Meaning of name:* Gnathonemus: jaw-thread; petersi for Dr. Wilhelm Peters, Berlin zoologist

*Length:* Up to 9 inches

Niger River to Congo River

Although this odd-appearing fish has a rather stiff body and often remains still, it is nervous and is capable of rapid movement. Should be kept in a large, well-planted tank. While aggressive toward its own kind, it seems not to kill. The extension of the lower jaw is flexi-ble and has taste buds which are probably used in locating worms in the soil. They take brine shrimp, white worms, or other live foods, eating in a manner similar to other fishes. Breeding habits unknown. Temperature about 75°.

## THE CHARACINS

### FAMILIES CHARACIDAE, ANOSTOMIDAE, GASTERO-PELECIDAE and HEMIODONTIDAE

The Characins form one of the largest families of fishes in the world. They are all from tropical America and Africa, They belong to the great order *Cypriniformes*, together with the Carps and Cat-fishes. Many Characins look much like some species of Carps (*Cyprinidae*), but the aquarist seldom has trouble distinguishing members of the two families. No Carp ever has any teeth in the jaws, or any adipose fin. Most Characins possess both teeth and an adipose fin. Some lack one or the other, but few or no species lack both, and if aquarists will remember this "one-or-the-other" combination, they will seldom be puzzled. The presence of teeth in a small live fish is easily determined by running a pin or needle lightly along the upper jaw of a fish held gently but firmly in a wet cloth or net. (Some Characins have teeth only in the upper jaw.) Internally they differ from the Carps in the bones of the throat. All Characins have scales, except-ing two very rare species from Ar-gentina.

While there is considerable varia-tion in members of the family as to size, shape and habits, ranging from the brilliant little Neon Tetra to the blood-thirsty Piranha, there is usu-ally a suggestion of uniformity that is not hard to discover.

Most of them are fairly hardy, considering that they come from tropical regions.

Generally speaking, they are not fighters, although any fish with good teeth is liable to use them. This sometimes results in a little sly nipping of fins. It takes place so seldom, and without any outward appearance of fighting, that it is hard to detect. On the whole they are peaceful and seldom kill.

## "Tetras"

In those earlier days of the exotic fish hobby, a number of Characins were included in the genus *Tetrago-nopterus,* a generic name still used for a small genus, but under which many of our aquarium fishes used to be placed. It became the trade practice to apply "Tet" or "Tetra" as a blanket name to all Characins, especially the small ones, such as "Tet from Rio," "Lemon Tetra," "Black Tetra," and "Neon Tetra". The name "Tetra" has become well entrenched in popular usage, but has no present scientific standing.

## Care and Breeding

In the matter of food, most Characins are easily pleased with an average fish diet. They appreci-ate variety especially when it tends

towards live foods, but seem to en-joy various freeze dried and frozen foods as well.

Few of them demand special water conditions for their well-be-ing, as long as the water does not become too hard.

In general the Characins do very well in water at from 70 to 75 de-grees, although for breeding, it should, in some instances, be raised to 80.

Very few of the species are easily bred. They offer an interesting chal-lenge to the aquarist in that respect. A number of them yield to skillful handling, yet several of the most desirable species, such as Cardinal Tetras (*Cheirodon axelrodi*), Rum-my-nosed Tetras (H.rhodostomus), Bleeding Heart Tetras (*H.rubro-stigma*), and many of the African species still oblige us to import wild specimens in order to keep up our stocks.

With the few exceptions to be noted, Characins drop adhesive or semi-adhesive eggs, to which they pay no attention, except, perhaps, for the doubtful compliment of eat-ing them. Failing this, they are likely to make up for the oversight by devouring the young. Very few of them fight in defense of their fry, as do the Cichlids and Bubble Nest-builders.

Only fishes in the best physical condition should be used for breed-ing. In many cases it is almost im-possible to distinguish between the sexes unless the fishes are in excel-lent shape.

In general the requirements for breeding the various species of Characins are similar. The aquar-ium should have a reasonable amount of open space, but with thickets of plants having finely di-vided leaves, such as Myriophyllum,

Nitella, Fontinalis or artificial spawning grass. To ensure cleanliness, and for better observation of eggs and fry, no gravel should be used. Water in the breeding tank should be clean, well aged, and possibly a little softer than the water in the aquarium where the prospective breeders are normally kept.

It has been found that some of the species spawn more readily in "soft" water. Indeed it may be hoped that this is the key to unlocking the difficulty of breeding this large and important family of fishes.

Many fishes are more apt to spawn if previously separated a few days from their mates. "Absence makes the heart grow fonder." It is usually best to place the female in the breeding tank a day or two in advance of the male.

If all goes well, spawning will take place the morning after the male has been placed in the breeding tank. If the fishes do not spawn within a few days, try a partial change of water. If that does not stimulate spawning, remove them and try again in a week or two. In the interim, feed rather often with the best foods available.

If the fishes have spawned, remove them immediately.

*The greatest problem in fish culture is the first food.*

Most fishes when hatched are more egg than fish. Some of them seem like a splinter attached sidewise to a ball. Gradually the fish enlarges and develops fins, while the ball contracts until it is a mere lump on the abdomen. It is the yolk sac. So long as it is visible it is nature's reservoir of nourishment. Usually the babies are not much in evidence during this period. Being helpless to avoid enemies, they hover or hop about the bottom. Sac soon absorbed, the fish becomes more streamlined and takes to the open water. It is on its own.

The aquarist's problem right here, and for the next week or two, is to have enough of the right sizes and kinds of food ready. Standard directions say "feed infusoria." Sounds simple enough, and it *is,* if we are lucky. Infusoria covers a multitude of sizes and kinds of organisms. The predominating one in most prepared cultures is Paramecium, which happens to be a fair food. In addition, many other tiny organisms are usually present in such cultures, providing a varied menu.

Having passed the feeding point where infusorians are outgrown, something larger must be found. Newly hatched brine shrimp is the food of choice. For hatching instructions, see the chapter on fish foods. With newly hatched brine shrimp, the youngsters can be raised until big enough to handle the normal food for the species.

Repeatedly it has been found that more youngsters can be brought through early infancy in an oversized, long-established tank. This is no doubt due to its containing more microscopic food of suitable sizes and quality. About the only way to bring through a large proportion of very small fry in a *small* tank is to feed them often on natural pond infusoria. As these organisms appear in usable quantity at unpredictable times, we have here an element of luck. It may be asked why scientific aquarists do not make continuous pure cultures of the best of the live micro-foods. This would indeed solve a problem and at least quadruple the output of fishes. It has been tried, but not successfully. However, it is the observation of experienced breeders that pond infusoria gives much better results than the cultured kinds.

Despite the difficulties considered here, the fact remains that most species of aquarium fishes *are* successfully reared.

*How much* infusoria to feed is an important question that cannot be answered in any exact way. *The bellies of the babies should bulge.* One soon learns to judge this. On the other hand, there ought *not* be *too much* live food present. It depletes oxygen and annoys the fishes. The amount of liquid to feed depends on the richness of the culture and the number of fry. It might be a spoonful or a cupful. A low-power microscope is important here. Examine the culture. It should be rich in life. Use with judgment. A test drop of water taken from the surface of the light side of the aquarium should show plenty of organisms.

Unfortunately it must be recognized that many, many ambitious aquarists are unable to secure even a few Daphnia, nor any good infusoria. By care they can succeed in a lesser degree. As has been mentioned elsewhere, there are fairly good substitutes for Daphnia, such as finely minced White Worms or grated raw shrimp. Some fishes have been reared on prepared dry foods, starting with flour size. Mashed yellow of hard-boiled egg, shaken in a bottle of water, sparingly fed, is an acceptable early food. It is almost impossible not to overfeed with prepared foods, so when using them it is well to have a number of small snails present to consume the surplus, but only after the eggs have hatched.

Inequality in the size of youngsters always puzzles the beginner. None can tell why it is any more than in human beings. Some fishes are no doubt born more vigorous than others. They get "the jump" by bolting the biggest and best food. Presently they become large enough to eat the smallest of their brethren. As these make the best of food, the disproportion increases. It is nature's way. A plentiful early supply of the small live foods tends to equalize growth.

Ordinarily the young should not be placed with their parents or other fishes if there is enough difference in size so that they *might* be eaten!

### *Hyphessobrycon callistus*
BOULENGER

*Popular name:* Serpae Tetra

*Meaning of name:* Hyphessobrycon: little Brycon; callistus, pretty sail, in reference to the dorsal fin. Formerly known as H. serpae

Length: 1½ inches

Parana-Paraguay System

The Serpae Tetra, overall soft red set off by the black of the dorsal fin and shoulder spot, is one of the most beautiful of small aquarium fishes. The black marking on the dorsal fin suggests *Pristella riddlei,* but fins are a little shorter and more intensely red. For those who like their fishes quiet, and restful to contemplate, this species is perfect. They seem to prefer a level about a third of the way up from the bottom, but are always on the alert to dash upward to catch falling food. Adipose fins are transparent.

They were first imported to Germany in 1931 and into the United

*Hyphessobrycon callistus*

States two years later. As they were hard to spawn, they disappeared for some years. We were without them until large fresh importations to the United States in 1948. They are now bred with good success and are usually available. They breed like *Hyphessobrycon flammeus,* but it seems that only a small proportion of females spawn. A charming species, neither timid nor aggressive, and an ornament to any collection of fishes of its own size. They respond well to feedings of "color foods" which intensify the red and are now on the market. Temperature, 70° to 80°.

## *Hyphessobrycon flammeus*

MYERS

*Popular name:* Tetra from Rio, Red Tet, Flame Tetra, and Flame Fish

*Meaning of name:* Hypessobrycon, little Brycon; flammeus, flame-like

*Length:* 1½ inches

Vicinity of Rio de Janeiro

The beauty of a fish by no means depends on bulk. In fact, many aquarists consider the inch-and-a-half length of this Flame Tetra the ideal size at which a fish can be viewed and appreciated. In addition, the Flame Tetra's brilliant color pattern is so simple that nothing is sacrificed to its small size. It is harmless, reasonably hardy, easily cared for, and can be bred—but not so easily as to become uninteresting.

Like many other exotic fishes, *H. flammeus* needs favorable conditions in order to develop its best colors. Plenty of room in a well-planted aquarium, an occasional

*Hyphessobrycon flammeus*

extra meal of Daphnia or other live food, and a temperature of about 75° will soon bring on "show condition."

The sexes may be told in several ways. The males have the Characin hooks on the end of the anal fin which stick to a fine-mesh net when the fish is turned out. The anal fin of the male has a more pronounced black edge, and the female appears fuller in the body outline. Color is not a dependable index.

This species should be bred where at least a part of the aquarium has a thicket of finely divided leaves, such as Myriophyllum. After lively driving by the male, the fishes take a close parallel position among the plants. Accompanied by a little trembling, about ten eggs are dropped and fertilized. This is repeated until 100 or more small, nearly transparent eggs are produced. The eggs are slightly adhesive and they will stick fairly well to the plants if not disturbed. Those that fall may also hatch. The young, kept at a temperature of 75°, appear in three days and are almost as transparent as the eggs. They will feed on infusoria and flour made of ordinary fishfood. Considering the almost microscopic size of the young when hatched, it is surprising to find that they will be two-thirds grown in less than six months when well fed.

When two males are used with a female, a higher percentage of eggs have been found to hatch.

For small fishes they are rather long-lived, attaining a ripe old age of from three to four years.

Dr. Myers found them not far from Rio de Janeiro in gorgeous color in brown, swampy waters at temperatures in the low seventies. He believes it would be well worth the attempt to breed them in the acid, brown waters of the pine barrens and cedar swamps of New Jersey or elsewhere.

### *Hyphessobrycon herbertaxelrodi* GERY

*Popular name:* Black Neon

*Meaning of name:* Hyphessobrycon, little fish with teeth; herbertaxelrodi, after Dr. Herbert R. Axelrod

*Length:* 1¼ inches

Brazil

A small Characin requiring much the same care as the Neon Tetra, *P. innesi.* Fairly soft and slightly acid water, a diet rich in newly-hatched brine shrimp or daphnia, some thickets of fine-leafed plants such as Ambulia, Myriophyllum or Cabomba, a dark background and peaceful tank mates bring about a feeling of well-being and therefore the most pleasing colors.

Sexes are easily distinguished as long as the fishes are mature and healthy. Females are somewhat larger and deeper bodied than males. They are more easily bred than the Neon, and eggs are less prone to fungus. Fry can take newly-hatched San Fransisco brine shrimp immediately after becoming free-swimming. (Brine shrimp eggs from the Great Salt Lake in Utah are larger, and the fry of small fishes are not able to swallow them.) The brine shrimp should also be offered as soon as they hatch.

Temperature, 75 to 80 degrees.

*Hyphessobrycon herbertaxelrodi*

## Hyphessobrycon pulchripinnis
AHL

*Popular name:* Lemon Tetra

*Meaning of name:* Hyphessobrycon, little Brycon; pulchripinnis, pretty-fin

*Length:* About 1¾ inches

Amazon basin

*Hyphessobrycon pulchripinnis*

The popular name of this species is well given. While the fish has a faint yellowish overtone, the color character is accentuated and brought out mostly by the intense yellow edging in the anal fin and, to a lesser extent, in the dorsal. Both those fins are usually well spread, giving the species a lively, saucy bearing. As seen here, bodies are somewhat translucent, the only spot of warm color being the bright red in the upper half of the eye.

Eggs are quite small and the spawning fishes are very successful in gobbling them almost as fast as dropped, which is not surprising in this family of fishes. For this reason it is desirable to provide them with dense plant thickets and with water that is not too deep—say about six to seven inches. They have been known to spawn on the exposed roots of plants.

An average temperature of about 73° to 75° suits them very well, but for breeding it should be raised to 78° to 80°.

*Hyphessobrycon rosaceus*

## Hyphessobrycon rosaceus
DURBIN

*Popular name:* Rosy Tetra

*Meaning of name:* Hyphessobrycon, little Brycon; rosaceus, rosy, sometimes known (in Germany) as H. ornatus

*Length:* 1¾ inches

Guyana and Brazil

A fish flying a black flag, but by no means a pirate. In fact it is one of the gentlest and best of aquarium species.

The handsome, over-arching dorsal fin with its great, black blotch, made more vivid by contrasting whites, is nearly always carried with military erectness as the fish darts about the aquarium in its busy way.

The fish is somewhat translucent, the color, consequently, varies according to whether it is viewed by transmitted or reflected light. At one time, it is pale yellow; at others, it is gently suffused with red. The red shown along the spinal column seems to be an internal color. Like other species of this type, it appears best under strong overhead artificial light.

The male (bottom fish in illustration) at maturity develops the longer dorsal fin, while the female shows a brighter red tip atop the white edging. Breeds the same as *H. flammeus*. Difficult to spawn. Temperature range, 72° to 82°. Ahl identifies a similar fish as *H. ornatus.*

## Hyphessobrycon rubrostigma
HOEDEMAN

*Popular name:* Bleeding Heart Tetra, Tetra Perez

*Meaning of name:* Hyphessobrycon, little Brycon; rubrostigma, with red mark

*Length:* 2½ inches

Colombia

When fully grown, this is one of the most handsome Tetras. They develop best in medium to large tanks in water of low hardness and slightly acid pH. Their tank mates should not be too active or aggressive, since Bleeding Heart Tetras seem to dislike having to compete for food. In more serene surroundings, they feed well on many kinds of food. Males develop long, flowing dorsal fins, sometimes reaching beyond the tail. They are not commercially bred, and our stock consists only of wild specimens.

## Hyphessobrycon scholzei   AHL

*Popular name:* Black-line Tetra

*Meaning of name:* Hyphessobrycon, little Brycon; scholzei, in honor of aquarist, Scholze

*Length:* 2½ inches

Lower Amazon

Through no fault of its own, nor of Ahl, who correctly named it in 1937, this species was later introduced to aquarists as *Aleta nigrans,* This name was probably concocted

*Hyphessobrycon rubrostigma*

*Hyphessobrycon scholzei*

*Hyphessobrycon simulans*

by some dealer who made "confusion twice confounded" by stating that it came from Africa, instead of South America, thus confusing it with *Nannaethiops unitaeniatus,* a somewhat similarly marked Tetra from that continent.

Usually the white first rays of the anal fin are more pronounced in the female, but this is not a dependable means of telling the sexes.

Black-line Tetras are prolific and easily bred. They are active, vigorous, and hardy in all ways. Individuals are apt to develop bad chasing habits in a community tank, but if kept in small groups of four or more, this does not become a problem. Temperature, 65° to 80°.

## *Hyphessobrycon simulans*

GERY

*Popular names:* Blue Neon, Long-lined Neon

*Meaning of name:* Hyphessobrycon, little Brycon; simulans, imitative

*Length:* 1 inch

Brazil

This is a comparatively new introduction, having been discovered only a few years ago. It differs from the regular, well-known Neon Tetra for it has a blue-green line extending the whole length of the body—from the gills to the tail—with a much fainter red band below it that only covers the area from the anal fin back to the caudal peduncle. It grows to about the same size as the Neon and can be kept under the same conditions.

Feeding them presents no problem at all, as they eat all types of live, frozen, and dried food as long as the particles are small enough. The breeding habits of these fishes are unknown at present, but we suspect they are not much different

*Paracheirodon innesi*

from those of other small Hyphessobrycons. However, proof of this is lacking and it may well turn out that they are one of the toughest fishes to get to spawn. Temperature 75° to 82°.

## *Paracheirodon innesi* (MYERS)

*Popular name:* Neon Tetra

*Meaning of name:* Paracheirodon, resembling Cheirodon, innesi: for the author of this book, William T. Innes

*Length:* 1¼ inches

Brazilian-Peruvian border; far western Brazilian Amazon; extreme eastern Peruvian Amazon

As this fish is generally regarded as the aristocrat of small aquarium personalities, some comments regarding its introduction and its peculiarities should be of interest.

Early in 1936 a young French banker, J. S. Neel, in the course of correspondence with the author, wrote that he had received from Brazil, through M. Rabaut, a French collector, "the most beautiful of aquarium fishes," and offered to prove his case by sending two pairs. The offer was accepted, but casually with mental reservations born of former disappointments. They arrived in due course and made an instant hit; the universal acclaim with which they were greeted established history in our hobby.

Other larger importations followed, the second being of 10,000. As these were sold to a New York importer at an unheard-of high price for a wholesale quantity, this probably constituted the largest single deal in the history of the trade. Dealers quickly dried up the apparently inexhaustible supply and everybody was happy, except perhaps the breeders who hoped to cash in on the young of this new, sensational fish.

Nothing would please us quite so much as to be able to give our readers a simple, sure-fire method of breeding this little beauty, but no such formula is known. Enormous numbers have been imported since their introduction, and thousands of aquarists have tried to breed them. Very few have succeeded, and still fewer have been able to repeat their success.

The old "law of compensation" seems to be at work here. Thus, for its surpassing beauty, hardiness, and perfect disposition the Neon Tetra pays with two weaknesses. First, it is subject to a mysterious "Neon disease," causing body wasting and loss of color. Second, of concern to us here, is the dissolving of the eggs that is caused by the penetration of bacteria. Overcoming that tendency among these frequent spawners is the most important and difficult step toward success.

Select young, and, if available, tank-raised breeders. Water should be slightly acid, soft, and reasonably sterile. Distilled water with two level teaspoons of salt to the gallon is one way of producing such conditions.

Sexes look alike, but the ripe females are easily told by their increased girth. Prepare breeders by separating them and feeding them live foods, such as brine shrimp or white worms. The breeding tank should first be treated with salt brine or other germ deterrent that can easily be washed away with distilled water. The tank should be bare (no gravel), and a small bunch of fine-leaved plants or artificial spawning grass should be placed at the bottom. Use light aeration. Place the pair together in the breeding tank in the evening, and arrange for very soft light the next day. Spawning is difficult to detect; the use of a flashlight will help. Eggs are non-adhesive and may be lifted by a dip tube. Whether left where they fall or transferred, they must be kept in virtual darkness until they hatch in two days and are free-swimming. Gradually increase light.

Their first food should be the yellow of hard-boiled eggs strained through fine cloth and placed in a half-filled, stoppered bottle of distilled water. Boil bottle and contents ten minutes; cool and place in refrigerator. It will keep for two weeks. To feed, shake the bottle and use single drops very sparingly. Artificially raised infusoria should also be used (See pp. 28-29.) In two weeks they should be put on newly hatched, brine shrimp (from the San Francisco area), which are small enough for the fry and which can also make an excellent food throughout the life of the adult fish. Once they are on brine shrimp they are as good as raised.

During the past few years, fish breeders in the Orient have developed a method of breeding these little fishes. They are now supplying hundreds of thousands of Neons every year for the European and United States markets.

Suitable temperature for Neons is between 72° and 76°.

## *Cheirodon axelrodi*    (SCHULTZ)

*Popular name:* Cardinal Tetra

*Meaning of name:* Cheirodon, with fins and teeth; axelrodi, in honor of Dr. Herbert R. Axelrod

*Cheirodon axelrodi*

*Length:* 1½ inches

Upper Rio Negro, Brazil

Until a decision made by the International Commission of Zoological Nomenclature, this fish was known as *Hyphessobrycon cardinalis* (Myers and Weitzman). The species appeared on the aquarium scene in the winter of 1955-56. It has since filled a similar position in the hobby as does *Paracheirodon innesi* which it resembles. The red of the *Cheirodon axelrodi,* however, is more radiant and runs the entire length of the fish; the bluish green line is more brilliant, and slightly longer. According to Dr. Harold Sioli, who collected the fish in the Upper Rio Negro in 1952, the original discoverer was probably Mr. Praetorius. It was not until its first importation in 1955 that the fish was seen in the United States.

The fish comes from brown, very soft, very acid water, pH 4.8 to 5.2,

according to Dr. Sioli, and it is probably due to the lack of such water that most of the first shipment to the United States did not live. Temperature, 75°-82°.

## Nematobrycon palmeri
EIGENMANN

*Popular name:* Emperor Tetra

*Meaning of name:* Nematobrycon, having a spike; palmeri, after a personal name

*Length:* 1¾ inches

Colombia

Introduced in the early 60's, the Emperor Tetra became a favorite as soon as it was available. A black line running from the eye to the caudal peduncle fades and picks up again to reach the center point of the three-pronged tail. The tapered dorsal, the prongs of the tail and the anal and ventral fins are all out-

*Nematobrycon palmeri*

lined in black, giving the species an ethereal beauty. Blue and red shadings follow the black body line. The females carry the same distinguishing features but are less vividly colored and the prong in the middle of the tail is much shorter.

A rather hardy fish with no critical water requirements. A few days of live-food feedings seem to promote spawning activity, but for a successful group spawning, the males should be of equal size. One large male will have a tendency to herd the females away from the others. Mops or bunch plants such as *Nitella* or *Myriophyllum* may be used as a spawning medium. The male attracts the female by trembling movements. The actual spawning takes place when the male pursues the female into a mop or plant, and as the fishes emerge the eggs are expelled.

Within three days after becoming free-swimming, the fry are ready to take newly hatched brine shrimp. Growth is rapid.

## Hemigrammus armstrongi
### SCHULTZ AND AXELROD

*Popular name:* Gold Terta

*Meaning of name:* Hemigrammus, half-line; armstongi, personal name

*Length:* 1¾ inches

Guyana

Newly imported fishes glitter with a most intense golden luster. They are active, playful fishes, and a small school of them in a well planted tank is a delight to watch. Unfortunately, all that glitters is not gold, for in a few months, the golden luster gradually fades to a dull silver color. It has been found that the golden color is produced through some harmless bacterial action in the skin of the fish, and that aquarium conditions inhibit this process. Much research is needed to explain this phenomenon fully.

The fishes, however, are very hardy and have a wide tolerance for different water conditions. Feed on all types of dried, freeze-dried, frozen and live foods.

Temperature, 75 to 80 degrees.

## Hemigrammus caudovittatus
### AHL

*Popular name:* Buenos Aires Tetra

*Meaning of name:* Hemigrammus, half-line; caudovittatus, with tail stripe through middle

*Length:* 3½ inches

Argentina

This is the largest of the *Hemigrammus* known to aquarists. Although it has its defenders as a community tank fish, there are known cases where it has been convicted of fin-nipping, particularly after it grows large. It devours many types of plants.

Breeds similarly to the Goldfish, the male chases the female to thickets where she drops rather ad-

*Hemigrammus armstrongi*

hesive eggs. Parents must be removed after spawning. Not difficult
to spawn, but ought to have a tank
of at least fifteen-gallon capacity.
Breeding temperature should be in
the neighborhood of 72° to 74°.
The species is easily fed and cared
for, as may be surmised from its
wide temperature range.

The female is slightly the larger
and is fuller in outline. Except at
the moment of spawning she is the
aggressor in chasing the male,
sometimes killing him. Temperature range, 60° to 85°.

*Hemigrammus caudovittatus*

### *Hemigrammus erythrozonus*
DURBIN

*Popular name:* Glowlight Tetra

*Meaning of name:* Hemigrammus,
half-line, in reference to the incomplete lateral line; erythrozonus, with
a red zone (stripe). Formerly known
as Hyphessobrycon gracilis

*Length:* 1¾ inches

Potaro and Mazaruni Rivers, Guyana

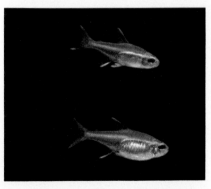

*Hemigrammus erythrozonus*

Glowlight Tetras distinguish themselves by a brilliant red line that runs from the eye to the peduncle. This marking and the white edging of their fins makes them highly attractive fishes, especially against a darkish background and a top electric light. Although they are well suited to life among other fishes of about the same size, they make a beautiful picture as a small school limited to their own kind.

The original importation was discovered by chance in a temporary overflow pool bordering the Mazaruni River in Guyana. The fishes proved to be both hardy and prolific, resulting in a firmly established and well-distributed breeding stock.

Their breeding action is a little different from most of the Characins, in that they quickly lock fins, embrace, and do a "barrel roll," while about a dozen eggs are extruded and fertilized. This is repeated. Eggs are slightly adhesive. A fairly large but loose bunch of Myriophyllum, other fine-leaved plants, or artificial spawning grass are ideal for catching them. They are being bred in large quantities. They will take ordinary foods, but love newly-hatched brine shrimp, live or frozen. Temperature, 70° to 80°.

## Hemigrammus nanus
### (LUETKEN)

*Popular name:* Silver Tip Tetra

*Meaning of name:* Hemigrammus, half-line; nanus. dwarf

*Length:* 1¾ inches

Lagoa Santa, Minas Gerais, S.E. Brazil

This new little fish, with its metallic bronze scaled body and complementing silver-tipped fins, is apt to be underrated unless seen against a dark background and preferably under top lighting. Otherwise, the effect of the fins is largely lost. Silver Tip Tetras are delightfully active and playful, but may frequently nip the fins of slower-moving fishes, such as Veiltail Guppies or Siamese Fighting Fish.

The species occurs both with and without an adipose fin which has led to some confusion and caused one of Europe's leading ichthyologists to classify it wrongly as *Hasemania marginata,* a name known only in the European trade. It was brought to Germany just prior to World War II, and to the U.S. in 1949.

The species has been freely bred by amateurs as well as professional wholesalers. The procedure is the same as for other small Characins. The male has somewhat brighter tips on fins. Temperature, 70° to 80°.

*Hemigrammus nanus*

## Hemigrammus ocellifer
### (STEINDACHNER)

*Popular name:* Head-and-tail-light Tetra

*Meaning of name:* Hemigrammus, half-line; ocellifer, with eye-like spot

*Length:* 1¾ inches

Guyana

"Head-and-Tail-Light," an appropriate name because the glitter in the eyes and at the base of the tail seems luminous. This is one of

*Hemigrammus ocellifer*

*Hemigrammus pulcher*

the popular fishes in the trade. The illustration shows a female, as the fullness of the body indicates.

These fishes are rather easily bred for Characins, following the method described at the beginning of this chapter. Suppliers are also usually supplied with these good and attractive aquarium species. Their temperature range is about 67° to 84°. They breed best at approximately 76°. They are not fussy about diet, but, like most fishes with teeth, they ought to have occasional meals of fresh animal substances.

## *Hemigrammus pulcher* LADIGES

*Popular name:* Pretty Tetra

*Meaning of name:* Hemigrammus, half-line; pulcher, pretty

*Length:* 1¾ inches

Upper Amazon

With so many small Characins nearly alike to the amateur, it is always a relief when a new introduction has at least one clear identifying characteristic. So far among aquarists' fishes, we have seen none with which this one might be confused. The illustration shows the tell-tale marking—a broad wedge of black on the posterior part of the body, extending about one-third its length. Body itself is also rather deep. In back of the gill plate will be seen two small light spots; also a light area just above the black wedge. All these markings have a light golden metallic glow; lower fins, lemon; dorsal, flecked red. Unfortunately, with increasing size the brillance of the black mark decreases. They breed like the other small Characins but do not spawn often. A grown female throws a large number of eggs. Temperature, 72° to 82°.

## *Hemigrammus rhodostomus*
AHL

*Popular name:* Rummy Nose

*Meaning of name:* Hemigrammus, half-line; rhodostomus, rosy-red-mouthed

*Length:* 2 inches

Brazil

First imported to America in 1933, we included this interesting fish in our first five editions. As no more were forthcoming, and as none had been bred, we dropped it, especially as our black-and-white photograph represented it poorly.

As the fish is again in stock and seems likely to remain, we are glad to include it.

The reddish glow on the snout, extending over the top of the head, varies in intensity, sometimes barely showing. A small school of them in good color, preferably under a top light, makes a charming picture.

It is unaccountably strange that certain members of a family, outwardly similar, are so much more difficult to breed than some of their cousins. After years of the apparently happy domestication of this attractive species, we have no record of its successful propagation. Temperature, 72° to 78°.

A very similar species, *Petitella georgiae,* is often imported, and sold as Rummy-nosed Tetra. This species grows just a bit larger, the red color of the mouth region does not extend beyond the gills, and the markings in the tail are not quite as distinct as in *H. rhodostomus.*

## *Pristella riddlei*          (MEEK)

*Popular name:* Pristella

*Meaning of name:* Pristella, a little saw, referring to the teeth; riddlei for Dr. Oscar Riddle, U.S. biologist, the collector

*Length:* 1¾ inches

N.E. South America

*Pristellas* stand out among small aquarium species for the distinct black-and-white contrast of the fins, particularly the dorsal. As the fish nearly always bears itself well, like a miniature yacht with sails spread, it can be depended upon to look its best. Without any loss to itself, it sets off some of the more colorful species. The fish in our picture are of the golden variety, developed by aquarists some years ago.

The uncommon white decorations of the fins can best be brought out by providing a dark background of abundant foliage, such as the leaves of Sagittaria, Vallisneria, or Cryptocoryne. The fish looks most

*Hemigrammus rhodostomus*

*Aphyocharax rubripinnis*

*Pristella riddlei*

attractive when playing in and out of the shadows. When against lighter backgrounds, the black markings become prominent.

General comments regarding breeding habits, commercial supply, etc., are the same as for *Hemigrammus ocellifer*. (see p. 86) Temperature, 70°-80°.

## *Aphyocharax rubripinnis*
PAPPENHEIM

*Popular name:* Bloodfin

*Meaning of name:* Aphyocharax, small Charax; rubripinnis, with red fins

*Length:* 1¾ inches

Argentina

Few of our more showy aquar-

ium fishes either come from or can endure cold water, but the popular Bloodfin from Argentina is an outstanding exception. In situations where a temperature below 60° is liable to occur, this is one of the safest fishes. Singly or in a group especially, they always make a pleasing picture. They are well-mannered, easily fed, active, and long-lived.

Although they breed like other Characins, they seem to do best in certain districts. In Chicago, for instance, where the water is alkaline, they are produced in quantity. Here some of the breeders successfully use a large breeding trap with screen bottom. Eggs are nonadhesive. The sexes are hard to distinguish except by the full body of the female prior to spawning and the well-developed anal hook in the male, as in all Characins. The red in the fins of the male is generally a little deeper, but since this is variable from time to time in both sexes, it is not a dependable guide. Temperature 60°-78°

## *Prionobrama filigera*   (COPE)

*Popular name:* Translucent Bloodfin

*Meaning of name:* Prion, saw tooth; brama, bream (a fish); filigera, bearing a filament on anal fin

*Length:* 2 inches

Amazon Basin

*Prionobrama filigera*

To the careless observer this fish might easily be mistaken for the much better-known. *Aphyocharax rubripinnis,* but a closer examination will show it to have distinct, beautiful characteristics of its own. Its strikingly translucent body has a glass-like quality. The anal fin in adults is long and pointed, the first ray being opaque white. The red in the fins of the female is confined to the base of the tail, in the male this coloration extends well into the lower and partially into the upper lobe. The red of *P. filigera* is more vivid and the length is slightly greater than *A. rubripinnis.* As in many fishes with partially transparent bodies, the Translucent Bloodfin has a little heart-shaped design at the end of the lower spinal column. This is the fan-shaped end of the back-backbone, technically known as the hypural fan.

Breeding habits are probably similar to *A. rubripinnis,* but so far no spawning of this fish has been recorded. Temperature range, 72° to 85°.

## Anoptichthys jordani
HUBBS and INNES

*Popular name:* Blind Cave Fish or Blind Characin

*Meaning of name:* Anoptichthys, fish-without-eyes; jordan, after C. B. Jordan

*Length:* 3 inches

San Luis Potosi, Mexico

In 1936 Mr. Basil Jordan, of Dallas, Texas, sent the author an eyeless fish. Obviously, it is a Characin, the only blind one. With the aid of Professor Carl L. Hubbs, the authority on cave fishes, it was found to be a new species, no doubt descended from *Astyanax mexicanus.* It was found in a Mexican cave and aroused such scientific interest that several expeditions were sent to study it in its native habitat. Elaborate reports may be found in the publications of The New York Zoological Society and the New York Academy of Sciences, the latter for April 5, 1943.

The fish is a whitish translucent with an underglow of pink. It has been commercially pushed as a "scavenger fish," and really is one. It finds bits of food at the bottom of the tank, either lost or spurned by other fishes. Gets along well in the aquarium, seldom bumps into anything (never with force), is perfectly peaceful and hardy. Most aquarists feel a needless pity for it at first, but they end by regarding it as a special pet.

Generations of influences which destroyed sight also changed breeding methods to an extent. They have trouble in keeping spawning contact, but in general they act like their prototype, *Astyanax mexicanus,* with which they can be crossed, but with difficulty, for the actions of each breeding partner seem to irritate the other. Young from this cross have varying degrees of sight which is seldom, if ever, perfect. Adult *A. jordani* will devour inch-long fishes if, by chance, they get hold of them. They are ravenous eaters and will accept any type of food.

### *Moenkhausia oligolepis*
(GUENTHER)

*Popular name:* Red-eye Tetra

*Meaning of name:* Moenkhausia, after W. J. Moenkhaus; oligolepis, with few scales

*Length:* 4 inches

Brazil and Guyana

A flashing red upper half of the

*Anoptichthys jordani*

*Moenkhausia oligolepis*

eye contrasts with a leaden gray body to give this fish an individuality easily remembered. It has other features, too. The large, black spot at the tail root and the black edging of the scales, presenting a laced effect, are pleasing points. The front ray of the anal fin, as with so many of the Characins, is white. There is a small golden spot in back of the adipose fin, just above the tail.

The market is mostly supplied by foreign breeders, who send quantities of them here at a size of about one and one-half inches. Purchasers are usually surprised to find how large and how rapidly they grow.

In two-inch size, it makes a fairly good community-tank occupant, but as it reaches maturity it is not to be trusted among other fishes.

The species is not easily spawned, but when it does breed, large numbers of fertile eggs are produced. Breeding habits similar to those of *Hemigrammus caudovittatus.* Temperature range, 70° to 85°. Breeds best at about 75°. Should often have chopped worms or minced raw fish, but will take any food.

## Moenkhausia pittieri
### EIGENMANN

*Meaning of name:* Moenkhausia, for Dr. W. J. Moenkhaus, Indiana University; pittieri, for H. Pittier, a botanist of Venezuela

*Length:* 2½ inches

Venezuela (Lake Valencia)

The small iridescent sparkles of green set upon a body of glistening silver give this fish its distinct beauty. These colors together with the ventral area, which under certain lights displays a light shade of blue, are sharply contrasted by the fiery red of the eye, especially in

*Moenkhausia pittieri*

the upper half of the iris. Less obvious, but no less distinctive, is this fish's boldly prominent dorsal fin with its unique contours and its equally handsome anal fin.

In adult specimens the sexes may be distinguished by the males having longer and more pointed dorsal and anal fins. The lower fish in the illustration is the female. The species has been bred by European aquarists, and its habits are the same as for similar Characins. It is a good community tank fish. Temperature range, 70° to 82°.

## Gymnocorymbus ternetzi
**BOULENGER**

*Popular name:* Black Tetra

*Meaning of name:* Gymnocorymbus, naked (unscaled) nape; ternetzi, after its collector, Carl Ternetz

*Length:* Up to 3 inches

Paraguay

While preserved specimens from nature come as long as three inches, aquarium specimens rarely reach two inches fortunately. After the fish attains a length of 1½ inches, its chic black markings progressively pale as the fish gets bigger. At the size shown in the illustration, they look their snappy best. When swimming, they look like little black fans moving about, for the tail fin is so translucent that it is rarely seen. Black Tetras are pert-looking fishes that contrast well with other tank mates. They are not aggressive and are able to take care of themselves. Though they have been bred at 1½ inches, the two-inch ones are more apt to produce. For breeding methods use the standard procedure described in the introduction to Characins. Black Tetras are always available and in good supply. Temperature, 68° to 80°.

*Gymnocorymbus ternetzi*

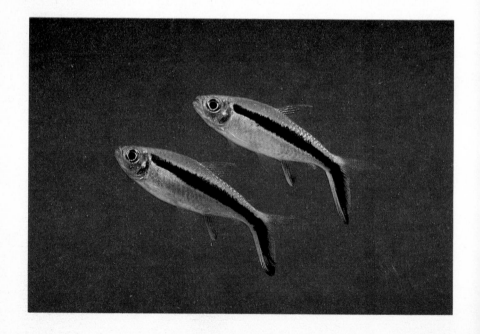

*Thayeria boehlki*

***Thayeria boehlkei***   WEITZMAN

*Popular name:* Penguin Fish

*Meaning of name:* Thayeria, for Nathaniel Thayer; boehlkei, a personal name

*Length:* 2½ inches

Amazon Basin

This rather odd and attractive fish has recently become very popular in the United States and Europe. While in motion it maintains a horizontal position, but when relaxed it assumes an oblique, head-up angle. The bold black stripe is edged above and below by iridescent pin-stripes. No other coloring. Sexes look very similar but, with experience, it is possible to differentiate the slightly slimmer shape of the male.

They are easily bred and are now produced in large quantities by breeders in the Orient. A breeding pair drift about slowly in open water, then they do a spirited love dance, nudging each other on the sides prior to the actual spawning. Very small fry hatch in two days and require the smallest sizes of microscopic live foods.

Adult specimens accept a variety of foods. Peaceful, but expertly gobble baby fishes. Temperature, 70° to 78°.

***Megalamphodus megalopterus***
(EIGENMANN)

*Popular name:* Black Phantom Tetra

*Meaning of name:* Megalamphodus, with large tooth on both sides; megalopterus, large fin

*Length:* 1½ inches

Brazil

*Megalamphodus megalopterus*

The Black Phantom Tetras are among the loveliest of the small Characins. They are pleasantly, if not brilliantly, colored and are very interesting to watch in a medium-sized, well-planted community tank. The water should be slightly acid and not too hard, *i.e.,* somewhat below 100 p.p.m. total hardness. Thickets of fine-leafed plants such as Myriophyllum (Milfoil or Foxtail), *Cabomba,* or *Ambulia* will greatly enhance the well-being of this species; the males establish territories and are a delight to watch as they defend them, spreading to the utmost their large, almost flowing dorsal and anal fins. They dance around one another, each one trying to gain an advantage over the other.

When on a well-balanced diet, these little fish will even spawn in a community tank as long as it is not too crowded or no larger fishes are present to bully them. Of course, the chance of raising fry in such a situation is almost nil. The eggs as well as any fry that might hatch would, in ordinary circumstances be greedily eaten by other fishes as well as by the parents themselves. They are easy fishes to breed, however, and are usually quite prolific. Fry are very tiny when first hatched and require infusoria as a first food, but soon graduate to newly hatched brine shrimp. Both of these foods should be on hand if raising the fry is contemplated. Sexes are easily distinguished at a fairly early age. Males are slightly larger, have larger dorsal and anal fins, and the adipose fin (the small fin between the dorsal and tail) is black in the males and a pretty red in the females. Temperature, 78° to 82°.

## Metynnis species

*Popular name:* Silver Dollar

*Meaning of name:* Metynnis, with a plough

*Length:* 4 inches

Amazon Basin and Guyana

Metynnis is a genus distinguished from *Colossoma* and *Mylossoma* by the *long, low* adipose fin (see photo). Several species have been imported, all sharing the appropriate name of Silver Dollar and all looking quite similar. The only apparent difference among them is the length of the adipose fin.

All *Metynnis* are silvery in color, sometimes with dark spots or bars that disappear with age. There is usually some orange or yellow in the tail and anal fin. All will take prepared foods, but in nature they feed on aquatic plants and fallen fruit. They will create havoc with aquarium plants. Plastic plants do well for such herbivores.

Peaceful, attractive, and hardy. Almost never bred. They are said to scatter non-adhesive eggs. Temperature, 72° to 82°.

## Mylossoma aureum          (SPIX)

*Meaning of name:* Mylossoma, body shaped like a millstone; aureum, golden

*Length:* 3½ inches

Amazon

One of the most attractive and enduring of the disc-like Silver Dollars, as they are popularly called. *M. aureum* is so flat that it seems emaciated. The fact that it keeps living happily in what appears to be a thin condition reminds one of the

*Metynnis spec.*

old saying, "a lean horse for a long race."

The dark portion of the anal fin is a rich, golden brown, and the broadest part of the fin is up towards the tail, this is an exceptional feature. In life, it is difficult to tell just where the body edge ends and the anal fin begins. Imagine a continuation of the curve of the lower belly line to approximate where one ends and the other begins. The scales are very small and very silvery. The soft vertical bars are gray and the back is light olive. A speck of color appears on the adipose fin. The eye is warm golden.

The ventral fins are incredibly small. Sex differences are not known; the fishes have never been bred.

Silver Dollars make good community fish, especially when kept with companions that are not diminutive. Comfortable between 72° and 85°. Easily fed. They eat plants.

*Mylossoma aureum*

### *Colossoma nigripinnis* (COPE)

*Popular name:* Pacu

*Meaning of name:* Colossoma, huge body; nigripinnis, with black fins

*Length:* 2 feet

Amazon Basin

In pet shops, very young, one inch long Colossoma are sometimes mistakenly sold as Piranhas, since

*Colossoma nigripinnis*

they resemble them very closely in shape, color and fins. The aquarist who takes them home however, soon realizes that these "Piranhas" are the most gentle fishes he ever owned. Pacus consume enormous quantities of food of any kind, and grow at a phenomenal rate but they never fight with any other fish. They make no demands on water conditions and become quite friendly with the owner who feeds them. They do demand space though, and an eight to ten inch specimen should have at least a 50 gallon tank. Temperature 72° to 80°.

### Serrasalmus species

*Popular name:* Piranha

*Meaning of name:* Serrasalmus, salmon-like

*Length:* 10 inches

Amazon and La Plata Basins

Tales of how swarms of blood-thirsty Piranhas skeletonize large wading or swimming animals in a matter of minutes have created a rather morbid public interest in them as aquarium fishes.

These fishes have razor-sharp, triangular teeth that interlock between lower and upper jaws. They bite out chunks of flesh that are swallowed whole. The wound is said to be painless. They can cut nets and fishing lines.

There are several species, varying in ferocity, some are even harmless. The most savage are those with the shortest, bulldog-like muzzles.

Single specimens are shy and easily scared. When raised together they constantly attack each other. For this reason, they need a large and well-planted tank. They are fond of all types of live food and may be fed on raw meat, liver, and fish. Color varies with species, from

*Serrassalmus spec.*

*A Close-up of a Head of a Piranha*

lemon trimmings on silver to some with bright red bellies.

Occasionally stocked. Temperature, 75°-80°

## Chalceus macrolepidotus

*Popular name:* Red-tailed Chalceus

*Meaning of name:* Chalceus, made of copper; macrolepidotus, with large scales

*Length:* To 12 inches

Guyana

Red-tailed Chalceus have to be handled with extreme care after they have arrived from the collecting grounds in Northern South America. They become extremely frightened and at the slightest disturbance may jump out of the tank or smash against the glass sides. Fins, scales, and lips damage easily. It is best to purchase young, immature fishes of about two to four inches, since they adapt best to aquarium conditions at that size. As they adjust, they become more and more intolerant towards each other. It may become necessary to separate individuals. However, if they have settled down and adjusted to the tank, they are gorgeous creatures indeed. Their tails and fins are a subtle raspberry color while their handsome rows of large, rounded scales radiate a pearly luster.

Their food consists of most types of frozen and living foods with blood worms (red mosquito larvae), black mosquito larvae, glass

*Chalceus macrolepidotus*

larvae, and brine shrimp either live, freeze-dried, or frozen as the first choices. Tubifex worms are less readily accepted. The fish grow at a fast rate if fed frequently and plentifully. Temperature, 75° to 80°.

## Triportheus elongatus
(GUENTHER)

*Meaning of name:* Elongatus, elongated

*Length:* 5 inches

Guyana and Amazon Basin

This is a robust and reasonably hardy fish which unfortunately is not too often seen. The young of this species look much different from the adults, having a tan body, black pectoral fins and a completely clear tailfin. They grow quickly on various types of food, but prefer to feed at the surface. An excellent jumper. Temperature 70° to 80°.

## Micralestes interruptus
BOULENGER

*Popular names:* Feathertail, Congo Tetra

*Meaning of name:* Micralestes: small fish which can escape quickly; interruptus: interrupted, referring to the incomplete lateral line

Also known as Phenacogrammus interruptus

*Length:* 3 inches

Congo River

This interesting tetra from Africa grows what look to be feathers on the tail, hence the popular name. This happens only in the male, as the fish matures. The female, when adult, has shorter fins and never grows quite as large as her mate.

This fish might be said to have many color phases, but more truly they are prismatic effects according to how the light strikes their scales, and the relative position of the ob-

*Triportheus elongatus*

*Micralestes interruptus*

server. With a dark background and the light coming from in back of the observer, brilliant prismatic colors follow each other in endless variety, mostly blue, green and yellow. Held in the air in net, under flashlight the color effect is startlingly gaudy. To enjoy its full beauty, the aquarium reflection should be put over the front of the tank.

The Congo Tetra is one of the larger tetras and should not be kept with much smaller species. It prefers soft, acid water and a temperature between 75° and 82°.

### *Arnoldichthys spilopterus*
(BOULENGER)

*Popular names:* African Red-eyed Tetra, Red-eyed Characin

*Meaning of name:* Arnoldichthys, after Johann P. Arnold, a German aquarist; spilopterus, with spot on fin

*Length:* Approximately 4 inches

Tropical West Africa, Lagos to Niger estuary

This is a somewhat delicate, easily frightened fish which should be handled with extreme care until it becomes used to aquarium conditions. Large, well-planted tanks are necessary to help them lose their nervousness. Water that has been used in an aquarium for some time is good, but such water should be slightly acid. Live foods such as daphnia, brine shrimp, or blood worms should be offered when specimens are first acquired, but later they will accept a good quality of dried and freeze-dried foods. They prefer to feed at the surface or in midwater. Has not yet bred in captivity. Temperature, 76° to 80°.

## FAMILY ANOSTOMIDAE

This is a group of medium sized Characins which has become quite popular in recent years. Some swim in a very characteristic head down position and are popularly called Headstanders. All come from South America. With the exception of *Chilodus punctatus,* none has been bred with regularity.

### *Anostomus anostomus*
(LINNAEUS)

*Meaning of name:* Anostomus, turned-up mouth

*Length:* 4 inches

Common in Guyana, rare in the Amazon

In coloration this fish looks like a cousin of *Nannostomus trifasciatus,* though a large and rather sluggish one at that. The dark portions of the forked tail root are deep blood-red as are the dark parts in the dorsal, the adipose, and the beginnings (at the body) of the ventral and anal fins. In addition to these strongly characteristic markings, there are three bold, broad, black stripes along the body.

The fish is related to the genus *Leporinus* and swims in somewhat the same fashion. Although this species was described by one of our earliest great naturalists, it was not imported for aquarists until 1933. As yet we know nothing of its breeding habits. It is a generally peaceful fish, but some individuals become dangerous and aggressive in a community tank, mercilessly chasing and nipping their victims. It possesses an extremely upturned mouth and in an upside-down position frequently scrapes at algae-covered rocks. It will eat most

*Arnoldichthys spilopterus*

*Anostomus anostomus*

foods, however, and even bits off the bottom by turning its whole body sideways and pulling them in laterally. Temperature, 75° to 80°.

## Leporinus fasciatus (BLOCH)

*Meaning of name:* Leporinus, with a snout like a rabbit; fasciatus, banded

*Length:* Up to 12 inches

Amazon and Guyana

Because this very striking fish is extremely difficult for collectors to gather in the wild and because it has not been bred in captivity, *Leporinus fasciatus* has never been commonplace. It is an enormous leaper and jumps over the nets of natives. To illustrate its acrobatics and toughness, one kept in a public aquarium jumped obliquely upward a distance of five feet, landing in a marine tank of a different temperature. After several hours it was returned undamaged to its own tropical freshwater tank.

As the fish is rather sluggish in its movements, the aquarist is apt to become careless about keeping the tank covered. One should not forget, however, that the most able jumpers, such as *Pantodon* and the reedfishes, appear to be slow movers.

The light bands in the photograph represent ivory yellow, while the dark bars are black. The fish has and needs no other colors. An interesting feature is that with age the number of bands increases. The young have five, while fully grown adults show ten. The species usually maintains a slightly head-down angle, common in the family. Eats anything, harmless, but quarrelsome among each other. Nibbles at plants. Temperature, 70° to 80°.

## Chilodus punctatus
MUELLER and TROSCHEL

*Popular name:* Headstander

*Meaning of name:* Chilodus, with teeth on lips; punctatus, spotted

*Length:* 3 inches

Guyana

Some fishes, without possessing any actual brightness of color, are nevertheless brilliant. An arrangement of contrasts or of designs in blacks, grays, olive, or brown tints, combined with sparkles of silver can be very effective. Such a fish is *Chilodus punctatus*. The middle band is clear black while the spots on the scales and the markings in the dorsal fin are brownish. This is one of those species that maintains an oblique balance most of the time, head downward. Whether absorbed in thought or merely looking on the bottom for food is a question any aquarist can answer for himself without fear of contradiction.

The species has been bred in captivity. It is said to lay glass clear eggs in fine-leaved plants near the bottom. Its mouth is rather small, but the fish is not fussy about diet. Peaceful and not very lively, but capable of lightning speed when pursued with a net. Temperature, 75° to 80°.

## Abramites microcephalus
NORMAN

*Meaning of name:* Abramites, like Abramis, the bream; microcephalus, small headed

*Length:* Up to 5 inches

Lower Amazon

Distinctly a novelty. Its assortment of markings range from white through shades of gray to heavy

*Leporinus fasciatus*

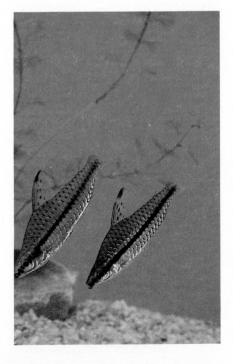

*Chilodus punctatus*                    *Abramites microcephalus*

black, thus it easily catches and holds the eye. The crescent in the tail fin is white. The other parts are mostly grays and blacks, pretty much as the photograph shows. Going about with the forepart of the body tilted downward is a characteristic pose; from this peculiarity one would expect them to be bottom feeders. While they do feed off the bottom, they feed equally well in mid-water, but dislike floating foods. They also nibble on live plants and usually select the most expensive ones.

The fish has been kept with other species and occasionally, fins of long-finned species were nipped. When among their own they tend to be belligerent toward each other. Happiest at an average temperature of 75°.

## THE HATCHET FISHES
### FAMILY GASTEROPELECIDAE

Strange little creatures, these Hatchet Fishes, with their bulging bellies, yet so thin from the front view. They seem to be built on some highly specialized plan, not unrelated to the principles employed in airplane construction. They are indeed known as Dwarf Freshwater Flying Fishes, for in their native waters, when alarmed, they skim lightly over the surface for considerable distances. Although in the aquarium they will eat live Brine Shrimp, Daphnia, and even prepared food that floats, it seems to be their nature to catch insects on or near the surface of the water. They never pick up food from the bottom.

All Hatchet Fishes for sale in pet shops are imported from South America. Like all fish caught in the wild, they can be easily frightened and often dash against the glass cover or sides of the tank, causing serious injury. Specimens once well acclimatized live rather long even when fed only on dry-prepared foods that float on the surface. Few have been bred in captivity. They are attractive novelties, well worth a place in a mixed aquarium, provided one does not hope to breed them.

They are not related to a well-known genus of marine Hatchet Fishes, nor to the famous Flying Fishes of the seas.

It has been pretty well established after centuries of argument that marine Flying Fishes, despite their amazing performances, do not voluntarily move their wing-like fins while sailing through the air. Our little Hatchet Fishes, however, are equipped with a deep, thin breast keel of bone, supporting relatively huge muscles attached to the "wings." It is known that this equipment enables them to vibrate their plane-like pectoral fins when in flight.

In the matter of temperature they seem, on the average, to prefer water in the neighborhood of 75°. Like most fishes that hang about the surface of the water, they are not very active, but can move fast enough when occasion demands.

*Carnegiella strigata*

## Carnegiella strigata
(GUENTHER)

*Popular name:* Marble Hatchet Fish

*Meaning of name:* Carnegiella, named for Miss Margaret Carnegie; strigata, streaked

*Length:* 1¾ inches

N.E. South America

This Hatchet Fish is considerably smaller, more whisp-like, and colorful than *Gasteropelecus levis*. No adipose fin is present. While not hardy, it is often more durable than *Gasteropelecus levis*. Requirements are the same.

One breeder reports several large spawnings at a temperature of 83° to 87° with the male courting by circling the female and dashing closely past her. The pair did much leaping out of the water, but the actual spawning took place in a side-to-side, head-to-tail position, the small transparent eggs being scattered among floating plants, such as Riccia. The species takes a variety of dry and living fishfoods.

The only way to distinguish the sexes is to take a top view of the fish and look for the broader body of the female.

## Gasteropelecus levis
(EIGENMANN)

*Popular name:* Silver Hatchet Fish

*Meaning of name:* Gasteropelecus, axe-belly; levis, smooth

*Length:* 2¼ inches

Amazon Basin and Guyana

This is the commonest of our Hatchet Fish importations. The lower part of the body is mirrored silver, while the top is olive. These colors are separated by a pleasing blue-black stripe which itself is enclosed between two narrow, pale silver lines. All fins are clear, in-

*Gasteropelecus levis*

cluding the long, arching, graceful pectorals or "wings."

These fishes like clear water at temperature of about 75°.

There is a similar species, *Gasteropelecus sternicla,* which is so similar that a count of fin-rays, teeth, and scales is needed to detect the difference—a job for an ichthyologist. The aquarist may regard them as one fish.

Like many of the fishes with marked ability at leaping, it spends most all of its time near the surface of the water. It is probably looking for small insects which have either fallen on the surface or are flying near it. Since it feeds off the surface, it should be given floating foods such as freeze-dried Brine Shrimp. When frightened, they often smash against the tank walls and death can occur.

## FAMILY HEMIODONTIDAE

This is another group of South American Characins. They differ from the family Characidae by having no teeth in the lower jaw. Characidae have a full set of teeth. The family contains some of the most exquisitely colored Pencilfishes. Unfortunately, they have become very scarce, due to export restrictions in some of their native countries in South America. Only *Nannostomus anomalus* remains plentiful, since many breeders of tropical fish have mastered the art of propagating this species.

### Nannostomus anomalus
STEINDACHNER

*Popular name:* Anomalus Pencilfish

*Meaning of name:* Nannostomus, little mouth; anomalus, abnormal, referring to lack of adipose fin; also

known as N. beckfordi, a Guyana species which may be identical with this one.

*Length:* 1½ inches

Amazon and Rio Negro

The long dark body-band of this fish comes through with an intense black and is bordered above by a vividly glistening gold. The eye is light gold divided by the black line that extends to the tip of the mouth. The red ornamentations in the dorsal, tail, and anal fins are unclear in the photograph. But the bluish white tips of ventral and anal fins show very well. The back is "fish olive," the belly is bright white. The fish is sprightly in its movements, standing still momentarily and then moving forward briskly.

They are stubborn spawners and breed like the average egg-dropper, depositing spawn among rootlets of floating plants and plant thickets. The babies adhere to plants and glass sides somewhat longer than most, taking about five days before they become free-swimming.

Commercial breeders in Europe and the Orient are raising these Pencilfishes, so that we no longer depend on imported wild stock. Any food for this species, living or prepared, but it should be small for they have tiny mouths. Temperature range, 75° to 80°.

### Nannostomus trifasciatus
STEINDACHNER

*Popular name:* Trifasciatus Pencilfish

*Meaning of name:* Nannostomus, little-mouth; trifasciatus, with three bands

*Length:* 1¾ inches

Amazon

One of the most satisfactory and beautiful of fishes. Our illustration

*Nannostomus anomalus*

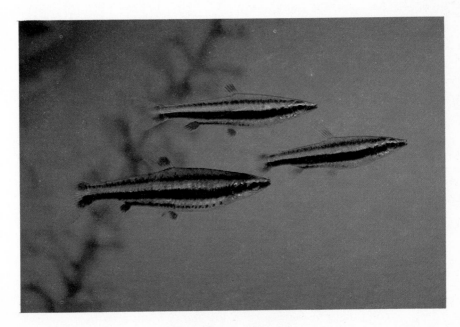

*Nannostomus trifasciatus*

depicts the colors correctly, but obtainable stock is usually a little smaller than shown here. Some specimens are less slender than these and may be a different species.

They have a good aquarium temperament and are peaceful toward other fishes, except for an occasional nip at a long fin. They are, however, a bit unfriendly toward each other. The tank should therefore be well planted, especially with fine-leafed plants, so that smaller individuals can escape harassment. They are omnivorous, but prefer smaller types of live foods.

Spawning, which is rather rare, usually takes place among loose Riccia. The eggs hatch in three days at a temperature of 75°. The babies are long and narrow and do not resemble the parents for several weeks. They poise themselves at odd angles.

Unless very hungry, the parents do not eat the eggs. With good feeding and plenty of room the young become adults in seven months.

The species went through a period of scarcity following its first introduction, but new importations have been made since 1945. It continues to be stubborn about spawning. Temperature range, 70° to 80°.

### Poecilobrycon espei   MEINKEN

*Popular name:* Barred Pencilfish

*Meaning of name:* Poecilobrycon, variable fish that can bite; espei, after a Mr. Espe

*Length:* Approximately 2 inches

Amazon Basin

The Barred Pencilfish apparently is the only member of the family having a color pattern fundamentally different from that of all other Pencilfishes. While most of them are

*Poecilobrycon espei*

marked with more or less horizontal lines, *P. espei* exhibit five vertical bars on a tan body. Interestingly, many other Pencilfishes assume a similar pattern at night when dark vertical bands replace the normal day pattern of horizontal lines.

Barred Pencilfishes are not often imported nor bred commercially and are, therefore, a rare sight in the dealer's tank. They have been bred on occasion, however, but the young are said to be rather delicate. Nevertheless, when free-swimming they can be started on newly hatched brine shrimp instead of the smaller infusoria. Temperature, 78° to 82°.

### Peocilobrycon harrisoni
(EIGENMANN)

*Meaning of name:* Poecilobrycon, variable fish that can bite; harrisoni, after Harrison

*Length:* 2½ inches

Guyana

These Pencilfishes have become quite plentiful in recent years. They are not bred commercially, but imported in large numbers since they are found in an area fairly accessible to collectors of tropical fishes in Guyana.

*Poecilobrycon harrisoni*

They grow larger than most other members of the genus, but require the same care. Adult specimens are a bit quarrelsome at times, but they do no harm to any but the most long-finned tank mates. Therefore, they should not be kept with Veiltail Guppies or such sluggish swimmers as Veiltail Angel Fish. Temperature, 75° to 82°.

## FAMILY CITHARINIDAE

This is an exclusively African group containing some brilliantly colored large fishes. We have included two of the most striking species.

### *Distichodus lusosso*  SCHILTHUIS

*Meaning of name:* Distichodus, with two rows of teeth; lusosso, probably a native name

*Length:* About 15 inches

Central Africa

These fishes, as well as the slightly smaller but very similar *D. sexfasciatus,* are the most brilliantly colored species of the genus *Distichodus* that are imported. The pattern of the body, bold black bands against a warm orange background, is sure to arrest even the most disinterested viewer. While they grow a bit large for most community tanks, they are comparatively peaceful until they reach maturity. At that time it is difficult to keep more than one of these scrappy specimens, unless the tank is large and thickly planted. Many plants, however, are eaten by these fishes, and only tough-leaved varieties such as Sagittaria, Cryptocorynes or Ludwigia are safe. Both species of *Distichodus* are sensitive to water conditions when first imported, doing best in soft and acid water. After they have become acclimated, their hardiness leaves nothing to be desired. They are not the least fussy about food, and all

*Distichodus lusosso*

*Distichodus sexfasciatus*

types are eagerly eaten, but, as usual, live and frozen foods, especially insect larvae, are preferred.

Spawnings of these beautiful Characins have not been reported, and secondary sex characteristics are not apparent. Temperature, 75° to 82°.

## THE GYMNOTID EELS
### FAMILY GYMNOTIDAE

The Knife Fishes, as aquarists call the Gymnotid Eels, are not Eels at all, but close relatives of the Characins, as has been determined by anatomical studies. From the Characins, and, in fact, most other fishes, they differ in having the vent placed at the throat, and by their elongate body and long anal fin. All of them are from South America or southern Central America. Most aquarists confuse the Gymnotids with the African and Asiatic "Knife Fishes" (*Notopterus* and relatives) which are occasionally brought in as aquarium fishes. The Notopterids have the vent in the normal position and do not even belong to the same order as the Gymnotids.

These Knife Fishes, so-called on account of their blade-like appearance, are, in some species, entirely too large for the household aquarium, the adult size in nature being 2 feet or more. It is therefore only the smaller sorts we aquarists occasionally possess.

There are many species looking closely alike, so that positive identification is not easy. However, they are so similiar in their ways, that, so far as the aquarist is concerned, they may be treated as a group.

The most interesting thing about them is their ability to swim forwards or backwards, seemingly with equal ease. A graceful rippling of the long anal fin propels them in either direction, slowly or rapidly as occasion requires. The way in which they instantly reverse themselves in the aquarium when pursued by a net is most interesting.

Nothing is known of their breeding habits. We do know that they are tough and can live in pretty bad conditions. They seldom die.

The best known member of the family is the "electric eel" (*Electrophorus electricus*) of South America, often seen in public aquaria but too large (up to six feet) for a home aquarium. The family Gymnotidae is sometimes split up into several families by ichthyologists, but we prefer to keep it intact in this book.

## *Eigenmannia virescens*
(VALENCIENNES)

*Popular name:* Glass Knife Fish

*Meaning of name:* Eigenmannia, after Eigenmann, famous American ichthyologist; virescens, green

*Length:* To about 12 inches

South America, (Guyana, Surinam, Northern Brazil)

Most Knife Fishes, including this one, are rather secretive, becoming more active at dusk than during daylight hours. They are odd creatures, rightly bearing their most descriptive common name. They have only three fins: two pectorals and one anal, the latter extending almost the whole length of the body to nearly the very tip of the tail. Knife Fishes are not very safe in the community tank, since they occassionally nip the fins of other fishes. Even though their eyesight appears to be poor, they are quite able to pursue other fishes (particularly their own kind), probably by means of the very weak electric field all Gymnotids are able to generate around their bodies. Disturbances in this field are then picked up by special receptor cells that are part of the lateral line system. Whether or not these fishes locate food in this manner has not

*Eigenmannia virescens*

*Sternarchus albifrons*

been proven, but watching them hunt for food in an aquarium certainly gives the impression that eyesight plays a very minor role.

Knife Fishes are hardy creatures once acclimated to aquarium conditions, but they do prefer neutral to slightly acid water and lots of hiding places. A cover of floating plants will help greatly in overcoming their shyness. Their food consists mainly of worms and crustaceans which, to the hobbyist, means Tubifex Worms, White Worms, Daphnia, Brine Shrimp, and Blood Worms either live or frozen. Their mode of reproduction is completely unknown. Temperature, 72°–80°.

## Sternarchus albifrons
LINNAEUS

*Popular names:* Black Ghost Fish, Ghost Knife Fish

*Meaning of name:* Albifrons, with white forehead, referring to white stripe on back

*Length:* Up to 16 inches

Amazon and tributaries

This is, without doubt, the most agile of all Knife Fishes. The acrobatic feats it can perform in trying to avoid the net are astonishing. It can take off instantly in any direction and swim several times around a rock or stump, tail first and with incredible speed, without bumping into other objects. And all this is accomplished with just the use of the two pectorals and the long waving anal fin, since its tail and one-rayed dorsal are of no use for locomotion. The fish does have a dorsal fin which cannot be seen in the picture since it is folded tightly against the body.

All South American Knife Fishes are imported directly from their native waters. Breeding habits are unknown for the entire family, and secondary sex characteristics have not been observed. The Black Ghost is a long-lived fish; specimens already mature have been kept in captivity for over 5 years. Temperature, 75° to 82°.

# THE CARPS OR MINNOWS
## FAMILY CYPRINIDAE

The Carps form the largest family of fishes known. Nearly all have scales, but none has teeth in the jaws. In place of jaw teeth, they have curved pharyngeal bones in the throat which bear grinding teeth. Many Carps have barbels (whisker-like structures about the mouth) but only a few rare ones have more than 2 pairs. No Carp has an adipose fin, and no Carp ever occurs naturally in South America or Australia.

The Carps vary in size from the giant Mahseer of India, which grows to 6 feet in length, to such tiny creatures as *Rasbora maculata,* of scarcely more than an inch. By far the greater number of species are small and minnow-like, and among these we find many of our best small aquarium fishes. The genera and species are most numerous and varied in Southeastern Asia, tropical Africa, and the United States, in the order given. Towards the north the species are much fewer in number.

Some of the minnow-like ones are among the most brilliantly colored of all fishes. This is particularly true of the minnows of the Southern Appalachians, the gorgeous colors of which, at times, equal or surpass the showiest of the exotics. Unfortunately most of the more gaudy American minnows live in swift-running water and would not be well suited to the ordinary still-water aquarium.

The Barbs give gaiety and grace to an aquarium. Their large, mirror-like scales constantly catch the light and flash it back from many angles, for they are seldom still.

A sparkling appearance is only one of their merits. They are peaceful, playful, most of them are easily bred, and they prosper at moderate temperatures, being quite happy within a range of 68 to 76 degrees.

So simple are the temperature requirements of the Barbs that they are included among exotic fishes which may be bred in outdoor pools in the summer climate of our states where the nights are not cold. If placed in a large, well-planted space and constantly supplied with live food, they will prosper and breed without further attention. It might be added that most of them are of popular aquarium sizes. Despite their general similarity, it is not dificult to detect the interesting differences in the many species known to the aquarist.

Nearly but not quite all of them have short whiskers or barbels about the mouth, a characteristic for which the genus is named.

In some books it will be noticed that our small Barbs, for which we use the generic name *Barbus,* are placed in the genus *Puntius (Puntius conchonius* instead of *Barbus conchonius,* for example). Dr. George Myers, who helps us with nomenclature, says this is an unimportant matter, and that aquarists are justified in sticking to *Barbus.* The reasons are several, partly ichthyological and partly a matter of convenience.

A sunny situation not only suits them, but shows them off best. Old water and plenty of plants should be provided.

They are rather long-lived, four to eight years under favorable conditions. Any kind of food is accepted. Another point of value is that they usually are not "scary" fishes.

Breeding *Barbus* is a simple matter. The female, naturally a little bigger than the male in many species, becomes noticeably larger as she fills with spawn. When this evidence is apparent, she should be placed with one or two males in an aquarium thickly planted with fine-leafed plants. The breeding is similar to that of the Goldfish, which is related to Barbs. The males chase the female and when she becomes sufficiently excited, she scatters or sprays adhesive eggs on the plants or wherever they may fall. As both sexes soon eat what eggs they can find, it is well to have the plants densely arranged to discourage this. The aquarist, of course, should promptly remove the fish when spawning is finished. The eggs hatch quite quickly, requiring only about 38 to 40 hours. The young are easily reared since most of them are abe to take newly hatched brine shrimp as a first food.

## *Barbus arulius*    (JERDON)

*Popular name:* Arulius Barb

*Meaning of name:* Barbus, from the barbels present in some, but not all species

*Length:* 4 to 5 inches

Southeast India

The color pattern of young Arulius Barbs strongly resembles that

*Barbus arulius*

of *B. filamentosus,* the species described on page 119, except that the black bars are not quite clear cut. While growing up, these bars fade considerably, but not completely, as in *B. filamentosus,* and no black spot ever appears on the caudal peduncle. The body coloring at maturity is about the same for both with a slightly more intense greenish lustre for Arulius Barbs. The body outline is somewhat deeper, not quite as streamlined, and close examination reveals the presence of two barbels.

They exhibit the same secondary sex characteristics, i.e., the longer dorsal of the male. Spawning takes place mostly at dusk in fine-leaved plants such as *Myriophyllum,* Willow Moss (*Fontinalis*), *Ambulia,* or artificial spawning grass. As with some other Barbs, a partial embrace takes place at each spawning act. Temperature, 75° to 80°.

*Barbus conchonius*

### Barbus conchonius
HAMILTON-BUCHANAN

*Popular name:* Rosy Barb

*Meaning of name:* Barbus, from the barbels present in most Barbs; conchonius, after a native name

*Length:* 2½ inches

India

For many years, the Rosy Barb has been without doubt the best

*Barbus everetti*

known and most popular Barb among aquarists. As shown in the photograph, this very familiar fish becomes brilliant when breeding. With just a little experience anyone will be able to identify the lower fish as the male. However, from the colors shown, it should not be assumed that the sex is always so easily distinguished. When lovemaking is over, the male lays aside his gay courting costume. Even outside breeding season the tops of those fins which are shown here as dark have a tendency to be darker than those of the female. On average, the male is also a little smaller.

Usually in good supply and is one of the hardiest of the Barbs. Temperature, 68° to 80°.

***Barbus everetti***     BOULENGER

*Popular name:* Clown Barb

*Meaning of name:* Barbus, from the barbels present in some, but not all species; everetti, after the collector, Everett

*Length:* 5 inches

Malay Peninsula and Borneo

The Clown Barb, named for the conspicuous spots that decorate its body, is one of the bigger Barbs and one of the more difficult to spawn. The immature fish have four vertical bars against a tan body.

Aeration, a little fresh water, and plenty of live food help put it in breeding condition.

The colors develop when the fish is about two inches long. At that size, or a little larger, the big blue-black spots are more clearly defined than in the fully mature fish. They have two pairs of barbels. They require a large, well-planted aquarium with a temperature range of 72° to 82°.

***Barbus fasciatus***     (BLEEKER)

*Popular name:* Striped Barb

*Meaning of name:* Barbus, with barbels; fasciatus, striped

*Length:* Up to 5 inches

Borneo, Sumatra, Malay Peninsula

Instead of the vertical slashes we are more used to in Barbs, this brilliant, silvery fish has well-defined, blue-black stripes running horizontally. It has been much favored by American aquarists ever since it was introduced in 1935. The fish also has a stripe along the middle of its back which cannot be shown in a side-view illustration.

The sexes are easily distinguished, the female has a fuller form, less pronounced stripes, and a broader middle stripe. They have not been bred. Temperature, 70° to 80°.

## Barbus filamentosus

(CUVIER AND VALENCIENNES)

*Popular name:* Filamentosus Barb

*Meaning of name:* Barbus, with barbels; filamentosus, with thread-like extension of dorsal fin

*Length:* 4 to 5 inches

Southern India and Sri Lanka (Ceylon)

Immature specimens of this fish look so different from their parents that it is easy to see why some aquarists in the past have mistook them for a separate species. When young, Filamentosus Barbs are adorned with four distinct black vertical bars. The body is silvery and the fins are very often dark red. As the fish matures, the bars fade leaving only a large black spot on the caudal peduncle; the sides turn a mother-of-pearl lustre with hints of green and blue. In the male some dorsal fin rays become long and drawn out and reach almost as far back as the tail.

Filamentosus Barbs, like most barbs, are very active fishes and not easily frightened. They require me-

*Barbus fasciatus*

dium to large tanks to reach full size and to mature properly. Water conditions are not very important as long as extremely hard and alkaline conditions are avoided. These barbs will eat prepared, frozen, freeze-dried, and live foods and they can be brought to breeding condition with the same foods if the supply is kept adequate. Males drive wildly at breeding time. Fairly large eggs are laid in fine-leaved plants. Temperature, 75° to 80°.

## Barbus nigrofasciatus GUENTHER

*Popular name:* Black Ruby Barb

*Meaning of name:* Barbus, with barbels; nigrofasciatus, black-banded

*Length:* 2¼ inches

Sri Lanka (Ceylon)

Although collectors of this interesting fish tell us of having to endure sultry equatorial heat, the fishes themselves do not seem to like it either, for they are captured while taking refuge under shady banks. When naturalized in the aquarium they are happy in comfortable room temperatures, although breeding is most successful at between 75° and 80°. They breed like the other Barbs (already described).

*Barbus filamentosus*

*Young of B. filamentosus*

If this species would appear in its best color at all times; we would not hesitate to rate it as the most beautiful Barb now known to aquarists. The rich glow of ruby in the forward part of the body seems to force itself through a stubborn film of near-black and is simply stunning. Only the males assume this color, but not for long. A partial change of water or other stimulation may start the magic. The contrasting blackness of the fins and body accompanies the glowing dark red; when one color goes, the other vanishes. Then we have a rather drab, barred Barb. Temperature, 70° to 80°.

### *Barbus oligolepis* (BLEEKER)

*Popular name:* Checkerboard Barb

*Meaning of name:* Barbus, with barbels; oligolepis, having few scales

*Length:* 1½ inches

Sumatra

The beautiful black-bordered, orange dorsal instantly identifies this fish. No other known Barb has markings even slightly similar.

Unfortunately, this feature does not show well in our illustration.

The lower fish is the female. Sexes are easily distinguished by the differences in color. The species has a small pair of barbels.

At breeding time the orange in

*Barbus nigrofasciatus*

*Barbus oligolepis*

*Barbus orphoides*

*Barbus schwanenfeldi*

the dorsal of the male intensifies. His body blackens and his scales sparkle blue and green. Breeding as per other Barbs. There are about 200 eggs to a spawning. The young hatch in sixty hours at 78° and are very small and translucent. They require the finest sizes of live food. When several females are ripe at the same time they may be bred together with an equal or a greater number of males.

In contrast to other Barbs, *B. oligolepis* is somewhat less playful and spends most time in the lower half of the tank. Temperature, 72°–82°.

### Barbus orphoides
(CUVIER AND VALENCIENNES)

*Popular name:* Red-cheeked Barb

*Meaning of name:* Barbus, with barbels

*Length:* 7 to 8 inches

Indonesia, Thailand, probably Malaysia

Fast-growing, handsome, hardy, and robust best describes these fishes. They are somewhat plump, quite strong, very agile, and are capable of swimming at great speed. One can witness their strength by the struggle they put up when netted. They grow quite large on practically any type of food provided it is abundant and the fish are given plenty of room.

Some of the Florida fish farms are breeding these fishes, but information on how it is done is lacking. It should not be too difficult to get them to spawn in an aquarium, since they often reach maturity at a rather young age and at half their full size. Water conditions for rearing Red-cheeked Barbs are not critical. They do equally well in slightly acid as

well as mildly alkaline water. Differences in secondary sex characteristics are not well known, except that females are much more rounded in the outline of the ventral region. Temperature, 70° to 80°.

### Barbus schwanenfeldi
(BLEEKER)

*Popular name:* Tinfoil Barb

*Meaning of name:* Barbus, with barbels; schwanenfeldi, after a personal name

*Length:* 12 to 14 inches

Thailand, Malaysia, parts of Indonesia

This is a large deep-bodied Barb suitable only for very large tanks sparsely planted with strong, tough-leafed plants. They will eat all tender plants and by their vehement motions uproot any which are not well established. Even though Tinfoil Barbs are perfectly peaceful toward other fishes, it is not a good idea to keep them with fishes much smaller than themselves. At feeding time, their gluttonous appetite will seldom permit small or shy fishes to get their share of food.

Secondary sex characteristics are not apparent. Certain variations in the intensity of the markings of the median fins, i.e. dorsal, anal, and caudal fins, are sometimes thought to represent sexual differences, but this has not been verified. Temperature, 70°–80°.

### Gold Barbs
(*Probably a mutant of Barbus semifasciolatus*)

Length, 2½ inches

This fish has been kept for years in our tanks, but we are still not certain of its ancestry. In the trade

*Gold Barb*

*Gold Barbs (Albino Form)*
*An albino form of the Gold Barb which appeared on the market a few years ago*

*Barbus tetrazona*

it is known as Barbus schuberti, but that is not a valid scientific name. It is said to have been developed by a Mr. Thomas Schubert of Camden, N.J., hence the trade name.

Whatever the name, the fish is beautiful, peaceful and easily cared for. It breeds readily in typical Barb fashion and is very prolific. Between 400 and 500 eggs per spawning are normal for a full grown female. Temperature 68° to 82°.

## Barbus tetrazona          BLEEKER

*Popular name:* Tiger Barb

*Meaning of name:* Barbus, with barbels; tetrazona, four-banded

*Length:* 2 inches

Malaysia to Borneo

Tiger Barbs are unusually high-spirited fishes. This trait has both advantages and disadvantages: it provides liveliness to the aquarium

and stimulation to other fishes, but when *B. tetrazona* become too exuberant, they nip the flowing fins of slower-moving fishes, such as Bettas, Angelfish, and Veiltail Guppies. From our experience, it is best to keep this fish only with its own kind; even then, the tank should be a rather large one, say ten or preferably fifteen gallons. A twenty-nine gallon tank containing about fifty of these beauties makes a strikingly lively and colorful sight.

Our illustration shows a male.

*Male Albino B. tetrazona*

*Barbus titteya*

*Barbus viviparus*

Females can usually be distinguished by their fuller outline. She also shows less red in the ventral fins as well as the nose.

Breeding is typical (described on page 116), with the exception that they are keen spawn-eaters. Males are liable to nip anal fins of females prior to spawning, even to the extent of killing them. Temperature, 70°–80°.

### *Barbus titteya*    DERANIYAGALA

*Popular name:* Cherry Barb

*Meaning of name:* Barbus, with barbels; titteya, native name

*Length:* 1⅞ inches

Sri Lanka (Ceylon)

Due to the considerable changes in color that this fish goes through, no single picture does it justice. Our photograph of the male Cherry Barb (lower fish) misses the impression he sometimes gives of being entirely suffused or overcast with a blush of deep red. Some strains of the fish show more color intensity than others.

The species is best bred in pairs in the usual Barb manner, but they are avid egg-eaters. Shallow water and plenty of plants help prevent this. The young are very small, but in a large, established tank they get enough natural infusoria to give

them a good start. The parents, of course, should be promptly removed after spawning. To rear fifty is considered good. A school of about that number is a pleasant sight.

This species in spawning sometimes jumps out of the water or even out of an uncovered aquarium. Temperature, 70°–80°.

### *Barbus viviparus*    (WEBER)

*Popular name:* Zig-Zag Barb

*Meaning of name:* Barbus, with barbels; viviparus, having live young

*Length:* Up to 3 inches

Southeast Africa

Its curious body markings distinguish this Barb from other species of this large genus. The second horizontal line does not run parallel to the first which is rather unusual for fishes of this type. Both lines meet just beyond the gills and at the caudal peduncle, a marking that has given this fish its common name, which, however, is not a very exact description. Zig-Zag Barbs are otherwise not very colorful, the fins are clear and the body is drab olive above and silvery below. On the other hand, they are very hardy and seem very resistant to disease.

Weber, the ichthyologist who first described these fishes in 1897,

*Tanichthys albonubes*

found well-developed young inside a specimen. He concluded that they were live-bearing fishes, hence the name "viviparus." Later, after Weber's preserved material was re-examined, it turned out that he had opened the gut of the fish and that the "young" were some type of baby cichlid which had been swallowed as food. This does not mean, however, that Zig-Zag Barbs are carnivorous—they readily eat all kinds of prepared foods. This simply shows that they, like most other fishes, will not reject any wiggling morsel, fish or not, as long as it is small enough. Zig-Zag Barbs are, without doubt, egg-laying fishes and spawn like most other Barbs in fine-leaved plants. Mature males are easily recognized by their slimmer body. Temperature, 70° to 80°.

## *Tanichthys albonubes*   LIN

*Popular name:* White Cloud Mountain Fish or White Cloud

*Meaning of name: Tanichthys,* for Tan, a Chinese boy scout who found the fish; ichthys, fish (Tan's fish); albonubes, White Cloud

*Length:* 1¼ inches

White Cloud Mountain near Canton, China

Seldom has a fish so many good points. In addition to being attractive, peaceful, active, and easily bred, it also stands a great range of temperature, 40° to 90°. It eats anything, but prefers small food given often. Breeds best at 68° to 75°. The male, distinguished by a longer and more colorful dorsal fin, chases the female as she scatters eggs freely. White Clouds have been successfully bred both with and without the use of plants. It is entirely possible to raise many young in the presence of their parents, since cannibalism is not a well-developed trait in these fishes. But, if large numbers of fry are desired, it is safer to use plants and remove the breeders after spawning.

At ages from two to ten weeks the babies are extremely beautiful, looking like young Neon Tetras, *Paracheirodon innesi,* with a dazzling streak of electric blue-green from eye to tail.

A very similar fish, *Aphyocypris pooni,* has been imported and become established in our tanks. It requires the same care as *Tanichthys albonubes.* Temperature, 65°–80°.

## THE RASBORAS

Of the approximately forty-five species of *Rasbora* known to science, only a few have been tried in aquariums. Those listed here are the only ones that have become established in any degree of popularity. With the exception of the Scissor-Tail, they have been bred only occasionally and more or less accidentally. Aquarists fortunate enough to propagate them have found no reliable method that has brought repeated success. However, imports have been fairly plentiful in recent years which might have caused a lack of incentive for hobbyists to try to breed these beautiful fishes.

Wing Commander Marsack, an experienced aquarist, has made personal field studies of the Malaysian region and the conditions under which most Rasboras live and breed. The waters are generally acid, going as low as 5.5 on the *p*H scale. This is very likely produced by humic acid generated by the decomposition of leaves and dead wood as the streams pass through dense jungles before emerging into the open where these fishes mostly live.

Broad-leaved Cryptocorynes grow in such profusion that their roots creep out of the soil and form mats over the bottom, making a perfect refuge for newly hatched fishes. Eggs of *Rasbora heteromorpha* (and probably others) are spawned against the underside of the leaves where they adhere until hatched.

The fact that most of the species are observed in large schools in nature, leads the author to suspect that they are "community breeders," spawning in such large numbers that liberal space is required. In aquariums we get them into seemingly perfect condition, loaded with spawn, yet nothing happens. This also applies to the hard-to-spawn Characins. Certainly we have missed some trick, for in natural conditions both of them are tremendous breeders. What makes it all the more puzzling is that they both take kindly to aquarium life and live for years in splendid health.

Except for a very few little-known species from Africa, all the Rasboras are native to southeastern Asia, from India to Borneo.

### *Rasbora elegans*          VOLZ

*Meaning of name:* Rasbora, a native name; elegans, elegant

*Length:* 5 inches

Malaysia and eastern parts of Indonesia

A central black body spot below the first dorsal ray, more or less oblong in shape and varying in intensity, roughly distinguishes this species. In addition to the ocellated dot at the tail base there is a horizontal, narrow, dark line just above the anal fin. The fish does not have the glittering appearance of burnished silver common to such individuals as *Mylossoma aureum*, but instead has more of a leaden gray with a touch of warmth.

The central body spot in the female is paler and she is also more aggressive than the male. The anal fin of the female is clear; it is yellow in the male. *R. elegans* seldom breeds. It spawns on fine plants.

This species grows rather large, and when it reaches maturity at five inches it makes an especially attractive show fish. Edged dark gray, the large scales show like a sleek coat of armor, which, of course, is what they are.

In its native habitat it can be found in small streams where it reaches great numbers.

*R. elegans* enjoys a mixed diet, will live peacefully in a community tank and will do well in any temperature of from 70° to 80°.

### *Rasbora heteromorpha* DUNCKER

*Popular names:* Rasbora, Red Rasbora, or Harlequin

*Meaning of name:* Rasbora, a native name; heteromorpha, differing in shape from most members of the genus

*Length:* 1¾ inches

Malaysia and Sumatra

For many years *R. heteromorpha* has occupied a prominent place in the minds of all advanced fish fanciers. It has been the open or secret ambition of many to own this unique, beautiful fish which stands in such relief to its paler cousins. Today the trade name "Rasbora" is taken for granted to mean *R. heteromorpha* as if no other species existed.

The lure of financial returns has spurred collectors and importers to such elaborate efforts in bringing them alive from Asia that they now

*Rasbora elegans*

*Rasbora heteromorpha*

arrive by the thousands; previously dozens were considered an event. They ship well and are a leader in sales volume. Many experts have tried to breed them, but few have had success. Reports of spawnings vary somewhat in detail but, in the main, they agree. The successful temperature is from 78° to 82°. The action takes place within a day or two after a ripe pair has been placed in a planted tank containing water that has aged only a few days. The male swims over the female for a time. She assumes an upside-down position, contacting to her belly the underside of leaves, such as *Cryptocoryne* or large *Sagittaria*. She is apparently searching for a suitable place on which to spawn. She is possibly preparing a place to which her eggs can adhere. On the other hand, she may be coaxing the male, for presently, but not immediately, he joins her under a leaf. He quickly clasps her in the crescent he makes of his body; the female continues in

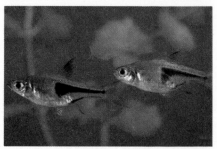

*Rasbora hengeli*

an upside-down position. During the momentary, trembling embrace, several small, crystal-clear eggs appear and are attached to the underside of the leaf. The action is repeated at intervals under different leaves for about two hours by which time thirty to eighty eggs have been ejected. Kept at a temperature of 80°, the eggs hatch in eighteen hours.

It is probable that clean, new leaves best serve the purpose. If they are coated with algae, the eggs are apt to fall and be eaten. One successful breeder uses water at $p$H

*Rasbora trilineata*

6.5, has *Bacopa* as a spawning plant, and conditions his breeders on brine shrimp and white worms.

The surest method of telling the sex in breeding-sized fish is the golden line along the top edge of the black triangle. By overhead artificial light, the line of the male will be found to be more brilliant and deeply colored. A less dependable indication is the ventral side of the triangle which points forward along the belly in the male.

*Rasbora heteromorpha* moves about the aquarium easily and without nervousness. It is adaptable in diet and temperature, a range from 68° to 88° produces no ill effects. It lives for about five years.

A very similar, if somewhat smaller species, *Rasbora hengeli,* has been imported from the same general region in large numbers in recent years. The black triangular spot is much narrower, often only indicated by a line somewhat broadened at the front end. Care and maintenance

*Alb. R. trilineata*

appears to be the same as that given for *R. heteromorpha*. No breeding accounts have been published as yet.

### *Rasbora trilineata* STEINDACHNER

*Popular name:* Scissor-Tail Rasbora

*Meaning of name:* Rasbora, a native name; trilineata, three lined

*Length:* Up to 3 inches

Johore in Malay Peninsula

Although a number of the Rasboras are difficult for the amateur ichthyologist to distinguish from one another, the distinctive markings on the tail fins of *R.*

*trilineata* should end any confusion about this species. Each lobe is whitish towards the outer part, then tipped black. Many fishes partially close the tail fin when starting to move. The markings of the Scissor-Tail make it very apparent that it uses a sort of clipping action when it starts to move, hence its popular name. The body is somewhat translucent.

They are frequently bred by commercial breeders at a length of two to three inches and are always available. The young are easily raised on newly hatched brine shrimp, Temperature, 70°-80°.

## THE DANIOS

This group of lively and spirited little fishes has been popular with hobbists practically since the early beginnings. They are beautiful, hardy, and among the easiest-to-breed egg laying fishes. The name Danio, which is the generic name under which they were first described, has stuck with them as the popular name, much like the name Tetra has stuck with the many popular small Characins.

*Breeding the Danios*

The spawning of the Danios is interesting because it challenges our ingenuity and resourcefulness in overcoming the strong tendency of these active fishes to eat their own eggs as they fall.

The scheme is (1) to have the water so shallow that the fishes have no chance to spear them as they sink, and (2) to have the eggs fall into a trap where the fishes cannot follow. The trap consists simply of small marbles or pebbles to a depth of about an inch. The eggs are non-adhesive and drop between the

marbles to the bottom. One danger with marbles is that the fishes are liable to wriggle among them in fright and be unable to get out. In that respect, quarter-inch rounded stones are better.

As spawning time approaches it is well to separate any promising-looking female and feed her for a week on choice food. Have the aquarium prepared and seasoned; ready for her and two or three lively males. Place the aquarium where it will get good light, introduce the female a day ahead of the males. If there is no spawn in three or four days, separate and try again. The spawning action is easily recognized. It is a wild chase, similar to that indulged in by Goldfish. If a glass-bottom tank is used, the aquarist can look up through the base to see whether eggs are scattered among the marbles. To a practised eye the shape of the female is sufficient indication of a spawning.

The fishes, of course, are removed after spawning. At this time an infusoria culture should be started for the young will hatch in about two days. They adhere at first in odd positions in their beginning efforts to move about, but in two more days they act like fish and have appetites. As the spawns average about 200 eggs, it is desirable to give the babies plenty of room. They should be continuously pushed in growth. It is the only way in which to produce fine, large specimens, and they are well worth the pleasant effort. While it is possible to raise them entirely on prepared foods, graded according to size, the result does not produce a robust fish. They are apt to be small and even deformed. Live food is better, newly hatched brine shrimp being ideal. The best age for breeders is about one year. At two years, they are old. They seldom live beyond an age of three years.

*Brachydanio albolineatus*

## Brachydanio albolineatus
(BLYTH)

*Popular name:* Pearl Danio

*Meaning of name:* Brachydanio, short Danio; albolineatus, white lined, an erroneous designation due to description from a preserved specimen which had changed color

*Length:* 2½ inches

Burma

To be seen at their best, many fishes should be viewed by reflected light, that is, with the light coming from the observer towards the fish. This is especially true of *Brachydanio albolineatus* whose exquisite mother-of-pearl colors can be appreciated only under those conditions. Particularly interesting are the colors in the anal fin which ordinarily pass unnoticed. Some aquarists claim that this fin shows colors in the male only, but this is not in accordance with the observations of the writer who finds that both sexes possess it. Possibly, it is a little stronger in the male. The ruddy glow about the lower rear part of the body is deeper in the male.

A strain is now available on the market having golden bodies and faint markings.

For breeding see "Breeding the Danios," (p. 132). Temperature, 68° to 78°.

*Brachydanio frankei*

## Brachydanio frankei MEINKEN

*Popular name:* Leopard Danio

*Meaning of name:* Brachydanio, short Danio; frankei, after Franke

*Length:* About 2 inches

Precise location unknown

This little Danio has been the object of much controversy since it was first imported and given its Latin name in 1963. We do not know at the present time exactly where the fish comes from. It first appeared in hobbyists' tanks in Czechoslovakia and from there was brought to Germany, Holland, and the United States, but its natural habitat remains a mystery at the present writing. Some aquarists call it a mutant, while others regard it as a subspecies of the old favorite, the Zebra Danio *(Brachydanio rerio).* It is said to produce fertile offspring when crossed with *B. rerio,* which is not the case with crosses between other species of *Brachydanio.*

Good-sized, vigorous specimens should be chosen when breeding the Leopard Danio as there is a tendency in this species for successive generations to mature at smaller sizes. Sexes are easily distinguished. Mature males are much more slender than the females and exhibit a distinct golden glow over the entire body. Females, on the other hand, are silvery.

On occasion, a curious disease crops up among these Danios. The males, particularly, become thin and emaciated, refuse food, and then die within a week or two. It is probably caused by intestinal parasites, but much research is needed to establish the real cause and to suggest ways of treating sick individuals.

Nevertheless, we can consider the Leopard Danio a very hardy fish, not at all demanding in water conditions, food a n d temperature, which makes it a perfect fish for the beginning aquarist. Temperature, 70° to 75°.

*Brachydanio rerio*

### Brachydanio rerio
(HAMILTON-BUCHANAN)

*Popular names:* Zebra Fish, Zebra Danio

*Meaning of name:* Brachydanio, short Danio; rerio, a native name

*Length:* 1¾ inches

Bengal, India

Of the various small egg-layers this fish is, no doubt, the most

permanently popular and with good reason. In an exceptional degree, it has all the points which make an ideal aquarium occupant. It is unusually active without being nervously annoying. It is a fish to show to advantage when moving in schools, in fact it scarcely has an equal, for its beautiful horizontal stripes—repeated in each fish—give a streamlined effect that might be the envy of our best automobile designers.

The sexes can be distinguished, but not at a glance. As is usual in many species, the females are noticeably fuller as spawning time approaches. This is particularly true of all of the *Brachydanios,* but it is possible to tell the sex of adult *B. rerios* by the fact that there is a more bluish cast over the female particularly in the tail fin. In adult males, the horizontal stripes tend to acquire a more golden hue.

Zebra Danio is a misfit name, since the stripes on Zebras are mainly vertical. The fish has extraordinary temperature tolerance, from a low of 60° to a high of 110°, but it breeds at 72° to 77°. Takes any food. See also "Breeding the Danios," page 132.

### Danio malabaricus        (JERDON)

*Popular name:* Giant Danio

*Meaning of name:* Danio, a native name; malabaricus, from Malabar

*Length:* 4 inches

India

Giant Danios are admirable fish, always on the move, easily fed and bred, rather long-lived, ordinarily peaceful and a standard member of a "happy family" tank. We have

*Danio malabaricus*

heard of their eating much smaller fishes, but this is liable to occur with many species when the difference in size is great. *D. malabaricus* is the largest of the imported Danios.

Distinguishing the sexes is not easy except at breeding time when the female is fuller in her belly outline. The ruddy hue in the fins and anal region of the male is a breeding color and ordinarily does not appear. The same breeding color in the female is less pronounced. In mature fish the golden vertical and horizontal bars and stripes are more broken in the female. In addition, she is usually slightly larger than the male. Unlike the other popular Danio, the Zebra Fish, *D. malabaricus* has adhesive eggs and breeds like Barbs. Temperature, 68 to 80°.

## Labeo bicolor

*Popular name:* Red-tailed Shark

*Meaning of name:* Labeo, lips; bicolor, two colors

*Length:* 4¾ inches

Thailand

The position of the rather triangular dorsal fin occurring anteriorly to the ventral fins and the ventral mouth have led aquarists to dub this fish, as well as some other species, shark. Nothing in the disposition or personality of these fishes warrants the designation. The elongate and somewhat compressed body as well as the fins of *L. bicolor* are black; the forked tail is a contrasting bright red. A velvet black and brilliant red are indications that the fish is in good condition. Inferior color occurs when conditions are faulty. The point of the dorsal fin is edged in white. There are two sets of barbels.

*Labeo bicolor*

The fish likes slightly alkaline water, $pH$ 7.1 - 7.3, and prefers a temperature in the high seventies. Algae that have grown on leaves or aquarium walls are good news to this species.

They are omnivores and not choosey about food. They play rather roughly among themselves, but do not harm one another seriously as long as the tank is thickly planted and enough hiding places are provided. They may have bred in captivity, but no details are available.

the fish shown in the illustration indicates a juvenile fish. Adults of this species change to a dark gray color, with numerous but faint red spots. The fishes feed on algae and other vegetable matter, but seem to prefer other foods in the aquarium. All live and frozen foods are relished, but floating dry foods are only reluctantly taken. They are peaceful towards other fishes, but among themselves very quarrelsome. It is best to keep only one in a community tank. Temperature, 72° to 82°.

## *Labeo variegatus*       PELLEGRIN

*Popular name:* Varigated Shark

*Meaning of name:* Labeo, lips; variegatus, variegated

*Length:* 6 inches

Central Africa

The pleasing marbled pattern of

## *Morulius chrysophekadion*
(BLEEKER)

*Popular name:* Black Shark

*Meaning of name:* Morulius, black; chrysophekadion, chryso, golden

*Length:* 12 inches

Sumatra, Java, Borneo

*Labeo variegatus*

*Morulius chrysophekadeon*

This species when first introduced to the aquarium scene
caused considerable excitement. Its
black shark-like appearance set it
apart and its high price indicated
rarity. As it became more available,
the price became less formidable
and when the Red-tailed Shark
*(Labeo bicolor)* was introduced
sometime later, *M. chrysopheka-*

*deon* lost its popularity. It is an excellent species, however, for a large aquarium and its hardiness and willingness to accept all types of aquarium fare make it a fish worthy of consideration. It is a bottom feeder and is somewhat shy. Although it feeds on algae, it does not remove it from leaves. We have found no reports of its breeding in captivity. It is apt to be aggressive with its own kind. See *Labeo bicolor* (p. 135) for water temperature, etc.

## Balantiocheilus melanopterus
(BLEEKER)

*Popular names:* Tricolor Shark, Bala Shark, Burnt Tail Fish

*Meaning of name:* Balantiocheilus, with pouch-like mouth; melanopterus, with black fins

*Length:* 14 inches, usually 7-8

Western Indonesia, Malaysia, Thailand

All Tricolor Sharks offered for sale at the time of this writing are imported, because all attempts at breeding them have so far been unsuccessful. Their mode of reproduction, even in their natural habitat, is largely unknown and sexes cannot be determined. They are somewhat delicate when first acquired and an occasional individual may refuse to accept food for several weeks. Offering live foods, such as Daphnia, Brine Shrimp, or Blood Worms (the larvae of Chironomus), plus applying the standard procedure of temporarily raising the temperature a few degrees above the normal range are the best means of persuading these strikingly beautiful, graceful fishes to become established in the aquarium. Once this has been successfully done, they are hardy and long-lived, fairly peaceful towards other fishes, but somewhat quarrelsome among themselves. Tricolor Sharks are avid jumpers and capable of lightning

*Balantiocheilus megalopterus*

speed. They should, therefore, be kept in spacious, well-covered tanks.

The unfortunate, but popular name "shark" has been applied to this and a number of very un-sharklike fishes, probably because the dorsal fin of these fishes is shaped somewhat similar to a true shark's dorsal and is, particularly in this species, always held erect. But in other respects, they do not resemble true sharks in either appearance, manner, size, or ferociousness. Temperature, 75° to 80°.

## THE LOACHES
### FAMILY COBITIDAE

The Loaches are much like the Carps, but they differ from them in having three or more pairs of barbels. They never have jaw teeth. Most of them have a movable spine just below the eye, with which they can inflict a painful wound when handled carelessly. They are bottom-dwelling fishes, often rather secretive, and should be given rocks or pieces of driftwood for hiding places.

### *Misgurnus anguillicaudatus*
(CANTOR)

*Popular name:* Japanese Weatherfish

*Meaning of name:* Misgurnus, from Misgurn, old English name for Loach; anguillicaudatus, with an eel-like tail

*Length:* Up to 8 inches

Japan, China

This fish differs from *Botia* and *Acanthophthalmus* by the absence of the movable spine below the eye. It is light gray with irregular blotches of darker gray, while the European form, *Cobitis fossilis,* is light brown

with several dark stripes along the body. They are virtually the same fish both from the scientist's and the aquarist's viewpoints.

Before the merits of *Corydoras* as aquarium scavengers were so well known, the "Weatherfish," as well as other forms of Loaches were much used for this purpose. Some aquarists still utilize them, but seldom in sizes over four inches in length. Their movements are wild and unpredictable, somewhat like a "chicken with its head cut off." When these fishes are fully grown, their strange, lashing actions are intolerable to the aquarist, for the sediment is whipped into a state of suspension and sand is shifted without regard to scenic effect. However, it would be incorrect to give the impression that this fish is always on the rampage. It is quiet for periods, often buried in the sand with its head looking out cutely. Then it will emerge and begin a peculiar, interesting action of "combing" the sand surface in search of food. Sand and dirt are taken into the mouth and rapidly expelled through the gills.

Will stand temperatures from 40° to 80° and has seldom been bred. They spawn on the bottom and the young bury themselves for a long period, no doubt feeding on microscopic life and vegetal decomposition.

### *Botia macracantha*   BLEEKER

*Popular name:* Clown Loach

*Meaning of name:* Botia, not known; macracantha, big spine, from the spine on the face below the eye

*Length:* 5 inches or more

Borneo

Loaches are usually thought of

*Misgurnus auguillicauda*

*Botia macracantha*

as long and eel-like, such as the Weatherfish, but there are others of more usual fish form, like our present subject.

The hinged spine, which lies in a groove beneath the eye, is a vicious weapon that makes other fishes keep their distance.

By nature a shy fish, largely nocturnal, but by association with other

*Botia lucas-bahi*

sorts it can be "reformed," as it were, especially if there are no places where it can completely hide. The fish has a quaint habit which is alarming when first seen. When any fish lies on its side at the bottom, it usually means *finis.* Clown Loaches love to rest this way and do so frequently, especially under the shallow shelter of an overhanging stone. Lives eight years or more.

Eats anything and is a good, long-lived "scavenger." Efforts to breed it have all met with failure. Temperature range, 68° to 82°.

### *Botia lucas-bahi*    (FOWLER)

*Popular name:* Tiger Loach

*Meaning of name:* Botia, unknown; lucas-bahi, personal name

*Length:* Up to 6 inches

Thailand, Malaysia, Indonesia

Like most other members of the family, Tiger Loaches are bottom-dwelling fishes, inhabiting streams and rivers with sandy or gravelly bottoms. They are extremely swift swimmers and are equally good at digging and undermining stones. They do this most efficiently and the tank should be set up accordingly to make them feel at home. The fishes use anal and tail fins to fan the sand away. Occasionally, with wide-open mouths, they "push" gravel from underneath stones to make hiding places where they spend much time. At times, for lack of space, the fishes lie on their sides, giving the impression of being sick. This, however, is quite normal behavior and no cause for concern.

The fishes are omnivorous, eating prepared as well as live and frozen foods. They are quite efficient in extracting tubifex worms from gravel as well as eradicating pond and ramshorn snails.

Temperature, 72° to 80°.

## Botia sidthimunki   KLAUSEWITZ

*Popular name: Dwarf* Checkered Loach

*Length:* About 1½ inches

Thailand

This is probably the smallest of all Loaches, usually reaching only an inch or a little more in length. It is pleasantly marked with a somewhat variable checkered pattern above the horizontal black line running the entire length of the body. Though a bottom dweller, this Loach spends more time than other members of the family foraging among plants in the middle reaches of the tank.

There is a strange similarity between this species and the Pigmy Catfish of South America, *Corydoras hastatus.* Both are the smallest members of their respective, but widely different, families and the only ones not exclusively feeding on the bottom. This is possibly another case of convergent evolution where two geographically separated species have evolved in the same way, resulting in amazingly close similarities in form and behavior. Dwarf Checkered Loaches are fair "scavengers," accepting almost any kind of food.

Because of their small size and hardiness, attempts at breeding them might be more successful than with the large species, but raising the fry will probably be more difficult. Hints on how to set up a tank for spawning cannot be given, however, since nothing is known about the reproductive habits of the genus *Botia.* But success with one species will certainly contribute to our knowledge of Loaches in general and might lead the way to successful spawnings of other species. Temperature, 72° to 80°.

## Acanthophthalmus semicinctus   FRASER-BRUNNER

*Popular names:* Kuhli Loach, Coolie Loach

*Meaning of name:* Acanthophthalmus, with spine near eyes; semicinctus, half-banded

*Length:* 2¾ inches

Malaysia and parts of Indonesia

An odd little Loach and rather pretty. It is also an active, durable fish. The bands across the back and sides are black on the edges and shade into dark gray in the middle. The eye, occurring in one of the dark patches, is not easily seen. A rather comical set of bushy barbels, looking like an obstinate little moustache, adorns the mouth.

The fish is a fair scavenger of rather limited capacity. Although nocturnal by nature, it readily learns to eat in daytime. Unlike other aquarium Loaches it never grows too large. It should be provided with rocks and crevices for hiding. Other similar species have been imported and although distinct differences can be found in their markings, for the aquarist's purposes, the popular name of "Coolie" may be applied to all of them. A few spawnings are recorded, but none observed. They almost certainly breed in the mulm at the bottom of the aquarium. Temperature, 70°-80°.

## Acanthopsis choirorhynchus   BLEEKER

*Popular name:* Horse-faced Loach

*Length:* 5 inches, seldom up to 8 inches

Burma, Thailand, Malaysia, Indonesia

*Botia sidtimunki*

*Acantophthalmus semicinctus*

*Acanthopsis choirorhynchus*

This Loach is certainly not the most colorful of the family, but its shape and amusing antics make it worthwhile keeping. The fish spends a considerable amount of time buried in the gravel with only the eyes and mouth showing, ready to disappear at the slightest sign of danger. While searching for food, however, it becomes extremely active and, from an aquarist's point of view, it is very useful in maintaining a clean tank. Sifting the gravel through its mouth and gills, much like some of the South American "earth-eating" Cichlids of the genus *Geophagus,* the fish leaves no corner of the tank untouched. When disturbed at this activity, it dives head first into the gravel. It disappears with lightning speed and most amazingly, literally seems to be able to swim through the gravel only to emerge safely on the other side of the tank. This is standard behavior of most of the Mastacembelids, the spiny eels, but unusual for Loaches. Of course, only well-rooted plants can withstand such activity and new plants should be protected from uprooting by means of rocks or flowerpots.

These Loaches are very enduring and peaceful. They usually outlast other tank mates. They can be offered almost any kind of food as long as it sinks to the bottom. Sex differences have not been observed and their means of reproduction are unknown. Temperature, 75° to 80°.

## FAMILY GYRINOCHEILIDAE

This family contains but one genus, and probably only one species. The peculiar structure of the mouth allows these fishes to attach themselves to smooth stones by suction, even in swiftly running water, and continue to breathe. They inhale water through an opening with a valve-like flap, and pass it over their gills without releasing the suction of the mouth.

*Gyrinocheilus aymonieri*

## *Gyrinocheilus aymonieri*
(TIRANT)

*Popular names:* Indian Sucker, Chinese Algae-eater

*Meaning of name:* Gyrinocheilus, with lips arranged in circle; aymonieri, after a personal name

*Length:* Usually up to 4 or 5 inches, larger in nature

Reportedly from Northern Malaysia and Thailand

These suckermouth fishes have not been reported from India, but the strong possibility exists that their range includes Burma and even Southern China. Their fairly recent importation came just at the time when the previously plentiful South American *Plecostomus* species became scarcer due to government-ordered, seasonal embargos, chiefly by Trinidad. Indian Algae-eaters consequently became very popular and are now being imported on a large scale.

Young fishes are perfectly peaceful and can do a fair job in keeping plants and rocks free of algae, but older ones frequently attack large, deep-bodied fishes, such as Angelfish,

Discus, or larger Gouramis. They seem to be fond of the slime produced by them and are often seen scraping away at the sides of these poor creatures, sometimes injuring them to such an extent that a serious wound develops. This seems to attract *Gyrinocheilus* even more, since they often return to the same spot. This may cause death to the victim once bacterial or fungus infections take hold. Temperature, 70° to 80°.

## THE CATFISHES

The Catfishes, made up of many different families which do not even resemble each other, nevertheless have distinguishing features only Catfishes possess. For example, no Catfish ever has scales, though some are more or less covered with bony plates. Many of them have very conspicuous barbels. Most people recognize a Catfish when they see one, but few know, that not every Catfish is a scavenger.

Most Catfishes are more or less nocturnal fishes. They hide or are quiet during the daytime but move about very actively at night. This often terrorizes the other fishes in an aquarium, who like to rest or sleep at night. The Smooth Armored Catfishes, such as *Corydoras,* seem to be an exception to this rule.

## THE SILURID CATFISHES

### FAMILY SILURIDAE

These Catfishes are easily identified by the extremely long anal fin and by the dorsal fin which is either very small and far forward or altogether absent. All Silurids are from Europe or Asia.

*Kryptopterus bicirrhus*

*Synodontis nigriventris*

## Kryptopterus bicirrhus
(CUVIER AND VALENCIENNES)

*Popular name:* Glass Catfish

*Native name:* "Limpok"

*Meaning of name:* Kryptopterus, hidden fin, an allusion to the almost invisible one-rayed dorsal fin; bicirrhus, with two hairs (whiskers)

*Aquarium size:* 2½ inches

Java, Borneo, Sumatra, Thailand

As one of the most nearly transparent fishes kept by aquarists, the Glass Catfish lives up to its popular name with the truly glass-like flesh of its long tail section. But when a light is held to shine through the body, it displays a wealth of prismatic colors. The skeleton is fairly visible. The internal organs are set in an extraordinarily forward position as is the barely perceptible, hair-like dorsal fin just above the body cavity. The fish maintains a constant rippling motion with its long anal fin even when it is standing still in midwater.

Were it not for the opaque, silvery sac containing the internal organs, it would be difficult to see this fish at all.

Brine Shrimp, Daphnia, Tubifex, Glassworms, Enchytraeids are eagerly (although at first shyly) eaten. Harmless. Not bred. Temperature, 72° to 82°.

Doradidae. Many Mochokids swim upside down.

## Synodontis nigriventris (DAVID)

*Popular name:* Upside-down Catfish

*Meaning of name:* Synodontis, with fused tooth plates; nigriventris, black belly

*Recorded length:* 3¾ inches

Lower Congo River, Africa

This entertaining little character, completely unconcerned as to whether it swims top-up or top-down, was introduced to aquarists in 1950. As will be seen in the illustration, its pupils are extremely large which would lead an ichthyologist to suspect that it is the young of a larger species. However, after nearly three years of being well fed in various aquariums, we have learned of no specimens over 3¾ inches long, about twice the importation size. Markings are in shades of gray and black on a changing background, ranging from olive to light yellow.

They have proved peaceful and interesting; few died, none bred.

As with many Catfishes, they tend to be nocturnal. They have a keen sense of ownership of a favorite location. The underside of an elevated flat stone, if provided, is a favorite perching spot. Easily fed. Temperature 74° to 80°.

## THE MOCHOKID CATFISHES
### FAMILY MOCHOKIDAE

The Mochokid catfishes form a small family confined to the fresh waters of tropical Africa. Most of them have the barbels on the lower lip fringed or branched, like some (but not all) of the South American

## THE BAGRID CATFISHES
### FAMILY BAGRIDAE

The Bagrids are "ordinary" looking Catfishes with dorsal fin present and of usual place and size, anal fin of moderate length, no "armor" on the body, and the "whiskers" usually long. All are from Africa or Asia. The differences between the Bagrids and the South American Pimelodids are small and internal, so that, for the aquarist, the best distinguishing feature is the habitat.

### *Mystus tengara*
(HAMILTON-BUCHANAN)

*Meaning of name:* Mystus, derived from mystax, meaning whiskers; tengara, the native name in the Punjab is "ting ga rah"

*Length:* 4 inches

N. India, the Punjab, and Assam

This species, to be correct, should have eight barbels, two of them nasal. Our photograph does not show that many, but otherwise the fish looks very much like correct figures of the species as listed above. It is not impossible that some of the barbels were out of view when the photograph was taken. At any rate, this illustration will serve to indicate the fish now being sold under the name. It is an interesting, attractive aquarium fish. Easily fed and cared for. Harmless. Seems happy at a temperature ranging at about 72° to 80°.

## THE SCHILBEID CATFISHES
### FAMILY SCHILBEIDAE

Representatives of this family are found in Africa and South East Asia. Most of them are schoolfishes, more active at dusk than during the day. None have been bred in aquaria. Some have been nicknamed "Sharks" for their erect dorsal fin, their silver-gray color, and their sharklike movements. They are not at all aggressive fishes.

*Mystus tengara*

*Etropiella debauwi*

### *Etropiella debauwi* (BOULENGER)

*Meaning of name:* Etropiella, small Etropier (another genus); debauwi, after a personal name

*Length:* 3 inches

Central Africa

This is one of the few Catfishes that spends most of its time in midwater, not near the bottom. It is also a typical schoolfish and becomes very shy when kept alone. All types of foods are accepted. There are no external sex differences and we have had no report of their breeding habits. Temperature, 75° to 80°.

### THE PIMELODID CATFISHES
### FAMILY PIMELODIDAE

The Pimelodids are Catfishes very similar in most features to another family (Bagridae) but come from South and Central America.

*Pimelodus clarias*

## *Pimelodus clarias* (BLOCH)

*Meaning of name:* Pimelodus, fat toothed; clarias, like the Indian catfish, Clarias

*Length:* To 12 inches

All of South America east of the Andes from Panama to Buenos Aires

This is one of those fishes that is most attractive when small, but when fully grown, it is neither good looking nor suited to the aquarium. Adults not only lose those stunning big spots, but reach a length of ten to twelve inches. Varieties from different locales of South America are spotted differently; some are altogether unspotted. Only smaller specimens are imported and, in an ordinary-sized aquarium, they retain both their dimensions and their decorative dots which are dark brown placed on a golden background. They are harmless, moderately active fishes having the novel characteristics of the South American Catfishes, including that of being difficult to breed. We know nothing of their reproductive habits. They are rarely imported and, thus, are infrequently found in the stocks of dealers. Easily fed. Temperature, 70°-80°.

## *Pimelodus pictus*

*Popular name:* Polka Dot Pimelodus

*Meaning of name:* Pimelodus, with wide teeth;

*Length:* 4 inches

Northern South America

Fast moving catfish, and like many similar species, a gluttonous feeder. It does not require special water conditions, but seems to be more comfortable at a higher temperature. 78° to 82° is a good range. They are rather susceptible to "Ick" (lchthyophthirius) and, once afflicted, difficult to cure.

*Pimelodus pictus*

Hiding places should be provided, but the fish uses them only intermittantly.

## Sorubim lima
### (BLOCH and SCHNEIDER)

*Popular name:* Shovel-nosed Catfish

*Length:* Up to 20 inches

Brazil

A rather strange-looking Catfish with a mouth resembling a duck's bill. The Shovel-nosed Catfish is not a scavenger, as most Catfishes are thought to be, but a predator, especially when large. For this reason, it is not suited for a community tank containing fishes of up to Swordtail size. It is a nocturnal fish and should be provided with hiding places.

This fish prefers to feed near the bottom and should not be given dried food. Occasional specimens, however, learn to take lumps of freeze-dried brine shrimp at the surface. In large tanks they often "cruise" or glide just above the bottom with outspread barbles, much in the manner of true sharks. Capable of considerable speed when alarmed. Temperature: 75° to 82°.

## THE BANJO CATFISHES
### FAMILY BUNOCEPHALIDAE

The Bunocephalids are small unarmored Catfishes with very wide, flat heads. They are similar in appearance and difficult to tell apart; for this reason, they are rarely identified correctly by aquarium dealers. All are from South America.

## Bunocephalus species

*Popular name:* Banjo Catfish

*Meaning of name:* Bunocephalus. with hills (bumps) on the head

*Length:* 5 inches

Amazon

*Sorubim lima*

*Bunocephalus spec.*

This is one of several very similar species of Banjo Cats that are imported from time to time. The colors are dark and mottled above and light beneath. They have very small, beady eyes. When the tail fin is spread, which is seldom, it shows a rounded form.

Seldom bred. Catfishes of this family in the past were reported to carry their eggs adhering to the abdomen. Though this has been observed in the aquarium with one species of Banjo Cat, others have been found to lay their eggs in sand. They are very sluggish fishes, but

able to bury themselves in gravel by powerful and slow lashing movements. When held in the water or even lifted out of the tank they play "possum." Temperature, 70°–80°.

## THE ARMORED CATFISHES

### FAMILY CALLICHTHYIDAE

This is a large group of mostly South American Catfishes which, instead of having ordinary scales, are covered with two main rows of overlapping, bony laminations or plates.

They share with all other Catfishes the needle-sharp, often serrated first spines of the dorsal and pectoral fins. Being pricked by one of those spines when trying to extricate them from a net is a rather painful experience.

They occasionally dash to the surface for a gulp of air. This neither indicates distress, nor that they are full-fledged air-breathers.

The most important group of the armored Catfishes, at least from the aquarist's point of view, are the various members of the genus Corydoras.

Although many of us like these fishes for their own marked individualities and their contrast to other aquarium species, it is as scavengers that they have permanently established themselves in popular favor, largely replacing snails for that purpose.

They are droll, gnome-like little beings going about their business of life in what seems to us a serio-comic fashion. This business, as far as the aquarist is concerned, is that of scavenger. It would hardly be going too far to give them the title of health officers, for their self-appointed task is going about the bottom of the aquarium seeking bits of food that other fishes have overlooked and which would soon contaminate the water. They go further than this as they consume dead leaves, dead snails, and even dead daphnia. True, they will not work on the side glasses as will snails, for they are strictly bottom-feeders. The important point is that few fish attack a *Corydoras* of moderate size, whereas many of our exotic fishes make short work of snails. Then, again, snails eat fish eggs. Finally, once established it is difficult to get rid of snails. This is not true of our little scavenger fish. However, under suitable circumstances, snails should be used as auxiliary cleaners, that is, in association with such fishes as will not kill them.

Unfortunately, many *Corydoras* in home aquaria lead a very meager existence. Especially since the advent of flake and freeze-dried foods which tend to float much longer than other foods, our little scavengers often remain hungry at feeding time. Some of them, of course, soon learn to turn upside down and feed at the surface, but they really prefer to eat in a more normal position. Furthermore, many new hobbyists even expect them to feed on the sediment which accumulates on the bottom of the aquarium, since the clerk at the pet store had sold the fishes with the promise that they would "keep the bottom clean."

This is a rather unfortunate state of affairs, since *Corydoras,* as well as the much larger *Hoplosternum,* make very interesting pets when properly cared for.

As should be observed by now, care must be taken that these Catfishes receive enough food where they most easily find it: on the bottom. By foraging for food on the bottom, they do stir up much of the settled dirt, which then is picked up by the filter. This alone is a valuable service. Armored Catfishes will eagerly eat all types of food, but in order to raise extra fine specimens, or to breed them, frequent feedings of live and frozen foods are almost indispensible.

We have good accounts of the breeding habits of *Hoplosternum thoracatum,* the Hoplo Catfish, and of *Corydoras aeneus,* the Bronze Catfish. *C. aeneus,* which is probably representative of the whole genus, exercises no parental care. *H. thoracatum* builds a nest which it guards with utmost vigor. Details can be found under the prospective headings.

### *Corydoras aeneus* (GILL)

*Popular name:* Bronze Cat

*Meaning of name:* Corydoras, spiny fish with helmet; *aeneus,* bronzy

*Length:* 2¾ inches

Trinidad

A very good scavenger fish freely introduced in 1933, it is easily distinguished from other members of the genus by the absence of any pattern markings on either body or fins. Now perhaps our commonest *Corydoras* as well as the hardiest. Temperature, 70°–80°.

In mature fish in good condition, the sexes are rather easily told apart. If viewed from above, the much wider girth of the female becomes quite obvious. At spawning time, the female—and occasionally the male as well—will clean either leaves of aquatic plants, the glass sides of the aquarium, or some other smooth object which she considers suitable for depositing eggs. Having prepared the site, the pair will go through an embrace of sorts, during which it is quite obvious that the female tries to bring her mouth as close to the vent of the male as possible. Through locking of pectoral fins, the pair holds this position for a few seconds. When they break apart, the female is seen resting with a few, usually four to five, rather large eggs in her cupped ventral fins. Presently she will swim up to the previously cleaned spot and deposit the extremely sticky eggs. This process is repeated until up to about one hundred eggs are laid. During this time, the male never goes near the eggs, and the question as to how and when the eggs are fertilized is still the subject of some debate. However, repeated close observation of the spawning process seems to leave no doubt that sperm is released by the male during the partial embrace. At the same time it is picked up by the female in her mouth, and then released while she deposits the eggs. After spawning, both fishes will resume their normal activity, and that

*Corydoras aeneus*

*Corydoras aeneus, Albino Form*

*Corydoras agassizi*

*Corydoras arcuatus*

includes eating Catfish eggs if they come across any. Therefore, the parents should be removed. The eggs hatch in about four days and fall to the bottom of the tank. In another four or five days, they will have absorbed their yolk sac and start foraging for food on their own.

Newly hatched Brine Shrimp is the best first food, but a finely powdered prepared food which sinks will do in a pinch.

## Corydoras agassizi

*Popular name:* Agassiz Corydoras

*Meaning of name;* Corydoras, spiny fish with helmet; agassizi, after Louis Agassiz, zoologist

Length, 2 inches

Northern South America

Like all other Corydoras, this is a very peaceful fish, and a busy bottom feeder. With proper lighting, the color of the body is a pleasing metallic green. Care is the same as for all other Corydoras. Has not been bred. Temperature, 70° to 80°.

## Corydoras arcuatus          ELWIN

*Popular names:* Bowline Cat, Tabatinga

*Meaning of name:* Corydoras, helmeted Doras; arcuatus, arched like a bow, with reference to the stripe

*Length:* 2½ inches

Upper Amazon

A very distinctive *Corydoras* with a bright pearly body traversed by a clear, arching black line. No need to confuse this with any other species. It was described and named by the English ichthyologist, Margery Elwin, and since its importation by the noted collector, Rabaut, in 1939 has not, to our knowledge, been bred. For lack of an established scientific name when first imported, dealers called it "Tabatinga," after the name of a tributary of the far reaches of the Amazon where it was collected. That name stuck and is still the popular designation.

Like the other *Corydoras,* it does not seem to have an atom of fighting spirit. Perhaps its defense, as with most other Catfish, consists in stiff fin spines. Always spread when caught or in danger, these make a

*Corydoras hastatus*

*Corydoras julii*

nasty wound in the throat of any fish trying to swallow it. Temperature, 72°–80°.

## Corydoras hastatus
EIGENMANN and EIGENMANN

*Popular name:* Pigmy Catfish

*Meaning of name:* Corydoras, helmeted Doras; hastatus, with a spear, in reference to the spearhead-like spot on tail root

*Length:* 1¼ inches

The Amazon

Though delicate-looking, this fish is really quite hardy. Its movements are unlike those of other Catfishes, possibly excepting the Glass Catfish, *Kryptopterus bicirrhus*. Instead of grubbing about the bottom, it balances itself by rapid motion of the pectoral and caudal fins, ready to dart quickly in any direction.

The body is translucent olive. Usually the dark stripe on the sides is a little clearer than shown here.

A few large, single eggs are deposited on the sides of the glass. Neither eggs nor young are eaten by the parents. The babies are about ¼ inch long when hatched and are easily reared on Brine Shrimp Nauplii.

These fish do best when kept in small schools. They take ordinary food and breed at about 75°.

## Corydoras julii    STEINDACHNER

*Popular name:* Leopard Corydoras

*Meaning of name:* Corydoras, helmeted Doras; julii, it is not known for what Julius this species was named. Formerly known as *Corydoras leopardus*

*Length:* 2 inches

E. and N. E. Brazil

A distinctive importation of 1933. They arrived in large numbers and promptly gained many friends, who, for the most part, consider them to be the best of the *Corydoras*. They are prettily marked, very active, hardy, and not too large. They can be roughly recognized by the triple stripe on the sides, the black spot above the center of the dorsal fin, and the spots extending over the nose. Temperature, 72°–82°.

## Corydoras schwartzi

*Meaning of name:* Corydoras, spiny fish with helmet; schwartzi, after the name of the collector

*Length:* 2¼ inches

Northern Brazil

A strikingly patterned Corydoras of fairly recent discovery. The fishes are hardy, active and somewhat less shy than other newly acquired Catfishes. They have not been bred in captivity, but there is no reason to believe that they spawn in a much different manner than C. aeneus. Temperature, 72° to 82°.

### Brochis coeruleus        COPE

*Popular name:* Hump-backed Catfish

*Meaning of name:* Coeruleus, blue

*Length:* 3 inches

Amazon Basin

This species is the largest of the *Corydoras* type of Catfishes. The young specimen might be confused with *C. aeneus,* but its body is chunkier, its dorsal fin is higher (like a sail), and its head is more pointed. The Hump-backed Catfish is very useful for cleaning out Tubifex Worms that have become established in gravel. It is very hardy, fast growing, peaceful, and good for larger community tanks. Nothing is known about its breeding habits, but most likely it spawns similarly to species of *Corydoras.* Temperature, 75° to 80°.

### Hoplosternum thoracatum
(CUVIER and VALENCIENNES)

*Popular name:* Hoplo Cat

*Meaning of name:* Hoplosternum, armed sternum; thoracatum, refers to the thorax

*Length:* 6 inches

Panama to Brazil

Often wrongly known as a spotted *Callichthys.* While *Callichthys callichthys* was reputed to be a bubble-nest builder, we personally know of no successful breedings.

*Corydoras schwartzi*

*Brochis coeruleus*

*Hoplosternum thoracatum*

When this fish built its nest at the water's surface, it was taken for granted that it was indeed a spotted *Callichthys*. It is not but it *is* a close relative with certain differences in bony structure. In 1955, still another closely related fish appeared on the market, *Dianema urostriata*. It has a very deeply forked tail.

Hoplo Catfishes are very active

*Dianema urostriata*

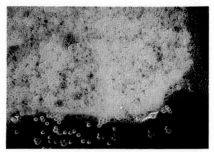

*Nest of H. thoracatum*

scavengers, well suited for large tanks. Their vigorous rooting leaves no section of the aquarium untouched, and only deep-rooted plants can withstand such activity. No Tubifex Worms will ever become established in tanks containing a Hoplo Cat.

Mature males can be readily distinguished from females by their generally larger size and the thickened, orange colored spines of the pectoral fins. When breeding, male Hoplo Catfish build large nests of froth at the surface, usually underneath a floating lily pad. In the aquarium, they readily accept substitutes. A piece of glass or plastic, suspended horizontally from the frame of the aquarium and touching the surface, or a floating but securely anchored plastic dish with a smooth bottom will do nicely. The nest-building is accompanied by much noise, caused by the slurping of air and the expelling of bubbles through the gills. Spawning usually begins during the nest-building period. In fact, the male enlarges the nest considerably after spawning is completed.

The spawning act itself is one of the strangest in the world of fishes. The pair will circle each other a few times under the nest in mid-water, while the female is trying to gain a position to the side of the male.

He then stops and slightly tilts his body, turning his ventral side toward the female. Hanging from his vent, a thin, thread-like structure can be observed now, about one half inch long. This appears to be a very elongated genital papilla. The female takes the papilla into her mouth, and at that very moment releases from three to ten eggs into her tightly cupped ventral fins. At the same time, the male releases sperm, which the female apparently stores in her mouth until she deposits the eggs she is now holding between her ventral fins into the nest. After resting on the bottom for a few seconds, she swims up to the nest, turns upside down, blows a few bubbles, (and, presumably, deposits the sperm at this time) and with a few quick thrusts of her body glues the eggs to the underside of the lily pad. This process is repeated from twenty to thirty times, resulting in an average spawn of two hundred fifty eggs. Large spawns can consist of almost five hundred eggs.

After all eggs have been deposited, it is best to remove the female.

The male busily enlarges the nest and, taking a position in mid-water below the nest, guards the eggs with utmost vigor. Keeping the sharp, serrated pectoral spines fully spread and locked in position, he drives off even the largest intruder with powerful whip-like movements of his body.

The eggs hatch in three to four days, and helplessly sink to the bottom. The male, whose guardianship instinct is much diminished by now, should be removed. In another four to five days, the fry are ready to take food. They can consume copious amounts of newly hatched brine shrimp.

It is possible to let the eggs hatch artifically. Since they stick so tenaciously to whatever was used in nest-building, the whole "nest" can be removed and submerged in a separate tank for hatching and rearing. This tank should be well aerated. A word of caution: a guarding male will attack the hand removing the nest!

# THE SUCKERMOUTH CATFISHES

## FAMILY LORICARIIDAE

The Suckermouth Cats are elongate, flattened Catfishes with a full coating (except on the abdomen) of bony plates that are rough with a thick coating of fine prickles. The mouth forms a sucking disk under the head. The adipose fin, if present, is supported by a bony spine covered with fine prickles. The Suckermouth Cats inhabit South America as well as Central America to Nicaragua.

### Plecostomus species

*Popular name:* Suckermouth Catfish

*Meaning of name:* Plecostomus: folded mouth

*Plecostomus spec.*

*Length:* Up to 10 inches

Nearly all of South America East of Andes

There are many species of this genus and several have been imported. With their peculiar mouths, they can cling tenaciously to any smooth surface. They are well equipped for eating algae which they do industriously, even going up and down Sagittaria leaves without injuring them. They are most active at night.

Color, gray with brown markings. Eats anything. They have a keen sense of property rights and bully or kill other scavenger fish, even their own smaller brethren. One to a tank is best. Temperature, 62° to 80°.

## *Loricaria species*

*Popular name:* Whiptail Loricaria

*Meaning of name:* Loricaria, armored one

*Length:* 3-5 inches

Tropical South America

Many species of *Loricaria* have been imported, but few identified. Purchasers of this species need not suspect damaged goods because there is no thread on the lower half of the tail. The "whip" is on the upper part only. Body markings are olive grays and near blacks. Body quite shallow and rather broad. Not a very active fish, but good algae eater.

Few people have bred them. Forty very large amber-colored adhesive eggs were placed in the form of a narrow triangle on top of a clean rock. Temperature, 78°. Male sits over eggs, crudely fanning them for the incubation period of eight days. He cleans them with his mouth, removing any fungus. Ignores the babies.

*Loricaria species*

## *Farlowella species*

*Popular name:* Twig Catfish

*Length:* 8 to 10 inches

Southern Guyana

These are highly specialized fishes whose diet consists almost exclusively of algae. Very few individuals accept other foods. They should not be kept together with other algae eaters, such as *Plecostomus* or *Gyrinocheilus*, the Indian Algae Eater, since they cannot compete with such active species.

The mature males develop bristles on side of head. Not bred in captivity. Temperature, 72° to 80°.

## *Otocinclus species*

*Popular name:* Dwarf Suckermouth Catfish

*Meaning of name:* Otocinclus, sieve-ear, in allusion to the holes in the skull in the ear region

*Length:* 1¾ inches

Tropical South America East of the Andes

Many of these species have been imported but few identified. The one pictured is *O. affinis* which has become quite popular. An interesting little "scavenger fish," it goes over leaves more thoroughly, from top to bottom, than any other fish. When tired it seems to take a nap, perched in some odd posture, usually atop a leaf. Peculiarly, the fish sometimes swims upside down, clinging to the water surface as snails do and apparently clearing it with its sucker mouth.

*Otocinclus* has seldom been bred. A well-known American wholesale breeder who has been successful with the fish writes: "On the glass side of an aquarium, much in the

*Farlowella species*

*Mouth of Farlowella*

manner of *Corydoras aeneus*, they lay single eggs the size of a small pinhead. They hatch in about forty-eight hours, the transparent young sticking to the glass for two days before venturing to the bottom to look for food. It would be interest-

*Otocinclus affinis*

ing, but not important, to know whether they adhere by suction lips or from body tackiness like other baby fishes."

This species causes the large wholesaler much financial grief, for when newly received, crowded in bare containers, and lacking plant life, they die off like flies. Under the better conditions supplied by the retailer and the aquarist, they are more at home and live satisfactorily.

A most inoffensive fish and, once acclimated, seems fairly hardy. Temperature range, 68° to 82°.

## THE KILLIFISHES

### FAMILY CYPRINODONTIDAE

The Killifishes, or Egg-laying Tooth-carps, belong to the order *Cyprinodontiformes* along with their live-bearing relatives, the Guppies, Swordtails, Platies and Mollies. The Killies are well distinguished from the Livebearers by the absence of the external sex organ or gonopodium (the modified anal fin) of the males.

There are over 200 species of *Cyprinodontidae* known, most of them inhabiting Africa and America. Southern Asia has only a few species.

In the culture of the Killifishes are several specific features in which they differ from most other families. For one thing, few or none give one big spawning all at one time. Pairs usually spawn a few eggs a day over a more or less extended period. The eggs are tough-shelled, usually with some long thin filaments or "hairs" attached to them, and are more often placed singly among dense, bushy plant growths (such as *Riccia*), or (in certain genera) placed in the mud of the bottom. Finally the eggs take longer to hatch than those of most other small aquarium fishes. The shortest time is about one week, the average is about two weeks, while with some of the annual species, the eggs may take several months to hatch. With the tropical species, spawning often takes place in an aquarium for several extended periods throughout the year. Few of the North American species have been spawned extensively by aquarists.

After the sexes have been separated for one or two weeks and well fed with nourishing food, spawning will usually commence as soon as they are placed together in a well lighted, healthy aquarium containing the necessary bushy plants (see later under "Annual Species" for the mud spawners). Nylon spawning mops may be used instead of the plants. As the spawning goes on day after day, the easiest method of handling the eggs is to remove the bushy plants (or spawning mops) containing the eggs about once a week and place them in a rearing tank. The rearing tank should be large enough and well enough planted to enable smaller, more recently hatched young to escape their older brethren. Eggs laid over two or three weeks apart should not be placed in one rearing tank.

Spawning behavior is almost always the same throughout the family. The male comes up alongside the female and pushes her broadside against the plant growth. There, with fluttering fins and trembling bodies, a single egg is laid and fertilized. Then the process is repeated. Only one pair spawns together at one time. Extra males should not be present, but one male may spawn with several females.

The eggs are about the size of a pin head, which is considered fairly large, and consequently produce fry of good size. Newly-hatched Brine Shrimp can be used as the first food. Growth is rather rapid.

The large babies sometimes eat the small ones. While the dwarfs of any large hatching of fishes may as well be disposed of in that way, it must be remembered that there is usually a week's difference in age of a lot of Killifish young and it would not be fair to assume that the small ones are runts. To save the little fellows through their infancy they should be occasionally sorted for size. A female may produce 400 eggs during a breeding season.

The species of *Aplocheilus* and *Epiplatys* have flat heads and large mouths. With some others more or less similar in appearance, they are sometimes spoken of as "the *Panchax* group," but this grouping has no basis in classification. The eggs of these genera take about two weeks to hatch at 75° F.

Some Killies, such as the larger species of *Aplocheilus*, *Epiplatys* and *Aphyosemion*, and all or nearly all the annuals, possess a somewhat combative temperament, and males often attack and sometimes kill other Killies and occasionally even members of other groups.

Spawning females should always have a place to retire from the attentions of overly ardent or combative males. Species of such disposition are better left out of a community aquarium.

Many of the Killies are great jumpers, and will leap through very small openings left in the tank cover.

Killifishes are the favorites of many hobbyists, but unfortunately, very few species are offered for sale in pet shops. But an organization devoted to the study, propagation and maintenance of these fishes has been formed many years ago. Members of this organization—the American Killifish Association,—trade in fish and eggs of many species and publish information in monthly bulletins. Membership is available to anyone interested in Killies, and details about the organization can be found in current hobbyist magazines.

## *Fundulus chrysotus*   HOLBROOK

*Popular name:* Goldear Killifish

*Meaning of name:* Fundulus, bottom fish; chrysotus, golden-ear, with reference to golden gill plates

*Length:* 3 inches

S. E. United States

Although this handsome fish is very variable, it is easily recognized. On its olive sides are a few spangles of green gold, usually mixed, on the male, with round red dots. Sometimes added to these are irregular islands of black. Extremely beautiful specimens are sometimes seen in which the red dots strongly predominate, while a deep reddish hue extends into all of the fins, even with the female, which in the ordinary form has them clear.

*Fundulus chrysotus*

*Aplocheilus lineatus*

The light spot shown on the gill plate is green to gold. Eyes, usually yellow. There is another strain that is spotted heavily with black.

The species is a typical egg-dropper, preferring such plants as Myriophyllum for spawning purposes. The eggs at 75 degrees hatch in about 12 days, and the young are easily reared. Female is less colorful.

The fish is highly regarded by European aquarists and even by some Americans. A snail-killer, and sometimes rips fins of other fishes.

Temperature, 60°–80°.

## Aplocheilus lineatus
(CUVIER and VALENCIENNES)

*Meaning of name:* Aplocheilus, simple lip; lineatus, striped

Formerly known as Panchax lineatus

*Length:* 3½ to 4 inches

India

The colors of this species vary so much according to the light in which it is placed that no one picture can show a composite of the truth. At times the lines of metallic scales seem like rows of tiny mirrors of burnished gold. Both fishes may be of a uniform, pale green color, but the female always has more and

stronger vertical bars and very few red dots. The black spot at the base of the dorsal also identifies her.

This is the best known of the *Aplocheilus* species, as well as the easiest to breed. It has a mouth of considerable capacity and in its larger sizes the fish can suddenly dispose of a half-grown Guppy.

The eggs are laid singly in fine-leaved plants or spawning mops, and hatch in about 2 weeks. The fry are large enough to handle Brine Shrimp Nauplii.

## Epiplatys dageti

*Popular name:* Firemouth Killifish

*Meaning of name:* Epiplatys, very flat above, with reference to the head; dageti, after the French ichthyologist Daget. Formerly known as E. chaperi

*Length:* 2 inches

Gabon, W. Africa

One of the true old favorites, and while of recent years it has been crowded by more showy species, it holds a place in many collections. It is fairly hardy and of a popular size.

*Aphyosemion australe*

than those of *Aplocheilus lineatus.* Infusoria are recommended as a first food. Temperature, 65° to 90°.

## Aphyosemion australe
(RACHOW)

*Popular name:* Lyretail

*Meaning of name:* Aphyosemion, a fish with a banner; australe, southern

*Length:* 2½ inches

Cape Lopez, Africa

A small but very individual color characteristic of the male is the fiery appearance of the lower lip and sometimes also the throat, best seen from the front view. Another peculiarity of the species which makes it easy to recognize, and at the same time tell the sex, is the pointed extension, in the male, of the lower part of the tail fin. This is a peculiarity that sets the species clearly apart from any of its relatives, near or far.

Though a free breeder, its eggs and fry are considerably smaller

When not kept in conditions to its liking, it "folds up," becomes narrower, does not spread its fins and is apt to resign from life altogether. In a favorable environment, it is not a delicate fish.

Considering that it comes from tropical Africa, it stands water of moderate temperature very well, 68 to 70 degrees suiting it admirably, although for breeding it should be kept warmer, say 72 to 74 degrees. However, it is very particular about

*Epiplatys dageti*

*old* water, preferably a little acid, about pH 6.8. This is important in breeding.

Eggs are deposited, a few at a time, among such plants as Riccia, or on artificial, floating, spawning mops. They are rather easily seen, and parents do not touch them. There is no advantage, however, in keeping the breeders with the eggs, once they are through the spawning period, which is likely to last several weeks. Hatching period, about 10 to 12 days. The fry grow rapidly if fed plenty of newly hatched brine shrimp.

The color of the fish in the illustration is much darker than the usual rich, brown body color. It is a male. Females are tan colored and have unmarked fins.

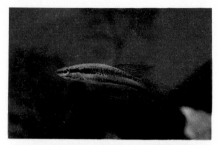

*Aphyosemion bivittatum, Male*

*Aphyosemion bivittatum, Female*

## Aphyosemion bivittatum
(LOENNBERG)

*Meaning of name:* Aphyosemion, a fish with a banner; bivittatum, two-striped

*Length:* 2½ inches

Tropical W. Africa

The fish itself varies considerably in color, only showing its best in old water in a well-planted aquarium, and in not too much light. Live food is important to it.

It moves about the aquarium, darting and then standing still, balanced by a continuous movement of the pectoral fins.

By nature the species is suited to living with other fishes, but special care should be taken to keep it only in old water. On the whole, it is one of the "touchy" species, requiring skilled handling.

Like other members of the family, it deposits eggs among plant

thickets. These hatch in about 12 days, at a temperature of 72 degrees. The young vary much in size and should be graded to prevent cannibalism.

## Aphyosemion gardneri

*Meaning of name:* Aphyosemion, a small fish with a flag (referring to the fins); gardneri, after a personal name

*Length:* 2½ inches

Nigeria

A beautiful and hardy Killifish, but, as is the case with so many of them, males do not tolerate each other's company very well. On occasion, males of this species will attack fishes of different species.

They are prolific breeders, depositing eggs in fine-leaved plants or artificial spawning mops near the surface of the water. It takes about 10 to 12 days for hatching, and the youngsters are large enough for feeding on newly hatched Brine Shrimp Nauplii.

Temperature 70° to 78°.

## *Roloffia occidentalis*
### (LOENNBERG)

*Roloffia occidentalis*

*Popular name:* Golden Pheasant

*Meaning of name:* Roloffia, of the ichthyologist, E. Roloff; occidentalis, from the west.

*Length:* 3 inches

Tropical West Africa

Not often imported and rather difficult to breed, this striking Killifish may be considered in the "select" class among aquarium fishes.

It likes old water and a rather subdued light, and does best on live foods. Should not be placed with fishes much smaller than itself. Capable of jumping over an aquarium edge that is several inches above water level. Keep closely covered at all times.

As with most of the Killifishes, the sexes are easy to tell by the pronounced differences between the fins of the male and female. In this instance, the male has a pattern in the tail fin, while the female has none. As might be expected, his coloring is much the brighter.

The fish is rather slender up to two years of age, at which it becomes heavier. The colors continue to intensify, especially the indigo. The odd, lower extension of the anal fin also appears with late maturity. Single large eggs, deposited on the bottom, hatch in

*Aphyosemion gardneri*

*Jordanella floridae*

about sixty days. Temperature range 70°–80°.

## *Jordanella floridae*
GOODE and BEAN

*Popular name:* American Flag Fish

Named for David Starr Jordan and the State of Florida

*Length:* 2 inches

Florida

Aquarists have not always been as successful with this beautiful and interesting species as they could have been had the food requirements been better understood. Apparently *Jordanella* has been mistaken for a sunfish, a strictly carnivorous fish, and has been denied algae, an important part of its diet.

As the male is a strenuous courter, the breeding aquarium should be thickly planted, including, if pos- sible, some Riccia. A well-estab- lished 5-to-10 gallon tank contain- ing soft algae is best. For several days eggs are deposited in depres- sions or among rootlets at the bot- tom, and are cared for by the male, who fans them and then protects the babies. The young are easily raised.

The species is rather combative, and is a heavy eater. In absence of algae, some boiled spinach should be alternated with other foods. Florida dealers supply this attrac- tive, interesting fish. It prefers alka- line water.

Temperature, 65°–80°.

## THE ANNUAL KILLIFISHES

### (Mud Spawners)

The remaining Killifishes differ from the preceding ones in the fact that they do not deposit the eggs on plants, but place them in the mud or very fine sand at the bottom of the aquarium. Even more remarkable is that most of the species, including more especially the South American *Cynolebias* and *Pterolebias* and the African *Nothobranchius*, are annual fishes, completing the life span in less than one year. Whether they are completely annual or not, all of the fishes in this division are short lived. We know of no specimen that has lived to be two years old. On the other hand, these annuals include the most brilliantly colored of all Killifishes, and the males of some of them are among the most gorgeously colored of all fishes.

The information that some of these Killies are annuals became known to aquarists in Germany as early as the 1920's but the fact that there is a large group of annual species, all belonging to a group of closely related genera, was not generally known until Dr. Geo. S. Myers presented the evidence in two papers published in 1942 (in Stanford Ichthyological Bulletin) and 1952 (in the Aquarium Journal). It was he who first called them "annuals."

In their native habitats, these fishes live in mud-bottomed ponds and sloughs, sometimes connected with a permanent body of water, but more often not. Towards the end of the rainy season, they spawn in the mud, and the adults then mostly wither and die, usually because the pond simply dries up. The eggs, however, survive, buried in the damp mud under the surface crust. There they remain, for a month and a half to several months. The heat of the sun apparently *slows up* the development of the eggs, for it has been noticed that eggs kept in water hatch sooner in cooler water than in warmer.

When the rains again begin to fill the pool, hatching occurs almost at once, and a new generation of fishes, born of parents long dead, grows very rapidly. However, the same sort of life cycle is gone through even if the body of water in which the fish live does not dry up completely.

Although several species come from tropical Africa and South America it is well to remember that they naturally inhabit well-shaded, still pools where the temperature does not rise excessively. Many capable aquarists have failed with these fishes, because of the fixed idea that all exotic fishes must be kept at a high temperature, an error caused by a too inflexible interpretation of the word "tropical" as applied to aquarium fishes.

While these fishes are among the more tedious to breed and difficult to handle, their great beauty makes the effort worthwhile and challenges our ability as aquarists.

Breeding tanks need not be large, even two gallon bowls can be used for the smaller species. As a bottom layer to receive the spawn, peatmoss which has been soaked in water for a few weeks works best.

## Nothobranchius guentheri

(PFEFFER)

*Meaning of name:* Nothobranchius, with pseudo gills; guentheri, after A. Guenther, ichthyologist

*Length:* 2 inches

Eastern Africa

One of the most brilliantly colored of the annual Killifishes. They should be kept in fairly soft, slightly acid water and frequently fed with a variety of live and frozen foods. Tubifex Worms, however, should be fed sparingly, if at all. Adult males are rather belligerent toward each other and it is best to keep just one male per tank.

In nature, this species is found in very small bodies of water which often dry out completely during the dry season. This, of course, kills the fish, but their eggs survive the dry spell buried in the mud on the bottom. Within a few hours after the next rain has filled the pond again, the young fish will hatch.

Their growth rate is phenominally fast, and in about six weeks the young fishes are already spawning.

In the aquarium, we can imitate the conditions in nature by keeping these Killies in a small aquarium with a layer of well-soaked peat moss on the bottom. Temperatures in the seventies are best.

Mature fish in good condition will spawn daily, laying one egg at a time into the peatmoss. After about two weeks, the peat containing the eggs should be taken out with a fine net, gently squeezed to remove excess water, air-dried until it is just damp to the touch and

*Spawning N. guentheri*

*Nothobranchius guentheri*

then stored for about six weeks in a closed plastic bag or other container at a temperature of 70° to 75°. After that incubation period, the damp peatmoss can be placed into a tank containing freshly aged water and presto, within an hour or so, tiny young will appear. They are ready to feed immediately, but require Infusoria for a day or two before they can tackle freshly hatched Brine Shrimp.

*Pterolebias peruensis*

### *Pterolebias peruensis*   (MYERS)

*Popular name:* Peruvian Longfin

*Meaning of name:* Pterolebias, Lebias (type of fish) with wings; peruensis, from Peru

*Length:* 3 inches

Peru

This is a South American species of annual Killifish, but the conditions for life are the same as for the African *Nothobranchius* species. They also deposit their eggs in the mud on the bottom, but in doing so dive head first, side by side into it. Therefore, in the aquarium the layer of peat should be sufficiently high (at least 2 inches) whereas for *Nothobranchius* a one inch layer is more than enough. The egg-drying process is the same as for *Nothobranchius*, but eight weeks of dry-

ness usually gives better results. Fry are also larger and can handle newly hatched shrimp the first day. Growth is extremely rapid but an almost constant supply of food is needed.

Temperature 68° to 76°.

## THE LIVE-BEARING TOOTH-CARPS

### FAMILY POECILIIDAE

The live-bearing Tooth-carps are the "live-bearers" of the aquarist. They are easily distinguished from the Killies by the elongated gonopodium or intromittent anal fin of the male. It is largely by differences in structure of this organ that the various genera are classified. All the Poeciliids are from the New World, the greatest number of genera in the species occurring in Central America and the West Indies.

There are several groups of viviparous or "live-bearing" fishes, but many of them are not yet known to aquarists. However, the family includes most of the live-bearers kept in home aquaria, and we interrupt the sequence at this point to give a general account of live-bearer breeding.

### *Breeding the live-bearers*

Not many years ago the author was often in receipt of letters, usually to "settle a bet," asking whether fishes really have their young born alive. The popularity of exotic fishes has become so general that the public now accepts the phenomenon of viviparous or live-bearing fishes without surprise. No more letters on that point are received.

However, there is some basis of truth in the idea that only mammals give birth to their young, for, while many of our aquarium fishes do indeed present developed young to the world, apparently without going through the egg period, this is not precisely true. Fully formed eggs are in the egg duct of the female, where they become fertilized, are hatched and grown to the same point of maturity as the young of egg-laying fishes which have absorbed their yolk-sacs and are ready to swim freely. In other words, the eggs of viviparous fishes have the protective advantage of hatching within the body of the female, and of entering the world well equipped to meet life on a competitive basis.

While it is true that an egg is the medium through which every live-bearing animal (whether warm- or cold-blooded) transmits the spark of life, there is a great difference between the internal process in mammals and fishes. In mammals, the ovum or egg after fertilization becomes attached to and is part of the mother. Its life stream proceeds from her. Except for the mother's supplying oxygen to the eggs and young, no such relationship exists between ordinary viviparous fishes and their babies.

## Period of Development

Females have no definite period of gestation as do warm-blooded animals. The young develop according to temperature, and after maturity are delivered at somewhat variable times, dependent upon conditions. Possibly the urge of the mother is a factor, for we know that if one fish is selected from a number of apparently "ripe" females and placed in fresh water, she is liable, through stimulation or excitement, to deliver within an hour. The babies are likely to be just as perfect as those coming from the other females several days later, indicating that they have been well formed for some time.

In the mother they lie folded once, with head and tail meeting, and are delivered in this form, one at a time, or occasionally two. Very soon they straighten out and swim for the best refuge they can find. The young when first introduced to the world are about a quarter inch long, which is considerably larger than from most species whose eggs hatch externally.

As has been stated, temperature has a bearing on the period of incubation, but to give the reader an approximate idea of what to expect from average conditions, it may be said that at 75 degrees the time from fertilization to delivery is about 4 to 5 weeks. The time may be greatly protracted by a few degrees less temperature. At 67 degrees it may be as long as 12 weeks. As with the egg-layers, however, it is believed that fairly rapid incubation produces the stronger young.

## Maturity Age

Different species vary considerably in this respect, and all species vary according to the conditions under which they are reared. A young Guppy, male or female, raised at an average temperature of 75 to 80, given plenty of room and live food, will be ready for breeding in 6 to 8 weeks. Platies are almost as rapid, while the minimum time for the maturity of Mollies is approxmatiely twice as long. Early breeding of females does not affect final size.

*Fertilization*

Interesting as are the facts already related regarding the live-bearers, they would be incomplete without an account of the fertilization itself. Those not already acquainted with the process will find it instructive. Many aquarist friends have found the theme of reproduction of live-bearing fishes to be an easy and natural medium for preparing young people for the "facts of life."

To outward appearances the sexes are the same at birth. In a few weeks the anal fin of the male fish becomes just a trifle more pointed. As time for maturity approaches, it rapidly lengthens into a straight, rodlike projection, carried backward and parallel to the body, and usually close to it, although capable of being quickly moved at any angle, forward or sideways. All appearances of a fin have disappeared. This is now called the *gonopodium*. In form and length it varies with different fishes. In Platies it is small and not always easily seen. In Guppies and *Gambusia* it is unmistakable, while in such genera as *Phallichthys* and *Poecilistes* it is quite obvious. The tip of the gonopodium varies in shape in different species.

The male in courting grandly spreads all fins and excitedly approaches the female, usually parallel to her and a little from the rear. He may circle her, all the while on the *qui vive*, ready to make a quick thrust from a position of vantage. The act is over in a second. The female never seems to be flattered by these attentions. Perhaps she dimly realizes with true world-old feminine instinct, that she is only his desire of the moment. At any rate the author has never seen nor heard report of her willingly accepting his attentions, nor of responding to them. Nevertheless, "love finds a way," and live-bearing fishes continue to multiply even faster than the rapidly increasing ranks of aquarists.

The live-bearers do not mate in the sense that the Cichlids do, nor the Gouramis. They are not even polygamous, but strictly promiscuous. Reproduction with them is conducted on a basis of what might be termed *impersonal opportunism*.

*Subsequent Fertilization*

Here is a subject of which we know little, but we have an idea. Owing to physiological reasons not fully understood, a female is able to store sperm from one mating for fertilization of 4 or 5 successive broods of young. These will be about the same distance apart in time as the time between fertilization and the first delivery. Immediately after a female has delivered her young, the males are intensely attracted to her and double their attentions. Although she is able to deliver another brood without further male contact, the question is whether such subsequent contact would result in part or all of the young inheriting the characteristics of the last male mate. This is brought up for the reason that if a fish breeder wishes to establish the characteristics of a certain male in its descendants, such, for instance, as particularly attractive markings in a Guppy, he would not be safe in assuming that the first 4 or 5 broods are necessarily fertilized by him if the female has, prior to the fifth delivery, been exposed to another male. That presents an interesting subject for research.

It is, of course, also a possibility that a second male contact any time after the first delivery of young, but before the fifth, would have no influence on the first 5 broods, but might fertilize later ones.

### When Is a Female "Ripe"?

Except with those few live-bearers which are black, or nearly so, there is a contrasting dark area on the female's body, close to the vent. It varies in shape and clearness in different species, but tends towards a crescent form, or sometimes a triangle. This is called the "gravid spot," caused by the dark portions of the internal organs showing through the stretched abdominal walls. This, however, is by no means a sure sign of pregnancy. In some color varieties of Swordtails and Platies, no black spot develops. In others a male might have it as well. Occasionally, in a light colored variety, the abdominal wall is so thin and transparent that little heads with eyes can be seen inside, peeping into the outside world. In that case, of course, there can be no doubt about the state of affairs. Most important, however, the sides of the fish bulge when seen from a top or side view. A little experience will give an idea of how far matters have progressed. With fishes we have not all the guiding facts that help our own medicos to make their computations in timing human births, but sometimes our guess is just as good!

### Frequency

Frequent breeding does not seem to shorten the life nor affect the final growth of either egg-layer or live-bearers. Interference with nature is more questionable.

### Number of Young

Broods may be as few as 3 in number, or well over 100. A fair average for a grown fish to deliver is 40 to 50. Anything over 100 is considered unusual. Some species have fewer and larger young than others. As previously stated, while the size of the female greatly influences the number of young she delivers, it has no effect on the size of the babies. Twins, attached belly-to-belly, are occasionally delivered. They usually die within weeks.

### Saving the Young

With all prolific animals nature seems to set up some barrier so they do not overrun the world. With live-bearing fishes in the aquarium, it is cannibalism on the part of parents. Aquarists can easily circumvent this tendency and save the babies.

First of all, the fewer fishes present at the time of delivery, the better. This also includes the male, his function having been completed weeks or months previously.

There are two general methods of saving the young. One is by providing them with hiding places, such as plant thickets, and the other is by the use of some mechanical contrivance which prevents the mother from getting at her babies.

Many such mechanical devices have been developed for the preservation of newly-delivered baby fishes. They have their points of merit. The central idea with all of them is to confine the ripe female in a space where she can live and which provides a small opening (or openings) through which the young fall or swim, and through which they cannot easily return.

V-shaped arrangements of sheets of glass in aquaria, with the bottom of the V slightly open, can be used in a large way for a number of ripe females at one time. Also a single sheet of sloping glass with the lower edge nearly against one side of the aquarium glass is another variation. Special "Breeding Traps" can be purchased.

These various mechanical devices have their uses, especially if the aquarist is not in a position to place the expectant mother in a thickly planted tank. It will be found, however, that in well-equipped establishments, where the breeding of live-bearers is conducted on a large scale, traps are seldom used. Preference is given to the other method utilizing thickets of plants as hiding places. The ideal aquarium for the purpose is an oblong one of from 5- to 10-gallon capacity, one-half of which is thickly planted. At the surface should be some floating aquatics such as Riccia or Hornwort. Any planting which provides a thicket is satisfactory, such, for instance, as masses of Anacharis, Myriophyllum or Nitella.

The planted side of the aquarium should be *towards the light*, as this is the natural direction for the young to take. The parent will not give chase among the plants, or will do so only feebly. The young sense their danger and are pretty cute at dodging.

There are several advantages to this plan of delivery. The female can be placed alone in the aquarium well in advance of expected appearance of young, thereby avoiding a certain amount of danger in handling her at a later time which might cause injury, and more probably, premature birth. In such an aquarium she can be well fed and kept in fine condition. With the aid of the open space she can easily be caught and removed after the completion of her duty to her species—and to her owner. By this scheme practically no young are lost and they grow well when left in the planted aquarium.

Shallow water seems best adapted to the needs of the young of the live-bearing species, although this is not an absolute requirement. From birth to 2 weeks old they seem safer in depths of 7 inches or less.

## Premature Births

As has already been stated, the handling of a live-bearing female shortly prior to her time for delivery is liable to result in premature births, even with gentle care. Some kinds of fishes are more sensitive than others. Guppies are seldom affected, while Mollies are touchy. The invariable sign of a premature delivery is when the yolk-sac is not fully absorbed, and is to be seen attached to the belly of the baby. Such young are heavy, and unable to rise from the bottom without effort. Few of them survive. If the sac is small it is advisable to salt the water, one full teaspoon to the gallon.

## Feeding Young Live-bearers

Unlike many egg-layers, young live-bearers spare the aquarist the fuss of providing live microscopic food. Being born of good size, they can manage newly-hatched Brine Shrimp at once, or will do fairly well on finely powdered fish food of almost any kind. Manufacturers have grades especially for them, but this is only a matter of size. Any granular food can be pulverized for the purpose. Size of food can be increased as the babies grow. They like "Mikro" worms.

At a reasonably high temperature, say about 75 degrees, they should be fed from 2 to 4 times daily. Whether the food be prepared or living, there should be only enough of it to last a quarter hour. Excess prepared food fouls the water. Too many Daphnia reduce the oxygen content. Snails dispose of prepared food the fishes have not taken. For this reason it is advisable to have plenty of them with young fishes of all kinds that are being raised on prepared foods. As the fishes grow, some species will kill the snails. If there is evidence of this, the snails may as well be removed and *Corydoras* substituted.

Sometimes beginner aquarists write that their baby fishes have not grown appreciably in several months. This state of affairs is likely to end in permanently stunting them, even though better conditions are later provided. Some causes of retarded growth are: too small aquariums, too many fishes, too low temperature, too little food, too little live food, infrequent feedings.

### When May Young Be Placed with Adults?

The answer to this question de-pends much on the size of the parents. Large parents of a given species do not have larger young than small parents, but they can swallow bigger fishes. The offspring of average parents are safe to place with the parents when the young have tripled their length, which should be in a month, with correct feeding. When placing *any* small fish in *any* aquarium, consider what the largest fish in that aquarium might be able to do to the little stranger. Can the big fish swallow the little fish?

Live-bearers seem to be quite impersonal toward their own particular young or the young of their own species. They are neither more nor less liable to eat them than the young of other parents or of other species. Their own appetites and the size of the proposed victim are the only considerations.

Generally speaking, the live-bearers will not eat young fishes if they have a good supply of choice live food for themselves. And, while generally speaking, it should be said that any fish introduced into an aquarium is apt to fare better if its hosts and future companions are in that mellow humor which is produced by having had a good meal, particularly if the new arrival happens to be small!

### Keeping Species Separate

As a matter of avoiding later confusion, it is best to keep the young of all similar species separate. This is particularly true of the live-bearers. Many of them not only look alike before maturity, but they are liable to breed much earlier than would be expected.

Hybridization between different species is not very likely to occur in an aquarium of mixed fishes, but undesired crosses are quite liable to happen between different color strains of the same species, such, for instance, as between red and blue Platies. This causes a degeneracy of pure types. When crosses are wanted, they should be deliberate.

## *Poecilia reticulata*  PETERS

*Popular name:* Guppy

*Meaning of name:* Poecilia, variable fish; reticulata, net marked, or mottled. Formerly known as Lebistes reticulatus

*Length:* male, 1⅛ inches; female, 2¼ inches

Trinidad, Guyana and Venezuela

Artificially introduced into many other locations

"Missionary Fish" would be a fitting name for this little beauty, for it far exceeds any other species in the number of convert aquarists it has made. And many of these converts who branched out and became aquarists in a big way still keep Guppies, and still feel that, with their infinite variety of colors, they are the most interesting of all aquarium fishes. Each male is as individual as a thumbprint.

Besides its beauty the Guppy has other great merits. Scarcely any other fish combines so many cardinal points in such degree. It is a live-bearer, the most popular type of fish. It is an extremely fertile as well as a dependable breeder. It is unusually active. It will thrive in close confinement. It can stand foul water. It has an extreme temperature range of 40 degrees, from 60 to 100. It will take any kind of food. It does not fight. It is not timid. It matures rapidly, an important point for those aquarists breeding for special points. It is

*Red Veiltail Guppy*

*Blue Veiltail Guppy*

*Female Guppy*

*Half-Black Guppy*

subject to few diseases. It can be had everywhere at prices available to everybody.

The activity of the male is extraordinary. Whether flashing about in pure joy of living, or paying court to a female, he is ever the embodiment of intensity. He might well be termed "the playboy of the aquarium."

In highly developed stocks some females appear not only showing traces of color in the tail fin, but also shiny highlights in it, as indicated in the single illustration. Any color in female adds value to a show pair.

Many beautiful strains of long-finned Guppies have been developed in the U.S. and now, breeders in the Orient are mass producing a fantastic number of colorful Gup-

pies for shipments all over the world.

No fancy breed can long be maintained without tireless vigilance in quickly discarding imperfect males, and in the early isolation of virgin line-bred females. Maturity takes place very early, and a female once fertilized by an inferior male is "ruined" as a select breeder until she has dropped all his young—a matter of some 6 months—without attention from another male. Her previous mis-alliance then has no bad effects on offspring by a later and better mate.

Breeding all sorts of animals for points, whether done on scientific Mendelian principles, or by "rule of thumb," involves the continual mating of the best close relatives. Unrelated breeders, of just as high grade, will not give as good results. As before stated regarding fishes, this can be carried on for generations without apparent physical deterioration, but breeders having both quality and good size should be chosen.

Excessive fin development does not occur in the young. Half-grown males of promise are best to use as breeders. The act of fertilizing requires more agility than that commonly possessed by fin-laden males.

Besides, Guppies are old at two years.

We do not agree with those who theorize that color inheritance is carried only through the male line. According to sound principles the female, showing little or no colors, still transmits the influence of her ancestry.

At several points we have suggested that certain fishes appear to best advantage with the light striking directly on the side we see. That is, from the back of the observer toward the tank. This is especially true of male Guppies. With most aquariums the light comes from the wrong direction for that, but it is a rewarding effort to even temporarily place them in a viewing jar with the sun playing on them.

The Guppy seems to be the only exotic fish species with enough variety of fixable points to establish it as a basis for fish fanciers. Guppy societies exist, having set standards for judging points to be used in shows.

Most of their diseases yield to "salt treatment" (see chapter on diseases). This may be carried far, as they can easily stand enough salt to kill most external enemies (and other fishes). The fatal "Hollowbelly" can usually be avoided by feeding several times daily on varying foods; live, fresh and prepared. A good average temperature for Guppies, 70 to 88. They are apt to worry snails to death by nipping at them.

## Poecilia sphenops

CUVIER and VALENCIENNES

*Popular name:* Liberty Molly

*Meaning of name:* Poecilia, variable fish; sphenops, wedgeface

*Poecilia sphenops (Liberty Molly)*

*Length:* 2 to 4 inches

Gulf Coast of Texas to Venezuela

Coming unheralded from Yucatan and imported by Wm. A. Sternke to OpaLocka, Florida, in 1935, this color variety of *P. sphenops* created quite a stir, and was soon widely distributed, as it proved to be a good breeder. The fish turned out to have so much exuberance (to put it politely) that it became something of a pest in chasing other fishes. This caused its popularity to wane, and possibly the strain lost some of its intense coloring through inter-breeding with other varieties of *P. sphenops,* which could readily be expected. For many years it was impossible to procure specimens showing the original bright coloring. Then, recently new stocks have been imported, and fish farms have made them available.

Kept by themselves in a large aquarium they make a lively living picture. As they are jumpers their tanks should be covered with either screen or glass. Temperature; 68°– 80°.

*Poecilia sphenops* is the most widely distributed species of the genus, so it is not surprising that it is also the most variable as to size and color, and, to some extent in disposition.

*Black Yucatan Mollies*

*Male Black Lyretail Molly*
*("Yucatan" Form)*

*Female Speckled Molly of the*
*"Yucatan" type*

A black strain has been developed by professional breeders and marketed under the name Yucatan Molly. They are easier to keep than the common Black Molly, less prone to diseases and less selective in diet.

Some Yucatan Mollies have a strong orange crescent at the end of the tail fin, and some have beautiful dorsal fins as shown on "Liberties." None of these colors, nor their variations or combinations, has much bearing on the identification of the species. Even the ordinary color, an olive gray with darker markings, means little. The aquarist's usual problem it to tell *sphenops* from *latipinna*. Fortunately this is not difficult. In *latipinna* the first ray of the dorsal fin starts in *front* of the highest point of the back. With *sphenops* it starts in *back* of the *hump*. The males are the more easily classified.

Mollies are particularly subject to injury in shipment, resulting in Mouth Fungus, "Ich" and "Shimmies." Early salt baths are effective.

*Poecilia latipinna, Male*

## *Poecilia latipinna*   LE SUEUR

*Popular name:* Sail-fin Molly

*Meaning of name:* Poecilia, variable fish; latipinna, broad-fin

*Length:* 3¾ inches

Coast of North Carolina to Florida; Gulf Coast and N. E. Mexico

This is the usual "Molly" of commerce. Coming from a considerable geographic range, it varies correspondingly in appearance, especially in that point of importance—the dorsal fin. This varies so greatly that it may class the individual either as a super-fish or as simply "another Molly." In a highly developed specimen, his resplendent dorsal fin is truly a crown of glory. To witness this "sail" fully exhibited in its royal splendor is to see something unforgettable—at least to an appreciative fish fancier or ichthyologist. Naturally his best display is put on either in a sham battle with another male (they seldom come to blows),

or before what might be called his lady of the moment. With all sails set he comes alongside her with insinuating motions, and then takes a position across her path as if, with a flurry of quivering fins, to prevent her escape. The colors displayed in these rapid and tense actions do not seem to be produced by excitement. It is merely an unfolding of the hidden tints which are always present but displayed only on occasions. The dorsal shows a gentle blue iridescence, but it is in the tail fin that the real color display takes place. The upper and lower thirds become a flashing, light metallic blue, while the center is a beautiful golden yellow. Yellow also covers the forward part of the belly.

The body of the fish is olive, with 5 narrow brown stripes, separated by rows of a lighter, sawtooth pattern.

Mollies require more care in breeding than most of the live-bearing species, but that extra attention bears fruit. They must have plenty of room, a temperature close to 78 degrees and plenty of the right kind of food. Mildly alkaline or slightly salted water is desirable. By nature they are largely vegetarian and, being active, eat often. They almost constantly nibble at algae. For this reason alone the fish should be in a large, well-lighted aquarium, which is conducive to the growth of algae. If there is insufficient growth for the purpose, a flake food which contains much vegetable matter should be used. Live Brine Shrimp, Daphnia, or Mosquito Larvae should be given frequently but not constantly. Feeding 4 to 6 times in 24 hours is desirable, provided each meal is entirely consumed within 10 minutes. This frequent feeding is important, both to breeding stock and the growing young.

At the first sign that a female is ripening, she should be removed to a well-planted delivery tank of about 10 or more gallons capacity. Gravid

females of all Mollies are adversely affected by handling, and the results are reflected in the young being born dead or defective in some respect, usually too heavy to leave the bottom. In fact, Mollies in general and *P. latipinna* in particular, had best be handled and moved from one aquarium to another as little as possible. If things are going well with them, a good motto is "Let good enough alone." If only a single pair is being bred, it is preferable to keep the expectant female where she is and remove the male as a matter

*Albino Lyretail Molly, Female*

*Marble Sailfin Molly, Male*

of precaution, although in the majority of cases, *P. latipinna* does not eat its young.

No female Molly should ever be placed in a small breeding trap. They need room and plenty of greens. All Mollies fail if crowded.

One feat no one has been able to achieve so far is producing Sail-fin young from Sail-fin stock in the aquarium. For one thing. it requires two years' growth.

## Xiphophorus maculatus
GUENTHER

*Popular names:* Moonfish, Platy

*Meaning of name:* Xiphophorus, sword-carrier; maculatus, spotted

*Length:* male, 1½ inches; female, 2 inches

Rio Papaloapan, S. Mexico

Beyond doubt, the general awakening of public interest in exotic aquarium fishes is due in large measure to the outstanding characteristics of a few species. The Platy Fish is one of the true early leaders, and one, through its many good points, that has retained favor while others have come and gone. The Platy, in addition to being one of the most attractive and generally satisfactory fishes in its own right, has contributed to the aquarium a most interesting assortment of hybrids. It may be safely stated that no other fish has made possible such elaborate studies in the inheritance of characteristics. This valuable quality, however, is beginning to overwhelm us with complications and many finely-drawn distinctions. It is with that thought in mind that the writer here intends touching only on some of the well-recognized variations of the Platy.

It should be remembered that all color strains or varieties of the species *Xiphophorus maculatus* are still the same species, and that they themselves in breeding pay no at-

*Red Wagtail Platies*

tention whatever to the colors of their mates. In practical application this means that if the aquarist is interested in maintaining pure strains he should keep all breeders of each variety in aquariums containing only their own kind.

Platies are bred very much the same as Guppies, except that they are a little less likely to eat their young. Also they do not take very kindly to the breeding trap, but should be placed in thickly planted aquaria and fed liberally when young are expected. They have a temperature range from 65 to 90, but do best at about 74 degrees. They are among those fishes that like to pick at algae, and it should be supplied them if possible.

## *Xiphophorus hellert*　　HECKEL

*Popular names:* Swordtail and Helleri

*Meaning of name:* Xiphophorus,

sword-carrier; helleri, after the collector, Carl Heller

Eastern Mexico

One of the most important of aquarium fishes. Its striking appearance, interesting habits and lively ways have made many an aquarium convert of those who saw it by chance. Then its variable colors, combined with the fact that it is a good breeder, have made it useful in studying certain laws of inheritance. We have been able to create new strains and new hybrids of great beauty.

The original imported stock, selling at the then fancy price of 10 dollars per pair, was strongly overcast with iridescent green and had metallic green in the tail spike. The saw-tooth line along the centre of the body was red and distinctly formed. The tail spikes were straight and long. Only a small proportion

*Gold Crescent Platy*

*Gold Wagtail Platies*

*Bleeding Heart Platies*

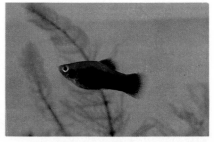

*Red Tuxedo Platy*

*Red Velvet Swordtail*

*Albino Swordtail*

*Green Swordtails*

*Red Wag Swordtail*

of the stock now available has these original characteristics in full measure. That variable quality which has made the Swordtail a good subject for experimentation has also made it difficult as to stability, so that clearly-drawn lines in varieties for purposes of competition in aquarium shows are hard to maintain.

The several Swordtails, in addition to being showy, are good aquarium fishes, but a few special characteristics should be remembered. They are wonderful jumpers, especially the males. Males are apt to bully one another, so it is best policy to have but one male in an aquarium. Like Mollies, they enjoy eating algae. It should be furnished them, if possible, even if it has to be scraped off another tank. In its absence a little finely chopped lettuce or boiled spinach is desirable. It is a species that feels the effect

of a single chilling for a long time and may never recover from the "Shimmies" resulting from that cause. They should have an average temperature of 72-80 degrees and frequent small meals.

Otherwise, breeding and care as per standard description. The sexes at first look alike, but as the male develops to maturity, not only does his anal fin change into an organ of sex, but the lower rays of the tail fin elongate into the well-known spike. If this change occurs while the fish is still small, it will never grow much more. Good-sized males are secured only by growing them rapidly while young. This calls for plenty of room (aquarium of 10 gallons or more), no overcrowding, a warm temperature and plenty of live food. The species likes a flood of light, and shows best in it.

A large female is liable to deliver more than 100 young.

*Black Lyretail Sword*

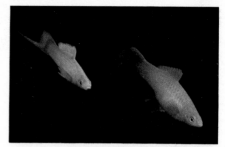

*Marigold Swordtails*

*Brick-Red Lyretail Swords*

*Red-Tailed Variatus*

*Black Variatus*

The males carry the colors, which begin to show at about 4 months, and are fully developed in a year.

This species is quite hardy and for short periods can stand a temperature as low as 50 degrees. It is a prolific live-bearer. If well fed the parents are not likely to eat their young.

### *Xiphophorus variatus*          MEEK

*Popular name:* Variatus

*Meaning of name:* Xiphophorus, sword carrier; variatus, varied or variable

*Length:* 2 inches

Rio Panuco to Rio Cazones, E. Mexico

The specific name of this fish, *variatus,* is surely appropriate. In coloration it is one of the most variable of aquarium fishes. For this reason it offers aquarists interesting problems in fixing colors.

### *Gambusia affinis holbrooki*
GIRARD

*Meaning of name:* Gambusia, worthless; affinis, related; holbrooki, after J. E. Holbrook

*Length:* males, 1½ inches; female, 2½ inches

Atlantic Coast States, Delaware to Florida

To many aquarists, at least in the United States, *Gambusia affinis* represents the beginning of an epoch. It was our first live-bearer. The

*Marigold Variatus*

*Gambusia affinis*

species was advertised by dealers as the eighth wonder of the world. All flocked with their $2 per pair to prove or disprove for themselves all claims for this strange fish. All placed them in with fancy lace-tail Goldfish. Soon the beautiful fins of the Goldfish were in shreds and the Gambusias were banished. But they were kept long enough to prove that they have their young born alive, and to demonstrate that they bred faster than purchasers could be found. This is not surprising, for in appearance they have no merit sufficient to offset the disadvantage of their destructive natures. Like other efficient fighters, they give no notice of attack.

G. affinis is a justly famed fish, for it has saved many human lives by eating mosquito larvae. It has been introduced into many parts of the world for this purpose, and its chief service to man has been in destroying the larvae of the mosquito which carries the germs of malarial and yellow fevers. In tropical countries in situations where the draining of mosquito ditches is impossible or too expensive, the little fish has been successfully brought into service. Its practical value is enhanced because it can live in good or bad water, and will stand a temperature range from 40 to 100 degrees. Success in building and maintaining the Panama Canal depended partly on the solution of the fever problem. G. affinis was and still is largely responsible for making Panama habitable to the white man.

There is much confusion in the minds of aquarists about the differences between the 2 common forms of Gambusia in our southern states. The worst error, and the hardest to eradicate, is the idea that the black-spotted Gambusias form a distinct species, holbrooki. The black spotting has nothing whatsoever to do with separating the two forms! The facts of the case are these: In the southern United States (excluding Texas for the moment), there are two forms of Gambusia, an eastern and a western, practically identical in color, form, size and habits. The eastern form (holbrooki), which is found in lowland streams of the eastern seaboard from Delaware to Florida and Alabama, has 8 rays in the dorsal fin and the third ray of the gonopodium shows a deep split when examined under the microscope. The western form (affinis) occurs in lowland streams from Alabama to southern Illinois and south in the Texas coastal region to Tampico, Mexico. It has only 7 rays in the dorsal fin and the microscopic split in the third ray of the gonopodium is absent. In Alabama the eastern and western forms meet and merge their distinctive features so that certain individuals from this area cannot be placed definitely as one or the other form. Hence they are not nowadays regarded as distinct species, the western one being known as G. affinis and the eastern one as a race of it, G. affinis holbrooki.

Both sexes of both affinis and holbrooki are ordinarily pale gray fishes, often with faint bluish metallic reflections. The dorsal and tail are usually marked with rows of tiny dark dots. The dots in the tail easily distinguish the plain females from female Guppies. Otherwise they look much alike.

The velvet black spotting or blotching which is prized in aquarium specimens may be present in either affinis or holbrooki. Dr. George Myers, who has collected affinis wild in North Carolina, says:

"Schools of several hundred Gambusias were to be seen swimming in shallow water near shore. In every second or third school a single, or at most 2, black males were observed; they were very conspicuous among their pale brothers. The original collectors who sent Gambusias north used to catch out these colored 'freaks' with a dip net, pair them with any large females caught in the schools, and ship them as a different species, the so-called 'G. holbrooki.' These black freaks seem in many cases to breed true, and at least some of our southern dealers seem to have developed strains which breed consistently. Wild black-blotched females are extremely rare, but in the course of man's selective breeding for black fish, a proportion of fairly dark females appear. So far as available data go, the black blotching of either sex occurs about as frequently in the western *affinis* as in the eastern *holbrooki,* but the black color, as can be seen from the foregoing, no more indicates specific difference than does the black color of the black Molly."

For breeding in the aquarium, it prefers a temperature of about 75 degrees. It conforms to the usual type of breeding described for "Live-bearers," but is one of the species which is particularly likely to eat its young if given the opportunity. Since they multiply with such tremendous rapidity when in the wild state, it must be that the young very quickly take themselves off to good hiding places. With plenty of natural food they soon develop to a size which is too large to be swallowed by the parents.

In the matter of food they are easily suited. While preferring animal substance, they will take any of the prepared articles.

The species is very seldom attacked by any kind of disease.

In some of the streams of southern and western Texas there are 3 or 4 other, very different species of *Gambusia,* at least one of which, the golden Gambusia *(G. nobilis),* has found its way into aquariums.

## *Belonesox belizanus*     KNER

*Popular name:* Pike Livebearer

*Meaning of name:* Belonesox, after the garfish, Belone, and the pike, Esox; belizanus, from Belize, Honduras

*Length:* To 6 inches; females somewhat larger

### Central America

Anyone attempting to maintain and possibly breed this species will have to solve first a very fundamental problem: how to supply a sufficient amount of food in the form of live fishes. Nothing short of live fishes will do, although a few individuals will sometimes take live Brine Shrimp, Bloodworms, Earthworms, and the like. The fishes are livebearers, but are not very likely to breed if not fed abundantly.

Since their native waters are often slightly brackish—they are mostly found near the mouth of rivers—the addition of a little salt to their tank water will be beneficial. About two teaspoonfuls of salt per gallon of water is not too much, and the hardier plants can withstand that amount.

Newborn young are already three quarters of an inch long, and nearly complete replicas of their parents. On their very first day of life, they are able to swallow fish of the size of newborn guppies, but will also do well for a while on live adult Brine Shrimp, live Bloodworms, Mosquito Larva, Glass Larva, and

*Belonesox belizanus*

large Daphnia. Youngsters grow at different rates, and if left together, larger ones will soon prefer their siblings over other foods. With good care, they will reach adolescence in about four months, and full maturity at about six. Full size is attained in about one year.

## FOUR-EYED FISHES
### FAMILY ANABLEPIDAE

This family contains but one genus, Anableps. They are highly specialized fishes, found only in Central America and the Northern Coast of South America. Few are imported, and when available, command a fairly high price.

### *Anableps anableps*      LINNAEUS

*Popular name:* Four-eyed fish

*Meaning of name:* Unknown

*Length:* 8 to 10 inches

Coastal Sections of Northern South America

Four-eyed Fishes are strange creatures, and if the name alone does not arouse the curiosity of the hobbyist, a look at a live specimen definitely will. Their eyes are divided into an upper part for vision above the water surface, and a lower part for underwater vision—hence their common name, Four-eyed Fish. They are surface dwelling fishes with positive buoyancy, which helps them float effortlessly just below the surface. In this position, the upper part of the eye is held above the water, but the fish regularly wets that part of the eye by dipping its head every few seconds. Four-eyed Fishes prefer brackish water, since their habitat is the lower reaches of rivers and streams, close to the sea.

Their food consists mainly of insects which have fallen into the water, but in captivity, they learn

*Anableps anableps*

very quickly to accept other foods, preferably the floating kinds. Although the fish will pick food particles off the bottom, they can only do so with great difficulty.

Shallow water is best for two reasons: one can observe the fish much better when the waterlevel in the aquarium is low, and the fish have less trouble in feeding off the bottom.

Anableps need a fairly roomy tank. It should be arranged with rocks, driftwood and/or plants which reach or protrude above the surface of the water. They are rather scrappy fish, at least among themselves, and should be able to get out of each other's way. Otherwise, the largest one will invariably take command and chase every other one to the point of exhaustion and eventual death.

There are no reports of them having bred in captivity, but we do know that they are livebearers. Interestingly, the gonopodium of adult males is movable to one side only, either to the right or to the left. In females, the genital orifice is also located either to the left or to the right, and right sided males can mate only with left sided females and vice versa. How this mechanism evolved or what purpose it might serve is not known. We do know that only up to 5 large, 1½ inch babies are born at one time, and that the period of gestation might last as long as 5 months. The fish are most comfortable at a temperature of 78° to 82°.

## THE SILVERSIDES
### FAMILY ATHERINIDAE

The Silversides are common saltwater fishes found on nearly all tropical and temperate coasts. A few permanently inhabit fresh water. The separate spiny dorsal fin and the Cyprinodont-like mouth will identify fishes of this family.

## *Melanotaenia fluviatilis*

*Popular name:* Red-tailed Rainbow fish

*Meaning of name:* Melanotaenia, with black band; fluviatilis, of the river

*Length:* 5-6 inches

Northern Australia

Of the three species of Australian Rainbow fishes which have been imported from that continent, this is certainly the most handsome as well as the largest and thus requires a slightly bigger tank. This is the species most often offered by petshops today. Red-tailed Rainbows are content with a variety of dried foods, but grow larger and develop more color on a diet of live, frozen, and freeze-dried foods. Water conditions are not very important as long as the water is not too soft or too acid.

They breed like other members of the Silversides. After a short courtship dance in which the male circles the female with his fins fully spread, the female deposits single, hard-shelled eggs among the fine leaves of plants such as *Myriophyllum* (Foxtail), *Ambulia,* Hornwort, *Cabomba* or on the roots of floating Water Sprite and Water Fern. Artificial spawning mops are also accepted. Fry hatch in about one week and immediately become free-swimming. They are very small requiring infusoria for a couple of days before they can handle newly hatched Brine Shrimp.

Contrary to most fishes of this shape, the male (lower fish in the illustration) is usually larger and more deep-bodied. His colors are more intense.

Temperature, 75° to 80°.

## *Melanotaenia maccullochi*    AHL

*Popular name:* Australian Rainbow fish

*Meaning of name:* Melanotaenia, with black band; maccullochi, named for the late Alan Riverstone MacCul-

*Melanotaenia fluviatilis*

loch, ichthyologist at the Australian Museum, Sydney, Australia

*Length:* 2¾ inches

Australia

Australian Rainbow fishes attain their beautiful coloration only when mature. The fishes pictured are young adults, not quite fully grown, and not yet in full color. Sexes are not two difficult to determine as long as the fish are in good condition. The male (fish to the right) is usually a bit more brilliant.

Rainbow fishes readily spawn in fine-leaved plants over a period of several days. The very small eggs hatch in about a week. Fry are tiny and require infusoria as a first food. Temperature 68° to 80°.

## *Telmatherina ladigesi*        AHL

*Popular name:* Celebes Rainbow fish

*Meaning of name:* Telmatherina, bony fish found in puddles; ladigesi, after

Dr. Ladiges, ichthyologist in Germany

*Length:* 2 to 2½ inches

Celebes (Indonesia)

For a fish coming from Indonesia, as this beautiful Rainbow fish does, one would expect it to thrive best in the same soft and acid water as do small species of *Barbus* and *Rasbora* and most other fishes from that area. Quite to the contrary, all Rainbow fishes—and this one is no exception—prefer water that is neutral to slightly alkaline in *p*H and medium hard. This is the quality of many tap waters, and all one needs to do to make it suitable for these fishes is to age it a few days. If only soft water is available, the addition of salt, about one teaspoonful per gallon, will improve it considerably.

These Rainbows are schoolfishes, preferring the upper half of the tank where they swim about tirelessly.

*Melanotaenia maccullochi*

*Telmatherina ladigesi*

*Chanda wolffi*

Because they live in swift-flowing streams, their tank should be well-aerated; they are uncomfortable in water of low oxygen content. Dried foods are readily taken, but preference is definitely given to Daphnia, Brine Shrimp, and Mosquito Larvae. Of the two dorsal fins, the second is the larger and more striking, a unique characteristic of all Rainbow fishes. In this case it is lemon yellow and in males the first rays are separated, much elongated, and jet-black in color. Spawning habits are similar to other members of the family. Single eggs are deposited in fine-leaved plants or roots of floating plants near the surface. Hatching time is approximately eight to ten days at a temperature of 78°. The fry become free-swimming immediately, but seem to grow rather slowly. A fairly high percentage of them never reach the free-swimming state, but become what the literature calls "belly-sliders." This failing is assumed to be caused by keeping the temperature too high, but no definite proof seems to be available. Temperature, 72° to 78°.

## THE CHANDIDS

### FAMILY CENTROPOMIDAE

The Chandids are small, brackish and salt-water fishes of the Indian Ocean and Western Pacific. They are very much like the salt-water Cardinal Fishes but differ in having the spiny and soft dorsals connected at the base. Most of the species are translucent.

## Chanda wolffi

*Popular name:* Wolff's Glassfish

*Meaning of name:* Chanda, a native name; wolffi, after a personal name

*Length:* 1¾ inches

Southeast Asia

These are calm and peaceful fishes unhappy in tanks containing many fast-moving fishes. They should only be kept wih fishes having the same temperament, or, better yet, entirely by themselves. Although an occasional specimen will take prepared foods, such fare is ignored by most of them. Live food must be offered to keep Glassfish in good health. In this species, there are no obvious secondary sex characteristics.

*Chanda wolffi* has replaced *Chanda lala,* the old favorite, in popularity with hobbyists, although it lacks the metallic sheen of *Chanda lala.* Apparently, it is more readily available to collectors in South East Asia. In addition, it is much more hardy. Temperature 75° to 82°.

## THE THERAPONIDS

### FAMILY THERAPONIDAE

The Theraponids are spiny-rayed, saltwater fishes of the East Indies which frequently ascend rivers into fresh water. They have two nostrils on each side, but differ from most related families in the absence of the small scale-like flap at the base of the ventral fins.

## Therapon jarbua        (FORSKAL)

*Meaning of name:* Therapon, shield-bearer; jarbua, a native name

*Length in nature:* 10 inches; usually much smaller in aquarium

Red Sea, E. Coast Africa to China, N. Coast Australia

The drooping concentric lines on

*Therapon jarbua*

*Monodactylus argenteus*

are marine fishes. Only *Monodactylus* enters freshwater. The deep forms and the scaly fins distinguish them from other aquarium fishes.

## Monodactylus argenteus
### LACEPEDE

*Meaning of name:* Monodactylus, with one finger, referring to appearance of dorsal and anal fins; *argenteus*, silvery one

*Length:* 4 inches

Indian Ocean

Not knowing that this is a marine fish, one would hardly suspect it. It is beautiful, but not with that gaudy display we have come to expect of marine tropicals.

The fish is extremely silvery, while the dark portions of the upper and lower fins represent a beautiful, rich yellow. Preference in purchase should be given to the younger specimens. They will grow rapidly in a large aquarium, *but should not be unnecessarily disturbed or moved about.* Salt water unnecessary. Never bred. Temperature, 75 degrees.

## Monodactylus sebae
### CUVIER AND VALENCIENNES

*Meaning of name:* Monodactylus, with one finger, referring to appearance of anal fin sebae, personal name

*Length:* to about 7 inches

Western coast of Africa

*Monodactylus* are mostly marine fishes, but do enter fresh water. They can be kept in either fresh or salt water, or anything in between. These are more quarrelsome than *M. argenteus* and are voracious feeders, needing plenty of live and frozen foods. They will also take freeze-

a ground of shining silver are dark gray to black. The large spot in the dorsal is particularly intense and adds to the already strange aspect of the fish.

Like the Chandids, to which it is closely related, it is a marine fish which enters fresh water; unlike the Chandids, it is an extremely active fish and will accept dried foods. It is very quarrelsome. Seldom imported and has never been bred in captivity.

Although a marine fish, it is easily kept in fresh water at a temperature of about 73° to 78°.

## THE BUTTERFLY FISHES
## FAMILY CHAETODONTIDAE

Almost all members of this family

**Monodactylus sebae**

it was not until the experiments of the late Dr. Hugh M. Smith, in Thailand, during the 1920's that the shooting was fully proved. In 1934 Dr. George S. Myers, while collaborating with Dr. Smith, worked out the structure of the shooting apparatus in the Archer's mouth. The illustration shows the best-known species of Archer. Long, colorful articles by Dr. Smith on this extraordinary fish appeared in "The Aquarium" (July, 1939 and August, 1944), and by Commander Alfred Marsack in January, 1952. Extinguishing distant lighted cigarettes at night by a pellet of water is one of their famous acts.

## *Toxotes jaculator*    PALLAS

*Popular name:* Archer Fish

*Meaning of name:* Toxotes, archer; jaculator, hurler

*Length:* 5 inches

Indonesia

Here is one of the unique showmen among aquarium fishes, and with the correct properties and settings supplied, it can be depended upon to do its act.

That a fish could accurately aim a mouthful of water as a missile and bring down a fly seems to strain one's credibility. Aside from the mechanical difficulties of such a feat, anyone with a slight knowledge of optics knows that, due to surface refraction, objects do not appear in their true positions when one is looking into or out of the water, unless, as might rarely happen, the object is directly above or below the observer. A bullet from a rifle aimed at an angle to the water and pointed at a small object below the surface could not hit it unless allow-

dried and other prepared foods. Nothing is known about reproduction, though they probably breed in the sea. Temperature, 75° to 82°.

## THE ARCHER FISHES

### FAMILY TOXOTIDAE

The Archer Fishes are a small family of four or five species from India, southeastern Asia, and northern Australia. The head is flat above and pointed, the dorsal is set far back, and the soft dorsal and anal fins are scaly.

Natives in Asia have long known that the Archer Fishes shoot water at insects above the surface, but ichthyologists long doubted it, even ascribing the habit to a different fish *(Chelmon)*. Early in the present century, European aquarists first saw captive, imported Archers shoot, but

*Toxotes jaculator*

ances were made for the optical "bend." The same is true from the under side of the surface, looking out. The Archer Fish has learned to compensate for this and will accurately splatter its prey from a distance of a foot or more and usually bring it down.

It shoots a few drops at a high speed, capable of reaching a distance of ten feet. If the first shot does not bring down the prey, it is followed by a rapid series until the insect falls. Few escape. The Archer's mouth is quite large, and the shooting is done while the lips are just above the surface of the water.

We are told that *Toxotes* varies considerably in color. Dorsal and anal fins are edged black. The six dark bars are a gorgeous black, making the fish easy to remember by its striking appearance as well as its original way of obtaining its food. It will eat live food which it has not knocked into the water. Meal worms

seem to be particularly relished. It will also eat live, adult Brine Shrimp and will readily learn to take lumps of freeze-dried Brine Shrimp.

Nothing is known as to sex distinctions or breeding habits. A temperature of 75° proves satisfactory. This is one of those species coming from salt, brackish, and fresh waters; we believe a mixture of sea water is advisable. They get along well together and even prove themselves sports by not quarreling when the shooter's victim is gobbled by another fish!

Like the various electric and walking fishes, the Archer Fish is a star attraction at a public fish show, for it will "knock off" live flies as long as the spectators choose to supply them.

## THE SCATS
### FAMILY SCATOPHAGIDAE

The "Scats" differ from the salt-water Butterfly-fishes to which they

*Scatophagus argus*

are most closely allied in various technical internal features. They cannot be confused with any of the other groups of freshwater aquarium fishes. Most "Scats" are imported from brackish or fresh water in Indonesia. They do enter the sea.

## *Scatophagus argus*    (PALLAS)

*Meaning of name:* Scatophagus, offal eater; argus, thousand eyed (from the spots)

*Popular name:* Scat

*Length:* 10 inches

Indonesia

Although we are told that in nature the fish comes in 10″ and even 12″ lengths, the usual size seen in the aquarium is from 2″ to 4½″.

The fish is rather flat in form, or "laterally compressed," as it is called. In markings it is so variable

that one would easily get the impression that the different patterns indicate various species. There are two principal types. Our photo shows the type known as the Tiger, or Red Scat, which is sometimes recognized as a variety called *rubrifrons*. Some aquarists believe the markings denote the male fish. While we believe this to be a mistake, we can offer no other evidence of sex. The subject is not important, as we have little prospect of breeding the species.

The second type or variety has numerous round black spots on a greenish silvery body. It is often described as Green Scat.

Of the two varieties, the Tiger Scat has the most striking appearance and brings the best prices. Neither species is cheap.

A renewed interest in marine household aquariums finds a considerable number of Scats doing well in ocean water at full strength.

There has been much discussion whether the species can be successfully kept in fresh water. The answer is that it can, although the addition of a moderate amount of sea water or sea salt is advisable. If this is not done, the water should at least be kept in an alkaline condition—say a pH reading of 7.4 or a little higher. This is a good fish to be kept in localities where the water is hard.

In nature the fish is one of the real scavengers of the sea, inhabiting the mouths of rivers and the docks of various tropical seaports. It is, therefore, not surprising to find that it will eat anything, although it is hard to account for the fact that it is extremely fond of Riccia and Nitella, plants entirely strange to its native brackish and marine waters. Temperature, about 70° to 78°.

Owners are usually very fond of the active and harmless fish, for it has "personality." It is a heavy feeder and always has a hopeful eye open for the appearance of the master. Quite a pet.

## Selenotoca papuensis
FRASER-BRUNNER

*Popular name:* Moon Scat, Silver Scat

*Meaning of name:* Selenotoca, selene: the moon; tocus, offspring—born of the moon; papuensis living in Papua (N. Guinea)

*Length:* 4 inches

New Guinea

A few aquarium fishes can live in either fresh or salt water. This is one that can. Of course, if a change is made from one to the other, it should be gradual.

The light portions in the illustration are brilliant, mirror-like silver, showing to especial advantage under strong light. The darker portions of the fish are black. No bright colors, nor even tints. Body flat, like that of a Scalare. Another species, *Scatophagus multifasciata*, occurs in Australia.

Altogether it is a very satisfactory

*Selenotoca papuensis*

*Scatophagus spec.*

aquarium fish; certainly a showy one.

Eats anything. Never bred. Suited to living with other fishes of about its own size. Swims about the aquarium industriously, always on the move. There is no known method of distinguishing the sexes. Temperature range, 70° to 80°.

## THE CICHLIDS

### FAMILY CICHLIDAE

The Cichlids are spiny-rayed, bass-like fishes found only in Africa, Madagascar, and tropical America, south of the Rio Grande in Texas. The sole exception is *Etroplus,* three species of which inhabit southern India.

In general the Cichlids are the big fishes of the aquarium. They are well represented by such species as the Oscar *(Astronotus),* Jack Dempsey *(Cichlasoma octofasciatum)* and the Jewel Fish *(Hemichromis bimaculatus).* Rather long fishes with slightly flattened, moderately deep bodies. The head, generally of good size, is armed with a strong, jutting lower jaw and small but sharp teeth, well suited not only to battle, but to the requirements of their remarkable habits in breeding, as we shall shortly see.

While a few of the Cichlids are peaceable citizens, most of them fight, especially with members of their own species, and more especially with those of the opposite sex. These battles mostly occur during courtship—terrific lovers' quarrels, as it were. Occasionally it is between mated pairs, as will be observed later.

No doubt feeling confident of taking care of themselves in open battle, most of the larger species tear out plants, especially at breeding time.

## Breeding

With the unique exception of the mouthbrooders (whose habits will be described under their own headings), the Cichlids breed so nearly alike that a general description will fit nearly all of them. The few traits that may be peculiar to a species will be noted under its own special text. For example, that popular favorite, *Pterophyllum scalare* (Angel Fish), requires separate consideration.

The typical breeding actions of Cichlids are certainly the most interesting and highly organized of any known aquarium fishes, especially when the habits of mouthbrooders are added to that which now follows.

Mating itself is with them no hit-or-miss affair. At the very beginning the ancient law of the survival of the fittest is put into practical operation. If raised from youngsters and left to themselves in a large group, pairs will mate themselves at maturity by natural affinity, which is one of the best ways of discovering pairs if one has the room and stock to carry out this plan. The usual procedure in trying to mate adult fishes which have not been raised together with a minimum of risk is to place them in a large aquarium with a glass partition between. That is their formal introduction. One fish is usually ready to mate before the other, and as fliration through windows is nothing new in the world, one of them makes the opening advances. As again in our world, it may be either the male or the female to make the first move. This consists in a wagging of the body, spreading of the fins and a variety of changes in coloring. When the "party of the second part" returns these salutations and shows signs of approval, it is time to take out the partition and note what happens. Usually the courtship continues and it is not long before the "kissing" stage develops. This is where one of the uses of strong jaws comes in. They grasp each other by interlocking the lips and then begins the first real test. Each tugs and twists the other, apparently in a test of strength. They may go through the performance several times. If they do this repeatedly without either losing its "nerve," they may be considered to be as well mated as though they have a marriage certificate. But it often happens that one of them takes fright and beats a retreat after one of those vigorous kisses. Fear is fatal, and the victim of it is liable to get killed unless a safe retreat is found, or a kind Fate in the person of the owner separates them.

Sometimes a subsequent trial will prove more successful, but it is advisable to try some other pairing, if substitutes are on hand. Certain fishes will reject or kill several proposed mates before meeting an agreeable affinity.

Owing to the physical tussle which takes place, an effort is usually made by the aquarist to match the candidates in size, but there are many instances of happy unions between fishes where disparity in this respect is great. Whether or not both fishes are ready to mate is the important thing. Their courtship promotes the elimination of the unfit.

To return to the actual business of breeding—let us consider the proper conditions which should be provided. Success is more likely in large aquaria. Among the larger species, 3 inches is about minimum breeding size. Some fishes should be bred in an aquarium of not less than 10 gallons. Twenty would be better. As size of the pair increases, follow with proportionate room. It will pay.

Water should be old and at a temperature between 75 and 80 degrees. The best bottom covering is approximately 2 inches of well-washed sand. Any moderately good light is satisfactory. Omit plants for most species. Exceptions in this respect will be noted.

For a few days prior to breeding, the fishes dig holes in the sand. They also start cleaning a surface which they regard as suitable to the reception of their adhesive eggs. This spot may be the side of the aquarium, a large stone, inside or outside of a flower-pot laid on its side, or even a spot on the bottom of the aquarium from which the sand has been fanned away. It has been observed that a light-colored surface is preferred to dark. For this reason some of our fish breeders place a piece of marble or other light-colored stone in the aquarium with mated Cichlids.

The breeding pair takes nothing for granted as to cleanliness. Regardless whether they select a mossy side of the aquarium or a piece of marble fresh from the quarry, the sacred spot to receive their eggs must be painstakingly gone over to insure its absolute cleanliness. They bite, scrape and polish it with their teeth until no flaw can be found. No Dutch housewife could make it cleaner.

A day or two prior to the actual spawning both fish develop from the vent a breeding tube, or ovipositor. It first appears as a very small point or nipple. Whether it is a Cichlid or certain other species which deposit their eggs in a like manner, the appearance of the nipple is regarded as a sure sign that the fish is ripe for breeding. The tube shortly before spawning increases in length. In large specimens it may be as long as a quarter inch. It disappears within a week after spawning.

In general it is not easy telling the sexes. In older specimens the males often have longer pointed dorsal and anal fins. Where there is any distinctive difference in markings, this will be described in connection with the species. When the females are ripe, they are slightly fuller, but not in a pronounced way. It will be found that the breeding tube of the female is slightly blunt, whereas in the male it is pointed.

All things now being in readiness, the female approaches the prepared spawning spot and touches it lightly with the breeding tube, depositing one or more eggs. The male immediately follows, and with like action sprays the eggs with his fertilizing fluid. This is repeated many times over a period of perhaps 2 hours, when finally there may be from 100 to 2000 eggs laid in close formation. As this whole operation is carried on by a sense of touch and the eggs adhere very lightly, it is quite remarkable how few are lost or knocked off.

The spawning operation being completed, each fish takes turns fanning the eggs with the pectoral fins or tail. They relieve each other every few minutes. It is a popular idea that this fanning is to supply oxygen to the embryo within the egg. We know that bird eggs need oxygen, but with fish eggs there is also another consideration. As fungus is the great enemy of the eggs and the parents go to no end of trouble to have everything immaculate, presumably to avoid this danger, it seems quite likely they are preventing fungus-bearing particles of dirt from settling on the spawn. Sometimes, despite care, fungus develops on a few eggs. It attacks all infertile eggs. Apparently sensing the danger of its spread, the fishes eat the affected eggs. This sometimes ends in all the eggs, good and bad, being eaten.

At a temperature of 80 degrees the eggs hatch in about 4 days. Now begins the next of the several remarkable stages in the breeding habits of these fishes. The parents scrape the eggs off and the fry are carried in the mouth of either of the parents and deposited in a depression in the sand. It may be newly dug or one left from the home-building connected with the early part of mating. The parents alternate in making the trips between the hatching place and the depression until all are transferred. In some instances the fishes set up a system so that neither end of the line is left unguarded. Each stands guard at one end and as everything is in readiness for the transfer of young, a signal is given in fish language and they dash past each other to the opposite terminus.

The young in the depression look like a vibrating, jelly-like mass not very easy to see. For several days they are moved from one depression to another, gently carried in the mouths of the parents. While it is generally conceded that the lower animals do not reason things out, the result is often the same as though they do. What they do "by instinct" is often wiser than our actions guided by reason. Whether the apparent reasoning in the actions of animals is of their own creation or is a reflection of the Master Mind in Nature makes little difference. Reasons for everything exist. It is interesting to speculate on them, and if we attribute higher thinking powers to our friends the fishes than they actually possess, we are only giving them the benefit of the doubt.

Cichlids have not only the most highly developed breeding habits from the social standpoint, but combine with them a seeming understanding of certain scientific principles which, as far as man is concerned, were discovered but yesterday. These are the recognition of the dangers from bacteria, and of their control through cleanliness. Reference has already been made to the scrupulous care in cleansing the spawning surface and to the eating of such eggs as have been attacked by fungus. Various interpretations may be placed on the practice of moving the young from one hole to another. As this is begun before the babies are old enough to eat anything, it cannot be to provide new pastures. One hole would be as safe from enemies as any other. Besides, in the open places where these fishes breed, they are absolutely fearless in the defense of their young, so the theory of safety may be dismissed. The theory which is in line with their other actions points to cleanliness as the motive—*scientific* cleanliness if you will. The babies are picked up in the mouth, a few at a time, and apparently chewed. They are only rolled around harmlessly and dis-

charged into the next depression. Every last one is so treated. It is the fish's baby bath. Each one emerges perfectly cleansed of any particles. By using a series of depressions for the purpose, the parents are absolutely certain that all babies were "scrubbed," of which they could not be sure if they were kept in one place.

After 4 to 10 days the yolk-sacs of the young have been absorbed and they swim up in a cloud with the parents, usually in formation, headed one way. Stragglers are gathered up in the mouths of the parents and shot back into the school. This family unit is very beautiful to see and gives the aquarist one of his biggest and most lasting thrills. How long the parents and young should be left together is a question largely of sentiment. In the wild the parents undoubtedly can be of much use to the young by protecting them after they are swimming about, but in the aquarium their usefulness ends at that point. The pleasure of seeing the parents and young together is the only reason for not separating them promptly. No hen could be more solicitous for her brood than are these devoted fish-parents for their fry. In their defense they are the very embodiment of savage fury, no matter what or how large the real or imaginary enemy. The owner himself had better not poke his nose too close to the water when peering into the domestic affairs of a large pair of Cichlids unless he wishes to have it shortened.

The young of the larger Cichlids are a fair size by the time the yolk-sac is absorbed and for the most part can get along without Infusoria if newly hatched Brine Shrimp or finely-sifted Daphnia are to be had. Theoretically these interesting pairs divide every domestic duty equally. It sometimes turns out that one is a better parent than the other, but resentment is clearly shown by the mate on whom the heavier part of the burden is shifted. An effort is made to drive the negligent parent to its duty. This failing, open warfare is liable to occur, resulting in the breaking up of matrimonial arrangements, the eating of eggs or young and the death of the principal at fault. In other words, these fishes seem to have and to carry out a sense of justice. Otherwise we may look at it as the elimination both of the unfit parent and of its progeny. The eating of the eggs by either fish is, for the same cause, liable to end in the same way. Here, as elsewhere in animal life, defective individuals are eliminated by normal ones.

With many Cichlids it is possible and even advisable to hatch and rear the young away from the parents. This method is described under the heading of *Pterophyllum scalare.*

Some tact should be shown in approaching an aquarium containing eggs or young, as the parents are liable to misinterpret the intentions of the interested owner and eat their young to thwart the imagined enemy.

When the young and parents are finally separated it is well to keep an eye on the old couple, as each may suspect the other of being responsible for the disappearance of the babies, and open an attack in reprisal.

Cichlids all tend towards carnivorous appetites, but few of them insist upon a diet exclusively of meats. While they do very well on live adult Brine Shrimp, live worms, Flies, Mosquito-Larvae, scraped meat, shrimp or fish (cooked or uncooked), Daphnia, etc., they will take various frozen and freeze-dried foods as well. In a warm temperature—75 to 85 degrees—the fishes are heavy eaters, and should be fed not less than twice daily.

Most of them will stand a reasonably wide range of temperature, about 65 to 90 degrees, although with valued specimens it might be unwise to risk anything below 68 degrees.

Cichlid parents, except Mouthbrooders, should be fed while caring for young. Live Daphnia have the double advantage that they drop young for the baby fishes, and are themselves eaten by the breeders.

Large Cichlids live long. It is not uncommon for them to reach 10 years, although after 5 years they are likely to develop certain signs of age not connected with feebleness. There are 3 such points which may be noted. The mouth does not close completely in breathing; a spinal hump forms just in back of the head; the colors become more fixed and permanent and do not change so readily under excitement.

Cichlids are commonly not good community fishes, although a number of big ones in a very large tank get along without trouble.

## *Aequidens portalegrensis*
(HENSEL)

*Meaning of name:* Aequidens, with teeth of same length; poitalegrensis, for Porto Alegre, Brazil

*Popular name:* "Port"

*Length:* 4 to 5 inches

S. E. Brazil

Usually considered to be the most kindly of this general type and size of fish. Quite easily bred, even in aquaria that are too small. That is,

*Aequidens portalegrensis*

it will manage in a ten-gallon aquarium, when it ought to have a fifteen gallon or larger.

The sexes are not easily told, but the male has more spangles, especially in the tail fin. The species is easily recognized by its blunt face and the peculiar pattern in the tail.

## *Apistogramma ramirezi*
### MYERS and HARRY

*Popular name:* Ram

*Meaning of name:* Apistogramma, in reference to peculiar lateral line; ramirezi, after Sr. Manuel Vicente Ramirez of Caracas, Venezuela

*Length:* 2 inches

Western Venezuela

One of the outstanding importations of 1947, this strongly individual little fish with a saddle-shaped dorsal, has attained permanent popularity. It is not only beautiful but also easily bred. It is free of that aggressiveness which marks most Dwarf Cichlids. While courting, males challenge and chase each other, but no harm is done.

The strong violet hue seen in adults is variable. It shows best in direct sunlight. Female shows rosy spot on sides when ready to spawn. She takes the lead in breeding and care of young. A tall spike at front of dorsal fin indicates the male. A cream-colored form of *A. ramirezi*, sometimes called Albino Ram, has recently appeared on the market. However, it is not a true albino, since it retains many of the iridescent spots of the wild form and also lacks the characteristic pink eye of true albinos.

Eggs are usually placed on a flat stone. Both parents fan the eggs, but the female takes a more active part in guarding the nest and young. Eggs can also be hatched in a separate container as described for Angel Fish. Soft slightly acid water preferred. Temperature, 70° to 80°.

*Apistogramma ramirezi*

## Astronotus ocellatus (AGASSIZ)

*Popular name:* Oscar

*Meaning of name:* Astronotus, marked with stars; ocellatus, with eye spot

*Length:* up to 10 inches

Guyana, the Amazon, and Paraguay

Allow us to present a strange Cichlid of such odd appearance and ways that one could well believe it to belong in another family. The scales are not very visible, the fish seeming more to be clothed in a sort of olive suede leather, handsomely decorated by a few fiery orange markings. Two color varieties have been developed in recent years: The "Tiger Oscar" with irregular red markings on a dark body and the "Red Oscar" with the entire body covered with copper-red scales.

When alarmed they have a peculiar habit of assuming a close head-to-tail position and doing a sort of slow roll.

When young, *A. ocellatus* will feed on live food of the usual kind; when adult, on one- to two-inch fishes. However, they can be raised just as well on lumps of freeze-dried Brine Shrimp, washed canned shrimp or small pieces of lean raw beef. Given a large tank, 55- to 100-gallon capacity, they spawn readily. They are excellent parents. Temperatures 70° to 80°.

## Cichlasoma festivum (HECKEL)

*Meaning of name:* Cichlasoma, thrush-body; festivum, gaily attractive, festive

*Length:* 5-6 inches

Amazon

The magnificent oblique bar, traversing the body from the mouth to the upper tip of the dorsal fin gives *C. festivum* a unique standing among aquarium fishes. The thread-like extensions or "feelers" seen on the ventral fins are a little longer than we commonly see among Cichlids. These increase with age, but nothing to compare with those on

*Astronotus ocellatus*

*Astronotus ocellatus, "Red Oscar"*

*Cichlasoma festivum*

Scalare. The general color of the body is silvery with a green cast. The fins have none of the color markings common to many species of the genus. This fish is at its best in a size of about three inches. When it gets larger the markings are apt to become less distinct. Breeding temperature, about 82°.

The fish is fairly hardy, especially as it becomes older and larger. It is difficult to mate. Although not a timid fish, it seems to prefer privacy when mating and caring for its young.

## *Cichlasoma meeki*    (BRIND)

*Popular name:* Firemouth

*Meaning of name:* Cichlasoma, thrush-body; meeki, for Professor Seth Meek

*Length:* 4 to 5 inches

Yucatan

Not every fish has a pronounced individual characteristic marking. *C. meeki* has two: the green-edged spot at the base of the gill plate and a fiery red color along the lower mouth which often extends into the belly. This color is present at all times and is brighter in the male, but becomes most vivid during mating, especially in the female.

Up to a size of three inches there are no external sex differences, except the belly coloring on the male may be a shade brighter. With another inch the male developed the usual long point on the dorsal fin, common to most male Cichlids.

It has now been successfully bred many times. The breeding habits are the same as with the other Cichlids. It is surely worthy of a place in any collection of fishes of this type. Breeding temperature, about 80°.

### Cichlasoma nigrofasciatum
(GUENTHER)

Popular name: Zebra Cichlid

Meaning of name: Cichlasoma, thrushbody; nigrofasciatum, black-banded

Length: 4 inches

San Salvador

For years this fish was considered to be the "Jack Dempsey" fish until the true "Dempsey" was found to be C. octofasciatum. Our present subject is sometimes known in the trade by the rather misleading name of "Congo Cichlid."

While they breed like other Cichlids, it is more necessary to give breeding pairs an aquarium liberally supplied with hiding places, such as flowerpots, or large stones arranged in arches. The female assumes most of the care of the eggs.

C. nigrofasciatum is one of the high-strung Cichlids that changes its colors rapidly. They are often very quarrelsome, but usually very devoted parents. Oddly enough, the female has most of the color—a unique trait among aquarium fishes. Her irregular pattern of dull orange scales on the posterior part of her body extends into the lower fins.

The species not only fights its own kind, but is unsafe among other fishes. Its attacks are swift and with little warning. Temperature 70°-80°.

### Cichlasoma octofasciatum

Popular name: Jack Dempsey

Meaning of name: Cichlasoma, thrushbody: octofasciatum, with eight bands. Formerly known as C. biocellatum

Length: Up to 8 inches

South America, probably Brazil

Before the reign of the Scalare, this fish, popularly and affectionately known as "Jack Dempsey," was the most popular of the Cichlids. Of its own type, with a long body and strong head, it is still the leader, for it has dazzling beauty, is hardy, is a good breeder and parent. One of the earlier introductions into the aquarium and a dependable showpiece.

With age, the colors of the Dempsey are particularly prone to become more fixed, brilliant, and less likely to change when the fish is frightened or excited. Our illustration shows an immature fish.

Often a large individual fish is kept as a pet in an aquarium by itself where it soon learns to beg, in fish language, for morsels of food from its master. Lives for ten years or longer. Our description of breeding of the Cichlids fits this species perfectly. Temperature, 65° to 90°.

*Cichlasoma meeki*

*Cichlasoma nigrofasciatum*

*Cichlasoma nigrofasciatum (A Pair of White Zebra Cichlids)*

*Cichlasoma octofasciatum*

*Cichlasoma severum*

## *Cichlasoma severum*   (HECKEL)

*Meaning of name:* Cichlasoma, thrush-
   body; severum, severe

*Length:* 5 to 6 inches

Amazon

Reference has already been made
to the great changeability in coloring
and marking of the various Cichlids.
This is particularly true of the *Cichlasoma severum*. The background
color in any individual may, in a few
seconds, change from pale gray to
deep green, brown, or nearly black,
or any imagined intervening shades.
Agitation of one kind or another
usually causes the color changes.

While the name *severum* means
"severe," it is no more militant than
the average large Cichlid.

Our illustration shows two immature fish fighting.

Undoubtedly this is one of the
more difficult Cichlids to breed. It
should have a large aquarium, plenty

*Cichlasoma severum, golden variety*

of warmth, about 80°; and be well
fed on Brine Shrimp and other live
foods in order to induce mating and
spawning. Otherwise, the methods
conform to standard. The sex is
easily told in adults, but not in the
young. The male has the regular
rows of dots on the side, whereas the
female has few, if any. When young
they show only dark, distinct vertical
bars. Temperature, 72°-80°.

## Cichla ocellaris
BLOCH and SCHNEIDER

*Meaning of name:* Cichla, thrush; ocellaris, with round spot

*Length:* To 2 feet

Widely distributed in South America

This is an important food fish in South America, and young specimens are rarely imported. Nevertheless, we do see them offered for sale occasionally and we include them here for those hobbyists who have large tanks and who are fond of big, ferocious carnivores. In behavior and food requirements, these fishes are much like the North American Basses. They are loners that preferentially feed on other fishes. Water conditions are not critical, but enough room is a must.

Temperature, 70° to 80°.

## Crenicichla lepidota    HECKEL

*Popular name:* Pike Cichlid

*Meaning of name:* Crenicichla, Cichla with teeth; lepidota, with scales on ear region (gill covers)

*Length:* To 12 inches

South America

Crenicichlas, of which there are a number of species, are unneighborly fishes and make poor members for a community tank. They are predators of the first order and require live fish for food when adult.

Although lacking brilliant coloring, they are decidedly attractive. The irregular markings on the back, observed in the photograph, are variable in their intensity.

The genus of *Crenicichla* is not often in supply commercially. They do not tear out plants. Temperature, 68° to 80°.

## Geophagus brasiliensis
HECKEL

*Meaning of name:* Geophagus, earth-eater; brasiliensis, from Brazil

*Length:* 6 inches

Brazil

Some Cichlids might well be the envy of mere man, for they become handsomer with age. *G. brasiliensis* is one of that kind. The high lights on the body and fins are electric blue-green and they will become much brighter as the fish grows older. The dark central body spot is larger and more showy than the photograph indicates. Breeds in standard Cichlid manner, but not often.

The fish is rather easily distinguished from the other popular Cichlids by the outline of its body. The head is large and the body tapers off sharply where it joints the tail fin. This end of the body is called the "caudal peduncle." The eye is dark gold and black. Temperature, 72°-82°.

## Geophagus jurupari    HECKEL

*Meaning of name:* Geophagus, earth-eater; jurupari, after a native name

Length: 7 inches

The Amazon

This *Geophagus* owes its peculiar appearance to a particularly long pointed head and a dorsal fin that is quite high along its entire length. The long, downward arching profile of the snout makes the lower line of the head and body seem somewhat flat. The eyes are very large and placed high and far back on the snout.

Like most Cichlids, their color and markings vary greatly in inten-

*Cichla ocellaris*

*Crenicichla lepidota*

*Geophagus brasiliensis*

*Geophagus jurupari*

sity. The average background is a rather light golden color while the spotted pattern on the body and in the fins is an iridescent green. One of the more peaceful Cichlids. Does not tear out plants.

The eggs of this peculiar mouthbrooder are laid and fertilized on the horizontal surface of a clean, flat, smooth rock. After a day or two, they are picked off by the female—rarely by both parents—incubated in her mouth for about ten days by which time the young emerge for brief periods to feed. Newly hatched Brine Shrimp are eagerly taken as a first food. At this time the male will also protect the fry against enemies by providing refuge in his cavernous mouth. The young, seldom pursued by their progenitors, enter the mouth of the parent upon a signal of flicking fins or simply when the parent opens its mouth.

Sexes are difficult to determine. In mature fish, the male has slightly larger and somewhat longer dorsal and ventral fins. Temperature, 72°-82°.

## Herotilapia multispinosa
(EIGENMANN)

*Popular name:* Rainbow Cichlid

*Meaning of name:* Herotilapia, resembling Tilapia (another genus of Cichlids); multispinosa, with many thorns

*Length:* About 4 inches; females usually smaller

South America

Rainbow Cichlids look very much as if they should belong to the genus Cichlasoma, but certain differences in the teeth justify their classification in a different genus. They do well under the same conditions as Cichlasoma, and breed in the same fashion. Females turn very dark

*Herotilapia multispinosa, Female*

during breeding time, as shown in the photograph. Both parents take an active part in caring for eggs and young. Temperature 70° to 80°.

## Pterophyllum scalare
(LICHTENSTEIN)

*Popular names:* Angel Fish and Scalare

*Meaning of name:* Pterophyllum, winged leaf; scalare, like a flight of stairs, referring to the dorsal fin

*Length:* 5 to 6 inches

Amazon and Guyana

Three "species" of *Pterophyllum* have been recognized: P. eimekei, P. scalare and P. altum. *P. altum*, from Venezuela, is very rare. It is probable that all three represent only subspecies or geographical races of one species.

To the untrained eye, *Pterophyllum* does not look like a Cichlid, but nevertheless it is one.

Except that it will eat small fishes of suitable size, it is quite a good "happy family" member. While the breeding habits are much the same as we look for in Cichlids, there are two distinct points of difference. Instead of depositing the spawn in or on such objects as flower-pots or stones, they prefer for this purpose a firm aquatic leaf, such as Giant Sagittarià, or some substitute that will approximate it. They will accept a heavy glass tube for the

*Herotilapia multispinosa, Male*

*Pterophyllum scalare*

*Angel Fish Spawning*

purpose, especially if it is opaque or, as in our illustration, the leaf of a plastic plant. They seem to have no confidence in the clear glass. Sometimes a glass tube is slipped over the aquarium drain pipe. Many commercial breeders use a strip of one quarter-inch slate, two to three inches wide and 8 inches long. It is placed against the aquarium side, sloping a few degrees off the vertical.

Unlike the great majority of Cichlids, Angels do not place their young in prepared holes in the sand. Wherever the baby Angel hatches, there it adheres suspended from the head by a sticky thread, vibrating its tail vigorously. The mass of young produces an appreciable current in this way, thus getting both exercise and a rapid change of water. During this period the parents pick up mouthfuls of young, retain them a few moments and gently spray them on another leaf, repeating the operation at intervals of perhaps an hour, until the babies can swim freely, which is in 3-4 days. One observes that the parents are most solicitous, and use great care to pick up any of the young which did not adhere to a new location. Babies seldom reach the bottom before rescue arrives.

As to how long to keep the parents and young together—if at all—is a matter for each aquarist to decide. Leaving them all together is a most interesting procedure if successful. Some families may remain together until the parents are ready to spawn again.

If the main object is to rear fish, and one is willing to forego the pleasure of witnessing their interesting family life, then the best thing to do is to remove the eggs to a hatching tray or aquarium containing water not over 8 inches deep. The container and water should be perfectly clean, for the babies are not to be freed of dirt particles in the laundry-mouths of their natural parents. The water, of course, should be seasoned. If fungus appears, boil the water next time and add 2 drops of 5% Methylene Blue solution per gallon after spawning. (This is bad for plants.)

Returning to the subject of artificial spawn receivers, it will now be apparent where their use is a practical convenience, for they are easily lifted out of the aquarium and laid sloping, egg side down, in the hatching tray. A light current of water about the eggs and young, produced by the mechanical liberation of air, is important. By the time the young have absorbed all of the yolk-sac and become free-swimming, they are able to eat newly hatched Brine Shrimp.

A number of other Cichlids may be reared in this way. It is worth trying when parents persistently eat eggs or young.

Newly hatched Scalares look nothing like their parents, but in a few weeks there is no mistaking their identity. Growth is rapid under the influence of liberal feeding and warmth.

## Peculiarities of Angel Fish

Several things about Angel Fish require special consideration. Perhaps the most outstanding one is an unaccountable loss of appetite. Try a change of food. They are particularly fond of live Mosquito Larvae, Daphnia, small or chopped Earthworms, White Worms and canned shrimp. If these fail to tempt, then try baby Guppies. Pretty bad case if these morsels fail to bring back the appetite. The only thing then left to do is to try a change of aquarium or of water in the present aquarium. Scalares seem to do best in slightly acid water, about pH 6.8. They seldom really starve.

There should be plants in the aquarium with Angel Fish. They tend to give the fishes a sense of security. When frightened, Angels

**Black Veiltail Angel Fish**

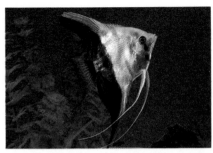

**Half-black Angel Fish**

**Angel Fish, Golden Variety**

**Black Lace Angel Fish**

**Marbled Angel Fish**

may dash against the aquarium glass and injure or even kill themselves.

Ordinarily when a fish lies over on its side on the bottom of the aquarium it is preparing to enter Fish Paradise. The Scalare is liable to do this from shock, fright or chill, but is likely to regain its equilibrium.

This fish is not very susceptible to Ichthyophthirius, but it is liable to a disease which causes the eyes to protrude. This sometimes leads to blindness and usually ends in death.

Under identical conditions some individuals of the original coloration will have brilliant black bars, while others are gray. Cause unknown. It is no indication of a state of health.

*Sex in Angel Fish*

This remains difficult to distinguish, but we can make a shrewd guess. Even mating is not a certain sign, for two females sometimes mate and have infertile eggs. The

*Symphysodon aequifasciata*

one method in use by practical breeders has reference to the space at the lower edge of the body between the "feelers" and the beginning of the anal fin. In the female this portion of the body outline is longer and straighter and the angle between the body and anal fin is more pronounced. As with other Cichlids, the breeding tube, which appears in both sexes just before egg-laying, is more pointed in the male, and is carried at a more forward angle. Also the female when filled with eggs looks fuller from an overhead view.

### *Symphysodon discus* (HECKEL)

*Meaning of name:* Symphysodon, with teeth at middle (symphysis) of jaw; discus, like a disc

*Length:* 5 to 6 inches

Amazon

At least two species of Symphysodon are recognized and imported: S. discus and S. aequifasciata. All require the same care. They are show fishes. Something that even the

*Symphysodon discus*

uninitiated remember. Their showy quality is increased by their large size.

At breeding times the male rivals the gaudy beauty of the most brilliant marine fishes. Occasionally the female is a brilliant golden yellow.

A considerable study has been made of various possible indications of difference in sex, but the only dependable point is that the blue pattern on the male is more pronounced and more extensive than on the female. Perfectly peaceful, but unexpected battles may occur between mated pairs.

Minimum breeding size, about 3 inches. The best way of securing a pair is to have say 6 in a 30-40 gallon aquarium and let them select their own mates. They are fussy feeders and should have a variety of live foods, including, if available, the shrimp-like Gammarus (see index). The new young have extremely small mouths. Before we learned that their first food is the slime they pick from the bodies of their parents, many of them died of starvation, because the eggs were hatched separately. The adults at this time seem to secrete a heavier slime on their bodies, an old provision of nature, akin to the fact that pigeons develop a "milk" in the crop as first food for their squabs. This recent discovery makes it clear that young should be tended by parents, even at the risk of their eating the spawn. Skilled breeders of tropical fishes now provide us with good tank-raised stock of these great beauties.

The species is subject to a few peculiar diseases, particularly abscesses about the head. Their water, especially for breeding, should be slightly acid and at a temperature of about 80 degrees.

### *Hemichromis bimaculatus*
GILL

*Popular name:* Jewel Fish

*Meaning of name:* Hemichromis, half-Chromis; bimaculatus, two-spotted

*Length:* 4 inches

Most of Tropical Africa

One of the typical savage Cichlids. It needs several redeeming traits to justify being kept, and it has them! A temperamental fish; a good parent; fairly hardy, and at times, gorgeously beautiful.

Although the fins and general coloration are the same in male and female, the sex is easily determined. The male has more and larger jewels on the gill plate, and those in the tail fin extend farther and form into a crescent. In her maximum redness at breeding time the female is a little brighter than the male, reversing the usual order of things. During courtship, the colors change rapidly, the dark spots become light or disappear altogether, and the jewel facets enlarge.

Out of breeding season both fishes are of a rather dark, nondescript color, lightly lined with blue jewelled scales and displaying a dark spot near the center of the body, one on the gill plate and one at the tail base. It is hard to understand why the specific name of the fish is not *trimaculatus*.

Mating time is difficult and dangerous. Whether working by group natural selection with several fishes or using only a pair, it is advisable with this species to have plenty of refuge places for the fish getting the worst of it. In addition to the flowerpot for receiving the spawn, there should be heavy plants like Giant Sagittaria or some large stones placed in formation for recesses.

The eggs of this species, if in clean condition, can be satisfactorily hatched and reared if the parents are removed, but then the aquarist loses one of his greatest pleasures by not witnessing the instructive and touching family life of the fishes.

The young grow rapidly and when about six weeks old begin attacking each other. For this reason they should be kept in an aquarium of at least ten-gallon capacity.

Temperature range, 60° to 90°. Breeding at 80°.

*Hemichromis bimaculatus*

### *Hemichromis fasciatus*    PETERS

*Popular name:* Banded Jewelfish

*Meaning of name:* Hemichromis, half-Chromis; fasciatus, banded

*Length:* 6 to 10 inches

Central W. Africa

We sometimes find a Cichlid that is suited to the aquarium only if the fish is not allowed to grow too big. *Hemichromis fasciatus* if kept in an aquarium of ten-gallon size can be held down to five or six inches, but if in a large tank, it reaches a length of ten inches. As it is a fierce digger, it can do a lot of damage when this size.

Contrary to *H. bimaculatus,* the colors are not bright. A brassy yellow or olive overlaid with five to six variable vertical bands constitutes the main pattern. Dorsal and tail fins, blue-black with narrow red edge. Ventral fins are clear to yellow; and the eye, brown. Black spot on opercle. At breeding time the forward part of the body becomes black and the belly pure white. The nose takes on a mahogany red color, while the anal and tail fins become red. Breeds like *H. bimaculatus.* The fish is a savage fighter.

### *Pelmatochromis guentheri*
(SAUVAGE)

*Meaning of name:* Pelmatochromis, Sole-Chromis, referring to a peculiar internal formation of the gill structure; guenther, after the naturalist, Guenther

*Length:* 4 inches

Equatorial W. Africa in coastal rivers

The dorsal fin on this fish is most striking and entirely different from that of any other known aquarium fish. It looks as if it were dusted with gold, especially in the female. As the body is a plain, drab purplish

*Hemichromis fasciatus*

*Pelmatochromis guentheri*

*Nannochromis nudiceps*

*Pelvicachromis pulcher*

hue devoid of pattern, the startling fins have the field to themselves. The fish is peaceful and will eat anything.

They are mouth-brooders, and both parents rear the brood. That is, the female will tend the eggs and fry, but the male will join her later in providing refuge in his mouth for the free swimming youngsters. When the young first emerge they are large. At the slightest sign of danger, they continue to use the mouths of their parents as a refuge, even after they have reached a length of 5/8 inch. It is quite an amusing sight to see them scamper in, especially when their size makes it impossible for all to enter. It is like a hen who is no longer able to hide all her chicks under her feathers.

Temperature, 70° to 82°.

## Nannochromis nudiceps
### (BOULENGER)

*Meaning of name:* Nannochromis, small Chromis; nudiceps, with naked head

*Length:* Up to 2½ inches; males to 3½ inches

Congo River

Compared to their South American counterparts, these little Cichlids from the Congo are extremely actives fishes. They dash with great speed from cave to cave, feeling at home only in a tank suitably set up with lots of rocks and hiding places. They tend to dig, mostly around and under rocks. To avoid uprooting, therefore, plants should be placed a few inches away from rocks. Mature females are a bit smaller than the males and, if in good condition, are almost always well-rounded and have a beautiful bluish-green patch on their sides.

They spawn in caves, or flowerpots, and the females tend eggs and young very carefully. The eggs are large, cream-colored, and attached to the walls of the cave by means of a short stalk. The eggs wave in the current while the female is fanning. Hatching takes place in about three days; thereafter, the fry are often moved by the female from one cave to another. They are free-swimming in another four or five days and are then ready to gorge themselves on newly hatched Brine Shrimp. Temperature, 76° to 82°.

## Pelvicachromis pulcher (BRULL)

*Meaning of name:* Pulcher, Pretty

*Length:* 3 inches

Western Equatorial Africa

One of the most popular and beautiful Cichlids from Africa. Our illustration shows a male, as evidenced by the straight belly lines and the markings at the end of the tail. The dorsal fin is normally more pointed in males, but our photograph is unclear in that respect. Females have a more brilliant patch of red on their sides, have a rounder belly and shorter dorsal. The tail is usually clear and unmarked.

The fish will accept many types of food, but they prefer to feed near the bottom or in midwater. Only reluctantly will they take food off the surface.

Eggs are almost always laid in hidden caves, and a flower pot laid on its side is readily accepted. The female, rarely both parents, cares for eggs and fry. The male takes a greater interest in guarding the nesting site.

Temperature, 72° to 80°.

## *Tilapia mossambica*          PETERS

*Meaning of name:* Tilapia, unknown;
mossambica, after Mozambique

*Length:* 8 inches

E. Africa, S. Africa and Mozambique

In this mouthbrooding species, the
female carries the eggs. The babies
first emerge from her maw in about
ten days, retreating as danger approaches much the same as described for *Pelmatochromis guentheri.*

The species is seen in dealer's
tanks only occasionally. They have
been introduced into different parts
of the tropics as food fish and
have multiplied greatly. We give
eight inches as the average aquarium
size, but the "Bulletin" of the Indo-
nesian Veterinary Association claims
that specimens in pond culture reach
an incredible six pounds. This fish is
a heavy feeder and takes any food.
Male at breeding time shows white
on lower part of head (as above),
while the tail and pectoral fins become deep red and the body turns a
dark charcoal gray. Temperatures,
70° to 80°.

Later reports indicate that the
fabulous poundage expectation from
the fish has not always been realized,
because their very productivity soon
overcrowds a pond, resulting in
much smaller fish.

Nowhere have we yet found an
exception to the axiom that great
growth needs not only heavy feeding
but also liberal water surface per
fish.

## *Steatocranus casuarius*          POLL

*Popular name:*  Bumphead Cichlid,
Buffalo Head

*Length:* Up to 4 inches; female slightly
smaller

Congo River

The first thing one notices when
observing these fishes in an aquarium
is the fact that they do not swim in
the normal manner of cichlids. They
dash in short spurts on the bottom
or hop from stone to stone in a way
similar to the native North American Darters. As the name "Bumphead Cichlids" implies, the male
develops a large fatty hump on its
forehead, of which the female only
shows a trace. Although this does
occur to some extent in other mature
male cichlids, it is extremely pronounced in this species. Their natural
habitat are the rapids of the Congo
River and they are unquestionably
very well adapted to live in such an
environment. In captivity they are
happiest in a tank containing lots of
gravel and rocks and few, if any,
plants. To simulate the natural environment even better, a large volume filter can be used to create a
fairly strong current in the tank. At
breeding time, which can be any
season of the year, they usually move
large amounts of gravel as they ex-
cavate breeding sites. Eggs are laid
in caves and both parents take an
active part in guarding the eggs and
fry. It has been reported that this
species provides pre-chewed food

*Tilapia mossambica*

*Steatocranus casuarius*

for the youngsters. This has been observed on other species of Cichlids, but only as an individual trait in some females and not as consistent behavior of a species. It is a very touching sight when one is lucky enough to observe it, and unique in the world of aquarium fishes.

## CICHLIDS OF LAKE MALAWI

The Cichlids of Lake Malawi have been known to ichthyologists for more than half a century, but only since the nineteen-sixties have they been imported for the aquarium hobby. Since then, they have become extremely popular, both due to their brilliant coloration and their interesting breeding habits.

Their way of life is much different from that of their South American cousins. They are much more active swimmers, and most of them do not establish clearly defined territories, as many south American Cichlids do. Neither do they form pairs, ex-

cept very briefly for the purpose of propagation.

These fishes live mostly along the rock-strewn shoreline of Lake Malawi, and the majority of them are found nowhere else on the continent. Being extremely agile in their rocky environment, they are very difficult to catch, and, before commercial breeders mass-produced them, were very high priced.

An aquarium set-up for these Cichlids should contain a large rock pile, that is, rocks should be piled up in a random manner to produce many passageways and crevices. In this way, any fight (and there will be many) does not end with the aggressor mercilessly chasing the looser through the aquarium, killing him in the end.

Water conditions are not very important. The fishes have been successfully kept and bred in hard and alkaline water as well as in soft and slightly acid waters. However, hard and alkaline water is preferred by most species, and acid conditions of 6.0 and below must absolutely be avoided.

For the most part the fishes are omnivorous, feeding on aquatic insects and crustaceans as well as algae and even some higher plants. A few are equipped with mouths specifically adapted for scraping algae off rocks. In the aquarium, they feed on all kinds of live and frozen foods, freeze-dried foods as well as flakes. As a rule, they are happier with frequent small feedings than with one or two heavy meals per day.

The breeding behavior of these Cichlids is a unique and interesting one. Almost all are mouthbrooders with the female carrying the eggs until the fry are hatched and completely formed.

Incubation takes about 3 weeks, during which time the female takes no food. Some individual females, however, have been observed to grab some food particles during this incubation time and go through chewing motions. Whether this is done to still her own hunger or to provide chewed food for the developing youngsters in her mouth is not clear, but both theories have been advanced. During this period, the female usually stays hidden among the rocks and rarely ventures into open water. At times, a female fails to find a secluded spot in the aquarium and is considerably disturbed by her tank mates. In that case, she should be removed to another tank. This needs to be done very carefully, since she will simply spit out the eggs or swallow them if she is too frightened by the procedure. Some breeders remove the eggs routinely from an incubating female and hatch them artificially. The eggs are placed in a separate container

and agitated gently by means of a slow stream of water, using the effluent from the filter.

When the young emerge from the mouth of the female, they are half inch long, fully formed replicas of their parents. For the first day or two, they still seek refuge in the mouth of the mother when danger approaches, but after that they are completely on their own. They are amazingly alert and, while searching for food, use the smallest nooks and crannies for protection. It is amusing to watch them—especially at this young age—go through the typical adult fighting behavior. With violent body wagging, fins and gillcovers spread to the utmost, they try to impress one another very much whenever two of them meet.

Newly hatched Brine Shrimp is the very best food for them, but any food of sufficiently small particle size can be fed.

Spawning takes place on a smooth, flat rock which is cleared of debris by both the male and the female. The pair will circle each other a few times and then the female will release from one to three eggs. They are large (about ⅛″ in diameter), irregularly shaped and of a dull yellow or pinkish color. The eggs are non-adhesive and often roll about in the current the fish produce while excitedly circling each other. Presently, the female picks up the eggs with her mouth and approaches the male who has taken a position squarely in front of her, presenting a side view of himself. On his widely spread anal fin a few yellowish or orange spots can be observed which look exactly like the eggs just laid by the female. The female will now peck at those egg spots, as they are called, apparently in the belief that they are more eggs to be picked up. At this very moment, the male will release sperm fluid, which gets sucked into the female's mouth to fertilize the eggs. This process is repeated a number of times until the female is depleted of eggs. The number of eggs varies from about ten to fifty or more, depending on the species and the size of the female. The best temperature is about 80°.

## Pseudotropheus auratus
(BOULENGER)

*Meaning of name:* Pseudotropheus, false Tropheus (another genus of Cichlids); auratus, golden

*Length:* 4 inches

Sexes look very much alike when not mature. Males undergo a dramatical change in color at breeding time, as shown in the illustration. Male below.

*Pseudotropheus auratus*

## Pseudotropheus elongatus
FRYER

*Meaning of name:* Pseudotropheus, false Tropheus; elongatus, elongate

*Length:* To 5 inches

This species is somewhat more quarrelsome than other members of the genus. Males lead a more solitary life. Diet consists predominantly of crustaceans and other aquatic organisms.

## Pseudotropheus zebra
(BOULENGER)

*Meaning of name:* Pseudotropheus, false Tropheus; zebra, with stripes

*Length:* To 8 inches

The fish shown represent only two color morphs, or color varieties, of the many occurring in Lake Malawi. Solid blue, orange, and white fishes are found in different parts of the lake. They all are *P. zebra,* and readily interbreed without regard to color. It is not clear how the different strains have evolved, and why the different colors remain distinct in the lake. Much research is needed in this field, and hobbyists breeding these fishes can provide much of the information we are now lacking.

*Pseudotropheus zebra white mottled*
*Female*

*Pseudotropheus elongatus*

*Pseudotropheus zebra*

*Labeotropheus fuelleborni*

*Labeotropheus trewavasae*

## *Labeotropheus fuelleborni*  AHL

*Meaning of name:* Labeotropheus, with distinct lips; fuelleborni, a personal name

*Length:* To 8 inches

*L. fuelleborni* occur in at least two color varieties, the blue one, pictured above and an orange mottled one. Orange mottled fish are often females and there is some doubt as to the existance of mottled males. The fish are well equipped for rasping algae off flat rocks.

## *Labeotropheus trewavasae*
FRYER

*Meaning of name:* Labeotropheus, with distinct lips; trewavasae, after E. Trewavas, British ichthyologist

*Length:* 5 inches

As in the foregoing, at least two color morphs exist in this species, and, again as in *L. fuelleborni,* mottled males are rarely, if ever, encountered. The fish benefit by the addition of algae in their diet, but will accept almost any type of food offered.

## THE NANDIDS

### FAMILY NANDIDAE

Most spiny-rayed fishes are found in salt water and very few families of this type are restricted entirely to fresh water. The Cichlids, Sunfishes, true Perches, and Gouramis are among such fresh-water families. The Nandids also share this distinction, and of all such groups they are the most widely scattered in range.

*Monocirrhus* (one species) is found over most of the Amazon Basin and in the Essequibo River, Guyana. *Polycentrus* (one species) is restricted to Guyana and the island of Trini-

dad. *Polycentropsis abbreviata* and *Afronandus sheljuzhkoi* represent the family in Africa, where it is confined to a relatively small area about the mouth of the Niger and in Cameroon. In India there are *Badis* (two species), *Nandus* (two species), and *Pristolepis fasciata* in Burma, Thailand, Laos and islands of the Malay Archipelago.

The Nandids differ technically from other related families chiefly in features of the skeleton. All of them (except *Badis*) have large mouths which can be opened out to a tremendous extent and all (except *Badis* again) have the peculiar feature of having the tail fin and the rear ends of the dorsal and anal fins so transparent as to be hardly visible in the live fish. The transparent dorsal and anal fin ends are almost constantly in motion. All except *Badis* are voracious fish-eaters, with large mouths and strong teeth. No member of this family can be maintained on a diet of prepared food. They all require live food.

## *Badis badis*
(HAMILTON-BUCHANAN)

*Popular name:* Badis

*Meaning of name:* a native name

*Length:* 2¾ inches

India

Many of our exotic fishes have extensive wardrobes of colored costumes which they wear according to whim on occasion, and an author attempting descriptions feels that he is helplessly repeating himself in saying very much the same thing about a number of species. However, *Badis badis* is one of the extreme cases. The usual color is brown with black or red bars in a chain-like pattern.

**Badis badis, Male**

Females never deviate from that pattern, but males are capable of considerable color changes. At breeding time, the barred pattern gives way to an overall bluish-black color with iridescent blue spangles in dorsal, anal and tail fin.

Sexes cannot be told positively, but the males (shown above) are more hollow-bellied and are apt to be darker and larger and have larger fins. *Badis badis* spawn underneath rocks or in small caves. There is an embrace similar to that of Gouramis, but unlike eggs of Gouramis, *B. badis* eggs are extremely adhesive. The female does not carefully place the eggs as most Cichlids do, but scatters them randomly during the spawing embrace. The eggs then become attached to the walls of the cave and the bottom. The male guards and vigorously defends the spawning site against any fish venturing too close. Eggs hatch in three days and the young are free swimming in another

**Badis badis, Female**

three days at a temperature of 80°. First food for fry is infusoria.

A ten-gallon tank can be used. Temperature, 78° to 80°.

## Monocirrhus polyacanthus
HECKEL

*Popular name.* Amazon Leaf Fish

*Meaning of name:* Monocirrhus, with one whisker; polyacanthus, many-spined

*Length:* 2½ inches

Amazon and Guyana

Although this extremely odd fish was first described by Heckel as long ago as 1840, for many years the type specimens in the Vienna Museum remained the only ones of which we had any knowledge. In an interesting reprint from the "Biological Bulletin" (November, 1921), Dr. W. R. Allen describes a sluggish brook overhung with tropical vegetation from which he captured three specimens. The fishes, of a leaf-brown, irregular mottled color, were difficult to see against a bottom matted with fallen leaves. They moved about peculiarly like drifting leaves and had the collector not thought it strange that leaves should move at all in such sluggish water, he would not have seen them.

The species is most peculiar and is a definite novelty of exotic character. It is really quite striking and is not confined to any particular shade of brown, but changes greatly. Whether this is a chameleon-like power of protective coloration, we can only surmise. The eyes are difficult to distinguish, owing to the dark lines radiating from them. Usually the fins are spread, their saw-edges contributing much to the leaf-like effect. The beard on the lower jaw adds a stem to the leaf. Even the natives call the species the Leaf Fish.

They move about sedately and pose themselves at unusual angles, frequently head-down as we see in the illustration. They do not seem to be particularly bored with life, but they gape or yawn prodigiously. Many fishes do this moderately, but the Leaf Fish puts on a startling act. The mouth seems to unfold from within itself until it becomes a veritable trumpet.

They deposit, fertilize, and fan their eggs somewhat like Cichlids, but their parental care is not nearly so intense. The first spawn of a pair, placed in a dark vertical corner

*Monocirrhus polyacanthus*

where the aquarium glasses join, was the most successful. Those later placed in pots did not do so well. The youngsters varied greatly in size and after three weeks began to disappear. Removed from the parents and graded for size, the trouble ended. They have barbels for the first months and when quite small are covered with tiny white dots which look like the parasitic disease Ichthyophthirius. This is common to a number of kinds of very young fishes; it is probably protective coloration.

The Leaf Fish is most interesting, but unless one is prepared to feed it exclusively and liberally on small live fishes, all thoughts of keeping it should be abandoned, for it will touch nothing else. As the fish has a voracious appetite, it usually either wears out its welcome or starves to death. Few fanciers are equipped to maintain royalty demanding such expensive food. A thousand grown male Guppies per year just about keeps one of these adult cannibal aristocrats from feeling neglected. It does not attack fishes too large to be swallowed, but one should not underrate its capacity! Temperature, 75° to 82°.

## THE GOBIES
### FAMILIES ELEOTRIDAE AND GOBIIDAE

The most noteworthy difference between the two families of Gobies is the fact that in the *Gobiidae,* the two ventral fins are *connected* and form a sort of suction cup. The fishes use it to attach themselves to rocks, plants and other submerged objects. The *Eleotridae* have no such suction cup. Their ventral fins are separated. All Gobies require live foods for their well-being.

## *Brachygobius xanthozonus*
### (BLEEKER)

*Popular name:* Bumble Bee Goby

*Meaning of name:* Brachygobius, short goby; xanthozonus, with yellow zones or bands

*Length:* 1¼ inches

Malaysia, Borneo, Sumatra, Java

Like so many of the Gobies, this little fish spends most of its time on the bottom of the aquarium hopping about in a droll way. It cannot be called a scavenger, however, since it has a distinct preference for Daphnia and Brine Shrimp. Reluctantly, it will take some dried foods.

They have rarely been bred. The breeders are conditioned on chopped earthworms and grown Brine Shrimp. Eggs are laid on upper side of an empty flowerpot which is on its side. The female takes an upside-down position in the pot while applying strings of eggs that adhere to the upper side. She drops to the bottom while the male does a "loop-the-loop," fertilizing the eggs as he passes them. Spawn hatches in five to six days at 75°. Male fans spawn and does not eat young. They must be fed on fine Infusoria for three days after their yolk sac has been absorbed.

The species prefers live food and they are apt to be fin-nippers.

*Brachygobius xanthozonus*

## *Dormitator maculatus* (BLOCH)

*Popular name:* Sleeper Goby

*Meaning of name:* Dormitator, sleeper; maculatus, spotted

*Length:* In nature, up to 10 inches; Aquarium size, 3 to 4 inches

Coast of tropical America, Atlantic side

Although the color of this species is made up of browns and grays, the fish is not lacking in character. The light spot in back of the gill plate is a sparkle of blue. The anal fin is ornamented with brown and blue spots, and is crisply edged with electric blue. A peculiarity is that in certain lights the center of the eye is a blind-looking stony blue. The fish appears to be able to "close" its eye on the inside, hence the name sleeper. It is often found in brackish water.

A peaceful, sluggish fish that has seldom been bred. Many small eggs are attached to cleaned stones. Tiny young are hard to rear. Especially the adults require large food particles. Temperature, 65° to 85°.

## THE ANABANTIDS. OR LABYRINTH FISHES

### FAMILY ANABANTIDAE

The Anabantids include the Climbing Perches and Gouramis. All have an auxiliary breathing apparatus, called the labyrinth, in addition to the ordinary gills. Although not capable of independent muscular action, this organ is comparable to the lung of an air-breathing animal, and serves the same purpose. It is called a labyrinth on account of its involved structure which brings a great many

*Dormitator maculatus*

fine capillaries into contact with the air forced through it. These capillaries absorb oxygen from the air and deliver it directly into the blood stream of the fish. The air, however, does not pass through the labyrinth in the same manner as we humans breathe, but is taken at intervals by the fish at the surface of the water. Simultaneously, a new bubble is taken in the mouth and the old one is forced out through the edge of the gill covers, having first passed through the oxygen-absorbing labyrinth. This is in the head.

These fishes use the regular gills for oxygenating the blood to a much greater extent than is generally believed. Experiments have shown that they extract almost as much oxygen from the water as do other species without labyrinths. However, it is a great advantage to a fish to be equipped with both kinds of breathing apparatus for in situations where the oxygen in the water is so deficient as to suffocate ordinary species, the labyrinth fishes maintain life without apparent distress. From this it will be seen why they may be kept in comparatively small containers.

On the mistaken theory that air-breathers take *no* oxygen from the water, aquarists sometimes add them to tanks which are already overpopulated.

The intervals at which air in the labyrinth is changed varies with species and conditions. When excited the fish may come to the surface several times a minute, but at other times, especially in cool water, it may remain below for several minutes at a time.

Nearly all of the labyrinth fishes are what are known as "bubble-nest builders." As the description of this peculiar method of breeding applies to the several species under the heading, it will not be needlessly repeated in each instance, but where individual characteristics vary from the following description, they will be pointed out as occasion requires.

The outstanding feature of the breeding of this family of fishes is the floating nest of bubbles which they construct and in which the eggs are placed, hatched and the young tended. These bubbles are formed by the male as he comes to the surface, draws a little air in his mouth and apparently mixes it with saliva of sorts. When released, many small bubbles float to the surface. Endless repetition of this act piles up what looks like a little mound of very fine soap bubbles. They often select a building spot just under some floating aquatic leaves or a large single leaf. The best temperature for breeding is 78°-82°. In the breeding tank it is advisable to reduce as much as possible any surface agitation caused by filters or aerators.

When a male starts building a nest, even in a small way, it indicates that he is about ready for breeding. Unless a female is already present, it is the proper time to bring a pair together. It is better to move the male into the aquarium occupied by the female. Most of these fishes are quite harmless to species other than their own, but at breeding time there is danger of one being killed, usually the female. For this reason it is desirable to have plenty of room and a liberal supply of refuge plants which, by the way, they never injure. The courting is conducted by a grand spreading of fins, first of the male, with ultimate response by the female if his suit is successful. His best holiday attire is used in courtship.

The male is often an impatient courter. After the nest is built, he drives the female towards it. If she is not ready for spawning her response will be slow, and it is then that he is liable to attack her, tearing her fins. It is at this time that the aquarist needs to be something of a strategist, as well as a diplomat, for the pair should not be separated at the very first sign of trouble. Like the wise judge at a Domestic Relations Court, he should give the contestants a reasonable chance to adjust their difficulties themselves. If matters grow worse, the strong arm of the aquarist should intervene, and give the parties an enforced separation. A later trial mating may prove more successful.

But let us assume, as we should, that the courtship has been a normal one, and that the pair is ready for the business of life. She follows him to a position just below the prepared nest. He bends his body into a crescent which encircles her. As they slowly sink through the water, rolling over, she drops several eggs which are immediately fertilized during the embrace of the male. He releases himself, picks up the eggs in his mouth, and pushes them into the nest. This act is repeated for perhaps an hour, at the end of which time there may be from 100 to 500 eggs in the nest. The male then asserts his rights as a father. He drives the female to the farthest limits of the aquarium and assumes full charge of the nest. At this point she should be removed, for she is likely to be killed, especially if the aquarium is a small one, say under 15 gallons.

To do this with as little agitation

*Spawning Sequence of Paradise Fishes*

*The female has joined the male underneath the nest, and the embrace begins.*

*The female, upside down, releases a few eggs which are immediately fertilized by the male.*

*The pair slowly rolls over until the female is in an upside down position.*

*After each spawning act, the male, occasionally the female as well, gathers the drifting eggs and deposits them into the nest.*

as possible, insert a glass divider between the pair. Female is then lifted without trouble.

With the presence of the eggs in the nest the male redoubles his efforts in producing bubbles, for the old ones gradually burst. In order to retard this evaporation, and for another reason to be explained shortly, the aquarium should be kept well covered with glass. The bubble-nest, originally about 3 inches wide and half an inch high, becomes perhaps an inch high and spreads out to 4 inches. The small eggs between the bubble suds can be seen, but sharp eyes are needed.

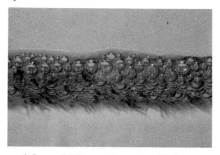

*2 Day old Fry of Paradise Fish*

The eggs hatch in about 2 days. At first they are like microscopic tadpoles among the foam, and are quite helpless. As they fall out of the nest through the water, the vigilant father gathers them up in his mouth and puts them back into their sudsy cradle. This continues about 3 days, the nest gradually becoming shallower and the young taking a position at the surface of the water just below it. By the time the young have absorbed the yolk sac and gained their balance the nest is nearly gone. No schoolmaster ever had a busier time looking after his charges and no children could have a more vigilant caretaker. He looks after the wanderers with an eagle eye, ever alert and willing to give his life in their defense. In perhaps a week he considers his task done and that the young should be able to protect themselves. So thoroughly does he seem to enter into this idea that he is liable to start eating them himself! Perhaps this is nature's method of eliminating those that can be caught. In the wild state his protection is no doubt necessary, but in an aquarium in which there are no fish enemies there is no reason to keep the father with the young after they are free-swimming.

There are several points of practical value in raising bubble-nest builders which may be covered briefly. It is a very, very common experience for beginners to become enthusiastic over prospects of raising a nest of these young, only to have them die off at an age of from two to four weeks. The principal reason for this is insufficient food of the right kind, and the causes in back of this are aquaria that are too small and too clean. These small fishes require a considerable amount of microscopic food, which can only be developed and maintained in old water. The proper aquarium for this purpose should be at the very least 15 gallons in size, well planted, containing old water from six to eight inches deep, and with a fair amount of natural sediment on the bottom. The presence of a few decaying aquarium plants is desirable. No snails should be used. When the eggs are laid it is advisable to sprinkle a little dried and crumbled lettuce leaves on the water, and also a very little of any finely powdered fish food. The decomposition of these organic substances keeps up the culture of microscopic life which will later be needed. It is a fact that very small fishes of this character have been raised on a fine flour made of fish food, but it is quite likely that the resulting Infusoria which feed on the decomposition of this substance have something to do with the success attained. At any rate, while it is a good idea to have a separate source of Infusoria culture, it is also desirable to cultivate a natural supply of it along with the baby fishes, especially when they are of a species which are extremely small. Aside from this suggested aquarium preparation, the young of labyrinth fishes may be raised as per the regular formula for egg-droppers. At the age of five to seven days they can also eat newly-hatched Brine Shrimp, previously described.

A reasonably successful substitute for live food is the yellow of a 20-minute boiled egg. It should be squeezed through a cloth and a bit as big as a pea shaken up in a bottle of about four-ounce size. A few drops of the agitated mixture may be lifted in a medicine-dropper and fed to the fry several times a day. These infusions should always be freshly mixed and should be fed with great care, as they can easily foul the water.

The other cause for losses is the failure to keep the aquarium well covered with glass during the critical period when the labyrinth is forming, for this organ does not begin to develop until the fish is about three weeks old. At this time they are particularly sensitive to draughts and temperature changes. Slight aeration should be used now to prevent scum from forming at the surface.

The writer has, with marked success, bred five kinds of labyrinth fishes outdoors in a six-foot lily pool, one species each season. Nests were always placed by the fish under a lily pad, with the exception of the *Colisa fasciata* (Giant Gourami), and

*Belontia signata,* both these species allowing their floating eggs to scatter loosely at the surface, to be freely blown about by the winds. Temperature ranged from 60° to 90°, averaging 73°. Females were never killed. Several overlapping nestings per season were raised, none interfering with or apparently eating the others. Sometimes two pairs of breeders were used. No artificial culture of infusoria was used. Daphnia occasionally. These were soon cleaned up by the parents or the young which were large enough to eat them. Never tried Bettas in the pool, distrusting our variable summer climate. The reader should not assume that conclusions from pond breeding are applicable to aquarium culture.

Members of this fish family are subject to much individual variation in temperament, especially in the action of males in breeding. Some kill one female after another; others devour their babies, while some refuse to mate at all. The most unpredictable is the Betta. Ingenuity by the aquarist is sometimes needed. A change of mates is often the answer.

The labyrinth fishes are by nature carnivorous, living principally on small crustacea and also on insects which fall on the water. They can be trained to take ordinary prepared dried foods, but this should often be supplemented by fresh animal diet, such as Daphnia, chopped worms, live and frozen Brine Shrimp, bits of fish, crab meat, or scraped raw beef liver.

They are all suited to life in a community tank with fishes of approximately their own size. But males of the same species sometimes fight. Male Bettas, of course, will invariably fight. Females may be kept together.

## *Macropodus opercularis*
(LINNAEUS)

*Popular name:* Paradise Fish

*Meaning of name:* Macropodus, large foot (fin), in reference to dorsal and anal fins; opercularis, with spot on the gill cover

*Length:* 3 inches

If ancient lineage is the true basis for aristocracy, then the Paradise Fish is undoubtedly the Exalted Potentate of all tropical aquarium fishes. It was introduced into Paris in 1868 by Carbonnier. This introduction undoubtedly marks the beginning of the study of tropical fresh water aquarium fishes as we have it today, and if any future enthusiasts wish to observe centenaries of the occasion, that is the year on which to base them. Goldfish and a few cold-water species, both fresh and marine, had been kept in European and American aquariums some years previously. It is now difficult to realize that in about 1850-60, especially in England, the household aquarium was a new and fashionable fad, and that many books appeared on the subject. Judging from the now comical misinformation contained in most of them, it is little wonder that the mushroom growth soon passed and left no trace, except for a few musty books. One of the earliest of them (Warrington 1850) contained the first correct statement of the principles of the balanced aquarium, and is worthy of commemoration.

For many years following its introduction into America in 1876 by the famous Adolphus Busch of St. Louis, the Paradise Fish was regarded as an aquarium novelty of doubtful value, for owners of Lacetail Goldfish rightly feared the pres-

*Macropodus opercularis*

ence of this menacing stranger among their highly developed but defenseless beauties. The Goldfish fins usually suffered when it was tried.

Because the Paradise Fish is so easily bred and can live in water down to 50°, it is held cheaply. If rare it would be considered a great beauty. When the male's fins are at their best, the long, sweeping filaments at the tail-ends are blue white at the ends. The females have shorter fin tips.

In contrast with Goldfish this species early acquired a reputation as a fighter, but in comparison with some other exotic fishes he is really not savage, but is untrustworthy in a small community tank.

A true albino strain of Paradise Fish with pink eyes was introduced from Europe in 1933. The bars on the sides are pinkish, becoming more red as the fish ages. Otherwise it is white, or cream colored. It breeds true and is prolific. What fight there is in the original stock seems to have mostly disappeared in the albino, the male not usually attacking the female after she has finished spawning.

*Macropodus opercularis,* or Paradise Fish, breeds true to standard form as described for bubble-nest builders. It is particularly suited to pond culture, as it is not injured by moderate chilly spells.

This fish is very tame, and while preferring animal food, will take anything. Like the Betta, in perhaps a slightly lesser degree, it seems to have no sense of fear. It is long-lived, and can endure very dirty water.

The species has been the subject of an unusual amount of discussion, by the systematists, having undergone, since its first description by Linnaeus in 1758, nearly a dozen changes of name, and been the subject of many hundred papers by ichthyologists and aquarists.

Paradise Fish are common in the rice fields of China, where they successfully endure a wide range of temperature. Here in America we have known them to be retrieved, nearly dead, from ice-coated ponds, then gently heated and brought to full health.

### *Macropodus concolor*

*Popular name:* Black Paradise Fish

*Length:* about 4 inches; female smaller

*Location:* Unknown

Paradise Fishes, the well-known *M. opercularis* as well as this one, are very hardy and durable fishes, able to survive the most adverse conditions. They are gorgeously colored, easily bred and raised, and accept almost any kind of food. Unfortunately, their popularity rating is very low, due to the undeserved reputation given them as aggressive and belligerent fishes. However, the risk in keeping them in a community tank is not much greater than that taken with a male *Betta,* the Siamese Fighting Fish. Of course, their tank mates should be of a comparative size or be sufficiently agile to be able to escape, if it should become necessary. Only while breeding, and this admittedly might easily take place in the community tank, does the male become so aggressive that he might inflict serious injury on other tank mates. This is the case with many fishes exercising parental care, especially with those who usually are devoted parents.

The outstanding features of Black Paradise Fishes are their deep brown (almost black) body color; the bright blue edging of dorsal, anal, and

*Macropodus concolor*

caudal fins, and their deep orange ventrals. While breeding or guarding the nest and fry, the male's colors are enormously enhanced, whereas the female's colors become a washed-out gray. The fish builds a large solid bubble nest and the fry are easily raised. Infusoria are necessary as a first food, to be followed by newly hatched Shrimp in five to six days.

Temperature, 75° to 85°.

### *Belontia signata*   (GUENTHER)

*Popular name:* Comb-tail Gourami

*Meaning of name:* Belontia, from native name of a related species in Borneo; signata, significant

*Length:* 3½ to 4 inches

Sri Lanka (Ceylon)

On reflection, most labyrinth fishes are easily identified; they have marked characteristics. In this one, we have not only a pronounced color pattern, but the long, soft-rays of the ventral fins are split and the rays of

The predominating color is reddish brown with some red in the fins, particularly the tail. Male is likely to kill female unless they have a large tank. Scattered eggs float with no nest. Both parents tend young. Temperature, 70° to 82°.

the posterior tip of the anal fin.

### *Colisa chuna*
(HAMILTON-BUCHANAN)

*Popular name:* Honey Gourami

*Meaning of name:* Colisa chuna: based on two native names

*Length:* 1¾ inches

Northeast India

*Colisa chuna* is a relative newcomer to the aquarium scene. In keeping with its popular name, the male is brick red with a yellow dorsal. A dark line passes from the eye horizontally to the base of the caudal, and a blue-black triangular area fades in obliquely from the eye to the tail fin extend well past the web.

*Belontia signata*

*Colisa chuna*

The female shows a more distinct band running from the eye to the peduncle on a washed silver-brown body. The dorsal and anal fins are edged with orange-red.

Breeding this species is accomplished by bringing the temperature of the water down from a normally 83° to 78°. A ten-gallon tank is large enough, and although plants may be present, the male builds his nest independent of plant fronds. Spawning lasts from an hour to two hours, during which time about 400 eggs are released. Within twenty-four hours the eggs begin to hatch and in seventy-two hours the fry are free swimming. First food consists of infusoria; within three days egg infusion may be offered. Newly hatched Brine Shrimp is taken five days later. The fry show the dark bands by four weeks. Growth is rapid and the youngsters mature by the time they are four months old, displaying their attractive colors.

*Colisa fasciata*

## Colisa fasciata
(BLOCH-SCHNEIDER)

*Popular name:* Striped Gourami

*Meaning of name:* Colisa, from a native name; fasciata, banded or striped

*Length:* 4½ inches

India

While the breeding habits of this *Colisa* are in general the same as for the family, there are differences. It does not build a very definitely formed nest, but blows a few scattered bubbles, preferably under a large leaf. The eggs are lighter than water and float to the surface where they are more or less scattered. For some reason which we are not even able to surmise, the male takes mouthfuls of sand and blows it

among the eggs. A male is shown in the illustration.

In the meantime, both before and after the hatching of the eggs, the male takes several gulps of air in his mouth, proceeds to a point below the surface, and expels a fine mist of air bubbles backward through his gills, scattering it with his pectoral fins. For a moment, it seems as though the bubbles are coming from all over his body. He busies himself with this procedure in all parts of the aquarium. We believe this is the first record of these facts.

Eggs hatch in two days at 78°. Remove female after spawning and male three days after eggs hatch. A peaceful, beautiful species, easily fed.

## Colisa lalia
(HAMILTON-BUCHANAN)

*Popular name:* Dwarf Gourami

*Meaning of name:* Colisa lalia, based on two native names

*Length:* 2 inches

Northern India

Before the discovery of *C. chuna,* *Colisa lalia* was the smallest of the genus *Colisa,* but it is still one of the most beautiful. A highly satisfactory and interesting aquarium fish with but a single fault. It is apt to be

timid and hide in the foliage. It is
too beautiful a flower to be allowed
to blush unseen. By associating it
with more forward fishes that rush to
their master for food, this little
beauty soon overcomes its shyness.

In breeding habits, this species
varies from the type description for
bubble-nest builders in one interesting particular. Bits of plant are incorporated into the nest, such as the
fine leaves of *Myriophyllum;* also
the female helps build the nest. In
addition to his much brighter colors,
the male may be distinguished by his
orange-red "feelers." Temperature
range, 68° to 84°. Breeds at about
80°. They are subject to dropsy.
Some males shoot water somewhat
like the archer fish.

*Colisa lalia*

*Helostoma temmincki*

# Helostoma temmincki

CUVIER and VALENCIENNES

*Popular name:* Kissing Gourami

*Meaning of name:* Helostoma, with turned-back mouth, referring to the thick curved lips, which are provided with series of small teeth; temmincki, for C. Temminck

*Length:* Up to 12 inches

Malaysia, Indonesia

This fish has been publicized both as a "kisser" and as an industrious eater of all kinds of algae. The latter claim is much exaggerated. The purpose of the kissing is not known but it much more appears to be a fighting gesture than a demonstration of affection. The larger ones are prone to persecute the smaller of their own kind. Only one or two in a community tank seems best, provided they are of equal size.

Breeding begins at five-inch size. They embrace like other Gouramies, build no nest and have from 400 to 2,000 floating amber eggs, the size of a pin head. Young hatch upside-down in a day. Parents may eat eggs, but will completely ignore young. Babies need Infusoria for a week, followed by newly hatched Brine Shrimp. In two weeks, fine floating food. Thereafter, they are surface feeders. Adults like powdered oatmeal with ground dried shrimp, they also like Pablum or crumpled dried spinach. They have few diseases, but decline if kept cool or not fed several times daily. There are two color phases: (1) silvery green and (2) a pinkish, iridescent white. It is the latter strain that does most of the breeding. There are no external differences in the sexes. Temperature, 75° to 82°.

# Sphaerichthys osphromenoides

CANISTRINI

*Popular name:* Chocolate Gourami

*Meaning of name:* Sphaerichthys, sphere-like fish; osphromenoides, resembling Osphronemus

*Length:* 2 inches, rarely larger

Indonesia, Malaysia

Much has been written in the aquarium literature of the past two decades about the Chocolate Gourami, but much remains to be learned about this beautiful, delicate, and still fairly rare fish. The accounts of its breeding habits vary tremendously, describing it as a live-bearer, a bubble-nest builder, and a mouthbrooder. Mouthbrooding accounts outweigh the others, at least, in quantity of material published. Since the structure of the fish rules out the possibility that it is viviparous, there remains the possibility that we are dealing with two very similar, yet different, species: (1) a bubblenester, and (2) a mouthbrooder. There is also the possibility suggested by Nieuwenhuizen, that fishes from different habitats, i.e., flowing stream vs. pond, breed in different ways. Since these discrepancies have not been cleared up, we can only provide suggestions regarding the conditions for keeping this little fish and hope that this will lead the way to resolving the mystery.

The water should be fairly acid (the fish are almost never comfortable in alkaline water), soft, and kept at a temperature of 80° or slightly above. A well-planted tank with a loose cover of floating plants to diffuse the light seems to enhance their well-being and therefore their color. Most types of live foods are accepted, but preference is usually given to Mosquito Larvae, Brine

*Sphaerichthys osphromenoides*

Shrimp, and Daphnia—in that order. Frozen foods are good substitutes, but are rarely eaten as eagerly. Some individuals will take dried foods, but this should never be used as the main diet.

Chocolate Gouramis are very peaceful and can be kept with other small mild-mannered fishes, but care should be taken to select fishes requiring the same treatment.

*Opaline Gouramis, A Color Variety of T. trichopterus*

## *Trichogaster trichopterus*
(PALLAS)

*Meaning of name:* Trichogaster, hair-belly; trichopterus, hair-fin

*Popular name:* Three-spot Gourami (the third spot being the eye); Blue Gourami

*Length:* 5 inches

Malay Peninsula, Thailand

For a time the Three-spot Gourami was known in the hobby only as a silvery fish overlaid with grey markings and with orange dots in the fins. The same species, as shown above, was later found in Sumatra and has become popular as the "Sumatra" or "Blue" Gourami. When the two color phases are crossed the blue in the babies is apt to be duller.

The species is one of the most easily bred of the bubble-nest build-

*Trichogaster trichopterus*

**Gold Gourami (*Another Mutant of T. trichopterus*)**

ers, although the nest itself is scattered and weak. This makes little difference as both eggs and young float. They are lusty fishes with such big spawns that the young are sometimes used as food for other fishes.

They also make excellent exterminators of that pest few other fishes will touch, Hydra. The male has a longer dorsal fin. Temperature, 65°-85°.

## *Trichogaster leeri* (BLEEKER)

*Popular name:* Pearl Gourami

*Meaning of name:* Trichogaster, hairbelly; leeri, after Leer

*Length:* 4 inches

Thailand, Malay Peninsula, Sumatra

If the male fish always maintained its full-breeding color, it could be fairly called the "Robin Redbreast Gourami," but it doesn't. Instead of being a flashy fish, it is one of exquisite refinement. The regularity with which the pearly dots are distributed over nearly the entire fish has given rise to two other popular names: (1) in Europe, Mosaic Gourami and (2) in England, Lace Gourami. Breeding is in the typical style of the bubble-nest builders. The male is not very insistent about driving the female away after spawning is completed. Neither of them eats the eggs or young. The eggs float.

The species shares hydra-eating

honors with the preceding fish, *T. trichopterus*. It is quite gentle and is well suited to community life among fishes of approximately its own size. Temperature range, 68° to 85°.

## Trichogaster microlepis

GUENTHER

*Popular name:* Moonlight Gourami

*Meaning of name:* Trichogaster, hair-belly; microlepis, with small scales

*Length:* 5 to 6 inches

Thailand

Moonlight Gouramis are softly colored, handsome fishes, perfectly suited for most larger community tanks. While young fishes are often inconspicuous in the dealer's tank because of their pale silvery color and sometimes unnoticeable dark horizontal line, mature specimens always catch the attention of the hobbyist. Males, especially, have bright red eyes and a deep orange on their feeler-like ventral fins as well as on the forward portion of their anal fins. Males also have long, fan-like dorsals, as is the case with other species of *Trichogaster*.

These fishes reach maturity at a rather late age. If one starts with young, one- to two-inch fishes it may take more than half a year before sexes can be determined. They thrive best in slightly acid water at a temperature of about 80°. Breeding can be encouraged by raising the temperature slightly to about 85°. The fishes, however, are not always very cooperative, probably because we are working mostly with wild, imported fishes that are always a little more difficult to bring to breed than those bred domestically for generations. They are bubble-nest-builders like most Gouramis, and much plant material is incorporated

*Trichogaster leeri*

*Trichogaster microlepis*

in their large nests. The young grow very irregularly which is also quite common with Gouramis. Most complete losses of the fry are probably due to a parasitic disease called "velvet" or "Oodinium" (the name of the organism causing it) which is very hard to detect and, unfortunately, not easily cured. (See chapter on diseases.)

## Trichopsis vittatus
CUVIER and VALENCIENNES

*Trichopsis vittatus*

*Popular name:* Croaking Gourami

*Meaning of name:* Trichopsis, with hair-like fins; vittatus, striped or banded

*Length:* 2 to 3 inches

Thailand, Malaysia, Indonesia

These interesting fishes are often neglected by hobbyists and dealers alike. Admittedly, they often are shy and drab-looking in dealer's tanks, but given a well-planted tank with fairly soft, acid water, they soon develop a certain grace and elegance of movement. An outstanding feature is their bright green, iridescent eyes. Males have the fascinating ability to produce a sound when sparring with another male or courting a female. With their fins spread to the utmost and the entire body quivering, they emit one or two short vibrating bursts of a somewhat rasping sound. In a quiet room, the sound is clearly audible several feet away from the tank.

*Betta spendens*

*Cambodia Betta*

The nest is usually built at the surface and passionately tended by the father. Spawning takes place in typical Anabantid fashion. The young, which are marked with a dark longitudinal line from the time they have hatched, are easily raised and able to take on newly hatched brine shrimp a few days after becoming free-swimming.

They are less demanding in proper *p*H, hardness, and temperature than *T. pumilus* a smaller, even more beautiful but much rarer species. Temperature, about 80°.

## *Betta splendens*                    REGAN

*Popular name:* Siamese Fighting Fish

*Meaning of name:* Betta, after a local native name, Ikan bettah; splendens, brilliant

*Length:* 2½ inches

Thailand

With all due respect to the Guppy for having aroused the interest of an enormous number of persons in aquarium study, there seems little doubt that the modern Betta launched the hobby in a big way in America. Its extraordinary, spectacular beauty made instantaneous conquests among those who would never have looked twice at any other fish, but who are now dyed-in-the-wool

fanciers and doing all in their power to interest others in the hobby.

But let us leave superlatives for a moment and have a look at the humble ancestor of this flashy fish. Its body is yellowish brown with a few indistinct horizontal bands. At breeding time the male becomes darker and rows of metallic green scales on his sides become plainer. Dorsal, metallic green tipped with red; anal, red tipped white. Ventrals always fiery red, tipped white. All fins of moderate size, tail fin being rounded.

Suddenly there appeared in our aquarium world a new comet—a cream-colored Betta with fiery, flowing fins. Two varieties, a dark and a light one. were in the shipment. These were brought into San Francisco in 1927 from Siam. Thinking he had a new species, Mr. Locke, the consignee who received and bred the fishes, called the light one *Betta cambodia*. This has since been proved, as have all the now numerous color variants, to be a race of *Betta splendens*. Other importations in varying colors soon followed, some of them coming through Europe. Breeders aimed for the darker colors and soon established the famous "Cornflower Blue," and finally a solid, rich purplish blue.

There are now so many shades of this fish in blues, lavenders, greens and reds that a decorator could almost find specimens to match the color scheme of any room, however, the majority of them have a pair of drooping, fiery red ventral fins.

Much misinformation exists as to the fighting qualities of this fish, some of it so amusing that we present it, even at risk of too much length.

The late Dr. Hugh M. Smith, ichthyologist and writer, former U.S. Commissioner of Fisheries and one-time Adviser in Fisheries to the then Siamese Government, was qualified to speak on this fish from any standpoint, especially as he had taken a particular interest in the species and personally brought to the United States some of the original long-finned Betta stock. In response to a letter asking to settle the point as to whether the fishes are especially bred for fighting or are caught from the wild for the purpose, the following extracts from his interesting and amusing reply should decide the matter finally, not only for newspaper columnists, but for aquarium writers, too.

"The literature of Betta as a fighting fish is replete with inaccuracies and absurdities. An unusually large number of these occur in a short paragraph in the article entitled 'The Heavenly-Royal City of Siam' by Florence Burgess Meehan (Asia, March, 1921).

" 'The fighting fish are about the size of goldfish. You catch one and put it into a bottle. Your neighbor does likewise. You put your bottle close to your neighbor's. Your fish becomes enraged. So does your neighbor's fish. They both flash all colors of the rainbow. They swell up. You bet on your fish. Your friends back you. After a time one fish or the other, hurling itself against the glass in a vain effort to reach its adversary, becomes so angry that it literally bursts. If it is your neighbor's fish that bursts, you win. If it is yours, you lose.'

"The writer of this paragraph certainly never saw what she was writing about, and the untrustworthiness of the account may be judged from the following facts:

"The Siamese fighting fish cannot properly be described as 'about the size of a goldfish' whatever may be the meaning of the expression. The fish are not matched while in separate 'bottles,' and when not fighting are usually kept in special rectangular jars about 4 inches square and 10 inches high, and a little larger at the top than at the bottom. When fighting, the fish do not 'flash all colors of the rainbow,' do not 'swell up,' do not 'hurl themselves against the glass,' and do not 'literally burst.'

"With these exceptions, the account quoted is nearly correct, but not quite. For instance, the impression is conveyed that if you wish to stage a fight, you and your neighbor go out and catch wild fish, whereas practically all the combats are between domesticated fish. Fighting fish have been cultivated and domesticated among the Siamese for many years, and all of the noteworthy combats on which sums of money are wagered are with selected, often pedigreed, stock. They have short tail fins.

"There are in Bangkok 10 or 12 persons who breed fighting fish for sale, and about 1,000 persons who raise fighting fish for their own use. A dealer whom I recently visited reports an annual production of 50,000 young, but only a small percentage of these are carried to the fighting age and sold. For the best males the current retail price per fish is 1 to 2 ticals, females half price (1 tical equals 44 cents gold).

"The native wild fishes from which the ordinary cultivated fish has been derived rarely exceed 2 inches for the males, the females being smaller. The cultivated fish reach a length of 2½ inches for the males.

"The way in which the male fish are matched and their method of fighting are well known. It will suffice to state that the combatants are placed together in a bowl or jar and quickly come to close quarters, expanding their fins and branchial membranes and displaying the gorgeous red, blue and green shades that have made the fighting fish famous. They approach one another quietly and may remain in close relation, side by side, for 10 to 15 seconds, or longer, without action. Then, in quick succession, or simultaneously, they launch an attack almost too swift for the observer's eye to follow, and this is repeated at short intervals during the continuance of the combat. The effect of the fierce onslaughts begins to be seen in the mutilation of the fins, which may soon present a ragged appearance and considerable loss of fin substance may occur. The branchial region (gills) may come in for attack, and blood may exceptionally be drawn. On two separate occasions my own fish locked jaws and remained in that position for a number of minutes. That fish is adjudged the victor which is ready to continue to fight while its opponent is no longer eager for the fray."

Dr. Smith's reference to the courage of the cultivated breed of *Bettas* may account for their truly remarkable absence of fear under a certain circumstance which frightens and

*A male Betta, attacking his image in the camera lens*

*Female Betta*

intimidates nearly all other fishes, especially the fighting sorts. This is the sudden confinement of the fish in a very small space such, for instance, a half-pint jar. Placed in such a situation he calmly surveys his miniature prison, makes a few eel-like turns in it, apparently to see whether it can be done, and is then ready for each or both of his twin interests in life—breeding and fighting. His movements are truly serpentine.

Owing to this intense fighting passion of the males, it is necessary, at the age of about 3 months, to rear them in individual jars or aquaria. This is the way all fine specimens are produced, for although fish fins recover from injuries, scars remain and the fish is never again perfect. For this reason the price of fine specimens will always remain fairly high.

Bettas conform to the described habits for bubble-nest builders. They like acid water, about 6.8, and do best in a well-planted aquarium with liberal light. Water should be clear, but with plenty of natural sediment.

*Betta splendens* are at their best appearance and vigor between the ages of 10 months and 2 years, and should be bred during that period. Prior to one year it is difficult to select the best specimens, and after 2 years they age rapidly.

*The male has constructed a nest in the styrofoam cup provided for the purpose*

There is no way of identifying the sexes until they are about an inch long, when the fins of the males begin to point and lengthen. Soon after this change is noted the males should be kept separately. The females may be placed together. Fin length is the result of inheritance—not food.

*During the embrace, the pair turns until female is upside down*

This fish is almost as adaptable to foods as it is to its surroundings, but nevertheless it does best on animal substances such as Daphnia, Brine Shrimp, Mosquito Larvae, chopped worms, bits of fish, crab, shrimp, etc.

A single male may be placed in a community aquarium, and possibly a female also, if the tank is 20 gallons or larger. In general the sexes should be kept separated; the males singly or else spread around so that 2 of the species are not in the same tank. Males placed in small adjoining aquariums with a cardboard divider between will always spread themselves when the board is removed. It is a show for visitors that never fails.

*From 10 to about 20 eggs are expelled at each embrace. Some eggs can be seen slowly sinking in the water*

The breeding actions of Bettas are unpredictable. Some males are killers, some egg-eaters. None should be trusted with the babies after they become free-swimming. Breeding temperature, about 78°, but stand 68° to 90°.

*Eggs are gathered and deposited in the froth nest.*

## THE BROAD-SOLES
### FAMILY SOLEIDAE

The Broad-Soles belong to the order Pleuronectiformes, all of which lie on one side and have both eyes on the upper side. The Soles differ from other Flatfishes in having a very twisted mouth. There are several families of Soles. The broad-soles are salt, brackish or freshwater fishes.

### *Trinectes maculatus*   (BLOCH)

*Popular name:* Freshwater Sole

*Meaning of name:* Trinectes, with three "swimmers" (fins); maculatus, spotted; also known as Achirus fasciatus, Common Sole

*Length:* To 8 inches

Coastal waters from Cape Cod southward

Due mainly to their curious method of swimming, an avid interest has developed for the young of this relative of the Flounders. By undulating its fins along the edges of the body, the fish glides in a horizontal position, like a pancake being propelled through the water. It is also able to bury itself by making wave-like, flapping movements, similar to a blanket being shaken, thereby churning up sand which settles down upon it. This accomplished, it lies in wait for small passing victims, remaining inactive much of the time. They can stick quite firmly to the sides of the tank by body suction.

All fishes of this type—and there are many of them—at first have eyes normally on each side of the head. At an early age, one of the eyes moves over to the other side, so that, eventually, we have a fish blind on one side and with two raised eyes on the other.

They can be fed Brine Shrimp (either live or frozen), Tubifex Worms, or bits of chopped clam. A novel and satisfactory fish. Temperature, 60° to 72°.

## THE SPINY EELS
### FAMILY MASTACEMBELIDAE

The Spiny Eels are not true eels. They are elongated tropical Old World freshwater fishes with numerous spines preceding the dorsal fin.

### *Mastacembelus erythrotaenia*
(BLEEKER)

*Popular name:* Fire Eel

*Meaning of name:* Mastacembelus,

*Trinectes maculatus*          *Mastacembelus erythrotaenia*

with armored beak; erythrotaenia, with red bands

*Length:* to 2 feet

An odd creature that is often imported today. We include it here for its interesting appearance and because it is the only member of this order that we have to show.

Like the Weatherfish, it spends much of the daytime buried in the sand, head peeping out. Probably, the Weatherfish does this for protection, but with *M. erythrotaenia* it is more likely a camouflage for attack as it is a strictly carnivorous fish. It swims about the surface of the sand at night. In common with most nocturnal fishes, it can be taught to eat in daytime, but as soon as it has had its meal of chopped Earthworms it quickly returns to its sandy hideout. Not interested in Daphnia or in raw meat. It will gladly take worms.

Similar species to the above, but smaller and better suitable, belonging to the genus *Macrognathus,* are being imported from tropical Africa and Asia in increasing numbers. Temperature, about 78°.

## THE PUFFERS

### FAMILY TETRAODONTIDAE

The Puffers are comical fishes. They can blow themselves up with air or water into a veritable balloon. No other fishes possess this remarkable ability. Their fused teeth (two above, two below) form a beak with which the larger species can give a dangerous nip. Most of the species are of good size and inhabit salt water throughout tropical and semi-tropical regions, but a few small ones inhabit fresh and brackish water.

## *Tetraodon fluviatilis*
### (HAMILTON-BUCHANAN)

*Popular name:* Spotted Puffer

*Meaning of name:* Tetraodon, four-toothed; fluviatilis, of the river

*Length:* 2 to 5 inches

Most of India, Burma, Malay Peninsula

Puffers of different species have a wide distribution throughout marine waters. This one occurs principally in fresh and brackish locations and in aquarium trade circles is known as the Freshwater Puffer.

The background color is light with a vivid sheen of green interspersed with large, dark blotches and spots. Belly white, or nearly so.

Although a fish of clumsy, thick appearance, it is extremely active, and never still a moment. It is also quite aggressive towards its own kind, but seems to do little harm.

The outstanding feature of these Puffers is their ability when frightened to puff themselves up balloon-like with air or water. Most but not all specimens will do it when removed from the water, placed on the hand, and tickled. Air is taken in at the mouth, in about a dozen noisy gulps, until the belly is fully inflated and hard. As the internal pressure increases, little hollow spines are projected from the scale spots. The fish is able to maintain this balloon for only about half a minute. When placed back in the water, it ejects the air with the same gulping valvular contractions and scurries to the bottom.

With ordinary care, it will live well in the aquarium, preferably with its own kind. Eats anything, but prefers meaty food, and lots of it. Never bred. Temperature, 70° to 80°.

*Tetraodon fluviatilis*

## *Tetraodon palembangensis*
BLEEKER

*Popular name:* Figure-eight puffer

*Meaning of name:* Tetraodon, four-toothed; palembangensis, from Palembang in Indonesia

*Length:* 8 inches

Indonesia

This Puffer, together with the well-known *T. fluviatilis,* the Spotted Puffer, is the one most frequently imported. Although it is said to reach a size of eight inches in its natural habitat, specimens measuring three inches are seldom imported. Their strange common name results from the arrangement of greenish-yellowish lines on their back which often describe the figure eight. This species is fairly peaceful towards other fishes, but since most Puffers do best in slightly brackish water (i.e. a mixture of fresh and saltwater which in the aquarium can be duplicated by adding varying amounts of salt, usually up to four teaspoons per gallon) many tank mates are eliminated.

All Puffers are gluttons, requiring copious amounts of live and frozen foods to support their husky frames. Best foods are Blood Worms, Brine Shrimp, some Meal Worms, pieces of raw or frozen fish, shrimp, or liver and beef heart. Snails are particularly relished and smaller ones need not be crushed, since Puffers have teeth fused into a strong, beak-like structure.

These Puffers have not been bred. The only information we have is of other members of the family which are said to exercise some form of parental care. The male parent is reputed to guard the non-adhesive eggs. The young appear to be very difficult to raise, and most breeders report failure in this area. Many hobbyists, however, find it well worth the time, effort, and space to provide a tank for these fascinating creatures alone. Temperature, 75° to 82°.

*Tetraodon palembangensis*

*Colomesus psittacus*

## *Colomesus psittacus*
### (BLOCH-SCHNEIDER)

*Popular name:* South American Puffer

*Meaning of name:* Colomesus, round fish; psittacus, parrot-like

*Length:* To 4 inches

Northern South America

The most important, single factor to be considered when attempting to keep any puffer is the availability of food. They are bulky fishes with a high metabolic rate and cannot be kept healthy and vigorous on a diet of dried foods, although some puffers will take them. Large amounts of live and frozen foods are required, and they especially relish bits of frozen or fresh shrimp (the kind used for cocktails) lean meat, fish, Earthworms, Meal Worms, snails, etc.

South American Puffers are the most active members of the family and the only ones found in South America. With powerful strokes of their pectoral fins as well as their dorsal and ventral fins which are set far back on their bodies, they can sustain a speed far greater than that of their Far Eastern counterparts. Large, roomy tanks are, therefore, necessary to maintain this species.

When very young and about an inch long, they have four broad black bands across their white backs. These bands change into irregular black and green patterns as the fishes mature. These puffers sometimes bury themselves up to their heads in sand, if that is used in the tank. Coarse gravel usually prevents them from doing this. Water conditions do not seem to be very important as long as extreme acidity is avoided. They will live equally well in either fresh or saltwater as well as all stages in between.

Sex differences have not been observed and there is no record of them having spawned in captivity. Temperature, 73° to 78°.

## THE TRIPLETAILS

### FAMILY LOBOTIDAE

These are mostly marine fishes of tropical regions. Datnioides is an exception being found in freshwaters of Thailand, Malaysia and Burma.

## *Datnioides microlepis*    BLEEKER

*Popular name:* Tiger Fish

*Meaning of name:* Microlepis, with small scales

*Length:* To 15 inches

Tiger Fishes can only be kept with other fishes of approximately the same size. They have cavernous mouths and are capable of swallowing a surprisingly large fish. However *Datnioides* do not need a diet of only fish. Earthworms, frozen or live Ghost Shrimp, and even chunks of freeze dried Brine Shrimp will be accepted. They require large amounts of food, and grow at a very fast rate. Sometimes they are a little happier in slightly brackish water (about 5 oz. of salt for ten gallons of water).

Temperature 72° to 82°.

## THE NEEDLE FISHES

### FAMILY BELONIDAE

Most members of this family are marine fishes. All are strictly carnivorous, feeding on other fishes. Very few enter freshwater. None have even been bred in captivity.

## *Xenentodon cancila*
(HAMILTON)

*Popular name:* Needle Fish

*Meaning of name:* Xenentodon, with odd teeth

*Length:* 12 inches

These are easily frightened fishes, and extreme care is necessary while handling them. They are capable of tremendous speeds, and often injure themselves by crashing against the aquarium glass. They should be kept in large, well covered tanks. Live fishes are their only food.

Temperature, 70° to 80°.

*Datnioides microlepis*

*Xenentodon cancila*

## INDEX OF GENERAL SUBJECTS